LOGIC PROGRAMMING

A.P.I.C. Studies in Data Processing
General Editor: Fraser Duncan

1. Some Commercial Autocodes. A Comparative Study
   E. L. Willey, A. d'Agapeyeff, Marion Tribe, B. J. Gibbens and
   Michelle Clarke

2. A Primer of ALGOL 60 Programming
   E. W. Dijkstra

3. Input Language for Automatic Programming
   A. P. Yershov, G. I. Kozhukhin and U. Voloshin

4. Introduction to System Programming
   Edited by Peter Wegner

5. ALGOL 60 Implementation. The Translation and Use of ALGOL 60
   Programs on a Computer
   B. Randell and L. J. Russell

6. Dictionary for Computer Languages
   Hans Breuer

7. The Alpha Automatic Programming System
   Edited by A. P. Yershov

8. Structured Programming
   O.-J. Dahl, E. W. Dijkstra and C. A. R. Hoare

9. Operating Systems Techniques
   Edited by C. A. R. Hoare and R. H. Perrott

10. ALGOL 60 Compilation and Assessment
    B. A. Wichmann

11. Definition of Programming Languages by Interpreting Automata
    Alexander Ollongren

12. Principles of Program Design
    M. A. Jackson

13. Studies in Operating Systems
    R. M. McKeag and R. Wilson

14. Software Engineering
    R. J. Perrott

15. Computer Architecture: A Structured Approach
    R. W. Doran

16. Logic Programming
    Edited by K. L. Clark and S.-A. Tärnlund

A.P.I.C. Studies in Data Processing
No. 16

LOGIC PROGRAMMING

Edited by

K. L. CLARK

*Department of Computing
Imperial College, London*

and

S.-A. TÄRNLUND

*Computing Science Department
Uppsala University, Sweden*

ACADEMIC PRESS, INC.

(Harcourt Brace Jovanovich, Publishers)

London   Orlando   San Diego   New York
Toronto   Montreal   Sydney   Tokyo

ACADEMIC PRESS INC. (LONDON) LTD
24/28 Oval Road
London NW1

United States Edition published by
ACADEMIC PRESS, INC.
Orlando, Florida 32887

British Library Cataloguing in Publication Data
Logic Programming.—(A.P.I.C. studies in data
    processing; No. 16)
    1. Electronic digital computers—Programming
    2. Logic, Symbolic and mathematical
    I. Clark, K. L.   II. Tärnlund, S.-A.
    III. Series
    001.64'2'015113   QA76.6

    ISBN 0-12-175520-7
    LCCCN 82-71009

PRINTED IN THE UNITED STATES OF AMERICA

85 86 87 88   9 8 7 6 5

we   10 - 8 - 85

CONTRIBUTORS LIST

Bellia, M., Istituto di Scienze dell'Informazione, Università di Pisa, Corso Italia, 40, I56100 Pisa, Italy

Bowen, K.A., School of Computer and Information Science, Syracuse University, Syracuse, NY, 13210, USA

Bruynooghe, M., Katholieke Universiteit Leuven, Afdeling Toegepaste Wiskunde en Programmatie, Celestijnenlaan 200A, B-3030 Heverlee, Belgium

Clark, K.L., Department of Computing, Imperial College, 180 Queen's Gate, London SW7, England

Colmerauer, A., Groupe Intelligence Artificielle, Faculte des Sciences de Luminy, Universite Aix-Marseille II, 13288 Marseille cedex 2, France

Davis, R.E., Electrical Engineering and Computer Science Department, University of Santa Clara, Santa Clara, CA 96053, USA

Degano, P., Istituto di Scienze dell'Informazione, Università di Pisa, Corso Italia, 40, I56100 Pisa, Italy

Gallaire, H., Laboratoires de Marcoussis, CGE Route de Nozay 91460 Marcoussis, France

Gregory, S., Department of Computing, Imperial College, 180 Queen's Gate, London SW7, England

Hansson, A., Uppsala University, Department of Computing, UPMAIL, Sturegatan 4A, S-752 23 Uppsala, Sweden

Haridi, S., Department of Computer Systems, The Royal Institute of Technology, Stockholm, Sweden

Hogger, C.J., Department of Civil Engineering, Imperial College, 180 Queen's Gate, London SW7, England

Kahn, K.M., Uppsala University, Department of Computing, UPMAIL, Sturegatan 4A, S-752 23 Uppsala, Sweden

Komorowski, H.J., Software Systems Research Center, Linköping University, S-581 83 Linköping, Sweden

Kowalski, R.A., Department of Computing, Imperial College, 180 Queen's Gate, London SW7, England

Lasserre, C., Ecole Nationale Superieure de l'Aeronautique et de l'Espace, BP 4032, 31055 Toulouse Cedex, France

Levi, G., Istituto di Scienze dell'Informazione, Università di Pisa, Corso Italia, 40, I56100 Pisa, Italy

de Lucena Filho., G.J., Departamento de Sistemas e Computacao
    Universidade Federal da Paraiba, Campina Grande, Paraiba,
    Brazil
McCabe, F.G., Department of Computing, Imperial College, 180
    Queen's Gate, London SW7, England
McKeeman, W.M., Wang Institute, Tyngsboro, MA 01879, USA
Mellish, C.S., Department of Artifical Intelligence, Univer-
    sity of Edinburgh, Hope Park Square, Edinburgh EH8 9NW,
    UK
Pereira, L.M., Departamento de Informatica, Universidade Nova
    de Lisboa, Quinta da Torre, 2825 Monte Da Caparica,
    Portugal
Porto, A., Departamento de Informatica, Universidade Nova de
    Lisboa, Quinta da Torre, 2825 Monte da Caparica, Portugal
Robinson, J.A., School of Computer and Information Science,
    Syracuse University, Syracuse, NY 13210, USA
Santane-Toth, E., Institute for Co-ordination of Computer
    Techniques (SZKI), H-1368 Budapest, P.O.B. 224, Hungary
Sebelik, J., Institute for Application of Computing Technique
    in Control, Prague 1, Husova 8, Czechoslovakia
Sergot, M., Department of Computing, Imperial College, 180
    Queen's Gate, London SW7, England
Sibert, E.E., School of Computer and Information Science,
    Syracuse University, Syracuse, NY 13210, USA
Sickel, S., Logical Paradox, Inc., 26 Moreno Drive, Santa
    Cruz, CA 95060, USA
Simmons, R.F., Department of Computer Science, University of
    Texas at Austin, Austin, Texas 78712, USA
Stepanek, P., Department of Cybernetics and Operational
    Research, Charles University, Prague 1, Malostranske
    namesti 25, Czechoslovakia
Szeredi, P., Institute for Co-ordination of Computer
    Techniques (SZKI), H-1368 Budapest, P.O.B. 224, Hungary
Tärnlund, S-A., Uppsala University, Computing Science Depart-
    ment, UPMAIL, Sturegatan 4A, S-752 23 Uppsala, Sweden
van Emden, M.H., Department of Computer Science, University
    of Waterloo, Waterloo, Ontario, N2L 3G1 Canada

PREFACE

This collection of papers is intended to give an introduction to the relatively new research area of logic programming. The key premise of logic programming is that computation is controlled inference. This view of computation is proving exceedingly fruitful, as we believe the papers in this volume demonstrate. It leads naturally to the idea that we should design computers as inference machines, an idea that the Japanese have taken as the basis for the design of their fifth generation machines.

The stimulus to produce the book was the first International Workshop on Logic Programming held in Debrecen, Hungary in the summer of 1980. The forty or so presentations, from many different countries, demonstrated the extent of current research. Thereafter, the demand for the informally produced proceedings of the workshop (Tärnlund, 1980), which composed draft papers and abstracts, convinced us that the time was ripe for the publication of a collection of papers that would serve as an introduction to current research in logic programming. We invited everyone who gave a presentation at Debrecen, and others whom we knew were active in logic programming, to submit a paper for possible inclusion in the collection. Of the twenty papers that we selected, thirteen had their origins in the Debrecen workshop. The rest were either specially written for the book or are revised or rewritten versions of papers that have only been privately circulated. One paper, that by Colmerauer on Natural Language, is a specially rewritten English version of a paper that was previously published in French.

We should like to thank the referees: K. Bowen, M. Bruynooghe, A. Colmerauer, M.H. van Emden, H. Gallaire, R.A. Kowalski, L.M. Pereira, J.A. Robinson, P. Roussel, S. Sickel, P.Szeredi for helping us to select the papers included in the book. In all we considered about 40 papers, each of which was refereed by at least two people. Of course, final responsibility for the selection rests with us, the editors.

We should also like to thank M. Brunell and B. Hansson whose assistance in the production of the camera ready copy is much appreciated.

Finally, very special thanks are due to Anneli Holmsten. She did all the formatting. She also patiently tolerated many revisions of the text and changes in the format that involved much extra work.

The book was produced using the text formatters Vided and Videdp developed in Sweden by J. Palme.

January 1982
The Editors

CONTENTS

INTRODUCTION

A BRIEF HISTORY OF LOGIC PROGRAMMING

Logic programming has grown out of research into automated inference, in particular the work on resolution inference that followed the publication of Robinson's seminal paper (1965). Resolution is a generalisation of modus ponens coupled with a powerful pattern matching operation, called unification. Resolution, and a simplification step called factoring, are the only inference steps required to build a complete inference system for predicate logic providing all the statements are first translated into a special form, called clauses. This makes resolution inference highly suited to computer implementation.

Using a resolution system implemented in LISP, Green (1969b) showed how it could be used to answer questions, to "simulate" the computation of a program, even to synthesise a program from a specification. He was forced to view the computational use as a simulation because the theorem prover was not specialised for this use, nor was it implemented with efficiency in mind.

Work at Edinburgh University on resolution inference lead to more suitable theorem provers. The Boyer and Moore (1972) work on representation showed how the derived clauses of a resolution proof could be represented by pointers to initial clauses and binding environments, a representation similar to the activation records of conventional language implementations. Then the work of Kowalski on efficiency and goal directness (Kowalski, 1970; Kowalski and Keuhner, 1971) lead to the design of a resolution inference system, SL-resolution, more suited to computation. SL-resolution also incorporated ideas from Loveland's non-resolution model elimination inference system (1968). When applied to the Horn clause subset of predicate logic, SL-resolution behaved very like a conventional program executor. The difference was that it was non-deterministic, and the process of unification did the work of parameter passing, and of data structure access and construction. Finally, by fixing on a backtracking search strategy, Colmerauer's research group at Marseilles produced an extremely efficient implementation of SL-resolution for the Horn clause subset of predicate logic. This was in 1972. The theorem prover/program executor was called PROLOG (Colmerauer et al. 1973; Roussel, 1975).

The PROLOG implementation gave the final credibility to the idea that inference could be viewed as computation, an idea that was expounded by both Hayes (1973) and Kowalski (1974). Hayes considered sets of equations as programs, whereas Kowalski used sets of Horn clauses. Kowalski's paper, entitled "Predicate logic as programming language", marked the beginning of logic programming as a separate research area. That paper has inspired many people to explore the consequences of viewing computation as inference.

Since then there has been increasing research activity, mainly in Europe. There are now many implementations of PROLOG of which the most well known is the Edinburgh compiler/interpreter for the DEC-10 (Warren et al. 1977). Moreover, research on logic programming has developed far beyond the concerns of efficient resolution inference systems. It now covers application areas such as expert systems and natural language understanding, theoretic issues such as logic + control decomposition of algorithms, program transformation and program synthesis, and control concepts such as parallel computation, stream communication and intelligent backtracking. All of these new areas are treated in one or more papers in this volume.

THE PAPERS

The twenty three papers have been grouped into ten sections. The papers in each section have a common theme.

The first section, INTRODUCTION TO LOGIC PROGRAMING, contains just one paper by Kowalski. This is a general introduction to the concepts of logic programming. It introduces many of the ideas that are expanded upon by later papers. It should be the first paper read by someone new to logic programming.

The second section, APPLICATIONS OF LOGIC PROGRAMMING, contains two papers. The first is a survey by Toth and Szeredi of PROLOG applications in Hungary, where it has been

widely used for deductive data bases, expert systems and
artificial intelligence. The second, by Sergot, deals with
the representation of law in logic. It shows, through
examples, how logic provides a natural representation
language if one wants to computerise certain aspects of the
law.

A major application area of logic programming is natural
language processing. For this reason we have a separate
section, NATURAL LANGUAGE UNDERSTANDING. We include in this
section a paper by Colmerauer that develops a logical framework for the representation of a subset of natural language.
This logical framework has been used to build several natural
language interfaces to data bases, the interfaces being
written in PROLOG. The other paper, by Simmons, looks at the
problem of story understanding. It describes a logic program
that parses, summarises and answers questions about short
descriptions of flights. It does this by fitting the
description into an anticipated flight schema.

The fourth section, IMPLEMENTATION ISSUES, deals with the
implementation of PROLOG-like languages. The paper by
Bruynooghe progressively develops a runtime representation
for a conventional architecture from the description of an
abstract PROLOG interpreter. It also discusses two very
different ways in which variable bindings can be represented.
This binding representation choice is expanded upon in the
paper by Mellish. He gives runtime statistics for two
interpreters that differ in the way they represent variable
bindings. The last paper in this section, by Pereira and
Porto, discusses intelligent backtracking and a scheme for
its implementation.

Because logic programs are primarily sets of sentences of
predicate logic they often double as specifications of what
they compute. They can also be developed and transformed
using classical techniques of formal inference. The section,
SPECIFICATION AND TRANSFORMATION, deals with this feature of
logic programs. The paper by Hansson and Tärnlund illustrates
a deductive program transformation that uses a change of data
representation defined by a mapping function. The paper by
Clark, Sickel and McKeeman shows how several different
integration algorithms can be deductively developed from a
single, highly non-deterministic logic program. The last
paper in the section, by Davis, shows how Horn clauses can be
used to develop runnable specifications of abstract data
types.

The PROLOG language is not a pure first order inference system. It includes various meta level features that enable PROLOG programs to manipulate and execute other PROLOG programs. The section, METALEVEL INFERENCE, has two papers on this topic. The Bowen and Kowalski paper discusses the general problem of integrating meta-level and object level inference in a logically sound way. They exemplify the benefits and power of such an integration. The paper by Gallaire and Lasserre uses meta-level inference in a different way. They propose the use of a separate meta-level program to control the execution of a logic program.

Aspects of control are further explored in the next section, CONTROL ISSUES. The paper by van Emden and de Lucena gives a tutorial introduction to a parallel operational semantics for Horn clause logic in which conjoined conditions become parallel processes and shared variables become communication channels. This is "and" parallelism. The paper by Hogger deals with a logic program whose efficient execution requires "or" parallelism, where alternative evaluation paths for a single condition are explored in parallel. He then shows how the program can be systematically transformed into one that can be efficiently executed with only "and" parallelism. The paper by Kahn deals with control based on message passing. He shows how message handling processes, such as Hewitt's Actors, can be implemented in PROLOG. He argues that the amalgamation of Actors and PROLOG offers a powerful programming system.

The eighth section, LOGIC PROGRAMMING LANGUAGES, has four papers that treat four different logic programming languages. The first, by Colmerauer, describes a successor to PROLOG that has now been implemented at Marseilles. The major difference is that this version handles infinite data structures represented by self-referential bindings such as x=1.x. He gives a modified unification algorithm that can cope with such bindings, and shows how the inclusion of these infinite structures leads to some very elegant logic programs. The next paper, by Clark, McCabe and Gregory, describes a variant of PROLOG implemented at Imperial College, called IC-PROLOG. Its distinguishing feature is a rich set of control options expressed by program annotations. The third paper, by Hansson, Haridi and Tärnlund, describes a logic programming language not based on Horn clauses and resolution. The programming notation is a much more extensive subset of predicate logic and the abstract interpreter is a natural deduction inference system. The last paper of the section, by Bellia, Degano and Levi, describes a deterministic logic programming language of constrained Horn clauses. They give the language a lazy evaluation operation semantics and a fixed point mathematical semantics. This latter extends the usual model theory semantics for logic programs.

Section 9, LOGIC IN LISP, describes two logic programming systems implemented in LISP. LOGLISP, described in the paper by Robinson and Sibert, is an amalgam of logic and LISP. The logic ingredient differs from PROLOG in that it is not restricted to backtracking search, the search strategy can be specified by the programmer. The second paper, by Komorowski, describes a PROLOG implementation in LISP designed to inherit as much as possible of the rich programming environment - structure editors, trace/interrupt facilities, etc. - from the host LISP system. Both these papers cover aspects of the implementation of logic programming features in LISP.

The final section, HORN CLAUSE COMPUTABILITY, has just one paper by Sebelik and Stepanek. They treat the classic problem of bases for computability. They show that two special forms of Horn clause programs, stratifiable and binary, are both bases for computability. They also deal with transformations between the two forms and the potential change in complexity resulting from the transformation.

INTRODUCTION TO LOGIC PROGRAMMING

LOGIC AS A COMPUTER LANGUAGE

Robert Kowalski

Department of Computing
Imperial College, London SW7
England

1. INTRODUCTION

Symbolic logic was first designed as a formalization of natural language and human reasoning. As a result of its origins in natural language it has long been used in computing science as a specification language for computer programs and as a foundation for database query languages. Recent developments in automated deduction, however, have resulted in efficient schemes for processing logic by computer. These developments in turn have lead to the increasing use of logic as a very high level programming language (Hayes, 1973; Kowalski, 1974) and as a language for database description (Gallaire and Minker, 1978).

The computer language PROLOG (Programming in LOGic), based on symbolic logic, was designed and implemented by Colmerauer and Roussel in Marseille in 1972. It has been used for such varied applications as symbolic integration (Bergman and Kanoui, 1973), plan formation (Warren, 1976), computer aided building design (Markusz, 1977a), compiler construction (Warren et al. 1977), database description and query (Gallaire and Minker, 1978), the solution of mechanics problems (Bundy et al. 1979b), drug analysis (Darvas et al. 1978d) and natural language processing (Coelho, 1980; Colmerauer, 1973b; Dahl, 1979; McCord, 1980). Implementations of PROLOG on conventional computer architectures have achieved efficiency comparable with pure LISP (Warren et al. 1977). Research is also underway on implementations of logic programming languages on multiprocessor architectures.

The suitability of logic for expressing both programs and

their specifications makes it especially useful for program development.

In this introductory paper we survey various aspects of the use of logic as a computer language.

2. PROGRAM DEVELOPMENT

The problem of developing a correct but efficient program can usefully be decomposed into two simpler subproblems:

1. Specification. The first task is to specify the problem to be solved and the information which is needed for its solution.

2. Efficiency. Inefficiencies implicit in the problem specification can then be identified and removed, transforming the specification into an effective program.

The specification itself is easier to formulate and modify than the completed program, since it only needs to be "correct" whereas the program itself needs to be both correct and efficient.

Moreover, if, as is the case with symbolic logic, the specification language is machine-intelligible, then the specification can be tested by using it to solve simple problems. If the specification is incorrect or incomplete then it can be altered and tried again. Such debugging of specifications is more effective than debugging of programs, because concerns of efficiency need not be taken into account.

If, as is also the case with symbolic logic, the specification language itself is a programming language, then problems of efficiency can also be simplified. In some cases the specification might already behave as a tolerably efficient program. In other cases transformations may be needed to remove inefficiencies.

The program transformation techniques of Burstall and Darlington (1977) deal with assignment free languages such as NPL (Burstall, 1977) based upon recursion equations. These techniques have been extended and applied to symbolic logic by (Clark, 1977; Clark and Sickel, 1977; Clark and Darlington, 1980; Hogger, 1978, 1979, 1980; Hansson and Tärnlund 1979a,b). They resemble earlier methods of program synthesis but can also be interpreted as applying rules of logical deduction. Programs derived from specifications by such rules are logically implied by their specifications. Thus the derivations while aiming to remove inefficiencies are guaranteed to preserve correctness.

3. NATURAL LANGUAGE VERSUS FORMAL LANGUAGE FOR PROGRAM SPECIFICATION

Considerations of effective program development argue in favour of a high-level computer-intelligible specification language which can also be used as a programming language. Superficially at least, these arguments conflict with the requirement that the specification language be natural and easy to use. We shall argue that this apparent conflict can be reconciled by re-expressing the program specification in three successive formulations,

1. imprecise natural language,
2. precise, unambiguous natural language, and
3. precise formal language.

In the first formulation the problem specification may be incomplete, ambiguous and possibly contradictory. Several specification projects and most artificial intelligence projects for natural language take such imprecise language as input. Researchers involved in such projects have been inclined to use representation schemes for natural language based upon such structures as semantic networks, frames and scripts. It has been argued (Hayes, 1977; Deliyanni and Kowalski, 1979), however, that such schemes can usefully be reformulated in symbolic logic.

It is easier of course to process precise, unambiguous natural language. It makes a useful intermediate stage, in which ambiguities are removed and implicit assumptions are made explicit. Such precise natural language serves as computer input for several projects in program specification, data base query and legal information processing. These projects are more inclined than ones dealing with imprecise natural language to use symbolic logic directly.

It is easiest to process precise formal language directly. Considerations that the language be convenient both for translation from natural language as well as for transformation into efficient programs argue strongly in favour of symbolic logic. Logic reconciles the requirement that the specification language be natural and easy to use with the advantage of its being machine-intelligible.

4. LOGIC FOR DATABASES

The advantages of machine-intelligible specification languages are generally recognised in the field of databases. Database queries are regarded as problem specifications, which are formulated without any concern for efficiency. It is the responsibility of the database management system to optimize the query and to convert it into a program which accesses the database. Since symbolic logic blurs the distinction between databases and programs, it is no surprise that logic, often in disguised form, is increasingly favoured as a database query language. Relational calculus (Codd, 1972) and query-by-example (Zloof, 1975) are among the query languages most obviously rooted in symbolic logic. For a detailed investigation of different approaches to the use of logic for database query see (Pirotte, 1978).

5. THE HORN CLAUSE SUBSET OF LOGIC

The similarity between the use of logic to represent programs and its use for databases can be seen most clearly with the Horn clause subset of logic (named after Alfred Horn, who first investigated its properties). Horn clauses are both exceedingly simple yet surprisingly expressive. They provide the logical basis of PROLOG.

A program (or database) is a collection of sentences (also called Horn clauses) which express the information which can be used to solve problems (or to answer queries). A (Horn clause) sentence is either

(a)   a simple atomic assertion, e.g.
         The parity of 9 is odd.
         Manny is the manager of Bob, or

(b)   an implication, e.g. such statements as
         x is responsible for y if z does y
                                 and x is the manager of z.
         x inherits y if x is a child of z and z has y.

In general, every assertion is a simple atom, A.
whereas every implication has the form

         A if B_1 and B_2 and . . . and B_n.

where conclusion A and conditions B_1, B_2, ..., B_n are atoms, expressing a simple relationship among individuals. Individuals can be named by constants such as 9, odd, Bob or by variables such as x, y, z, etc.

To read a clause, such as A. or A if B_1 and ... and B_n., determine the variables x_1, x_2, ..., x_k it contains and interpret it as expressing that for all x_1, x_2, ..., x_k A or for all x_1, x_2, ..., x_k A if B_1 and ... and B_n respectively.

In addition to constants and variables, more complex names for individuals can also be constructed by using function symbols. For example the term cons(x,y) where "cons" is a function symbol, can be used to name the list

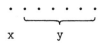

which consists of x followed by the list y. Thus if the constant "nil" names the empty list then the term:

cons(B, cons(0, cons(B, nil)))

names the list of characters: B O B.

It is common in mathematical notation to use <u>infix notation</u> for function symbols, writing for example 2+2 instead of +(2,2) and 2+2+3 instead of +(2,+(2,3)). Similarly it is convenient to write x.y instead of cons(x,y) and thus B.0.B.nil instead of cons(B,cons(0,cons(B,nil))).

The opposite convention (<u>prefix notation</u>) is also common in symbolic logic, writing for example Parity(9,odd). and Manager(Manny,Bob). instead of "the parity of 9 is odd." and "Manny is the manager of Bob."

Infix notation is more natural, but prefix notation is more precise. For example the infix assertion: "Bob is a salesman." can be interpreted in prefix notation either as a one place predicate Salesman(Bob). or as a two place relationship Is-a(Bob, salesman). For the sake of simplicity we shall use infix notation when it is convenient and not seriously ambiguous.

<u>Example</u>   The clauses
            x is a member of x.y.
            x is a member of u.v <u>if</u> x is a member of v.

constitute a definition of the relationship

    "x is a member of w ".

The definition can be understood simply in terms of the
natural language paraphrase involving the logical expressions
"for all", "if" and "and". Problems (or queries) can be posed
without needing to consider the operational problem-solving
behaviour to which the definition gives rise. To determine,
for example, whether 3 is a member of the list 4,2,3 it
suffices to ask the question.

    3 is a member of 4.2.3.nil?

In general, a query (or a program invocation) is a collection
of atomic conditions, written

    A_1 and A_2 and ... and A_n?

which is interpreted as the goal of finding a substitution of
terms for the variables in the query such that all of the
resulting conditions are implied by the database (or
program). For example, the query: x is a member of 4.2.3.nil
and x is a member of 2.4.1.nil? has two distinct solutions:
x = 2 and x = 4. When either substitution is applied to the
query the resulting variable-free atoms are logically implied
by the definition of membership.

Example. The following program was written by Moss (1980) at
Imperial College as one of several benchmark tests to compare
various PROLOG implementations with each other and with
PASCAL. The program itself is not particularly useful for
other purposes. It defines the relationship Revlist(x,y)
which holds when y is the list, in descending order, of all
the non-negative integers less than or equal to the integer
x. This relationship in turn is defined in terms of the
relationships Makelist(x,y,z) which holds when z is the list,
in ascending order, of all non-negative integers from x to y
inclusive and Reverse(u,v,w) which holds when the list w is
the result of appending the list v to the reverse of list u.

    Revlist(x,y) if Makelist(0,x,z) and Reverse(z,nil,y).
    Makelist(x, y, x.z) if x<y and Makelist(x+1, y, z).
    Makelist(x, x, x.nil).
    Reverse(x.y, v, w) if Reverse(y, x.v, w).
    Reverse(nil, w, w).

Here "x+1" is shorthand for a separate explicit condition

which determines the sum of x and 1. Written out in full, the second clause becomes

    Makelist(x, y, x.z) if x < y and Plus(x,1,u)
                        and Makelist(u, y, z).

The call Revlist(100, x)? computes x = 100.99 ... 2.1.0.nil. in .20 seconds when executed by Waterloo PROLOG (Roberts, 1977) on an IBM 370/135. The corresponding recursive PASCAL program takes .19 seconds on the same machine.

Example. The data in the table

Club	Name	Office	Dues	Birthdate	Date joined
	Mary	president	10p	4 Mar 77	4 Mar 77
	John	secretary	10p	2 Mar 78	2 Mar 78
	Bob	treasurer	10p	1 Apr 80	1 Apr 80

can be expressed by 3 assertions :

    Club(Mary, president, 10p, 4.Mar.77, 4.Mar.77).
    Club(John, secretary, 10p, 2.Mar.78, 2.Mar.78)
    Club(Bob, treasurer, 10p, 1.Apr.80, 1.Apr.80).

The clause   Club(x, y, z, 1.Apr.u, v)?   expresses the query "Was any member of the birthday club born on April fool's?"

However, the same database can also be expressed by means of binary relations using both assertions and implications:

    Member(Mary, Club).   Office(Mary, president).
    Member(John, Club).   Office(John, secretary).
    Member(Bob, Club).   Office(Bob, treasurer).
    Birthdate(Mary, 4.Mar.77). Birthdate(Bob, 1.Apr.80).
    Birthdate(John, 2.Mar.78).
    Dues(x, 10p) if Member(x, Club).
    Date-joined(x, y) if Member(x, Club) and Birthdate(x, y).

The same query can now be expressed by the clause

    Member(x, Club) and Birthdate(x, 1.Apr.u)?

6. HUMAN PROBLEM-SOLVING

The Horn clause subset of logic compares favourably with other formalisms studied by cognitive psychologists as a basis for information processing models of human problem-solving (Nilsson, 1980). The formulation of the farmer, wolf, goat and cabbage problem is a simple example.

State(x,y,u,v) expresses that there is a state in which the farmer, wolf, goat and cabbage are on banks x,y,u,v respectively of the Thames. Initially they are all on the north bank with a boat and want to cross to the south:

   State(N,N,N,N).   and   State(S,S,S,S)?

Opp(u,v) expresses that u and v are opposite banks and Safe(x,y,u,v) expresses that the state in which the farmer, wolf, goat and cabbage are on banks x,y,u,v respectively is safe. The farmer can cross from one bank to the other taking at most one passenger provided the new state is safe:

State(x,y,u,v) <u>if</u> State(x',y,u,v)
                <u>and</u> Opp(x,x') <u>and</u> Safe(x,y,u,v).
State(x,x,u,v) <u>if</u> State(x',x',u,v)
                <u>and</u> Opp(x,x') <u>and</u> Safe(x,x,u,v).
State(x,y,x,v) <u>if</u> State(x',y,x',v)
                <u>and</u> Opp(x,x') <u>and</u> Safe(x,y,x,v).
State(x,y,u,x) <u>if</u> State(x',y,u,x')
                <u>and</u> Opp(x,x') <u>and</u> Safe(x,y,u,x).
Opp(N,S).
Opp(S,N).

A state is safe if the farmer and goat are together on the same bank, so the farmer can protect the goat from the wolf and the cabbage from the goat. It is also safe if the farmer and goat are on opposite banks but the wolf and cabbage are together with the farmer:

   Safe(x,y,x,v).
   Safe(x,x,x',x) <u>if</u> Opp(x,x').

The preceding clauses constitute a complete specification of the problem. A natural, but efficient, solution can be obtained by applying the same strategy - the reduction of problems to subproblems - which is used for answering database queries and for executing programs.

7. PROBLEM-REDUCTION

The problem-reduction strategy for Horn clauses is identical with the procedural interpretation. An implication of the form

A $\underline{if}$ B_1 $\underline{and}$ ... $\underline{and}$ B_n.

is interpreted as a procedure which reduces problems of the form A to subproblems B_1 $\underline{and}$ ... $\underline{and}$ B_n. Each of the subproblems B_i in turn is interpreted as a procedure call to other implications. Assertions A. are interpreted as procedures A $\underline{if}$. which solve problems directly by reducing them to an empty collection of subproblems.

To apply a procedure to a procedure call, it may be necessary to instantiate variables, to make the procedure call identical to the conclusion of the procedure. Instantiating variables in the procedure can be regarded as transmitting input from the procedure call to the procedure. Instantiating variables in the procedure call can be regarded as transmitting output from the procedure to the procedure call and to all other procedure calls with which it shares variables.

If more than one procedure applies to a given procedure call then the problem-solver may need to explore the alternatives. The search can be pursued in parallel, trying all alternatives simultaneously; or it can be pursued sequentially, trying one alternative at a time, backtracking to try another if it fails. PROLOG (Roussel, 1975) and the majority of non-deterministic languages (Cohen, 1979) use backtracking to explore alternatives. Moreover the order in which clauses are written determines the order in which they are tried.

Logically, a collection B_1 $\underline{and}$ ... $\underline{and}$ B_n of procedure calls can be executed in any order and even in parallel. In PROLOG, procedure calls (for the sake of simplicity and efficiency) are executed left to right in the order in which they are written. In IC-PROLOG (Clark and McCabe, 1979a), however, facilities exist for executing procedure calls in pseudo-parallel and as coroutines.

8. IMPLICATIONS AS CONDITIONS

The expressiveness of Horn clauses can be improved by allowing conditions which are implications. In particular, explicit loops and recursions can often be avoided by using universally quantified implications instead. For example, whereas the Horn clause definition of the subset relation (where sets are represented by lists)

nil $\subseteq$ y.
u.v $\subseteq$ y $\underline{if}$ u is a member of y $\underline{and}$ v $\subseteq$ y.

involves an explicit recursion, the more natural definition

$x \subseteq y$ if for all z (z is a member of y if
z is a member of x).

does not. Here the expression   for all z   is a   universal
quantifier.

Notice that the procedural interpretation of the Horn clause
definition of the subset relation gives rise to an iterative
procedure which shows that $x \subseteq y$ by showing that the
successive members of x all belong to y. The second definition using the universal quantifier can be interpreted
similarly, except that it imposes no constraint on the order
in which the elements of x are investigated. It is even
compatible with an interpretation in which the members of x
are investigated in parallel.

The procedural interpretation of Horn clauses can be extended
to include the case in which a condition can have the form

for all x_1, x_2, ..., x_k (D if C_1 and ... and C_m).

To solve such a condition

find all substitutions (of terms for the variables
x_1, x_2, ..., x_k) which solve the query C_1 and ... and C_m?
and show that each such solution also solves the query D?

This procedural interpretation contrasts with the classical
interpretation:

To show for all x_1, ..., x_k (D if C_1 and ... and C_m)
assert the existence of arbitrary individuals named
a_1, ..., a_k, say, which satisfy conditions C_1 and ... C_m
and show that the same individuals also
satisfy the conclusion D.

The procedural interpretation is consistent with the classical interpretation on the assumption that the procedures
available for solving C_1 and ... and C_m? are the only ones
which are needed to define the relations. Reiter (1978) calls
this assumption for databases the closed world assumption. It
is intimately connected with the interpretation of negation
as failure.

9. NEGATION AS FAILURE

In the farmer, wolf, goat and cabbage problem it is more
natural to characterize a safe state as one which is not
sorry and a sorry state as one in which either the wolf and
goat are on the same bank and the farmer is on the other or
the goat and cabbage are on the same bank and the farmer is
on the other bank.

$$\text{Safe}(x,y,u,v) \quad \underline{if} \ \underline{not}\text{-Sorry}(x,y,u,v).$$
$$\text{Sorry}(x,y,y,v) \ \underline{if} \ \overline{\text{Opp}}(x,y).$$
$$\text{Sorry}(x,y,u,u) \ \underline{if} \ \text{Opp}(x,u).$$

It is natural to interpret the negative procedure call not-P?
as succeeding if the positive procedure call P? fails. Clark
(1978) has shown that such an interpretation of negation is
consistent with the standard interpretation, on the assumption that all of the procedures needed to solve P are present
in the database (program).

This justification of negation as failure can also be used to
justify the procedural interpretation of conditions which are
universally quantified implications. The definition of the
subset relation for example can be re-expressed in the form

$$x \subseteq \text{if } \underline{not}\text{-Nosub}(x,y).$$
$$\text{Nosub}(x,y) \ \underline{if} \ z \text{ is a member of } x$$
$$\underline{and} \ \underline{not}\text{-}(z \text{ is a member of } y).$$

The procedural interpretation of not in this formulation
gives rise to the same behaviour as the procedural
interpretation of the universally quantified implication in
the previous formulation.

10. THE DISTINCTION BETWEEN SPECIFICATIONS AND PROGRAMS

The preceding examples illustrate the way in which symbolic
logic blurs not only the distinction between programs and
databases but also the distinction between specifications and
programs. The following two definitions of ordered sequence
help to clarify the dual status of definitions expressed in
logic.

$$x \text{ is ordered } \underline{if} \ \underline{for} \ \underline{all} \ i, j \ (x_i \leq x_j \ \underline{if} \ i < j).$$
$$x \text{ is ordered } \underline{if} \ \underline{for} \ \underline{all} \ i \ (x_i \leq x_{i+1}).$$

Both definitions might be regarded as specifications. But

they can also be interpreted as procedures. The first
definition behaves as the inefficient procedure which runs in
time proportional to n^2 where n is the length of x. The
second definition, however, behaves as the optimally
efficient procedure which takes time proportional to n.

11. FUNCTIONAL VERSUS RELATIONAL NOTATION

The two definitions of ordered sequence above use functional
notation x_i to name the i-th element of the sequence x. Such
functional notation is often more natural and concise than
the corresponding relational notation. In relational notation
we would have to write something like

x is ordered if for all i,j,u,v ($u \leq v$ if i<j and
                                    u is the i-th item of x and
                                    v is the j-th item of x).

x is ordered if for all i,j,u,v ($u \leq v$ if Plus(i, 1, j) and
                                    u is the i-th item of x and
                                    v is the j-th item of x).

The functional and relational notations are virtually inter-
changable. It has been shown (van Emden and Kowalski, 1976),
moreover, that the fixpoint semantics normally associated
with functionally expressed recursion equations coincides
with the standard semantics of the same equations reexpressed
in relational notation as Horn clauses.

12. PROLOG

The language PROLOG provides, in addition to Horn clauses,
several extralogical features which extend its power but also
conflict with the classical semantics of logic. These
features allow control over the backtracking search strategy
and allow clauses to be manipulated, added and deleted from
the program during the course of execution. By means of these
facilities it is possible to define negation by failure and
other extensions of Horn clauses. The "PROLOG clauses"

    not(x) if x and / and fail.
    not(x).

for example define negation as failure. Here "fail" is any
atom which matches the conclusion of no clause elsewhere in
the program. "/" (called "cut" or "slash") is an extralogical

"evaluable predicate" which controls backtracking. The variable x in the first clause has two interpretations. The first occurrence of x is a term and the second occurrence is an atom. Although this use of x is not first-order logic it can be reinterpreted as syntactic sugar for something which is.

Given a goal   not (P)?   the first clause generates the subgoal P. If this succeeds then the execution of the evaluable predicate / restricts backtracking from later using the second clause to solve not(P). Execution of "fail" guarantees that the first clause then fails. If P does not succeed then / is not executed and backtracking successfully uses the second clause to solve not(P).

IC-PROLOG does away with the extralogical features of other PROLOG implementations. It incorporates directly a number of extensions, such as indexing, coroutining, negation by failure, conditionals and the construction and manipulation of all solutions of a subgoal, which are compatible with the semantics of logic.

A PROLOG compiler for the PDP10 has been written in PROLOG by Warren et al. (1977). They have shown that the compiler runs LISP-like Horn clause programs with similar efficiency to compiled pure LISP. PROLOG has also been implemented on several small computers, including a PDP11 by Chris Mellish in Edinburgh, a Motorola 6800 by Colmerauer et al. in Marseille and a Z80 by Frank McCabe in London.

13. OTHER DEVELOPMENTS

Especially noteworthy is work being done on selective backtracking, metalanguage and multiprocessor architectures. The first two topics are the subject of papers by (Bruynooghe 1978, 1980, 1981; Pereira and Porto, 1979a,b, 1980a,b,c; Bruynooghe and Pereira, 1981; Bowen and Kowalski, 1982). Work on multi-processor implementations of logic programming is being pursued at the University of Maryland, the University of California at Irvine and at Imperial College in London. In October 1981 a conference was held in Tokyo to explain the Japanese Fifth Generation Computer Systems Initiative. The project, which aims to develop the computer systems of the 1990's, proposes to use logic as the core programming language. A major objective is to produce a highly parallel multiprocessor implementation of an extended PROLOG.

14. LOGIC AS A COMPUTER LANGUAGE FOR CHILDREN

Since September 1980 I have been engaged with a colleague, Richard Ennals, in an SERC and Nutfield Foundation supported project to teach logic as a computer language for children. Logic is the single academic discipline which is common to all subjects taught in school. It provides a single uniform computer-intelligible language which is useful for expressing databases and programs for such diverse subjects as language, mathematics, the social sciences and the natural sciences.

In mathematics for example, transitivity of relations is just a special case of recursion: $x{\leq}y$ if $x{\leq}z$ and $z{\leq}y$. Moreover, the problem of solving several equations in several unknowns, e.g. $x+y=2$ and $x-y=0$? can usefully be introduced to children as the problem of answering a database query.

In English, logic clarifies, for example, the meaning of the commas in the sentence

All students, who study logic, like logic.

With commas the sentence means

x likes logic   if x is a student.
x studies logic if x is a student.

Without commas it means

x likes logic if x is a student and x studies logic.

The examples could be multiplied by considering all the other subjects taught in school. The development of logic as a computer language makes it especially appropriate, therefore, as a means of introducing children to computers. It contributes not only to the teaching of programming, databases and program specification but also to the application of logic to subjects traditionally taught in school.

ACKNOWLEDGEMENTS

The research reported in this paper has been supported by the Science Research Council. An earlier version was presented to the Infotech State of the Art Conference on Software Engineering, June 1980 (Kowalski, 1980).

APPLICATIONS OF LOGIC PROGRAMMING

PROLOG APPLICATIONS IN HUNGARY

E. Santane-Toth   P. Szeredi

Institute for Co-ordination of Computer Techniques (SZKI)
H-1368 Budapest P.O.B. 224.
Hungary

ABSTRACT

The paper makes an overwiew of the main PROLOG applications
in Hungary. For each application a short description of the
problem and the main characteristics of the implementation
are given. Finally the paper summarizes the experiences of
the described applications.

1. INTRODUCTION

Since 1975 (the implementation of the first PROLOG interpreter in Hungary) many problems have been solved using
PROLOG; problems previously either unsolvable (in traditional
programming languages) or solvable only by applying complex
algorithms and considerable effort.

PROLOG development and application was started in NIM IGUSZI
(Institute of Industrial Economy and Plant Organization of
the Ministry of Heavy Industries) on an ICL 1903A computer in
a batch environment. The interpreter for the language was
written in CDL (Compiler Description Language, Koster, 1977).
The first applications, in the areas of drug design and
architecture, were very succeessful. This lead to the wider
use and further development of the PROLOG system.

In 1977 the PROLOG interpreter was installed on a SIEMENS
7.740 (later 7.755) computer of SZKI under the BS2000
operating system. This installation is the most widely used

one, mainly because of the interactive environment and the
large virtual memory, and also because it introduced several
new built-in procedures. The BS2000 implementation served as
a basis for later installations on IBM 360 compatible
computers.

In 1978 KSH OSZI (State Institute for Application of Computer
Technique of the Central Statistical Office) provided support
for research to find new application areas for PROLOG and new
ways of solving problems in PROLOG. The PROLOG applications
in Hungary were studied in this framework (Santane-Toth,
1979) and the results of this research served as a primary
source of this survey.

In the following we begin with an enumeration of PROLOG
installations in Hungary and then we give a review of the
more interesting PROLOG applications. Finally we summarize
the experimental results and give some comments on the basis
of current PROLOG applications.

2. PROLOG INSTALLATIONS IN HUNGARY

Table I shows the existing Hungarian PROLOG installations in
time order. Due to the fact that the interpreter is written
in CDL there were no special difficulties when porting to
other machines. The reference and users' manuals are
(Szeredi and Futo, 1977; Koves, 1978; Laufer, 1979).

An improved PROLOG interpreter, the so-called MPROLOG has
also been developed (see Bendl et al. 1978, 1979b, 1980a;
Koves, 1979). One of its essential new features is that it
facilitates modular programming in PROLOG. It also offers
better interactive programming aids and an improved interpretation mechanism. Table II gives dates of early MPROLOG
installations.

It is worth noting here that an MPROLOG compiler is being
developed (see Bendl et al. 1980b).

3. PROLOG APPLICATIONS IN HUNGARY

PROLOG has been used for several purposes so far. The antho-
logy "How to solve it with PROLOG?" (Coelho et al. 1979)
surveys the fields where special problems could successfully
be solved using the language. Grouped according to topics, we
now give a list of the main Hungarian PROLOG applications.

For each of them we give the year of realization and the computer on which the program was developed or adapted. The relevant publications are given immediately after the title.

Table I. Hungarian PROLOG installations till 1980

Year	Machine	Op.Sys	Institute
1975	ICL 1903A	GEORGE	NIM IGUSZI (Inst. of Ind. Econ.)
1975	ICL SYSTEM 4/70	MULTIJOB	OTSZK (Nat. Planning Office)
1976	EMG 840	TMIN	NIM IGUSZI (Inst. of Ind. Econ.)
1976	HWB 66/20	GCOS	ASZSZ (Comp. Serv. of State Adm.)
1976	ODRA 1304	GEORGE	ELTE (Eotvos L. University)
1977	ICL 1905	GEORGE	MUM SZAMTI (Ministry of Labour)
1977	ODRA 1305	GEORGE	KGY (Chemical Works G. Richter)
1977	ODRA 1305	GEORGE	EGYT (Pharmaceutical Works)
1977	SIEMENS 7.755	BS2000	SZKI (Inst. Co-ord. Comp.Tech.)
1977	IBM 370/145	DOS/VS	SZAMOK (Comp. Education Centre)
1978	R22	OS/MFT	SZAMKI (Inst. Appl. Comp. Sci.)
1978	IBM370/145	OS/VS1	SZAMOK (Comp. Education Centre)
1979	SIEMENS 4004	BS2000	ETI-EGSZI (Inst. Building Sci.)
1979	R22	DOS	PMMF (Pollack M. Techn. College)
1979	R40	OS/MVT	KFKI (Centr. Res. Inst. Physics)
1980	IBM 3031	CMS	SZTAKI (Comp. and Automat. Inst.)

Table II. Early MPROLOG installations

Year	Machine	Op.Sys	Institute
1980	SIEMENS 7.755	BS2000	SZKI
1980	IBM 3031	CMS	SZTAKI
1980	R22	OS/MFT	NIM IGUSZI

3.1. Applications in the pharmaceutical research

3.1.1. CALCULATION OF PARAMETERS PREDICTING BIOLOGICAL ACTIVITY OF PEPTIDES
1979; SIEMENS 7.755; (Darvas et al. 1980).

Peptides compose a compound group of increasing importance in pharmaceutical research. For predicting their activity a model revealing the specific features of peptides is needed.

The mixed-language PROLOG-FORTRAN program system generates a family of structure activity models and, at the same time facilitates prediction of the biological activity on the basis of the models. The system infers chemical stuctural units (substuctures, fragments) from the aminoacid (i.e.

chemical) composition of peptides and assigns numerical parameters to the units. This is done by PROLOG programs. The relationship between the parameters and the biological activities of peptides is investigated by FORTRAN programs.

3.1.2. RESEARCH MANAGEMENT IN THE PHARMACEUTICAL INDUSTRY
        1979; SIEMENS 7.755; -

The system helps to solve research management problems in the pharmaceutical industry by information retrieval and automatic inference; the latter aiming at finding new applications for drugs and pesticides. The languages of the system are PROLOG and EDT (the editor of BS2000).

3.1.3. CALCULATION OF PHYSICO-CHEMICAL PARAMETERS FOR DRUG DESIGN PURPOSES
        1976-78; ICL 1903A, ODRA 1305, SIEMENS 7.755;
        (Darvas, 1978; Darvas et al. 1978a)

In computer-aided drug design, a considerable part of the calculations is based on the so-called logP value of components, a value indicating their lipophillic character. The manual calculation of this value is time consuming and results are of questionable accuracy. By 1976, when the PROLOG program was written, only one computer program for this calculation had been published.

3.1.4. PREDICTING DRUG-INTERACTIONS
        1975-79; ICL 1903A, ODRA 1305, SIEMENS 7.755;
        (Darvas et al. 1976, 1978c, 1979b; Futo et al. 1978a).

Modification in clinical effects may arise when drugs are parallelly administered. The so-called drug-interactions constitute an aspect of medical treatment. The present system considers the physico-chemical, pharmacological and chemical properties of drugs and, starting from these, infers the possible drug-interactions.

3.1.5. NUMERICAL ANALYSIS OF LIGAND-BONDING SYSTEMS
        1979; SIEMENS 7.755; (Kofalusi and Bartha, 1979b).

The PROLOG program generates a FORTRAN SUBROUTINE segment which calculates the proper initial value for the numerical analysis of ligand-bonding systems. The program is based on the program generator described in 3.7.2.

3.1.6. TESTING AND MODELLING OF SELF-REPRODUCING BIOCHEMICAL PROCESSES
1979; ICL SYSTEM 4/70, SIEMENS 7.755; -

The program permits the analysis and modelling of any biochemical self-reproducing cycle. With the replacement of the built-in data base any cycle can be examined. The input data of the program are the formal reaction equations; in the course of processing the nutriments, endproducts and attractors are selected. The program is an appropriate example for the fast and convenient definition of structural system models in PROLOG.

3.1.7. SEARCH OF ANALOGOUS SUB-STRUCTURES TO ENZYME SEQUENCES
1979; SIEMENS 7.755; (Matrai, 1979).

The program serves as a means of finding the sub-structures of enzymes with known sequences and similar mechanism, that are presumably relevant from the viewpoint of functioning. The program is suitable for the search of analogous primary sequence units of any size and having any number of error spots.

3.2. Information-Retrieval Systems

3.2.1. A LOGIC BASED CHEMICAL INFORMATION SYSTEM
1976-78; ICL 1903A, ODRA 1305, SIEMENS 7.755;
(Darvas et al. 1978b, 1979a).

The system consists of programs in FORTRAN for statistical calculations and PROLOG programs for automatic inference based on chemical structure and chemical and biological properties. The PROLOG environment provides tools for uniform knowledge representation and information handling for the two kinds of information (structure and properties).

3.2.2. AN INTERACTIVE INFORMATION SYSTEM FOR AIR POLLUTION CONTROL
1977; ICL SYSTEM 4/70;
(Bendl et al. 1979a; Futo et al. 1978a).

This program system handles data about the basic concentration of seven industrial pollutants in Budapest and in the counties of Hungary with each county having 15-20 districts. The system checks whether the air pollution of working or planned plants is below the permitted level. If not, it calculates the height of the chimney necessary to reduce the concentration, moreover it looks up in its data base and recommends industrial filtering equipment appropriate to the given industrial branch technology. The system works interactively; the basic motive of its planning was to enable people with different approaches (e.g. managers, designers and research workers) to use the system.

3.2.3. INFORMATION RETRIEVAL SYSTEM PROCESSING DATA ON PESTS AND PESTICIDES
1977; ICL SYSTEM 4/70; (Futo et al. 1978a).

This PROLOG program, aimed at the examination of results to be expected when applying different pesticides in given situations, can be used to determine interactions among the three following factors:
- diseases, pests, etc. detrimental to a culture;
- insecticides, pesticides, etc. against given diseases;
- cultures, application areas of given insecticides, pesticides, etc.

3.2.4. INFORMATION SYSTEM FOR THE "ANSWER" SOFTWARE DEVELOPMENT SYSTEM
1977-80; ODRA 1304, SIEMENS 7.755; (Ban et al. 1979).

The information system in question is a subsystem of the ANSWER software development system for CDL programs. The information system is being implemented in MPROLOG. Facilities of this system include: checking the connections between CDL program modules, tracing the effects of a modification of a CDL object, searching a CDL module for a given task.

3.3. Applications in the Building Industry

3.3.1. PLANNING OF A ONE LEVEL WORKSHOP BUILDING USING PREFABRICATED PANELS
1975; ICL 1903A; -

This program is the first PROLOG application in Hungary; it plans a one level workshop built of prefabricated panels. The ground-plan is a rectangle. The building is to be constructed from columns, beams and ceiling panels. The data of the available prefabricated elements (geometric size, net weight, supporting strength) are given in the form of assertions of the program. As initial data the geometric size parameters of the workshop and the intensity of the balanced load of the ceiling are given. The program determines the ground-plan (the distribution of the ceiling panels) and chooses the elements appropriate from the viewpoint of the geometric and statical conditions.

3.3.2. ARCHITECTUAL PLANNING OF PANEL BUILDINGS
        1976; ICL 1903A, R22; (Markusz, 1977a, 1977b).

The program generates the floor plan variants of flats with
given size, number of rooms or halfrooms, using the panel
elements stored in the data base. The program designs all the
possible variants of the floor plans of a flat with given
data.

3.3.3. PLANNING BUILDINGS WITH MORE THAN ONE LEVEL
        1980; SIEMENS 7.755, IBM 3031; (Markusz, 1980a,1980b).

The program system provides support in the stages of planning
of buildings with more than one level. First it generates the
variants of ground-plans of all flats according to the
special requirements of customers. The customer is given the
possibility to classify the variants, to choose the most
advantageous ones, and to exclude the less favourable ones.
The program assembles from chosen variants the plan of the
whole building satisfying requirements for the horizontal and
vertical arrangements, the given measurements, and the
conditions depending on the building site.

3.3.4. AUTOMATIZED SOLITAIRE FOUNDATION PLANNING
        1979; ICL SYSTEM 4/70, SIEMENS 4004; (Holnapy, 1979).

The problem solved by the program is the selection of bodies,
usable under columns, from a given fixed set of system
components (defined by assertions). An arbitrary system of
loads (load list) and a distance list can be given in the
goal statement and the result consists of the identifiers of
the foundation bodies to be used at the loading forces.

3.4. Software Applications

3.4.1. GENERATOR OF COBOL PROGRAMS FOR DATA VALIDATION
        1978; SIEMENS 7.755, ICL 1903A; (Lang, 1978).

The program generator is written in PROLOG and is applicable
for generating ANSI COBOL programs to be used for checking
input data. The generated program outputs the valid data on
an output file and prints the erroneous data (indicating the
cause of error). The structure of the files maintained by the
generated COBOL program and the aspects of validation are
defined by parameters from terminal or from a file.

3.4.2. GENERATING COBOL PROGRAMS
1979; SIEMENS 7.755; (Futo and Keresztely, 1979).

The program generators written in PROLOG generate programs according to standards used in SZKI. The generated COBOL programs solve data processing problems of the following types: listing data files, data maintenance, merging two data files and validation of primary input data. The structure of the input/output data maintained by the generated COBOL programs and the work to be done can be specified by uniform parameters.

3.4.3. PROM-MAPPING OF INTEL 3000 MICROPROGRAMS
1978; SIEMENS 7.755;
(Szeredi J. 1978; Balogh et al. 1978).

INTEL 3000 microprocessors have a special program addressing mechanism. The program can be thought of as a matrix, with every instruction in the matrix explicitly indicating its successor(s). There is only a limited set of matrix positions available for placing a successor (e.g. in the same column as the predecessor), furthermore the form of limitation depends on the sort of instruction. The PROLOG program performs the task of address assignment. Its input consists of a partially loaded store and a microprogram to be allocated to the given store. The PROLOG program gives either a possible mapping plan as output, or indicates the impossibility of mapping the given microprogram.

3.4.4. ANALYSIS OF PROGRAMMING STYLE AND EFFECTIVENESS
1980; IBM 370/145;
(Gero and Halmay, 1980; Halmay and Gero, 1981).

The aim of the program system is the evaluation of the quality of syntactically correct PL/I and COBOL programs by their analysis according to structure, style, effectiveness and complexity. In addition to the discovery of quality errors in the programs, the system suggests correct alternatives. During the structural analysis the system reveals and prints (in the form of hierarchy diagrams) the logical structure of the program being analysed, and notes the structural corrections to be performed. The program system was implemented mainly in PROLOG with the exception of the module drawing the hierarchy diagrams which is in optimizing PL/I.

3.4.5. A SYSTEM FOR VERIFYING PROLOG PROGRAMS
    1977-78; ICL SYSTEM 4/70, SIEMENS 7.755;
    (Balogh et al. 1977).

The system aims at proving partial correctness of PROLOG programs. A subsystem, consisting of a program for formula transformation and a program for general theorem proving can be used in itself, for interactive theorem proving. The interactive formula transformation program performs natural deduction on the basis of either built-in or interactively generated transformational (inference) schemas. The general theorem prover program is based on the resolution principle. The system is an experimental one. The studies (Balogh, 1979, 1981) deal with the conceptual side of the system.

3.4.6. DESIGN OF SOFTWARE AND HARDWARE OBJECTS
    1978; ICL 1903A, SIEMENS 7.755; (Balogh et al. 1978).

The experiences with PROLOG applications revealed the suitability of the language for solving problems manageable only with difficulties or not at all in other languages. The programs written in PROLOG reflect very clearly the structure of the problem and the way of solving it. This - and the possibility to run intermediate design results as PROLOG programs - led to the idea that applying PROLOG as a language for planning might be a worth-while experiment. The plans of sorting programs, a file maintenance system, a module library maintenance program and an RPG parser have been developed.

The experimental applications enumerated above proved that PROLOG is usable for planning software (and hardware) objects but the language lacks the data handling facilities, "real" means for interactive testing and an appropriate methodology of planning. Having drawn the conclusion a logic-based language (the LDM) for software development was designed (see Szeredi et al. 1980).

3.5. Supporting Computer Architecture Design

3.5.1. GENERATING ETALON PROGRAMS FOR TESTING COMPUTER
    ARCHITECTURE DESIGN
    1978; SIEMENS 7.755; (Kiss V. and Simor, 1978).

In designing and evaluating computer architecture supporting a particular high level programming language, good use can be made of small-sized runnable programs written in the language, that exhibit certain statistical features absorbed from the analysis of users' programming habits. Examples of such statistical features for given high-level language are the rate of occurence of instruction types or of data types. A PROLOG program was developed as an experimental tool, for the purpose of generating such etalon programs. The program input consists of the syntax rules of the given language and the statistical features we want the generated programs to have.

3.5.2. A SIMULATOR FOR EVALUATING THE DESIGN AND EXPERIMENTAL TESTING OF HIGH-LEVEL ARCHITECTURES
1979; SIEMENS 7.755; (Kiss V. and Simor, 1979).

The basic purpose of the development of the simulator was to provide computerized support for the design process of language-oriented computer architecture. The system can be used for:
- measuring quantitative factors characterizing the effectiveness of the given architecture;
- the experimental validation of the specified architecture by means of running test programs (see 3.5.1.);
- measuring the dynamic statistics of the use of the source language.

3.6. Simulation

3.6.1. AN INTERPRETER FOR THE LANGUAGE T-PROLOG
1980; SIEMENS 7.755;
(Futo et al. 1980b, 1980c, Futo and Szeredi J. 1981).

T-PROLOG is a PROLOG based simulation language with a capability for explicit and implicit time handling. The interpreter of the language is capable of running an arbitrary number of PROLOG like goals in parallel. The processes executing the goals can communicate through logical variables, through the data base and by means of a simple "demon mechanism". In the case of a deadlock further paths are explored through backtracking.

There is now a project underway to use T-PROLOG in the examination of the long-term regional models of VATI (an institute concerned with city development).

3.6.2. GENERATING MODELS OF TELEPROCESSING NETWORKS
1980; SIEMENS 7.755; -

A PROLOG program was developed for the generation of simulation models of data processing networks. The program generates a simulation model of the network in GPSS (SIAS) language. The description of the network (the topology, the line control algorithms, the type of channels, etc.) is entered into the system in a conversation with the user. The generated model traces the throughput of the system, the waiting queues at the nodes, etc.

3.7. Other Applications

3.7.1. COMPUTERIZED MORPHOLOGICAL ANALYSIS OF HUNGARIAN TEXTS
1979; SIEMENS 7.755; (Kiss Z. et al. 1979).

The problem of parsing Hungarian texts by computer hasn't been solved yet - because of the complexity of the grammar, especially the agglutinative character of the language. Due to the different verb forms, order relations, the assimilation of vocals and consonants it is very difficult to find an algorithm solving this problem. The first step of text parsing is the morphological analysis of the text. This part of the problem could be solved in PROLOG relatively easily. The program itself actually represents two automata - one for the morphological analysis of the Hungarian verb forms and the other for the morphological analysis of the tagged nouns.

3.7.2. COMPUTING THE FIRST N DERIVATES OF COMPOSITE REAL FUNCTIONS
1979; SIEMENS 7.755; (Kofalusi, 1979b).

Input of this PROLOG program is a composite real function of several variables and high complexity. The program generates the first n derivates of the function by symbolic differentiation. Possible simplifications are made at the symbolic level. The output of the program is a FORTRAN subroutine for computing substitution values of the derivates. Common subexpressions are evaluated only once. The PROLOG program is based on the state space concept (see e.g. Kofalusi, 1982; Kofalusi and Halmay, 1981).

3.7.3. SIMPLIFICATION IN MATHEMATICAL STRUCTURES
1979-80; SIEMENS 7.755; (Kofalusi, 1979a).

The objective of the program under development is the simplification of expressions allowed in a very broad class of mathematical structures (including groups, rings, fields, Boolean lattices, etc.). The program traverses the expressions represented by binary trees bottom-up, from left to right, and looks ahead for one level, backward for more levels. In the case of an associative chain of operators the program performs sorting according to the appropriate ordering aspects.

4. EXPERIENCES AND CONCLUSIONS

First, let us try to analyse the reasons for success of PROLOG in Hungary. The relatively large number of Hungarian PROLOG applications is due to several factors (we do not mention here the well known general advantages of PROLOG programming, listed e.g. in (Coelho et al. 1979):
- There were no other artificial intelligence languages available in Hungary.
- The Hungarian PROLOG interpreter was fast enough for starting real applications, it was fairly portable so that it could be installed on any computer chosen by the user.
- There was a good cooperation between PROLOG implementors and people working on applications; due to this a number of special built-in procedures and a good tracing mechanism (for batch environment) were produced.
- There were two successful "pilot" applications: drug design and architecture (see 3.1.3, 3.1.4 and 3.3.1, 3.3.2); these served as a basis for further similar applications.
- Most of the people involved in programming the PROLOG applications had little traditional (algorithmic) programming backround, this allowed them to learn PROLOG relatively easily.
- The installation of PROLOG on SIEMENS 7.755 with interactive environment and large virtual memory helped a lot in further development of existing applications and in the introduction of new ones.
- The interactive environment together with the good symbol manipulation facilities of the PROLOG interpreter (and also the lack of other symbol manipulation languages) promoted the development of a new PROLOG application area represented by the COBOL program generators (these are completely algorithmic programs, but make intensive use of symbol manipulation facilities).

There were, however, several problems with PROLOG applications:
- The simple implementation of PROLOG stacks (recovery of space only on backtrack) caused problems in smaller installations and forced programmers to use tricks for space recovery (by forcing a backtrack). Even on the largest installation (SIEMENS, 3 Mbyte stack) there were some occurences of stack overflow for some special programs.
- The demand for an interface with algorithmic languages (mostly with FORTRAN) arose a number of times. The problem was partially solved by communicating with separate FORTRAN programs through files (see e.g. 3.1.1), also an experimental

interpreter version was produced that allowed FORTRAN subroutines to be called from PROLOG (Kofalusi and Bartha, 1979a), but the real solution is still lacking.
- The need for handling large data bases (held in disk files) also arose. In some cases the problem was solved by using the system editor (that can be called from PROLOG in the BS2000 implementation), see e.g. 3.1.2.
- The naive backtracking mechanism of the implementation caused problems in programs involving combinatorial search (see e.g. 3.4.3). The difficulties had to be overcome by programming special backtrack and/or coroutine-like features in PROLOG itself.
- The speed of PROLOG also caused problems when some PROLOG systems were put to extensive use. This was the case for most of the drug design systems.
- There is great lack in a textbook for introducing PROLOG for people trained in traditional, algorithmic programming.

As a conclusion we claim that main reason of the success of PROLOG in Hungary is the existence of good connections between people of theoretical and practical attitude. With the additional help of other factors this enabled the exploration of various application fields and the starting of several concrete applications. For further work in this direction it is necessary to overcome the problems, most of which concern the (space or time) efficiency of the applications. We hope that with the help of present results in efficient implementation of logic programming these problems can be solved. In fact in the new MPROLOG system, which is now in experimental use, some of the listed problems are already settled. Hopefully the others will be solved in near future, also in the framework of PROLOG.

ACKNOWLEDGEMENT

We should like to thank everybody working in the development and application of PROLOG for their help in putting together this paper.

PROSPECTS FOR REPRESENTING THE LAW
AS LOGIC PROGRAMS

Marek Sergot

Department of Computing
Imperial College, London SW7
England

ABSTRACT

With growing interest in the applications of computing to
law, logic programming techniques provide a promising tool
for the implementor. In the first instance, much law can be
viewed as high-level specification which is relatively easily
formalized as logic programs. On the other hand, the construction of an intelligent legal expert system requires a
more powerful, but still human-oriented, framework for
expressing legal rules. An informal treatment of a simple
example illustrates the potential of logic in this area.

1. LAW AND LOGIC

Logic provides a natural base for a computer interpretable
formalism to express legal rules: law treats large sets of
complex rules that have long seemed suitable for logical
analysis, and once the law is expressed in some appropriate
subset of predicate logic, that formulation can function as a
program which interprets the law.

But legal provisions vary widely in their character, and it
is useful to distinguish two general kinds of law which would
require different treatments in logic. In the first instance,
substantial amounts of law can be viewed simply as high-level
descriptions which more or less precisely define legal
properties and relationships. A law which defines citizenship
or nationality would be mostly of this category, for example.
This kind of law can be relatively easily formalized as logic
programs, and in the short term practical legal systems could

appear in this area. The next section elaborates this point.

In contrast some law is of a quite different nature, and can
be regarded instead as a set of norms of conduct which state
what must or must not be done under certain circumstances. A
more ambitious approach might be to inspect the properties of
the norms that are found in law, and to examine how they are
used in legal reasoning. The rest of the paper presents an
treatment of a simple example, with the aim of indicating how
such norms might be modelled by logic programs and mentioning
several ways in which these models could be used.

2. LAW THAT ACTS AS A HIGH-LEVEL DESCRIPTION

Substantial sections of law, of modern legislation in particular, do not express norms describing what must or must not
be done. Rather, they define legal properties, relationships
and entitlements. Many tax laws and laws in areas like social
security are of this category for example. Nevertheless such
legal specifications are not expressed as detailed algorithms
and it is often a daunting task to construct suitable algorithmic implementations of them. In contrast, it is relatively easy to transcribe these high-level descriptions as logic
programs by defining the legal concepts they describe in
precise logical terms, in a style moreover which closely
resembles the original legislation. For example, the first
clause describing British nationality states that

A person born in the United Kingdom after commencement shall
be a British citizen if at the time of the birth his father
or mother is - (a) a British citizen; or (b) settled in the
United Kingdom. More precisely:

                x becomes (British Citizen) at t
                    if x born-in UK
                    and x born-at t
                    and t is-after Commencement
                    and y is-parent-of x
                    and (y is (British Citizen) at t
                                    or
                         y is-settled-in UK at t)

As above, predicate symbols will often be written in infix
form to aid readability. Constant symbols begin with a
capital letter, variables are written in lower case, and
function symbols are clear from context.

This example illustrates a general point, that the accurate application of a law may require access to facts spread over a long span of time. In this sense past history can never be deemed irrelevant for legal purposes. This point can be underlined by referring to the impact made in legal computing by LEGOL (Stamper, 1979), which is widely regarded as the most general legally oriented system available at present. LEGOL seeks to provide a (rudimentary) framework in which information can never be 'forgotten', and which gives the handling of time a special treatment unlike the other kinds of data present. The LEGOL language, while still inadequate for many types of legal rules, has nevertheless found a number of practical applications. In fact the LEGOL language, in versions to date at least, has been based on relational algebra, but there are significant advantages in viewing it instead as a logic programming language tailored for specific application areas (Sergot, 1980).

3. LAW AS A SET OF NORMS

A short introductory article cannot discuss in detail the structure of norms, what modalities such as 'must', 'should' or 'may' can mean, or how they may be used in legal reasoning. Some of the requirements and their difficulties can be explained however by considering the Library Regulations for borrowing books at Imperial College.

LIBRARY REGULATIONS

1. A separate form must be completed by the borrower for each volume borrowed.
2. Books should be returned by the date due.
3. Borrowers must not exceed their allowance of books on loan at any one time.
4. NO BOOK WILL BE ISSUED TO BORROWERS WHO HAVE BOOKS OVERDUE FOR RETURN TO THE LIBRARY.

Book Allowances: Undergraduates   6   Academic staff   20
                   Postgraduates   10

In comparison with most 'real' law of course this example is exceedingly trivial, but it can make some useful points, and it has the merits of being short and dealing with concepts familiar to most. Moreover, it is typical of rules and regulations to be found in many institutions and organizations, rules which are not part of "The Law", but which have the same character as legal provisions nevertheless. The

problem can be decomposed into two simpler sub-problems:
(1)   What do norms mean ?
      How can they be used ?
      How can they be represented by computer ?
(2) How can the norms in force be determined from the various
sources of law, which include legislation (statutes), and
unwritten law like case law and general legal 'principles'
("no man may profit by his own wrong-doing") by which judges
are 'guided' ?

The sections below are intended to address the first of these
sub-problems by reference to the Library Regulations,
although no attempt has been made at completeness. The general approach taken is to attempt computer program models of
law, which 'do' to the data in the machine what the law
'does' to corresponding entities in the real world.

3.1 The Library Data Base

In discussing the Library Regulations, it will be helpful to
imagine how they might be included in a logic data base which
the Library maintains to mechanize its administration. Information stored might include, amongst other things:

assertions describing each person's "borrower status"
            Undergraduate(John).
            Postgraduate(Amy).
            Staff(Jake).
            Librarian(Miss Page).
                      :
books which the Library has available
            Book(War and Peace).
            Book(Confessions of a Logic Programmer).
            Book(Alice in Wonderland).
                      :
and some general rules
            Person(x) if Undergraduate(x)
            Person(x) if Postgraduate(x)
            Person(x) if Staff(x)
            Person(x) if Librarian(x)

Clearly the contents of such a data base would change with
time, frequently as books are borrowed and returned, and less
often as new readers join the Library or leave. The aim here
is not to discuss how logic data bases should deal with time
information however. Without labouring the point, a time
parameter can be included in most of the data base relations.

Records are kept about the return of books, so the data base could contain, on the 1 September, say

(Miss Page) lent (War and Peace) to Amy on (9 July).
(Miss Page) lent (Confessions of ...) to John on (20 April).
John returned (Confessions of ...) on (21 April).

When books are returned, a corresponding 'due on' record is deleted from the data base, so also "(War and Peace) due on (23 July)." since Amy has not returned her book yet. Some more of the general rules in the data base are:

```
x has y at t if Librarian(z)
              and z lent y to x at t-one
              and t on or after t-one
              and not exists t' : (x returned y on t'
                                   and t' between t-one and t)
  Overdue(x,t) if x due on t' and t is after t'
  Has-a-book-overdue(x,t) if x has y at t and Overdue(y,t)
```

Here, 'not exists z: (conjunction of conditions)' means negation as failure, true if and only if the query "(conjunction of conditions) ?" has no solutions.

The Library data base can be used to answer various queries posed by either librarian or reader, in the usual way. But to help with a particularly common type of question which can be expected, a useful rule might be included which states

```
Possible(x,borrow(y),t) if Person(x) and Book(y)
                        and not exists z : z has y at t
```

The intended reading of Possible(x,y,t) ("it is possible for x to do y at t") expresses that only those books which the Library has in stock can be lent out, and then on condition that they are not already on loan. The representation of actions (like "borrow") is for illustration only, and no particular significance should be attached to it. So if 'Today' is a constant symbol with the obvious interpretation

```
  Possible(John, borrow(War and Peace), Today) ?
```

asks if a particular reader can have the book he wants, and is one of many similar questions that could be put.

3.2 Prohibitions and Obligations

Some insight can be gained into the nature of norms by

examining the ways in which they can be used. In the first instance then the Library Regulations could be used, by librarian or prospective borrower, to determine whether a particular person is allowed to have a chosen book.

The overall effect of the Regulations might be modelled by including in the Library data base a program of the form:

```
x allowed-to-borrow y at t if  Person(x)
                            and not At-limit(x,t)
                            and not Has-a-book-overdue(x,t)
where
At-limit(x,t) if Allowance(x,n) and Number-of-books(x,n,t)
   Allowance(x, 6) if Undergraduate(x)
   Allowance(x,10) if Postgraduate(x)
   Allowance(x,20) if Staff(x)
```

together with rules which allow the number of books a reader has borrowed at any time (Number-of-books) to be calculated from data describing which books he has borrowed (has). (Regulation 1, dealing with completed forms, has a different character, and would probably appear in another form in a realistic implementation. For present purposes, its existence can be safely ignored.) Now permission for any reader to borrow a desired book is established by asking, for example

Jake allowed-to-borrow (Alice in Wonderland) at Today ?

On the other hand it would be a fair criticism to say that this representation was possible only because the set of rules to be modelled was small. In general this approach would be less appealing because the interaction of provisions and their spread over pages of legislation would make this kind of formulation difficult. More attractive is a solution which lists the individual provisions one by one, but which behaves overall like the single allowed-to-borrow rule. It is generally useful to label individual provisions, so possibly:

```
Prohib(LR3, x, borrow(y),t) if At-limit(x,t)
Prohib(LR4, x, borrow(y),t) if Has-a-book-overdue(x,t)
```

where Prohib(x,y,z,t) is to be read as "rule x prohibits y from doing z at t". Now permission is expressed by the general rule

```
x allowed-to y at t if not exists z : Prohib(z,x,y,t)
```

enabling the earlier question to be phrased as

Jake allowed-to borrow(Alice in Wonderland) at Today ?

But most useful would be answers to questions like "Can I borrow this book ?", where 'can' is defined

x can y at t $\underline{if}$ Possible(x,y,t) $\underline{and}$ x allowed-to y at t.
Now
        Jake can borrow(Alice in Wonderland) at Today ?

checks first whether Alice in Wonderland is available, and then whether Jake is allowed to borrow it.

Implicitly, the reading given to the Library Regulations so far has been that they are directed at borrowers. They are also meant to be obeyed by the librarians. In this second interpretation

        Prohib(LR3',x, lend(y,z),t) $\underline{if}$ Librarian(x)
                                $\underline{and}$ At-limit(z,t)
        Prohib(LR4',x, lend(y,z),t) $\underline{if}$ Librarian(x)
                                $\underline{and}$ Has-a-book-overdue(z,t)

are rules which should be included in the data base also, together with, say

Possible(x,lend(y,z),t) $\underline{if}$ Librarian(x) $\underline{and}$ Book(y)
                $\underline{and}$ Person(z) $\underline{and}$ $\underline{not}$ $\underline{exists}$ z' : z' has y at t

This representation of prohibitions allows additional questions to be asked, for example "Is there anything I must not do ?", or more precisely, "Is there anything I could do, but which is forbidden to me ?"
        Possible(Me, y, Today) $\underline{and}$ Prohib(z, Me, y, Today) ?

An obvious extension is to attempt a formulation of obligatory acts in the same style, and regulation 2 provides just such an example. Approximately
        Oblig(LR2,x, return(y),t) $\underline{if}$ x has y at t and Overdue(y,t)

A supplementary general law to be included is
        x allowed-to y at t $\underline{if}$ Oblig(z,x,y,t)

so long as the set of laws being modelled is 'consistent', in the sense that

        Oblig(x,y,z,t) $\underline{and}$ Prohib(x',y,z,t) ?

has no solutions.

A fuller treatment of these ("deontic") modalities and their
properties is inappropriate here, but the possibility of
inconsistency in a set of norms could lead to definitions
like
    Unreasonable(norm) if Oblig(norm,x,act,t)
                       and not Possible(x,act,t)
and, with a sufficiently rich representation of the properties of acts, concepts such as
    Conflict(norm-one,norm-two) if Oblig(norm-one,x,act-one,t)
                                and Oblig(norm-two,x,act-two,t)
                                and Incompatible(act-one,act-two)
could be attempted.

3.3 Towards Extracting the Meaning of Norms

With the Library data base in its present form, the Regulations are represented in a way that merely describes what
acts are prohibited, obligatory and permissible, and under
what circumstances. The formulation of norms can be extended
as a first step in capturing what is meant by these terms.
Some of what norms 'mean' can be extracted by defining

x transgressed norm at t
            if Prohib(norm,x,y,t) and x did y at t
x transgressed norm at t
            if Oblig (norm,x,y,t) and not x did y at t

For the data base, with its crude representation of acts,
x did lend(y,z) at t if x lent y to z at t
x did borrow(y) at t if z lent y to x at t and Librarian(z)
x did return(y) at t if x returned y on t

So that, if as well as the 'lent' and 'returned' data above,
(Miss Page) lent (Alice in Wonderland) to Amy on (14 August).
holds, solutions to the query: x transgressed y at t ? would
indicate that Amy transgressed LR4 on 14 August, and Miss
Page transgressed LR4' on 14 August, and moreover, that Amy
had been transgressing LR2 since 24 July.

Typically, individual norms are linked together, and a
particularly common type of link in the legal context is the
sanction. Often, when one norm is transgressed, another
norm, the 'sanctioning norm', is activated. For example, the
Constitution of Imperial College might include a rule which
requires the Chief Librarian to punish (by dismissal with a
month's notice, say) any librarian who breaks the Library
Regulations. Since this norm affects the Library's
administration, it should be included in the data base.

Oblig(IC-Const-Lib,x,dismiss(y),t)
<u>if</u> Chief-Librarian(x) <u>and</u> Librarian(y)
<u>and</u> y transgressed norm at t'
<u>and</u> Library-Regulation(norm)
<u>and</u> t is-one-month-after t'

Now one solution to the question: Oblig(x,y,z,t) ?   would indicate that the Chief Librarian should dismiss Miss Page on 14 September, because she broke regulation 4 by issuing Alice in Wonderland to Amy when Amy had a book overdue.

4. LEGAL EXPERT SYSTEMS

Throughout this example the Library Regulations have been incorporated in a Library data base. On the other hand the very same representation of these norms could provide the knowledge domain for a rule based 'expert system'. Clark and McCabe (1982) describe how expert system features like inference generated requests for data and explanations of behaviour can easily be implemented in the logic programming language PROLOG. A system constructed in this way could give advice about the Library Regulations, asking for any information it requires, and giving reasons for its decisions. Indeed many types of regulations could not realistically be included as part of some data base, but they could be the basis for a useful legal expert system of this kind.

5. USING LEGAL NORMS TO CONSTRAIN DATA BASE UPDATES

The checking of attempted updates to preserve data base consistency is an important function of any data base management system. In the Library, an intelligent maintenance system should reject, for example, updates describing the return of a book which is not out on loan, or the borrowing of a book which does not exist. Earlier, meaningful actions were described by the 'Possible' relation, which was included as part of the data base. Now, the 'Possible' clauses could be used instead to define constraints on data base updates, which the maintenance system can use for checking purposes.

This scheme suggests an alternative role for the Library Regulations, and contrasts usefully with that described earlier. Here, legal norms can be represented as before, but included now, not as part of the data base itself, but as additional constraints to be taken into account before an update is accepted. There is an important distinction to be drawn however between constraints defined by legal norms, and, for lack of a better term, "physical" constraints. Thus, the 'Possible' relation defines constraints which represent "physical necessities", in the sense that they can never be broken: it is meaningless to describe, in the Library data base context, the return of something which is not a book, and one that is not out on loan at that time. Legal constraints are much weaker though. They can be broken, and, in the real world, often are.

The amalgamation of language and metalanguage proposed by Bowen and Kowalski (1982) allows powerful formalizations of data base maintenance, and suggests how these ideas can be sketched in brief. Here it is intended that

Assim(currdb,p-laws,l-laws,event,newdb,report)

holds when assimilation of an input describing some event description into a given current data base currdb with constraints p-laws (physical) and l-laws (legal) results in a new data base newdb. Success or failure is transmitted by report.

6. CONCLUSION

The success of projects like LEGOL confirms the intuitive impression that logic programming techniques provide a promising framework in which to attempt the computerized implementation of substantial sections of law. It would be of great interest if practising lawyer-programmers were to adopt a logic programming language like PROLOG as their programming tool.

The simple Library example sketched a treatment of norms and indicated how a single representation could be useful in a number of ways. A more rigorous presentation could not be undertaken here. More generally, the representation of how things behave in time is a central theme, since much law deals primarily with prescriptions of allowed and prohibited actions.

Finally, the norms expressed in law change so rapidly, and are derived from so many separate sources, that only an experienced lawyer could attempt the construction of a useful legal expert system. To expect him to learn unfamiliar computer languages in addition is unreasonable.

NATURAL LANGUAGE UNDERSTANDING

AN INTERESTING SUBSET OF NATURAL LANGUAGE

Alain Colmerauer

Groupe Intelligence Artificielle,
Faculté des Sciences de Luminy,
Université Aix-Marseille II
13288 Marseille cedex 2,
FRANCE

ABSTRACT

We are interested in defining a minimal natural language
subset which can be used, for instance, to create and consult
data bases. After examining the simplest statements that can
be based on a verb, a noun and an adjective, we go on to more
complex statements involving articles, relative clauses and
negations. Emphasis is laid on the systematic transformation
of a sentence into a semantic formula. It appears that such
semantic formulae can be interpreted correctly only in a
logical system with three truth-values. Moreover one must
suppose that the elementary relations associated with the
verbs, nouns and adjectives range not over individuals, but
over sets of individuals.

An early version of this paper can be found in the proceedings of the Workshop on Formal Base for Data Base held at
the Centre d'Etude et de Recherches de l'Ecole Nationale
Superieure de l'Aeronautique et de l'Espace de Toulouse,
Toulouse, France, 1977. A more elaborated version, which is
written in French, can be found in (Colmerauer, 1979a). This
third version differs in the way the logical system is
presented. Financial support for this work was given by the
Centre National de la Recherche Scientifique, (Equipe de
Recherche Associée 363).

1. INTRODUCTION

Our aim is to delimit and study a subset of natural language
that might serve as starting point for numerous applications,

such as the consultation, creation and updating of sophisticated data bases. Although the language examined here is
French the results presented ought to be transferable to
other languages. This has been partially done for Spanish,
English and Portuguese.

What we require of the subset is :

(1) a simple but natural syntax;
(2) rigorously defined semantics.

Nevertheless, in spite of our desire to formalise, we do not
want to prejudge the semantic representation. We shall
develop and motivate this through a series of examples.

First, we introduce the notion of elementary statements based
on proper nouns. We do not at this stage attach precise
semantic rules to them. We then show the fundamental role
played by articles in relating two statements and in the
introduction of a variable that behaves as a proper noun.
This leads us to three-branched quantifiers which permit us
to state clearly the quantification hierarchy problem.

After considering negation, conjunction between two statements and relative clauses, we specify which restrictions a
statement must satisfy in order to be easily translatable
into classical first-order logic. These restrictions being
too strong, we then abandon this logic and re-examine the
problem in a new light. This forces us to adopt two
hypotheses on the semantics of our natural language subset:

(1) In a given situation certain sentences are meaningless
    and it is therefore necessary to consider the truth value
    "undefined" in addition to "true" and "false". (This
    technique has been used by Keenan (1972) in order to
    formalise presupposition.)
(2) Properties introduced by sentences must apply to sets of
    individuals and not to individuals: this is mainly in
    order to treat plurals correctly. (Pasero, 1973, had
    already adopted this hypothesis.)

All this leads us to a special logical system for natural
languages. The semantics of a formula in this system are its
truth value variations (true, false and undefined), when we
place ourselves in different situations. We conclude by
showing how to associate a formula of this system with each
sentence in the French subset that we treat.

2. ELEMENTARY STATEMENTS

We first concern ourselves with the simplest statements that can be made involving proper nouns. We will distinguish three types:

Those constructed with a common noun and the verb "to be":

```
Garigou is (a) cat          Pierre is (the) son of Paul
       est (un) chat                est (le) fils de
```

Those constructed with a verb:

```
Garigou trots               Sophie lends Garigou to Anne
        trotte                     prête          à
```

Those constructed with an adjective and the verb "to be":

```
Garigou is striped          Anne is satisfied with Garigou
        est tigré                est contente  de
```

We will associate the following formulae with these six examples:

```
iscat(Garigou)              lendsto(Sophie,Garigou,Anne)
issonof(Peter,Paul)         isstriped(Garigou)
trots(Garigou)              issatisfiedwith(Anne,Garigou)
```

HYPOTHESIS 1: To each verb, to each adjective and to each common noun there corresponds a property with n arguments, each argument being a proper noun.

It must be noted that not only verbs, but also adjectives and nouns may introduce properties with more than one argument.

3. INTRODUCTION OF THREE-BRANCHED QUANTIFIERS

Let us consider the sentence: Arthur owns   a   car
                                       possède une voiture

We could associate with it the formula: owns(Arthur,a(car))

But then to the sentence: Otto owns   a   car
                                     possède une voiture
would correspond: owns(Otto,a(car))

and we might conclude that Arthur and Otto own the same car, when this is probably not the case. On the other hand, behind the sentence: Arthur owns a car, two elementary statements are probably hidden: one around the verb "to own" and the

other   one   around the noun "car". It would be interesting to
make them clearly apparent. We propose to replace the   statement by the pseudo-French paraphrase:

pour un x tel que x est (une)   for an x such that x is (a)
voiture il est vrai que Arthur   car it is true that Arthur
possède x   owns x

represented by the formula: a(x,iscar(x),owns(Arthur,x))

which is better illustrated by the tree:

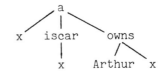

HYPOTHESIS 2:   In   a   general manner, to each article d will
correspond a "three-branched   quantifier"   q   which,   from   a
variable   x   and   two   formulae f_1 and f_2, creates the new
formula: $q(x,f_1,f_2)$

$q(x,f_1,f_2)$ corresponds to the statement:

for   d   x   such that e_1, it is true that e_2.

Here, e_1,e_2 are the statements corresponding to f_1,f_2.

By articles we mean words such as:

        a   every   the1 the2 the3 ...
        un chaque le   la   les

(where   the   numbers   1,2,3   represent respectively masculin-
singular, feminin-singular, plural)

and also groups of words such as:

        many   few   no   all the ....
        beaucoup de peu de   aucun (ne)   tous les

We use the expression "three branched quantifier"   as   a   re-
minder that this type of quantifier relates a variable to two
formulae, whereas the classical quantifiers E and A relate   a
variable   to a single formula. We will examine later the case
when it is possible just to use classical quantifiers.

4. QUANTIFICATION HIERARCHY

Consider the sentence: no   man   has   a   trunk
                        aucun homme (ne) possède une trompe

Should it be paraphrased by (1) or (2):
(1) for no x_1 such that x_1 is a man, it is true that
       for an x_2 such that x_2 is (a) trunk,
       it is true that x_1 has x_2
(2) for an x_2 such that x_2 is (a) trunk, it is true that
       for no x_1 such that x_1 is (a) man,
       it is true that x_1 has x_2

Case (1) is translated by: and case (2) by:

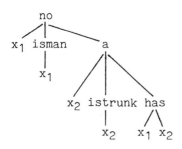
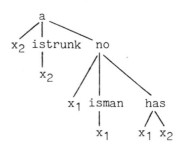

Of course, the correct paraphrase is (1). Paraphrase (2)
means something like: there exists a trunk that no man has.
By trying several examples with all sorts of articles we
arrive at the following hypothesis:

HYPOTHESIS 3a: The quantification introduced by the article
of the subject of a verb dominates the quantification(s)
introduced by the complement(s) closely related to that verb.
In speaking of complements closely related to the verb, we
exclude adverbial phrases, which will not be studied here.

This hypothesis permits a better grasp of the change of
meaning that might take place during the transformation of a
sentence from the active to the passive voice:

(1) few   persons   speak   several   languages
     peu de personnes parlent plusieurs langues

(2) several languages are spoken by few   persons
     plusieurs langues   sont parlèes par peu de personnes

are respectively translated by:

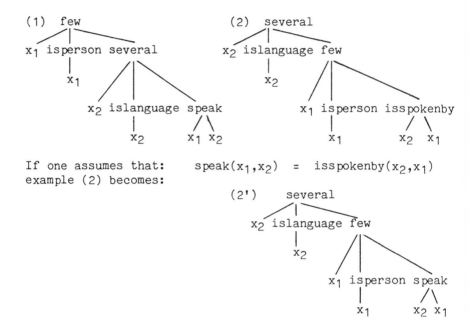

If one assumes that: $speak(x_1,x_2) = isspokenby(x_2,x_1)$
example (2) becomes:

This proves that change from active to passive voice inverses the hierarchy of quantifications.

Consider now the two sentences with their translations:

Garigou knows   the smell of each   bush
         connait l' odeur de chaque buisson

the desires of no   man   are   confessable
les désirs   d' aucun homme (ne) sont avouables

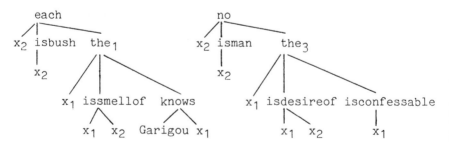

and also the sentence:

Pangloss recommends Candide to the captain   of each   ship
Pangloss recommande Candide au   capitaine de chaque navire

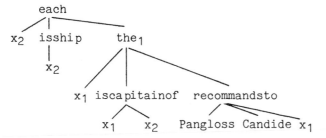

These examples suggest the hypothesis:

HYPOTHESIS 3b: In a construction involving a noun and a complement of this noun, the quantification introduced by the article of the complement dominates the quantification introduced by the article of the noun.

There only remains to consider the quantification hierarchy between several complements. Let us take the sentence:

Jacques gives a   gift   to each   child
      donne un cadeau à   chaque enfant

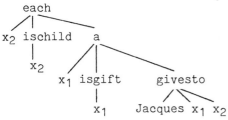

In this example the rightmost complement generates a quantification which dominates the quantification of the preceding complement. We will generalize this case by adopting the following hypothesis. We are fully conscious, however, that this may be an oversimplification.

HYPOTHESIS 3c: Whenever a verb, an adjective or a noun has two complements, the quantification is made in the inverse order of the natural order of their appearance; that is, the rightmost complement generates a quantification dominating the quantification generated by the other complement.

We will illustrate hypotheseses 3a, 3b and 3c by translating the following sentence e_1 into the tree $<e_1>$:

e_1 =   The vote of each elector gives some shudders to many
           members of the goverment

           le vote de chaque électeur procure des frissons a
           beaucoup de membres du gouvernement

The order of quantification corresponding to each article is:

e_1 = the(2) vote of each(1) elector gives some(5) shudders
        to many(4) members of the(3) government

We obtain successively:

$<e_1>$=   each(x_1,iselector(x_1),$<e_2>$)
e_2 =   the(2) vote of x_1 gives some(5) shudders to many(4)
            members of the(3) government
$<e_2>$=   the$_1$(x_2,isvoteof(x_2,x_1),$<e_3>$)
e_3 = x_2 gives some(5) shudders to many(4) members of the(3)
            government
$<e_3>$=   the$_1$(x_3,isgovernment(x_3),$<e_4>$)
e_4 = x_2 gives some(5) shudders to many(4) members of x_3
$<e_4>$=   many(x_4,ismemberof(x_4,x_3),$<e_5>$)
e_5 = x_2 gives some(5) shudders to x_4
$<e_5>$=   some(x_5,isshudder(x_5),givesto(x_2,x_5,x_4))

After we piece all these parts together, $<e_1>$ becomes:
$<e_1>$ = each

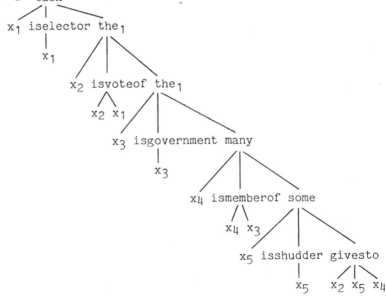

5. NEGATION

Given a statement e, consider the new statement:

it is false that e   il est faux que e

We shall translate it by: not(f), f is the translation of e.

We will study the connection between the negation "do not (ne pas)" and the operator "it is false that". Several negative sentences and their translations follow:

many   tourists do not   know   Marseille
beaucoup de touristes ne connaissent pas Marseille

some   grumpies are not   satisfied with any   broadcast
quelques grincheux ne sont pas contents de   chaque emission

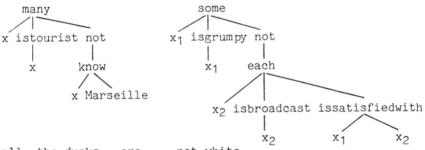

all   the ducks   are   not white
tous les canards ne sont pas blancs

every old-man   does not benefit from a pension
tout   viellard ne jouit   pas d' une pension

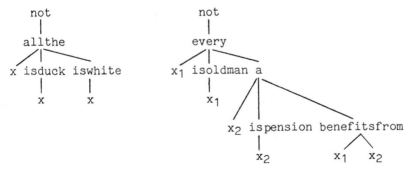

We will adopt the following hypothesis:

HYPOTHESIS 4: The negation introduced by "do not (ne pas)" is translated by the operator "not" placed immediately below the quantification(s) introduced by the subject. Nevertheless, if the article of the subject is "each (chaque)", "each of the (chacun(e) des)", "every (tout(e))", "all the (tou(te)s les)", the operator "not" applies to the whole statement.

6. CONJUNCTION BETWEEN STATEMENTS, RELATIVE CLAUSES

Given two statements e_1 and e_2 consider the new statement:
$$e_1 \text{ and } <et> e_2$$
We will translate it by: $and(f_1, f_2)$
where f_1 and f_2 are the respective translations of e_1 and e_2.

We can now deal with sentences containing relative clauses (we are only interested in the so-called restrictive type of relative clause):

Garigou appreciates the food that is contained in the can of Ron-ron
Garigou apprecie la nourriture qui est contenue dans la boite de Ron-ron

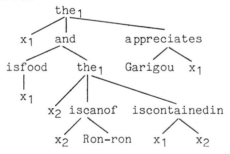

no   cat which eats many   fish   is unhappy
aucun chat qui mange beaucoup de poisson (n') est malheureux

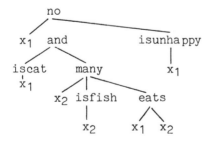

We shall adopt the hypothesis:

HYPOTHESIS 5: Every relative clause is treated as an ordinary statement; the relative pronoun is replaced by the appropriate variable and the whole is linked to the translation of the noun by the conjunction "and".

It must be noted that hypothesis 5 excludes the passing of a quantification from a relative clause above the "and" which links that relative clause to the noun. It is therefore incorrect to translate:

>   the cat that many   persons   like   is   striped
>   le chat que   beaucoup de personnes aiment est tigré

by: it must be translated by:

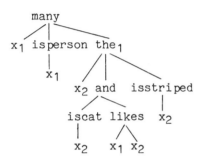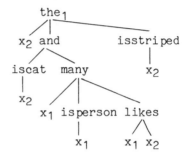

7. DIRECT USE OF FIRST-ORDER LOGIC

Let us restrict ourselves to the following articles and to their associated three branched quantifiers:

>   a <un,une>   -> $a(x,e_1,e_2)$
>   no <aucun(e) (ne)>   -> $no(x,e_1,e_2)$
>   every,each <tout(e),chaque> -> $each(x,e_1,e_2)$

Let us consider classical first-order logic with its connectors $\neg,\&,\supset$, its quantifiers $\forall,E$, its relational symbols, its constants and its variables. We will treat:
- proper nouns as constants,
- each verb,noun and adjective as a relationnal symbol,
- "and" as &,   "not" as $\neg$,
- the variables of the three-branched quantifiers as those of first-order logic.

The preceeding three-branched quantifiers can then be defined by:

$$a(x,e_1,e_2) \quad = \quad Ex(e_1 \ \& \ e_2) \ = \ \neg \ \forall x(e_1 \supset e_2)$$
$$no(x,e_1,e_2) \quad = \quad \neg \ Ex(e_1 \ \& \ e_2) = \ \forall x(e_1 \supset \neg \ e_2)$$
$$each(x,e_1,e_2) = \quad \forall x(e_1 \supset e_2) \quad = \ \neg \ Ex(e_1 \ \& \ \neg \ e_2)$$

We can now easily translate certain statements into first
order logic. For instance:

Haddock despises every man   who does not sail
       méprise   tout   homme qui ne navigue pas

    is first translated by: which turns into:

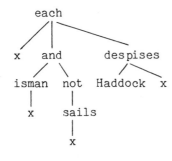
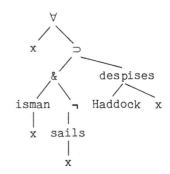

that is to say:

$\forall x \ (isman(x) \ \& \ \neg \ sails(x) \supset despises(Haddock,x))$

Similary: no   squirrel has   a nut-cracker
             aucun ecureuil ne possède un casse-noix

is first translated by: which turns into:

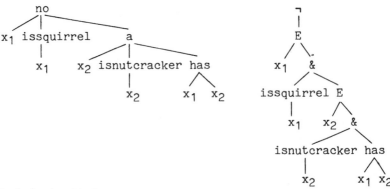

that is to say:

$\neg$ Ex$_1$(issquirrel(x$_1$) & Ex$_2$(isnutcracker(x$_2$) & has(x$_1$,x$_2$)))

which is the same as:

$\forall$x$_1$ $\forall$x$_2$ (issquirrel(x$_1$) & isnutcracker(x$_2$)) $\supset$ $\neg$ has(x$_1$,x$_2$)

The article introducing the plural form and the definite
article do not conform to such simple treatement and we will
be forced to develop a logic different from classical logic.

8. NEED FOR REASONING WITH MORE THAN TWO LOGICAL VALUES

Let us consider the statement:

   the cat   that Sophie is holding is mewing
   le   chat que   Sophie retient   miaule

In a situation where there is a cat which Sophie is holding,
this statement is true or false according to whether it mews
or not. On the other hand, in a a situation where there is no
cat held back by Sophie, the statement is neither true, nor
false, because

it is false that the cat that Sophie is holding is mewing
il est faux que le chat que Sophie retient   miaule

is not true. The statement in this case is meaningless. We
will attach the truth value "undefined" to it. This case does
not appear solely with the definite article. Consider the
statement:

                  Jacques meets <rencontre> Jacques

that is to say: Jacques meets himself <se rencontre>

It is difficult to imagine a situation in which this
statement is true or is false. It seems that the binary
property we will associate to the verb "to meet" will have
the value "undefined" each time its arguments are identical.

HYPOTHESIS 6: In a given situation, a statement will have
three possible values: "true", "false" or "undefined".

In this light we can already give the truth table for the
operations "not" and" "and":

```
not<true>                       =  false
not<false>                      =  true
not<undefined>                  =  undefined
and<true,true>                  =  true
and<true,false>                 =  false
and<false,true>                 =  false
and<false,false>                =  false
and<true,undefined>             =  unfdefined
and<undefined,true>             =  undefined
and<false,undefined>            =  undefined
and<undefined,false>            =  undefined
and<undefined,undefined>        =  undefined
```

We will also need a binary operator "if" defined by:
```
    if<p,q>    =    if   p = true   then   q   else   undefined
```

and another negation operator "nottrue":
```
    nottrue<true>               =  false
    nottrue<false>              =  true
    nottrue<undefined>          =  true
```

9. PROPERTY MUST APPLY TO SETS

Consider the sentence:

```
the beams      that the car      throws    are    parallel
les faisceaux que   la   voiture projette sont   paralleles
```

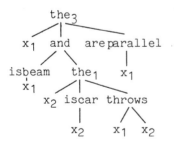

The 1-ary property "areparallel" makes no sense unless its argument x1 is a set. Of course one can, in a later stage, turn it into a binary property "isparallelwith" by assuming for instance that:

```
areparallel(X) = true    iff    X  is not the empty set and
                                 for all x,y elements of X
                                 isparallelwith(x,y) = true
```

areparallel(X)   =   false   iff X is not the empty set and
                                  for all x,y elements of X
                                  isparallelwith(x,y) = false

areparallel(X) = undefined in the other cases

But all properties over sets cannot be reduced so easily to
properties ranging over individuals, especially those
involving notions of cardinality. On the other hand, a
property on individuals can always be expressed in terms of a
property on sets by representing an individual as a set of
cardinality 1. We will in consequence adopt the hypothesis:

HYPOTHESIS 7: The n-ary properties introduced by verbs, nouns
and adjectives do not apply to individuals but to sets of
individuals.

Throughout the present article we will not be concerned about
the different more or less systematic ways to express these
properties over sets in term of properties over individuals.

10. A LOGICAL SYSTEM UNDERLYING NATURAL LANGUAGE

We shall now introduce a rigourous logical system the
semantics of which will be clearly definable. Naturally, such
a system will include, among other features, three truth
values, properties (or relations) on sets and the operators
"and" and "or". Quantification will be effected by a single
mechanism that consists in introducing the formula
"those(x,e,e')", meaning intuitively "those x's which satisfy
statement e". This will enable us to define the three-
branched quantifier "for(x,e,e')" signifying "for those x's
which satisfy the statement e, the statement e' is true". We
will then show how to transform the formulae we associate
with sentences into formulae belonging to this logical
system.

- Let K be a set of symbols called "proper nouns".
- Let R be a set of symbols called "relational symbols". With
  each element r of R a positive integer degree<r> is
  associated.
- Let X be a infinite set of variables.

We will define three types of formulae: e_i's, s_i's and n_i's:

DEFINITION: A <u>statement formula</u> e_i has one of the 8 forms:

(1) $r(s_{i_1},...,s_{i_p})$ with r element of R and degree<r>=p
(2) and(e_j,e_k) (3) if(e_j,e_k) (4) not(e_j)
(5) nottrue(e_j) (6) equal(n_j,n_k) (7) less(n_j,n_k)
(8) for(x,e_j,e_k) with x element of X

A set formula s_i has one of the 3 forms:

  (1) c   with c element of K
  (2) x   with x element of X
  (3) those(x,e_j) with x element of X

An integer formula n_i has one of the two forms:

  (1) j where j is a non negative integer
  (2) card(s_i)

The occurrence of a variable x in a formula f (of statement, set or integer type) is "free" if it does not arise inside a sub-formula of the form those(x,e) or for(x,e,e'). A formula which contains no free variable occurences is said to be "closed".

When we place ourselves in a well defined situation, a closed statement formula will have a truth value, a closed set formula will have a set as its value, and a closed integer formula will have an integer as its value. Let us clarify this notion of "situation" which is a simplification of the notion of "interpretation" in classical logic.

DEFINITION: A "situation" S is a mapping which, to each relational symbol r element of R and of degree n, associate an n-ary relation Sr, whose arguments E_i are the subsets of the set K of proper nouns, and whose values $(Sr)<E_1,...,E_n>$ are either "true","false" or "undefined".

The simplest way to define the value of a closed formula, in a given situation, is to express it recursively from the values of the immediate sub-formulae. These sub-formulae are not necessary closed. This forces us to define the value of any formula (even not closed) in an "extended situation".

DEFINITION: An "extended situation" S is a situation that has been extended in such a way that it also associates to each variable x of X a subset Sx of the set K of proper nouns.

If E is a subset of K then S' = S/(x:=E) denotes the extended situation which agrees everywhere with the extended situation S except on the variable x where S'x = E.

DEFINITION: Let S be an extended situation:

The "value" $valS<e_i>$ of a statement formula e_i is defined by:

(1) $valS<r(s_{i_1},\ldots,s_{i_p})> = (Sr)<valS<s_{i_1}>,\ldots,valS<s_{i_p}>>$

(2) $valS<and(e_j,e_k)> = and<valS<e_j>,valS<e_k>>$

(3) $valS<if(e_j,e_k)> = if<valS<e_j>,valS<e_k>>$

(4) $valS<not(e_j)> = not<valS<e_j>>$

(5) $valS<nottrue(e_j)> = nottrue<valS<e_j>>$

(6) $valS<equal(n_j,n_k)> =$ if $valS<n_j> = valS<n_k>$
    then true else false

(7) $valS<less(n_j,n_k)> =$ if $valS<n_j> < valS<n_k>$
    then true else false

(8) $valS<for(x,e_j,e_k)> = valJ<e_k>$ with
    $J = S/(x:=valS<those(x,e_j)>)$

(The connectors "and","if","not","nottrue" have been already defined in section 8.)

The "value" $valS<s_j>$ of a set formula s_i is defined by:

(1) $valS<c> = \{c\}$

(2) $valS<x> = Sx$

(3) $valS<those(x,e_j)> =$ the union of all the subsets E of K
    such that:
    $valJ<e_j> =$ true   for $J = S/(x:=E)$

The "value" $valS<n_i>$ of an integer formula n_i is defined by:

(1) $valS<j> = j$

(2) $valS<card(s_j)> =$ number of elements of the set $valS<s_j>$

It can be shown that the value of a closed formula in an extension S' of a situation S, does not depend from the way this extension has been done. This leads to:

DEFINITION: The value $valS<f>$ of a closed (statement, set or integer formula) f in a given situation S, is the value $valS'<f>$ that this formula takes in any extended situation S' of S.

The semantics of a closed (statement, set or integer) formula f are just the variations of its values $valS<f>$ in different situations S. From this system can be developed a simple and complete three valued logic (Colmerauer and Pique, 1981).

11. TRANSLATING INTO THIS LOGICAL SYSTEM

The formulae we have introduced at the beginning of this

article differ from closed statement formulae only in that
they include extra three-branched quantifiers. We shall show
how to eliminate them.

Consider the following list of articles and the three-
branched quantifiers they introduce:

a <un(e)>   -> $a(x,e_1,e_2)$
no <aucun(e)>   -> $no(x,e_1,e_2)$
every,each <tout(e),chaque>-> $each(x,e_1,e_2)$
the(singular) <l',le,la>   -> $the_1(x,e_1,e_2)$
the(plural) <les>   -> $the_3(x,e_1,e_2)$
all the <tou(te)s les>   -> $allthe(x,e_1,e_2)$
i: a non negative integer   -> $i(x,e_1,e_2)$
as in "peter has 5 cows"

HYPOTHESIS 8: We will choose the following equalities:

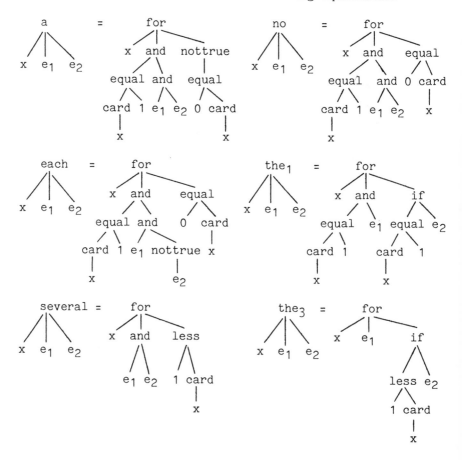

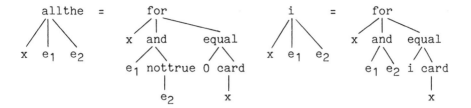

12. ANSWERING QUESTIONS

Let us consider the sentence:

    Henry appreciates the capital city of each   country
    Henry apprécie   la   capitale   de chaque pays

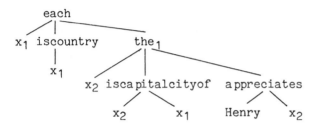

By using hypothesis 8 we obtain a formula of our logical system:

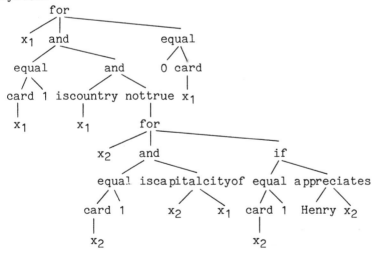

Let us imagine a data base dealing with cities, countries, names of persons and facts about them. This data base would describe a situation S in which the value valS<f> of a formula f would be either true, false or undefined. This

value would be nothing other than the answer to the question:
does Henry appreciate the capital city of each country?
est-ce que Henry apprécie la capitale de chaque pays?

In the same way we could find the answer to the question:
which countries does Henry appreciate the capital city of?
de quel pays est-ce que Henry apprécie la capitale?

starting from the formula:

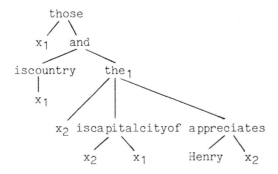

and transforming it into a set formula. The answer would then
be a set of proper nouns, each one representing a country.

To answer: how many cities does Henry appreciates?
                combien de villes est-ce que Henry apprécie?

it would be sufficient to compute the value of the integer
formula:

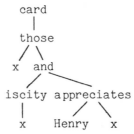

If one is therefore interested in writing an algorithm for
computing the answer to any question, in some situation, it
is sufficient to follow exactly our definition of valS<f>.

13. CONCLUSION

What are the limits of the present study? First of all,

hypothesis 1 which, in particular associates to each verb an n-ary property which applies neither to tenses nor to certain states, masks all the problems introduced by action verbs. Indeed, such of action verbs are only definable in terms of modifications of states. Our study, therefore, may not pertain to the use of natural language in robotics. Let us mention, on the subject, the very interesting paper by McCarthy and Hayes (1969) where they introduce "situational" variables.

We have not examined the problem of sentences with verbs that have arguments wich are sentences. A great part of the work done by Montague (1974) deals with this subject.

We also cannot deal with the problems illustrated by:

(1a) Jacques knows Paul's brother
(2a) Henry is Paul's brother
(3a) Jacques knows Henry

(1b) Jacques knows the number 427041
(2b) Paul's phone number is 427041
(3b) Jacques knows Paul's phone number

The sentence (3a) may be deduced from (1a) and (2a), but the sentence (3b) cannot be deduced from (1b) and (2b). For this kind of problem see Montague (1974) and McCarthy (1979).

On the other hand, we have not discussed the problem of pronouns. Although our variables allow us to easily represent certain cases as, for example:

every women intimidades the man   who loves her
toute femme intimide   l' homme qui l' aime

becomes: every

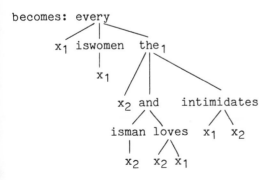

the sentence: every   man   who owns   a   garden maintains it
              chaque homme qui possède un jardin l'entretient
would become: every

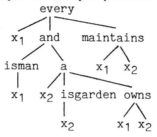

which is a formula containing a free variable: the occurence
of the variable x_2 in maintains(x_1,x_2) is not quantified. The
same problem arises for the representation of pronouns from
sentence to sentence. Pasero (1973) has studied this type of
problem in depth.

In addition we have not discussed the ambiguity of certain
articles, such as the article "a (un)" in subject position.
In: an elephant arrives (un éléphant arrive) the article "a
(un)" has its usual meaning, but in: an elephant is grey (un
éléphant est gris) "a (un)" means "each (chaque)". A similar
problem arises when it is necessary to reconstruct a missing
article; this is not too frequent in French, but it might be
in other languages.

Finally, we have not discussed all of the inconsistencies
between the different groups of articles. For example, as it
has been noted in (Coursaget-Colmerauer, 1975), a noun, which
is preceded by "no (aucun)", cannot be the complement of a
noun, which is preceded by "a (un)", as in: Victor has picked
up a leaf of no tree (Victor n'a rammasse une feuille d'aucun
arbre).

Other constraints on the combination of determiners in French
have been listed and studied by Gross (1977).

What about the applications of this study? Our work has
deeply influenced the conception of several systems for
consulting data bases in different languages:
- for French, the system of Pique (1975), the system of
Giraud et al. (1980) and also the system of Perichaud (1981);
- for Spanish, the system of Dahl (1977);
- for Portuguese, the system of Coelho (1979);
- for English, the system of Warren and Pereira (1981).
All these systems are programmed in PROLOG using metamorphosis grammars (Colmerauer, 1978).

A NARRATIVE SCHEMA IN PROCEDURAL LOGIC

Robert F. Simmons
Department of Computer Science
University of Texas, Austin
Texas 78712, USA

ABSTRACT

An approach is described for constructing a flight schema to organize the sentences of a narrative into an outline form. The flight schema is programmed in Horn clauses within LISP and applied to the syntactically analyzed text to result in a schema instantiation that approximates the desired outline. The instantiated schema is shown to have excellent properties for computing summaries and for answering questions about the narrative.

1. INTRODUCTION

Several procedural logic programs have been described for natural language processing at the isolated sentence level. In fact, one motivation for the original development of PROLOG as a programming language by Colmerauer and his colleagues, (Roussel, 1975), was its potential application to natural language processing problems. Since then papers by Perreira (1979), Dahl (1979), Silva et. al. (1979), and Pereira and Warren (1980) have described clausal grammars for the analysis of natural language sentences. Clausal grammars including semantic tests and transformations were used by Simmons and Chester (1979) to translate English sentences into networks of semantic relations in a LISP version of procedural logic called HCPRVR. That paper also presented a primitive approach for using clausal rules to relate successive sentences into a discourse structure. Discourse structures - structures that show how an entire article is organized - have been treated in detail by Beaugrande (1979),

and their computation using scripts, plans and themes is
described by Schank and Riesbeck (1981). This paper shows an
application of procedural logic that uses a variation of
direct clause grammars for computing a discourse analysis for
a story about a V-2 rocket flight.

HCPRVR - Horn Clause Prover - is a compiled program that
augments LISP to accept and evaluate Horn clause procedures.
Kowalski (1979), Clark and Tärnlund (1977), and others have
shown the effectiveness of logic programs for realizing list
processing, sorting, robot problems, data management, and
natural language analysis procedures. The logical syntax and
semantics of procedural logic is described particularly well
by Kowalski and by Clark and Tärnlund. Horn Clauses in LISP
have essentially the same semantic interpretation but are
expressed in LISP syntax, augmented with LISP functions, and
supported by the LISP environment. HCPRVR, programmed and
described by Dan Chester (1980), compiled in less than 2000
octal words, interprets the LISP Horn clause procedures.
Recently Robinson and Sibert (1980) have published a
description of LOGLISP that uses essentially the same syntax
as HCPRVR and the procedures presented in this paper will
probably run in LOGLISP as well.

2. THE FLIGHT SCHEMA

A honey bee sitting on a flower shakes herself, spirals into
the air and flies to her hive. A massive wooden flying boat
revs its engines, slowly begins to move down the bay, lifts a
few feet from the water, and soon settles back to the
surface. A great black and yellow V-2 rocket in a New Mexico
desert climbs amid a burst of flame, slowly at first then
rapidly disappears from sight; a few minutes later it plunges
to the desert floor.

Each of these examples briefly describes a Flight composed of
a Flightsystem, an Ascent, a Cruise and a Descent. This is
the schema of events common to all, although some elements
may be implied rather than explicitly mentioned in a text,
and the text may be enriched by much more detailed
descriptions of the time, location, and associated events.
The computational problem is to represent schemas as
procedures that can recognize a particular series of events

in such widely varying texts, then reorganize the text representation in terms of the schema, resolving pronouns and restoring ellipsis as it does so. Selecting an appropriate schema to account for a story, coping with a range of alternate vocabulary choices, with stylistic variations in ordering of events, with subevents, missing events, complications and interruptions, all add considerably to the problem. (See Schank and Riesbeck, 1980). No complete solutions to this formidable computation are presented here, but expression of schemas as procedures in clausal logic is shown to be an effective approach to the problem.

A V-2 rocket story was presented and analyzed as a network schema structure by Beaugrande, and Simmons and Chester presented a clausal logic grammar that transformed its sentences into semantic network structures. The first and third paragraphs of the rocket text which will be used to develop an abbreviated Flight schema are shown below.

A great black and yellow V-2 rocket forty-six feet long stood in a New Mexico desert. Empty it weighed five tons. For fuel it carried eight tons of alcohol and liquid oxygen.

With a great roar and burst of flame the giant rocket rose slowly and then faster and faster. Behind it trailed sixty feet of yellow flame. Soon the flame looked like a yellow star.

The three sentences of the first paragraph describe a rocket, its location, its weight and its fuel status. The focus of each sentence is the rocket, referred to by "it" in the second and third sentences. As readers, we accept this paragraph as a description of a __flight system__ that is prepared for flight. The second paragraph also contains three sentences; the first describes the action of the rocket's ascent, the second describes the appearance of the rising rocket, and the third expands that description. In this paragraph the subject of the first and second sentences is the rocket, then the focus is changed to the flame that it trails. As readers we can understand this paragraph to be a description of the __ascent__ of the rocket.

With this understanding we can form the following outline using abbreviations of the sentences:

```
FLIGHT
    FLIGHTSYSTEM
        V-2 ROCKET IN DESERT
                    WEIGHT FIVE TONS,
                    CARRIES  ALCOHOL AND OXYGEN
                                    FOR FUEL
    ASCENT
        ROCKET RISES WITH ROAR AND FLAME
            TRAILS FLAME
            FLAME LOOKS LIKE A STAR
```

It is a structure very similar to this outline that is wanted
in an instantiated schema. Such a schematic outline can be
truncated to give only the first and fourth sentences as a
summary:

A V-2 rocket was in a desert. It rose with a roar and
a burst of flame.

The structure can also be used to answer questions of
sequence:

When did the rocket trail flame?
After it rose.

By defining a schema as a set of rules or procedures to
compute such an outline, the sentences of the text are
organized and classified as to their place in an event
description and the resulting instantiated schema makes
explicit some of the relations which readers of the text use
for understanding how the sequence of sentences relates to
the event being described.

Rules for defining schemas examine the analyzed sentences and
depending on the nature of the focus and the verb for each
sentence, they assign the sentence to a category of the
schema. The sentences of this example were automatically
parsed into the following (abbreviated) case relations.

```
(STAND AE (ROCKET TYPE V-2...) LOC (DESERT...))
(WEIGH AE IT AMT (TON QU FIVE...))
(CARRY INSTR IT PU (FUEL PREP FOR) AE(ALCOHOL...))
(RISE AE(ROCKET...) AC (ROAR...))
(TRAIL INSTR IT AE (FLAME...))
(LOOK PARTIC LIKE AE (FLAME...) AP (STAR...))
```

In these examples the case relations AE, LOC, etc. have the
following meanings:

AE Affected Entity, LOC Location, AMT Amount,
QU Quantity, INSTR Instrument, PU Purpose,
PREP Preposition, AC Accompanying, PARTIC Particle,
AP Appearance.

Each semantic relation is a transformation of the English
sentence into a set of formal case relations among the
lexical entries for the words it contained. A semantic
relation is composed of a governing term, e.g. the verb and a
set of arguments (usually noun phrases) each labelled by a
convenient case-name describing the semantic relation between
it and the verb. Similarly, the noun heads a semantic
relation for representing noun phrases with each modifying
argument classified by a label, e.g. SIZE large, COLOR (black
and yellow). As a result of the transformation from English
into the case relations, each sentence becomes a network data
structure that easily answers such explicit questions as,
What did the rocket trail?, "Where was the rocket?" "What
type was the rocket?", "What trailed flame? etc. The question
answering is accomplished by first parsing the question into
a case relation form, e.g.,

        What trailed flame?
        (TRAIL INSTR   ?WHAT   AE FLAME)

then matching with a candidate sentence,

        (TRAIL INSTR ?WHAT AE FLAME)
        (TRAIL INSTR (ROCKET...) AE (FLAME...))

and returning the argument, (ROCKET...) that matches the
question term, ?WHAT. Instantiating a schema will be
accomplished by answering questions about each succeeding
semantic relation in the discourse.

To construct the schema we must write rules that capture the
informal operations we used to form the outline given above.
We noticed first that the initial sentence focused on a
rocket and asserted that it stood in a desert. The verb
"stand" describes a state rather than an action and so do
"weigh" and "carry" in the next two sentences. The first rule
we might write would be one for a Flight;

A Flight of ?FLIGHTFOCUS occurs
            IF there is a FLIGHTSYSTEM
                    about ?FLIGHTFOCUS
            AND an ASCENT of ?FLIGHTFOCUS

We now need a rule for a FLIGHTSYSTEM,

A FLIGHTSYSTEM is described in a sentence
        IF the FOCUS of the sentence is
                an instance of ?FLIGHTFOCUS
        AND ?FLIGHTFOCUS can fly
        AND the verb of the sentence is an instance of
                POSITION, WEIGHT, or SUPPORT

The term, ?FLIGHTFOCUS is a variable whose value is the focus
(usually the subject) of the first sentence. The condition
"?FLIGHTFOCUS can fly", is satisfied by matching the
assertions, "ROCKET CAN FLY", "HONEYBEE CAN FLY", etc. When a
pronoun such as "it" occurs in the focal position, it is
taken as an instance of the value of ?FLIGHTFOCUS, if it
agrees in class, gender and number. For example, the "it" of
the second and third sentences, agrees with "rocket" in
class, i.e. Physical Object, and in gender and number. This
rule is meant to account for the initial sentences describing
the V-2 rocket and others such as the following:
    "A massive flying boat floated by the dock."
    "A tiny honeybee was poised on a flower."
The verbs, "floated" and "poised" are instances,
respectively, of SUPPORT and POSITION and flying boats and
honeybees can fly.

An ASCENT rule can now be written,

An ASCENT of ?FLIGHTFOCUS occurs
            IF the FOCUS of the sentence is an instance
                of the ?FLIGHTFOCUS
            AND the verb is an instance of RISE.

This rule accounts for such sentences as "The giant rocket
rose", "A honeybee spiralled into the air", and "The flying
boat lifted". We now need some default rules to account for
such descriptive statements as "It trailed sixty feet of
yellow flame" and "The flame looked like a yellow star." Both
of these verbs can be classified as DESCRIPTORS (in these
usages), so a rule for DESCRIPTOR can be written.

A sentence is added as a DESCRIPTOR
            IF its FOCUS matches an argument of the
                preceding sentence,
            AND the verb is an instance of DESCRIPTOR.

To apply these rules to a set of sentence relations, we need
a procedure that will accept the set as an argument, and as

each relation is found to satisfy a rule, will add it to the instantiation of the schema that is being computed. To accomplish this in clausal logic, the rules are augmented with variables that stand for
1) the sentences to be examined,
2) the result of applying the rule, and
3) the sentences that remain to be looked at.

The following technical section, which can be skipped by the casual reader, provides a detailed examination of the logic procedure for applying schema rules to the two example paragraphs. The resulting instantiated schema is shown in Figure 1, and the discussion following that figure shows how it is used to compute summaries and answer certain classes of questions.

3. DETAILED TECHNICAL DESCRIPTION OF FLIGHT SCHEMA

The first procedure in the Flight schema is abbreviated to to define only a Flightsystem and an Ascent, as follows:

```
((FLIGHT X (FLIGHT TPC X LOC U SETT T1 SEQ T2 OUTC Z) S)
   <
   (FLIGHTSYSTEM X U T1 S R)
   (ASCENT X U T2 R NIL))
```

This procedure is composed of a Consequent relation, a left pointing arrow, and two Antecedent relations. The consequent is true if the antecedent relations are true. It will be seen later that the antecedent relations are each defined as relational procedures under the same interpretation. An assertion is a relation with no antecedents. Successful top-down evaluation of these relations forms a tree whose terminal elements are assertions. Each relation in a procedure is a list whose first element is a constant taken as a relation name; the arguments of the relation can be constants, variables, lists and other relations. Variables are the letters L-Z, optionally concatenated with numbers. A successful evaluation (unification) of the tree of relations results in obtaining bindings for each of the variables.

The relational pattern in the Flight schema is:

```
(NAME   TOPIC   COMPUTED-STRUCTURE      SENTENCES)
(FLIGHT   X     (FLIGHT TPC X LOC U...)      S   )
```

The relational procedure is called with a list of parsed

sentences given as the argument S, using the LISP function, PROVE:

```
(PROVE (FLIGHT X Y ((STAND AE (ROCKET...)...)
                    (WEIGH AE (IT NBR SING)...)
                    (CARRY PU (FUEL...) AE (IT...)...)
                    (RISE AE (ROCKET SIZE GIANT...)...)
                    ...) ))
```

The variable X will get bound to the topic, ROCKET, and the variable Y will first be bound to (FLIGHT TPC X LOC U SETT T1...) and then the variables in this expression will take on values as the antecedent relations are successfully evaluated.

The list of sentences is passed to the S variable in the first antecedent, (FLIGHTSYSTEM X U T1 S R), and the attempt is made to prove it:

```
((FLIGHTSYSTEM X U (FLTSYSTEM EVT (T1 T2 T3)) S R)
  <
  (LOCAT X U T1 S R1)
  (WT X T2 R1 R2)
  (SUPPORT X T3 R2 R))
```

This relation will be proved if its three antecedents are true. Before examining them, we should notice that FLIGHTSYSTEM introduces the variables, U and R. The variable, U, will pick up a location and transmit that value back up to FLIGHT, where it is the second element of a pair, LOC U. The variable, R, is more interesting. The first antecedent of FLIGHTSYSTEM is (LOCAT ... S R1). When LOCAT is evaluated, it will take the first sentence of S and bind the remaining sentences to R1. The second antecedent, WT, uses R1 as its list of sentences and returns the remaining sentences as R2, which are used in SUPPORT, which in its turn gulps a sentence from R2 and binds R to the remainder. So in FLIGHTSYSTEM, the variable, R, is eventually bound to the sentences remaining after its antecedents have been evaluated. These are passed to ASCENT as its sentence argument.

The result of evaluating FLIGHTSYSTEM will be the list, (FLTSYSTEM EVT (T1 T2 T3)). A new list is being formed of the elements T1, T2, and T3 simply by putting those elements in parentheses. The antecedents of FLIGHTSYSTEM are now to be evaluated.

```
((LOCAT X Y (X POSIT U LOC Y . Q) ((U . W) . R) R)
   <
   (RELATE U POSITION)
   (MATCHPR (AE (X1 . Q) LOC Y) W W)
   (RELATE X X1))
((WT X (X WT Y . Q) ((U . W) . R) R)
   <
   (RELATE U WEIGH)
   (MATCHPR (AE (X1 . Q) MSR Y) W W)
   (RELATE X1 X))
((SUPPORT X (X CO (Z PU Y)) ((U . W) . R) R)
   <
   (RELATE U SUPPORT)
   (MATCHPR (AE X1 CO Z PU Y) W W)
   (RELATE X1 X))
```

In the LOCAT consequent the argument bound to the sentences is ((U.W).R), and whatever is bound to R goes to the remainder argument, R. The dot notation is precisely that of LISP; (U.W) is the car of the sentences and R the cdr, and U is the first word of the first sentence, and W its cdr. Generally, (A B C.D) refers to the car, cadr, caddr, and cdddr, respectively, where list A B C is appended to list D. This is what is happening in the third argument of LOCAT, (X POSIT U LOC Y.Q), where various values are selected from the antecedents and arranged in a list with a particular ordering, including the final cons of Y to Q. One notable advantage of procedural logic lists is that car, cdr, cons and append are usually accomplished by designation rather than by explicit function calls. LOCAT is the first relation that will actually examine a sentence. The first parsed sentence is bound to (U.W) .

```
(STAND AE (ROCKET DET A SIZE (GREAT) COLOR (BLACK *AND
(YELLOW)) TYPE (V-2) LGTH (LONG LGTH (FOOT QU (FORTY-SIX) NBR
PL)) NBR SING) TNS PAST LOC (DESERT PREP IN DET A LOC
(NEW MEXICO) NBR SING))
```

The variable, U, is bound to STAND and W to the rest. The antecedents of LOCAT are RELATE, MATCHPR, and RELATE. The first RELATE is to establish that the verb of the sentence is in a superset relation to POSITION. It finds an assertion, (STAND SUP POSITION), and so is proved. MATCHPR with the given arguments establishes that the arcs, AE and LOC (i.e. Affected Entity and LOCation) occur at the top level of the sentence relation and so binds the values of (X1.Q) and Y, respectively. The second use of RELATE finds that X is an unbound variable and so gives it the value of X1 which is

ROCKET. The variable, Y, was bound to (DESERT
LOC(NEW MEXICO...)...). These bindings are the TPC and LOC
values which are passed on up to FLIGHT as well as to all
intermediate relations.

As a result of this evaluation, LOCAT binds (X POSIT U LOC
Y.Q), with the following value:

      (ROCKET POSIT STAND LOC (DESERT LOC (NEW MEXICO...)
            SIZE GREAT   COLOR(BLACK *AND (YELLOW)...)

thus transforming the sentence into a more convenient noun-
headed data structure for embedding into the schema.

In a similar fashion, WT and SUPPORT evaluate the next two
sentences, bind their arguments, and return values up to
FLIGHTSYSTEM. The RELATE function in WT is called with
(RELATE ROCKET IT), since X has by now been bound to ROCKET.
By finding that ROCKET is a physical object that matches "it"
in gender and number, RELATE solves the simple pronoun
reference. The second antecedent of FLIGHT is then evaluated:

    ((ASCENT X L (ASCEND TPC X FROM L SETT Y EVT Z SEQ W) S R)
      <
      (PREPAR X Y S R1)
      (ASCEND X Z R1 R2)
      (CRUISE X W R2 R))
    ((ASCEND X ((U TPC X . W) . V) ((U . W) . R) R1)
      <
      (RELATE U RISE)
      (MEMPR (AE X1) W)
      (RELATE X X1)
      (DESCRIP X V R R1))
    ((DESCRIP X ((U . W) . V) ((U . W) . R) R1)
      <
      (U SUP DESCRIP)
      (FOCUS W X1)
      (RELATE X1 X)
      (DESCRIP X2 V R R1))
    ((DESCRIP X NIL S S))

ASCENT is given the remaining sentences as its S argument,
and forms a structure summarizing the ascent, showing the
setting, from-location, the rising-event and a sequence arc
to the rest of the narrative. The first antecedent is PREPAR
which covers a paragraph we deleted from the original story ,
so we'll ignore it here. A rule for ignoring PREPAR is
                  (PREPAR X NIL S S)

which follows the other PREPAR rules and thus acts as a default for the missing schema event. The next antecedent is ASCEND which we'll examine, and the last is CRUISE which covers the continuation of the story and which we'll also ignore. ASCEND examines its sentence to insure that the verb relates to rise, that the AE (affected entity) is related to the current binding of X (i.e. ROCKET), and then calls DESCRIP. In DESCRIP we attempt to capture the linguistic generalization that an action may be followed by a series of descriptive sentences, such as "Behind it trailed yellow flame" and "The flame looked like a yellow star". DESCRIP doesn't do much but establish that a series of sentences is a description and returns them and a remainder as lists to the schema element that called it. DESCRIP also succeeds, returning a NIL value, if the sentence it is applied to is not a description but an act or a state.

ASCEND inserts the arcpair, TPC ROCKET, into its action sentence and conses that sentence onto any list of descriptive sentences that DESCRIP may have returned. ASCENT which is a main schema element constructs a summary structure,

```
(ASCEND TPC ROCKET FROM (DESERT...) SETT...
        EVT (RISE TPC ROCKET AE(IT...)...) SEQ (CRUISE...))
```

When these bindings for variables are passed up to the initial procedure, FLIGHT, the instantiated schema is the value of y in that procedure. The instantiated schema is shown in Figure 1 on the next page.

4.   USE OF THE INSTANTIATED SCHEMA FOR SUMMARIES AND
      QUESTIONING

The result of the evaluation of the Flight schema with the six rocket sentences is shown in Figure 1. The structure it imposed can be shown in the following summary form, which approximates the summary shown earlier.

```
(FLIGHT TPC ROCKET LOC (DESERT...)
        SETT (FLTSYSTEM EVT ((ROCKET...)(ROCKET...)(ROCKET...)))
        SEQ  (ASCEND TPC ROCKET FROM (DESERT...)
                     EVT ((RISE...)(TRAIL...)(LOOKLIKE...))
                     SEQ ...)
```

This can be appreciated as a structure of assertions about a flight event. A LISP function adds backlinks relating each

```
(FLIGHT TPC ROCKET LOC (DESERT PREP IN DET A LOC (NEW MEXICO)
                       NBR SING)
   SETT (FLTSYSTEM EVT ((ROCKET POSIT STAND
                                LOC (DESERT PREP IN
                                  DET A LOC (NEW MEXICO) NBR SING)
                                DET A SIZE (GREAT)
                                COLOR (BLACK *AND (YELLOW))
                                TYPE (V-2)
                                LGTH (LONG LGTH (FOOT QU
                                         (FORTY-SIX) NBR PL)) NBR SING)
                    (ROCKET WT (TON QU (FIVE) NBR PL)
                         ST (EMPTY) NBR SING)
                    (ROCKET CO (ALCOHOL WT (TON QU (EIGHT) NBR PL)
                             PREP OF *AND (OXYGEN STATE (LIQUID)
                                                     NBR SING)
                             NBR SING
                             PU (FUEL PREP FOR NBR SING)))))
  SEQ (ASCEND TPC ROCKET FROM (DESERT...)
            SETT...
       EVT ((RISE TPC ROCKET
                    AC (ROAR PREP WITH DET A SIZE (GREAT)
                        *AND (BURST OF (FLAME PREP OF
                                              NBR SING)
                              NBR SING) NBR SING)
                    AE (ROCKET DET THE SIZE (GIANT) NBR SING)
                    TNS PAST RATE (SLOWLY *THEN (FASTER *AND
                                                    FASTER)))
               (TRAIL LOC BEHIND INSTR (IT NBR SING)
                    TNS PAST AE (FLAME MSR (FOOT QU (SIXTY)
                                               NBR PL)
                                 PREP OF COLOR (YELLOW)
                                 NBR SING))
               (LOOK TIME SOON AE (FLAME DET THE NBR SING)
                    TNS PAST AP (STAR PREP LIKE DET A
                                COLOR (YELLOW) NBR SING)))
       SEQ (...                                              )
```

Fig. 1. Computed Narrative Structure

sublist to the list that encloses it, and asserts the
resulting structure so that each list and sublist can be used
as assertions to prove appropriate relations. The approach to
summarizing and questioning the instantiated schema will be
described briefly below. A detailed treatment of answering
questions from this schema is given by LeVine (1980).

The summary of a sentence can be obtained by using a rule

such as BREV which abbreviates case relations. Given the semantic relation, (ROCKET SIZE GREAT COLOR (BLACK *AND YELLOW) TYPE V-2 LGTH (FEET QU...) NBR SING), BREV selects only the Head, ROCKET, and values of SIZE, TYPE and NBR to produce the new semantic relation, (ROCKET SIZE GREAT TYPE V-2 NBR SING). Recursive application of this rule to an entire sentence relation produces a summary for the sentence. Thus the original sentence, "A great black and yellow V-2 rocket forty-six feet long stood in a desert in New Mexico", is reduced to "A great V-2 rocket stood in a desert."

Summaries for the entire schema are produced in a similar fashion using the rule, GIST. GIST takes the instantiated schema as an argument, finds each EVT arc (see Figure 1) and selects the first case relation in the list. It then uses BREV to abbreviate the semantic relation, and finally passes the resulting list to the grammar rules. These are the same rules that parsed the original sentences into semantic relations and because of their symmetry as logic expressions, they transform semantic relations back into English. An example summary (for the full story): (SUMMARIZE (FLIGHT)((A GREAT V-2 ROCKET STOOD IN A DESERT) (THE GIANT ROCKET ROSE WITH A GREAT ROAR AND BURST OF FLAME) (ROCKET PLUNGED INTO EARTH FORTY MILES FROM THE STARTING POINT))).

Additional utility of the schema is found primarily in using the temporal-causal relation, SEQ, to answer "Why" and "When" questions. If the question is asked "When did the rocket trail yellow flame", various answers such as "While it was ascending" or "after it rose" can easily be produced by looking at the enclosing subschema, ASCEND, or by the preceding event. "Why did the rocket trail flame" requires looking at the enclosing subschema, ASCEND, to give the answer, "Because it was ascending", or to the following event, CRUISE, to answer, "to cruise". While these examples only hint at the power and depth of inference that may be required in answering questions, LeVine's thesis examines the procedures much more thoroughly. Generally the process of questioning a semantic relation or an instantiated schema requires several steps.

1) Translate from English question to a semantic relation,
2) Analyze the semantic relation into
     a) a query term   e.g. (COLOR ?WHAT)
     b) an identifier e.g. (ROCKET TYPE V-2)
3) Find a set of candidate semantic relations that match the identifier. (In this example, all those that start with (ROCKET...))

4) Match the remaining terms of the question identifier with the candidate. e.g. is (TYPE V-2) one of the pairs in the candidate.

5) For the surviving candidates, match the constraints given by the query, e.g. (COLOR ?WHAT) and select any that give a value for the query term.

6) Pass the surviving candidates to the grammar to translate into English and print the resulting answer.

In matching terms from a question with those of a candidate answer, various transitivity rules are applied to relate classes of words with instances, e.g. RISE instance LIFT, and to backlink into preceding events to find default parameters, e.g. (RISE LOC ?WHERE) follows backlinks to the FLIGHTSYSTEM subschema to find (ROCKET LOC DESERT) as an answer.

5. CONCLUSION

We have shown an approach to constructing and computing schemas in a LISP version of Horn clause procedures. The example text that was used is a very simple one that led to the definition of a Flight schema which was designed to account for three simple examples including the rocket text, and comparable sentences describing the flights of a honeybee and a flying boat. It was argued that an instantiated schema should organize the sentences of a narrative into something approximating the outline that a human reader might construct and it was shown that such an outline was useful for producing summaries and for answering questions about sequences of events. A Horn clause procedure for the Flight schema was described in detail and its instantiation was shown to approximate the human produced outline of the text, and to have excellent properties for constructing summaries and answering questions.

The paper emphasized what is essentially the case study of an approach to defining and instantiating one schema, the Flight, using Horn clause logic. Without attempting to generalize beyond this limited goal, it is believed that the study shows that the programming of schemas in logic results in concise procedures that run rapidly to construct a data structure that is useful for summarizing texts and answering questions. The interpretration of the schema was strictly top-down, but other control structures have been studied that apply the rules in a bottom-up fashion as well.

IMPLEMENTATION ISSUES

THE MEMORY MANAGEMENT
OF PROLOG IMPLEMENTATIONS

Maurice Bruynooghe

Katholieke Universiteit Leuven
Afdeling Toegepaste Wiskunde en Programmatie
Celestijnenlaan 200A, B-3030 Heverlee, Belgium

ABSTRACT

We describe the top down execution of logic programs and the concepts of computation rule and search rule. We show that PROLOG's depth first search rule results in important simplifications of the necessary runtime structures. At a high level, we describe an interpreter with its runtime structure. This interpreter is intended to be a fair description of the best known implementations. At the same high-level - without considering the actual representation of the bindings of variables - we discuss the different opportunities to save space by popping the environment stack of the runtime structure. Finally, we discuss the problems of space saving that result from the representation of the bindings of the variables. We describe two possible representations: structure sharing and copying.

1. LOGIC PROGRAMS - PROLOG

Logic Programs (Kowalski, 1974)

A logic program consists of a set of procedures and a goal statement. A procedure or Horn clause has the form $B <-- A_1,...,A_n$ (n>=0) with B and A_i literals. Literals have the form $R(t_1,...t_k)$ (k>0) with R a k-adic relation and the t_i terms i.e. constants (first symbol an upper case letter), variables (first symbol a lower case letter) or expressions of the form $f(t_1,...,t_m)$ (m>0) with f a m-ary function symbol and the t_i again terms.

A procedure $B<\!\!-\!\!-A_1,\ldots A_n$ can be used to solve a problem when the heading B of the procedure matches the literal ('call') representing the problem. By 'match' we mean that the heading and the call must agree to consider the same problem, namely the most general instance of the call for which the procedure can be used. This matching process ('unification') creates a substitution consisting of components $x<\!\!-\!\!-t$.

To execute a program top-down, the <u>search rule</u> selects the initial goal statement $<\!\!-\!\!-A_1,\ldots A_n$, asks the <u>computation rule</u> to select a call $A_i = R(t_1,\ldots,t_p)$, applies a procedure $R(t'1,\ldots t'p)<\!\!-\!\!-B_1,\ldots,B_m$ matching that call with a substitution ('most general unifier') Θ and derives the new goal statement $<\!\!-\!\!-(A_1,\ldots,A_{i-1},B_1,\ldots,B_m,A_{i+1},\ldots,A_n)\Theta$. Then the search rule starts over again: selecting a goal statement, possibly activating the computation rule and deriving a new goal statement. New goal statements are <u>active</u>; goal statements become <u>inactive</u> once all procedures matching the selected call have been applied. The search can be represented by an OR-tree, the <u>search tree</u>. The nodes are goal statements. The descendants of a node are the alternative goal statements derivable from the goal statement in that node. The search is finished once all nodes are inactive. The terminal nodes of the tree are either unsolvable goal statements or empty goal statements. The empty goal statements represent solutions. The composition of the substitutions used on the path from the root node to an empty node, applied on the variables of the initial goal statement, gives the desired result. To complete the search, only the active goal statements are needed. An example of a search tree is given in Fig. 1.

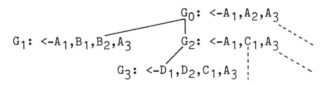

Fig. 1. Sketch of a search tree (substitutions are ignored).

The computation rule has selected the call A_2 in the initial goal statement. The search rule has derived the goal statements G_1 and G_2 from G_0; the dashed line shows there is another procedure to be applied on the call A_2 of G_0. The computation rule has selected the call A_1 in G_2. Three procedures are candidates to match A_1; at this point, only one has been applied.

A goal statement can be represented by an AND-tree, the proof tree. The root node has as immediate descendants the subgoals A_i of the initial goal statement $<--A_1,...,A_n$. A subgoal A_i being executed by a procedure $B<--B_1,...,B_m$ takes as descendants the subgoals $B_1,...,B_m$. The unifier θ is then applied to every node in the tree. The goal statement corresponding to a proof tree is given by the nonempty tips.

In Fig. 2 proof trees of G_0 and G_2 are subtrees of the proof tree of G_3. It is straightforward to reconstuct the previous proof trees from the final one when the order in which subgoals are selected is given. In general, the proof trees corresponding to the successive goal statements of a single branch in the search tree are a succession of proof trees, each of which is produced from the preceding one by extending the tip labelled with the selected call.

A proof tree and a sequence of its nontip subgoals (their selection order) defines a corresponding sequence of proof trees/goal statements. In the sequel, we shall often talk about the goal statement corresponding to a nontip subgoal of a proof tree, e.g. in Fig. 2, G_2 corresponds to subgoal A_1 and G_0 to subgoal A_2 of the final proof tree.

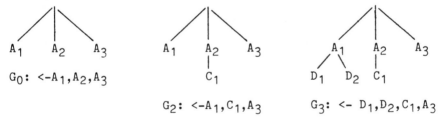

$G_0: <-A_1,A_2,A_3$

$G_2: <-A_1,C_1,A_3$

$G_3: <- D_1,D_2,C_1,A_3$

Fig. 2. The sequence of proof trees (substitutions are ignored) following a branch of the search tree of Fig. 1.

PROLOG

The search rule of PROLOG explores the search tree depth first, PROLOG always works on the most recent active goal statement (the current goal statement). This strategy greatly simplifies the needed runtime structures. Indeed, all active goal statements are on the branch leading from the root to the current goal statement. This means that we only need keep the proof tree corresponding to the current goal statement. If this becomes inactive, we can restore the most recent active goal statement by undoing the last extensions ("backtracking").

The computation rule of PROLOG always selects the left most
subgoal in the proof tree. This means that subgoals are
solved sequentially; execution of a subgoal A_{i+1} is only
started when the subgoal A_i is completely solved. The subgoals are expanded from left to right; on backtracking, their
expansions are removed from right to left. A node on the
proof tree corresponding to the selected subgoal of an active
goal statement (a goal for which there are untried procedures) is called a backtrackpoint. The nodes added to the tree
since the execution of the last backtrackpoint are part of
the current segment of the proof tree. On backtracking, the
current segment is removed and substitutions applied to the
tree during the growth of this segment are undone. What
remains of the proof tree becomes the current goal statement.

2. RUNTIME STRUCTURE - INTERPRETER

As discussed above, the run-time structure needs to represent
the proof tree corresponding to the current goal statement
and needs to be able to restore the proof trees corresponding
to the backtrackpoints.

On the proof tree the literals represent the subgoals.
Usually, these literals contain variables. Before applying a
procedure, it is necessary that the goal statement and the
procedure use different names for their variables. A
straightforward solution consists of making a copy of the
procedure with unique names for the variables. This results
in an inefficient use of memory; each time a procedure is
used, a new copy is made. It is preferable to use, like in
Algol, reentrant code for the representation of procedures,
such that all instances of the same literal share the code
describing that literal. This is possible by using binding
environments. The pure code is always accessed in the context
of a particular binding environment. When accessing a
variable in the reentrant code, the corresponding binding
environment is consulted. Thus, literals can be presented by
a pointer to the pure code and a pointer to the binding
environment. Because all literals of the same procedure body
share the same environment, it is convenient to store the
binding environment in the common father node.

We can distinguish two kinds of nodes in the proof tree. We
have the tipnodes which are the unsolved subgoals of the
current goal statement and the nontipnodes which are the
partially solved problems. Except for the leftmost tipnode,
the one to be selected by the computation rule (the current

subgoal), all tipnodes are part of instances of procedures $B \leftarrow B_1, \ldots, B_m$ with their first literal B_1 either as current subgoal or as nontipnode. Assuming that the pure code allows us to find the right-hand brothers B_{i+1}, B_{i+2}, ... of any subgoal B_i, and knowing that their execution demands the same binding-environment, an explicit representation of the tipnodes in the proof tree is not necessary. They can be accessed either through nontipnodes or through the current subgoal. For the nontipnodes it is convenient to use a stack ('environment stack'). The subgoals being executed are pushed on the stack, on backtracking, the stack is popped.

Finally, we have to consider the unification between call and procedure heading. Unification not only creates a binding environment for the variables of the procedure but also updates (binding variables) the binding environment associated with the call (and possibly other binding environments). Variables, and their bindings, are removed by popping the stack/proof tree on failure when they are part of the current segment. The others are not affected by this operation. To

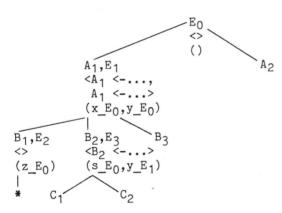

Fig. 3a. Complete abstract proof tree. Each nontipnode contains a subgoal, a binding environment E_i, a list $(<...>)$ of untried procedures and a list $((...))$ of the variables whose update is not automatically undone by popping the proof tree on failure. This figure describes the current active goal statement but, (knowing Prolog's computation rule) also the sequence of proof trees/goal statements forming a complete branch of the search tree. Due to PROLOG's search rule, this branch is the only one containing active goal statements. Thus the figure describes the whole search process.

allow the backtracking process to restore the original
situation, we have to record the bound variables which do not
belong to the current segment. In the abstract proof tree
(Fig. 3a), each node contains a list of variables to be
reset. In a concrete implementation (Fig. 3b and 3c), it is
easiest to collect these variables on a stack (the 'trail')
and to put a pointer to the trail in each backtrackpoint.

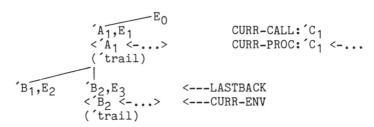

Fig. 3b. Concrete proof tree and global information about the
state of the computation. Only the nontipnodes are retained.
Each node contains a pointer ($'$) to the pure code of the
subgoal. The backtracknodes also contain a pointer to the
pure code of the first of the untried procedures and a
pointer to the trail. The given information (the trail is
given in Fig. 3c) completely determines the abstract proof
tree, indeed the nonempty tipnodes and the nonempty lists of
untried procedures are accessible through the given pointers.

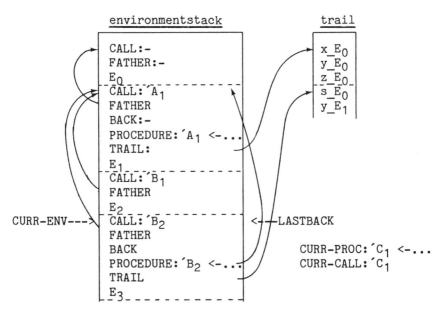

Fig. 3c.   The stack representation.

The nodes of Fig. 3b are pushed on the environmentstack and extended with navigational information, i.e. the fields FATHER and BACK.

The state of the computation is characterized by:
- CURR-CALL: a pointer to the pure code of the current subgoal.
- CURR-ENV: a pointer to the node containing the binding environment of the current call (the 'father' of the current call).
- CURR-PROC: a pointer to the pure code of the procedure to be applied on the current call.
- LASTBACK: a pointer to the last backtrackpoint.

The current goal statement is given by the current subgoal, its right-hand brothers and the right-hand brothers of all its ancestors.

To backtrack, the current segment of the environment stack is popped (the node pointed to by LASTBACK becomes the current subgoal), all updates noted on the current segment of the trail are undone and the current segment of the trail is popped.

To summarize, a 'deterministic' node contains:
- CALL: a pointer to the pure code of the call. This pointer also gives access to the right-hand brothers.
- FATHER: a pointer to the father of this node. This father node contains the binding environment associated with CALL, it also gives access to the right-hand brothers of all ancestors of CALL.
- a binding environment for the variables of the procedure applied on CALL.

A backtrackpoint also contains:
- BACK: a pointer to the previous backtrackpoint.
- PROCEDURE: a pointer to the pure code of the next procedure to be applied on CALL (gives access to all untried procedures).
- TRAIL: a pointer to the trail.

Algorithm
1. Push a node on the environmentstack with
- CALL := CURR-CALL
- FATHER := CURR-ENV
- Find 'the first successor of CURR-PROC which possibly matches' CURR-CALL, if none
then we have a deterministic node

else we have a backtrackpoint (a bit of CALL or FATHER can be
used to indicate the difference) and we have to   complete
the node with :
BACK := LASTBACK, LASTBACK becomes the new node
PROCEDURE := the next possibly matching procedure
TRAIL := top of the trail
- A binding environment for the variables of CURR-PROC
2. Unification between CURR-CALL with its binding environment
CURR-ENV and the heading of CURR-PROC with its binding
environment in the new node. All changes to the   environmentstack not restricted to the current segment are noted on the
trail.
CURR-CALL := first call in the body of CURR-PROC
CURR-ENV := the new node of the environmentstack
3. If successful unification
then find the   next unsolved subgoal (if none: a solution is
    derived): while CURR-CALL = NIL do
                CURR-CALL := the successor of CALL in CURR-ENV
                CURR-ENV := FATHER of CURR-ENV
else backtrack: (if LASTBACK = NIL then end of computation)
- use TRAIL pointer of LASTBACK to undo changes which are not
in the current segment of the environment stack and pop
current segment of the trail.
- CURR-CALL:= CALL of LASTBACK
- CURR-ENV := FATHER of LASTBACK
- CURR-PROC:= PROCEDURE of LASTBACK
- LASTBACK := BACK of LASTBACK and pop the current segment of
the environmentstack (all nodes inclusive the one pointed by
the old value of LASTBACK)

Notes
1. The first PROLOG implementation (Battani and Meloni, 1973;
Colmerauer et al. 1973) did not make a distinction between
deterministic nodes and backtrackpoints. Many, including
Warren (1977) prefer to have the binding environment at a
fixed offset from the start of the node. This is especially
desirable with structure sharing because of the frequent
switching of binding environment during unification. The
author's implementation makes the distinction and uses a bit
of the CALL field to indicate the type of the node.

2. The fact that a deterministic node is more space efficient
than a backtracknode, and, more important, that deterministic
nodes play a crucial role in the space saving techniques
described in the next section, makes it worthwhile to spend
some   effort(computation   or adequate representation) in
determining 'the first procedure which possibly matches a
call'. Warren (1977) uses an index on the first argument of

the procedure heading. Others (i.e. this author) use a slower but more accurate 'software' indexing on all arguments: a procedure is acceptable when the arguments in the heading and the corresponding arguments in the call are acceptable for each others. Two corresponding arguments are acceptable for each other when one of them contains a variable or both contain the same constant or both contain the same function symbol and the corresponding arguments of these function symbols are acceptable for each other.

3. OPPORTUNITIES TO POP THE ENVIRONMENTSTACK - PITFALLS

At this point, we ignore the existence of binding environments or, more accurate, we assume that pointers between binding environments, if present, are oriented from top to bottom of the stack (tips to root of proof tree). This means that we can pop the environmentstack without creating dangling pointers. Later, we return to this problem.

a. Completing a deterministic subgoal

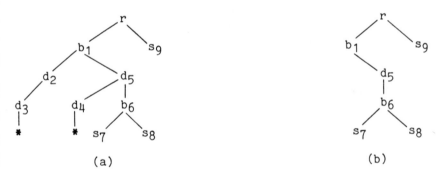

(a)   (b)

Fig. 4. Dropping a deterministic subtree

In Fig. 4. r denotes the root of the proof tree, the d_i denote deterministic nodes, the b_i denote backtrackpoints, the s_i denote unsolved subgoals and the * denote empty sets of subgoals. The subgoal corresponding to d_2 is completely solved, the solution is unique (no backtrackpoints in the subtree). This completed subtree can be dropped from the proof tree (Fig. 4.b) without affecting the behaviour of the algorithm. Indeed, we have the same current goal statement and the goal statements corresponding to the backtrackpoints (b_1, b_6) are also the same.

This technique corresponds to the situation in a conventional language: the activation record is popped when returning from a procedure.

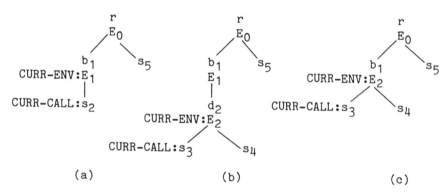

(a)   (b)   (c)

Fig. 5.   A call s_2, only one procedure matches the call, the procedure has an empty body.

Due to the detection and handling of 'tail recursion' (see section 3.b), the application of this technique only need be applied to the situation depicted in Fig. 5. where just one procedure matches the call and the body is empty.

Detection of the situation by the interpreter (Fig. 5.b): CURR-CALL = NIL and CURR-ENV is a deterministic node.

Action by the algorithm: CURR-CALL := successor of CALL in CURR-ENV, CURR-ENV := FATHER of CURR-ENV and pop the top node of the environment stack (new top is either CURR-ENV or LASTBACK).

b. Tail recursion

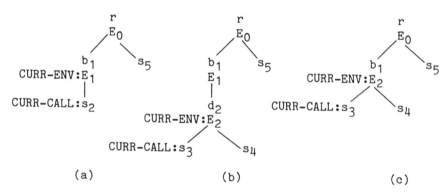

(a)   (b)   (c)

Fig. 6. Replacing tail recursion by iteration.

The situation is depicted in Fig. 6. The E_i denote the binding environments which are part of the nodes. In Fig. 6.a, s_2 is the last call of a procedure surviving in the proof tree (possible left-hand brothers have been popped).

Only one procedure is matching. (Fig. 6.b). The behaviour of the interpreter on the proof trees of Fig. 6.b and Fig. 6.c is the same. Because: (1) the same current goal statement (with the same binding environments!) and (2) the goal statements corresponding to the backtrackpoints are also identical. The node describing the call s2 has been collapsed with its father (E_2 replaces E_1 and the node s_2 is popped). The same node can now be used to execute s_3 (iteration over the same space). This situation is typical for recursive calls with tail recursion. The recursion is replaced by an iteration. It results in great savings when there is deep recursion.

Here we violate the assumption stated at the beginning of this section. We remove an environment E_1 which is not on the top of the stack. This can create dangling pointers. To be able to remove E_1, either we have to perform a complex update of the pointers going from E_2 to E_1, or we have to add a special control mechanism assuring that pointers created between E_1 and E_2 go from E_1 to E_2. We can avoid this problem by swapping E_1 and E_2 before creating any pointers between them. This restores our assumption.

Detection of the situation by the interpreter: (prior to unification, Fig. 6.a). The successor of CURR-CALL is NIL and LASTBACK is at least as far from the top as CURR-ENV (thus CURR-CALL is deterministic and its left-hand brothers have been popped).

Action prior to unification: swap binding environments of the new node and the node CURR-ENV. Moving environment E_1 has to be done with care. It is not impossible that E_1 contains pointers to itself, a simple update (adding a constant) of such pointers is necessary.

Action after unification (Fig. 6.b) : CURR-ENV : = FATHER of CURR-ENV, pop the top node (CURR-ENV is the new top).

Notes
1. When executing s_3 or s_4 (Fig. 6.c), their FATHER field will refer to node b_1, although b_1 is not the real father but a further ancestor. This is important when executing a cut ('/'), a special operation in PROLOG which transforms all backtracknodes of the subtree with the (real) father of the cut as root into deterministic nodes. A false father (e.g. b_1 when s_3 or s_4 is a cut) has to be saved from this fate. A bit of the FATHER or CALL fields (in b_1) can be used to indicate whether a node is the real father or a further ancestor of

its immediate descendants (s_3 and s_4).
2. There are cases where tail recursion optimisation is prevented due to the nondeterminism of the last call. Execution of a cut in the body of the applied procedure removes this nondeterminism. Then it becomes possible to perform a (delayed) application of tail recursion optimisation. This is a complex task due to the necessary updates of pointers.
3. Tail recursion optimisation is important when there is only a small amount of workspace available. It is less important when there is plenty of workspace because the workspace is released anyway. For the positive effect on speed, see (Warren, 1980).

c. Pitfalls

Up to now we have neglected the actual representation of the binding of a variable. The above optimisations are based on the assumption that all pointers between environments are oriented from the top to the bottom of the environmentstack. The first PROLOG interpreter (Battani and Meloni, 1973) violated this condition, as a consequence it could only pop the stack on backtracking. The attempt to pop the stack when completing a determinate subgoal drove the author (Bruynooghe, 1976, 1979) and David Warren (1977) to develop other methods for the handling of the binding environments. The author was the first to implement 'tail recursion optimisation' (end 1977). It is also implemented by Warren (1980).

4. THE REPRESENTATION OF THE BINDING ENVIRONMENTS

Structure Sharing

In the first PROLOG interpreter (Battani and Meloni, 1973) the representation of the binding of a variable is a variant of Boyer and Moore's structure sharing (1972). As with the subgoals, the binding of a variable is represented by two pointers, one to the pure code, the other to a binding environment. This binding environment in turn contains the bindings of the variables in the pure code. (Some implementations only use two pointers for a variable bound to a compound term. For other values they use a type field and either the address of the value (pointer) or a direct representation of the value, i.e. a variable: the address on the stack).

With this scheme, there are three cases when the unification algorithm has to bind a variable.

1. A variable x which is free in environment E_i and a variable y which is free in environment E_j. Suppose that E_i is more recent (or identical) than E_j, then, the variable x in E_i is bound to the pure code of y and to the environment E_j. The pointer from E_i to E_j is oriented to the bottom of the environmentstack.
2. A variable x which is free in environment E_i and a term t with environment E_j and E_i more recent than E_j. x is bound to the pure code of t and to the environment E_j. Also this pointer is oriented to the bottom of the stack.
3. Same as (2) but E_j is more recent than E_i. Also here, x has to be bound to the pure code of t and the environment E_j but the pointer from E_i to E_j is oriented to the top of the environmentstack. As a consequence, the space saving techniques of the previous section are impossible.

Example
A call with pure code $P(r,s,t)$ and a binding environment E_i consisting of:
- r: $'f(...)$,E_r: a pointer to the pure code representing the term f(...) and a pointer to the binding environment E_r.
- s: free.
- t: free.
A heading with pure code $P(x,y,g(x,u))$
A new binding environment E_j is created with free variables x,y and u.
The matching process results in the following bindings:
- x of E_j: $'f(...)$,E_r (case 2) (same value as r of E_i).
- y of E_j: $'s$,E_i (case 1) (a pointer to the pure code in the call of the variable s).
- t of E_i: $'g(x,u)$,E_j (case 3)(a pointer to the pure code of the heading).

To solve the problem, Warren (1977) observes that the trouble is due to the variables occurring in the terms of the pure code. He calls such variables global, the others he calls local. He divides the binding environment into a global part and a local part. Also in the pure code, he makes the distinction between global and local variables. Local environments are placed on the environmentstack but the global ones are placed on a special global stack. This stack is only popped on backtracking. Now unification starts with two literals of pure code, each with a local and global environment. The algorithm takes care that pointers between environments are either oriented from top to bottom in the environmentstack or, from the environmentstack to the global stack. This is possible, because, whenever a free variable is matched against a term, all variables occurring in the term are, by convention, in the global environment.

In our example, y belongs to $E_{j-local}$; x and u to $E_{j-global}$ and the problematic binding becomes
t of E_i: $'g(x,u),E_{j-global}$.

Note: The user can declare ('mode declaration') that some terms will never be matched against a free variable, this makes it possible to classify more variables as local.

<u>Copying pure code</u> (Bruynooghe, 1976, 1979; Mellish, 1980)

The binding of a variable can be represented by a single pointer to a direct representation of the value. However, pure code containing variables cannot be a part of such a direct representation. Whenever a free variable is matched against a term of pure code containing variables, a copy of that term is made. In this copy, the pure code for the variables is replaced as follows.
- if the variable is free in the corresponding binding environment, then the copy gets a free variable and the variable in the binding environment is bound to this new free variable.
- if the variable in the corresponding binding environment is already bound to a part of a copy, a pointer is placed (a 'bound' variable) from the new copy to the existing copy.

Using a special copystack only popped on backtracking, this assures that pointers are either oriented from top to bottom in the environmentstack, from the environmentstack to the copystack, or have any direction in the copystack. Again, the environmentstack can be popped without danger of dangling pointers.

Repeating our example, the given binding environment E_i now consists of
- r: $'f(...)$: a pointer to the direct representation of the term $f(...)$.
- s: free.
- t: free.
The matching process now results in
- x of E_j: $'f(...)$: a pointer to the existing direct representation of $f(...)$.
- y of E_j: $'s$ a pointer to the variable s of the binding environment E_i.
- t of E_i: $'g('f(...),u')$: a pointer to a created direct representation of a term g with two arguments, the first argument is a pointer to the existing direct representation

of f(...), the second argument is a new free variable called
u' and we also obtain:
- u of E_j: ´u': a pointer to the new free variable u'.

Notes
1. Warren has pointed out that he can drop variables from the
local environment once they will not be referenced during the
further execution. More specifically, local variables with
only one occurrence ('void' variables) do not need a place on
the environmentstack, the unification algorithm knows they
are free; local variables occurring only in the heading can
be dropped after unification of call and heading. Indeed,
they are not referenced in the body of the procedure. The
same, but for all variables, is true in the copying method.
2. Some parts of the global/copy stack can become
inaccessible. Garbage collection and compaction is possible.

5. DISCUSSION

To get an idea of the space efficiency of both approaches, we
can compare the storage needs of nodes and binding environments.

With copying, a deterministic node needs 2 fields (CALL,
FATHER); with structure sharing, 3 fields are needed (also a
pointer to the global binding environment), usually 6 are
used (frequent changes of binding environments - speed).

A backtrackpoint needs 6 fields with both methods (CALL,
FATHER, BACK, PROCEDURE, TRAIL, pointer to global/copystack).

With structure sharing, the binding environment associated
with the use of a procedure needs 2 fields for each variable.
The division between local (on the environmentstack) and
global (on the global stack) variables is determined by the
definition of the procedure. With copying, one field for each
variable is needed on the environmentstack. The space needed
for copies is harder to determine. The number of copies being
made depends on the pattern of the call. The space needed by
a copy depends on the chosen representation. We give two
possibilities:
a. To copy a term containing variables, of the form
$f(t_1,...,t_n)$, we can use n+1 fields, one field to identify
the functor f and one pointer to the representation of each
argument. Such a representation gives fast access to the i-th
argument.
b. With nested terms, it is possible to avoid the pointers to

the arguments by placing the arguments one after another. Then, only one field for each symbol is sufficient. This representation is more compact but the access to the i-th argument is slower. With both representations, the copy of a variable is either a free variable or a pointer to the value of the variable.

For each typical call of the procedures given in the benchmark of Warren (1977) we calculated the space occupied by the binding environment. Making the sum for 23 typical calls, we observed that the total amount of space was slightly smaller with copying (184- 216) and that structure sharing needed mode declarations to reduce the global stack to a comparable size (from 130 to 82). However, individual cases where copying is substantial worse than structure sharing are possible, i.e. when large terms need to be copied. Also the reverse is possible, i.e. a large number of variables but no copies to be made, but seems less likely in practice.

The paper of Mellish (1982) studies the behaviour of several programs under the two representations. A complete comparison between both approaches has also to consider the problem of speed. We have to restrict ourselves to the observation that structure sharing is faster in building new compound terms but slower in accessing those terms.

Notes
1. In our analysis of the storage needs of both approaches, we have considered the number of necessary fields. Machine dependent details are discussed in (Mellish, 1980; Warren, 1977).
2. Mellish (1980) discusses a variant of structure sharing. He observes that the two fields representing the binding of a variable are only needed when the pure code refers to a structured object (neither a variable nor a constant). He proposes to use only one field. When both fields are needed, a 'molecule' containing the two fields is created on the global stack and the variable points to this molecule. In most cases, this approach reduces the total amount of space (for our benchmark, the total is very close to that of copying), but increases the size of the global stack, especially when combined with mode declarations. In view of the different opportunities to pop the environmentstack, especially tail recursion, a method giving a small global stack seems preferable, particularly when there is no garbage collector for the global stack.

AN ALTERNATIVE TO STRUCTURE SHARING IN THE IMPLEMENTATION OF A PROLOG INTERPRETER

C. S. Mellish

Department of Artificial Intelligence
University of Edinburgh
Hope Park Square,
Edinburgh EH8 9NW, UK

1. INTRODUCTION

In this paper we discuss an alternative to "structure sharing" (SS) as a technique for representing binding environments in a Prolog interpreter. Our non structure sharing (NSS) approach, which uses a system of "copying", is used in a practical interpreter running on the PDP-11. This interpreter is capable of running substantial Prolog programs, even though the PDP-11's address space is limited to 32K, 16-bit words. We compare the space efficiency of this interpreter with that of a structure sharing version that was constructed later. It turns out that the "copying" approach compares very favourably, although the comparison would be less favourable on a machine capable of holding two addresses in one word. Our comparison shows that the decision whether or not to use structure sharing in a Prolog implementation is not simple and must take into account a number of factors. This paper has been condensed from a longer research report (Mellish, 1980).

2. STRUCTURE SHARING AND NON STRUCTURE SHARING

A standard technique in Prolog implementations is to represent a complex value of a variable as a pair of pointers, called a <u>molecule.</u> The first pointer is to a <u>skeleton</u> value which may reference other variables, and the second is to an <u>environment</u> specifying the values of these variables. Because environments for interpreting skeletons are specified explicitly, this scheme allows a single skeleton to be used in the representation of many different terms. Because of this sharing of information, the scheme has become known as **structure-sharing** (SS). Structure sharing was used in the first Prolog implementations (Battani and Meloni, 1973) and is also the basis of the DEC System-10 Prolog system (Warren et al. 1979).

The alternative, non structure sharing (NSS), system that we have investigated is much closer in spirit to the methods of storage allocation used by conventional programming languages like POP-2 and Algol68. In this system, when a variable comes to stand for a complex term, a concrete copy of the term is created, and a pointer to it is returned. Once a concrete copy has been constructed, the values of its component parts can be simply read off, without the necessity of consulting environment pointers. Any cells corresponding to unbound variables in the copied term are linked to the existing cells for those variables by pointers. This NSS approach, which Bruynooghe (1982) calls "copying pure code", is what we use in our PDP-11 interpreter (Mellish and Cross, 1979).

3. THE GLOBAL AND LOCAL STACKS

In order to explain our findings, we need to mention some important facts about the storage management of Prolog systems. It is common to divide the storage used by a running program basically into two stacks, called the local and global stacks. The local stack is used to hold administrative information (like "return addresses"), as well as data that need not be kept after a deterministic subgoal has been completed. The global stack is used to hold all other data (variable bindings, etc) generated by the program's execution. When backtracking takes place, both stacks are popped back to where they were at the last choice point. When a deterministic subgoal has been completed, only the local stack is popped back to where it was when the goal was started. It can be seen from this brief description that, for optimal space efficiency, a Prolog interpreter must ensure that as little as possible goes on the global stack if it can possibly go on the local stack. For more details about the memory management of Prolog implementations, the reader is referred to (Warren, 1977; Bruynooghe, 1982; Mellish, 1980).

In a SS system, every variable in a clause is classed at "compile time" as either "local" or "global", and is at run-time allocated a cell on the appropriate stack. This determination is based on whether the variable could be needed for the interpretation of a molecule. Because molecules represent complex terms that may need to be kept after the completion of a deterministic subgoal, any variable value that is needed for the interpretation of a molecule must appear on the global stack. Other variables can appear on the local stack.

In an NSS system of the kind we are considering, every variable is allocated a cell on the local stack. In addition, all concrete copies appear on the global stack, because they may have to be kept after the completion of a deterministic subgoal.

4. GENERAL COMMENTS

Let us start by making some general comments about what kinds of differences we might expect between the SS and NSS systems.

4.1. Constructing Complex Terms

When a complex term becomes accessible (as the value of a variable) for the first time, we can talk of the term being constructed. The whole point of SS is that there is a very low space overhead in constructing complex terms. As far as the global stack is concerned, the only pieces of information represented for a constructed terms are the values of the variables occurring within it. Moreover, each variable is only represented once, even if it appears several times in the term or in multiple constructed terms. On the other hand, the NSS approach needs to copy ground parts of a complex term and to have a location for every occurrence of a variable in a complex term. So structure sharing definitely seems to require less global stack when a term is constructed. It is clear that an NSS system could be optimised to avoid copying ground subterms, but it would still lose by having to copy functor information and pointers for ground subterms of terms which are not themselves ground.

4.2. Accessing the Components of Complex Terms

When a pattern is matched against a complex term that is already accessible, we can talk of the components of the term being accessed. When it comes to accessing the components of already constructed terms, SS does not perform so well. It allocates space on the global stack for the variables referring to the components, because at compile time there is no way of telling that an accessing, rather than a construc- ting, operation will be involved (unless use is made of "mode declarations" (Warren, 1977). On the other hand, the copying approach only puts items on the global stack when constructing takes place.

4.3. Overall Stack Usage

From the last two paragraphs, we can see that the relative merits of SS and NSS as regards global stack usage will depend on the types of programs that we wish to run. On the one hand, we can construct a pathological program where huge terms containing repeated variables are continuously constructed but never accessed - on this, structure sharing will gain by arbitrary amounts. On the other hand, we can construct a pathological program that constructs a single complex term and repeatedly accesses its subterms - on this, structure sharing will lose by arbitrary amounts. Presumably, "real" programs fall somewhere in between these extremes.

As regards local stack usage, SS is clearly superior, since it allocates space for only some variables on the local stack, whereas NSS allocates space for all. Since local stack space can be reclaimed at the end of a determinate computation, NSS might be expected to do best with determinate programs. The hope of this approach is to reduce the global stack usage at the expense of the total amount of stacks used. This clearly will not pay off if the local stack space can only rarely be reclaimed.

4.4. Representing Molecules in Machines with Small Word Sizes

Our discussion so far has assumed that it is possible to store a molecule (two addresses) within the space allocated for a single variable value. In general, the most economical and simple unit of space to use is the machine word (here taken to be the smallest independently addressable unit of storage above some minimum size). In a machine with a small word size, we may be able to store things like atom representations and (smallish) integers in single words, but a molecule is really out of the question. This is a problem that we had to confront for the PDP-11, and in fact it was one of the main reasons why we turned to an alternative to structure sharing.

If we wish to stick to a structure sharing approach, how are we to represent molecules on a machine of small word size? One possibility is simply to take a larger unit, such as 2 words, for the value of a variable. Another is to have a molecule as a 2-word item to be separately allocated on the global stack and to which variable cells can point. The second of these will take up less storage if at all times the number of variables allocated on the global stack is at least twice the number of molecules. This has proved to be the case in all the examples we have tested.

It should be noted that the overhead in representing molecules sometimes affects a structure sharing approach even when the components of a constructed term are accessed. When structure sharing has to represent a complex subterm of a constructed term, it needs to produce a molecule, of course. Sometimes the appropriate molecule is already available as the value of a variable occurring in the constructed term. Otherwise a new one must be constructed. Such an action incurred no overhead previously, when we considered a molecule as something that could be stored in any variable cell.

5. SOME FIGURES

How do all these factors interact, and what are the relative merits of structure sharing and its alternatives in practice? When we decided to investigate this question, we had already developed a non structure sharing interpreter for the PDP-11 (Mellish and Cross, 1979), and so we decided to construct a structure sharing version of it and make some comparisons. The structure sharing interpreter copes with the small word size of the PDP-11 by using the second approach for representing molecules, with a molecule being allocated as a separate object on the global stack. In spite of these particular details, our figures provide a basis for a comparison between SS and NSS in general.

We took 7 different, already existing, programs and ran them on the two interpreters. Three of the programs (numbers 2, 3 and 4) represent a selection from the examples given in the appendix of Warren's paper (1977). Numbers 2 and 3 ("naive reverse" and "quicksort") intuitively seemed to involve roughly equal amounts of "accessing" and "constructing" (with a bias towards the latter), whereas number 4 ("serialise") was expected to involve a higher proportion of "accessing". For reasons that are not of interest here, we reduced the "quicksort" problem to deal with only the first 30 elements of the list given by Warren. Because our simple interpreter (without the aid of Warren's "mode declarations") regarded these programs as highly non-deterministic, we introduced for contrast a version of program 2 ("naive reverse") with added "cuts" as number 7. Next, we decided to investigate the claim that the real disadvantages of NSS would become apparent when we tried to write a Prolog interpreter in Prolog. We thus took the very simple Prolog interpreter given in (Warren et al. 1979) and presented it with programs 2 and 3, giving numbers 5 and 6. Finally, we wished to try something a bit different from these rather "toy" examples. We took the natural language parser from Dahl's (1977) program, as modified by Warren and Pereira to deal with a new language (English) and a different domain (computer operating system queries). This program reads an English sentence, character by character, from the terminal, converting it to a list of atoms, and constructs a logical formula expressing its "meaning" (This can then be used in conjunction with a database of facts about the world to produce an appropriate response). This program, when presented with the question "What files dating from Tuesday does the owner of the file dating from Monday possess?" forms our first example.

With each program, we measured various parameters of the space used. We did not measure runtime or the amount of space occupied by clauses. The parameters (all measured in machine words) are given in Fig. 1 below. They are:

A - The size of local stack on termination.
B - Local stack maximum size during computation.
C - The amount of space occupied by molecules (2 words each) on termination.
D - The amount of space occupied in the global stack on termination. This corresponds to the total amount of space that would be taken up in the long term if the program were invoked as a "subroutine" and all choice points were then discarded (for instance, with a "cut"). It is a reasonable measure of the maximum amount of global stack in use at any time.
E - The total amount of global stack in use, ignoring the space taken up by molecules (D-C).
F - The total amount of space that would be taken up in the long term if the program were invoked as a "subroutine" but all choice points were kept (A+D).
G - The total amount of space needed (B+D).

6. CONCLUSIONS

It is hard to know how to select a representative sample of programs for such an experiment. As it was, the programs were selected in advance as easily accessible programs that

Program		Local (A)	Local Max(B)	Mols (C)	Global (D)	D-C (E)	A+D (F)	B+D (G)
(1) Natural	SS	620	700	510	1235	725	1855	1935
Lang Prog	NSS	780	907	-	805	-	1585	1712
(2) Naive	SS	2820	2823	988	2353	1365	5173	5176
Reverse	NSS	4185	4192	-	1454	-	5639	5646
(3)	SS	907	913	340	763	423	1670	1676
Quicksort	NSS	1270	1280	-	482	-	1752	1762
(4)	SS	267	311	338	924	586	1191	1235
Serialise	NSS	454	512	-	467	-	921	979
(5) Interp	SS	4975	4992	2046	4995	2949	9970	9987
running (2)	NSS	7892	7913	-	3414	-	11306	11327
(6) Interp	SS	2715	2732	1188	2757	1569	5472	5489
running (3)	NSS	4252	4276	-	1839	-	6091	6115
(7) (2)	SS	0	214	988	2353	1365	2353	2567
with "cuts"	NSS	0	278	-	1454	-	1454	1732

Fig. 1. Comparison of SS and NSS Systems

covered a range of different situations. Assuming that they are not too unrepresentative, we can conclude:

- Comparing columns C and E, we see that in each case the number of variable cells on the global stack in SS is at least twice the number of molecules. (Since C is the amount of space used by the 2- word molecules, this result follows from the fact that C<E in all cases). This provides justification for our choice of the representation of molecules as separate items on the global stack. It also suggests that Prolog implementations making use of long words to store molecules may not be very efficient in terms of the number of bits used, unless the extra length is used significantly for the representation of large integers, say.

- Comparing column D for NSS with column E for SS (and columns A and B for both), we see that if there were no overhead in representing molecules then SS would be better everywhere (except in program (4)). This suggests that SS is the more efficient technique in terms of the number of words used, given a machine of large word size.

- Comparing column D for the two systems, we see that (given the molecule overheads) NSS is in each case better than SS for global stack usage. This suggests that for determinate programs (where local stack is eventually reclaimed) NSS is superior in the amount of storage occupied in the long term.

- Comparing columns A and B for the two systems, we see that NSS always uses more local stack than SS. However, when this is added to global stack usage (giving columns F and G), the systems are fairly similar. Differences now depend on the particular task - (1), (4) and (7) are better for NSS; the others are better for SS. But the differences are small.

- It should be noted that most of these programs include "false choice points" where the interpreter cannot detect that a clause chosen will be the only one that matches a goal. These would disappear with a more intelligent interpreter that used indexing on the main functors of a predicate's arguments. The great difference that this would make is illustrated in the difference between programs (2) and (7). From our point of view, the important thing is that NSS comes out better in the program with "cuts" (see columns F and G), whereas it is worse off in the one without. Thus certain obvious improvements in our interpreters can be expected to make NSS an even more favourable option. Of course, other improvements (such as, perhaps, garbage collection of the global stack) may well work in favour of SS.

7. SOME FINAL REMARKS

As we have seen, the comparison between structure sharing and its alternatives is not a simple one, and no quick answer can be given as to which approach is best. It is interesting, however, that a significant factor in the decision is the relationship between the word size and address size of the machine on which the system is implemented. Unfortunately, neither of the systems discussed is optimal in its use of the local and global stacks. It remains to be seen whether mixed approaches can be devised that have the advantages of both.

8. ACKNOWLEDGEMENTS

I am grateful to Fernando Pereira, David Warren and Lawrence Byrd for many fruitful discussions, as well as for comments on earlier versions of this paper.

SELECTIVE BACKTRACKING

Luis Moniz Pereira   Antonio Porto

Departamento de Informatica
Universidade Nova de Lisboa
Quinta da Torre
2825 Monte da Caparica
Portugal

ABSTRACT

In (Pereira and Porto, 1979a,1979b) we presented a method for performing selective backtracking in Horn clause programs as applied to Prolog (Roussel, 1975; Warren et al. 1977). It is, in fact, a specialization to the depth-first strategy of a more general form of intelligent backtracking (Bruynooghe and Pereira, 1981). In this paper we review selective backtracking and address general implementation issues.

1. BASIC IDEAS

The basic ideas of selective backtracking are illustrated and explained in the figures and text below. In Fig. 1 we depict each goal execution as a box with four ports, following Byrd (1980b). The DO port is entered when the goal is first activated, whereas the DONE port is exited on complete execution of the goal. On backtracking, control re-enters the goal execution box via the REDO port, and exits at the UNDONE port on unsuccessful execution. The goal execution box itself decomposes into two similar boxes: the clause head matching box and the clause body execution box.

After matching goal G with a clause head, the clause body execution box for G becomes one of the boxes of Fig. 2. Backtracking to a goal G actually consists in entering the REDO port of the clause head matching box for G.

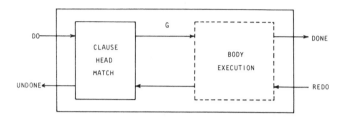

Fig. 1.

no goal   single goal   conjunction of goals

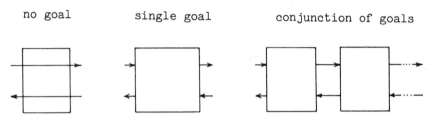

Fig. 2.

The main idea of selective backtracking is to select, at each failed goal, a single goal to backtrack to, not necessarily the previous goal as in standard backtracking. Consequently, entry into the REDO port of G is allowed only if G has been selected as the backtrack goal for the last failed goal; otherwise control flows directly to the UNDONE port of G (see Fig. 3).

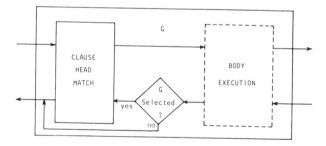

Fig. 3.

At the UNDONE port of the clause head matching box, i.e. after failure, selection of the backtrack goal takes place. Deselection of the backtrack goal is done when backtracking to it occurs, i.e. at the REDO port of its clause head matching box (see Fig. 4).

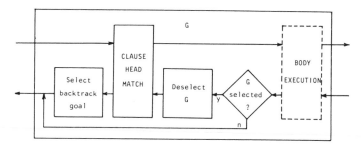

Fig. 4.

2. SELECTION OF THE BACKTRACK GOAL

How is the backtrack goal selected?

Upon failure of a goal G, the backtrack goal is chosen among the candidate goals for backtracking. These are:

1) The <u>ancestors</u> of G - These are the goals whose alternative clauses avoid reactivation of G.

2) The <u>modifying goals</u> for G - These are the goals whose match if undone will undo failure-originating bindings in the arguments of G. In the sequel we refer how they are obtained.

3) The <u>legacy set</u> of G - This is the set of candidate backtrack goals inherited from failed goals that selected G as the backtrack goal; they must be kept as candidates for backtracking to ensure completeness of the search.

Among all the candidates, the most recently activated one is selected as the backtrack goal. The remaining ones become part of its legacy set.

Refining the set of candidates

The set of candidates for backtracking can be refined as specified next.

The ancestors - Among the ancestors, it suffices to retain the parent as candidate, since if and when the parent fails, then its parent becomes a candidate. This way no ancestor will be left out.

The modifying goals - Rather than the whole set of modifying goals, some subsets may be used instead, without loosing completeness; they are the global modifying sets.

A global modifying set is the union of local modifying sets, where each of these is associated with the mishmach of the goal with a clause head.

A local modifying set is obtained from the unification conflicts in the mismatch. To each conflict is associated an elementary modifying set, and it is argued in (Pereira and Porto, 1980) that taking as the local modifying set any one of the elementary modifying sets is sufficient to maintain completeness; it is also pointed out which is the best elementary modifying set choice.

An elementary modifying set is the set of modifying goals for variables whose links to non-variable terms were followed in accessing the two conflicting constant symbols.

The modifying goals for a variable linked to a non-variable term are goals whose matches produced bindings part of that link. (More on this later.)

A further refinement in this case is achieved by discarding from any modifying set, because redundant, all goals which are ancestors of another goal in the set. In fact, all ancestors are eventually backtracked to when their descendants fail. We now deal with one more important refinement.

Goal determinism - We say a goal is strongly-deterministic if some constant symbols in its arguments only allow the goal to possibly match one clause, and those symbols cannot be replaced. (The unreplaceable symbols are those textual in the goal or acquired at strongly-deterministic matches.)

It is irrelevant to backtrack to a strongly-deterministic goal since no alternative clauses exist for it, and analysis of its failed matches is irrelevant since the unreplaceable symbols will never allow it to match other clauses even after backtracking. Accordingly, the modifying goal for a variable bound in a strongly-deterministic match is not the matching goal but its most recent non-strongly-deterministic ancestor, called its avoiding goal. Naturally, whenever a goal fails, the avoiding goal replaces the parent as a candidate for backtracking.

3. REPRESENTATION OF DEPENDENCIES

In this section we present one solution to the problem of storing the information to be used by an interpreter for identifying modifying goals. DEC-10 Prolog syntax will be used for terms, ie. names beginning with an upper-case letter will denote variables, otherwise constants, functors or predicates. Terms are transformed to contain information on their own binding dependencies, and are unified through a special unification algorithm.

Let us sum up what dependencies must be remembered:

1) Because ancestors of failed goals are always backtracking candidates, the goal dependencies created by simple transmission of terms up and/or down the derivation tree (through chains of ancestors possibly linked by coomon variables at brother goals) need not be noted explicitly.

2) A goal in whose match a goal variable becomes instantiated must be kept as a modifying goal for that variable.

3) A goal in whose match two uninstantiated goal variables become bound together (through a double occurrence of a variable in the clause head) must be kept as a modifying goal for the two variables.

4) Strongly-deterministic goals do not create dependences. Accordingly, should the goal in cases 2) and 3) be strongly-deterministic its avoiding goal, rather than itself, should be kept as a modifying goal.

Thus, only non-strongly-deterministic goals are modifying goals. In order to be referenced, they are numbered from 1 onwards, in the order they are activated. During backtracking this numbering is undone.

To convey dependencies, any binding of a variable X in the goal is represented in the form   TX : DX

DX is the dependency tag of X. TX is the term bound to the variable, possibly comprising other bindings of variables in this form.

The dependency tag DX is a list   IX . BX

IX, the instantiation variable of X, shows the type of bindings performed on X:

IX = d(N) if X was directly instantiated (that is, without any intermediate binding to another goal variable) during the match of a goal G. N is the number of G, or that of G's avoiding goal in case G is strongly-deterministic.

IX = i if X was indirectly instantiated (that is, through an intermediate binding to another goal variable).

IX remains free while X is free or bound to variables alone.

BX is a (possibly empty) list of the relevant dependencies of X created by unification with other variables. Each such dependency, created by binding X to Y, is of the form b(N,D) where N is the number of the goal G in whose match the binding is done, or that of G's avoiding goal in case G is strongly-deterministic.

If Y, bound to TY:DY, is instantiated, then D becomes DY. If Y is uninstantiated then D becomes DY1, and DY is updated to include the element b(N,DX1), expressing the dependency of Y on X. DY1 is the result of deleting b(N,DX1) from DY, and similarly DX1 is obtained from DX by excluding b(N,DY1) from it. Thus circularity of reference is prevented.

What happens is that when several goal variables get bound together through several explicit bindings among them, the graph of those bindings is a tree-like structure with unspecified root. The dependency tags we build are, for each variable, a representation of that tree having the variable as the root.

All this is best seen with an example. Suppose we have the goals and clauses:

```
        1       2       3           p(V,V) <-

    <- p(X,Y) , p(Y,Z) , q(Y)       q(a) <-

    After goal 1:

X = T : IX.b(1,IY.BY1).BX1          X --1-- Y
Y = T : IY.b(1,IX.BX1).BY1

    After goal 2:

X = T : IX.b(1,IY.b(2,IZ.BZ1).BY2).BX1    X --1-- Y --2-- Z
Y = T : IY.b(1,IX.BX1).b(2,IZ.BZ1).BY2
Z = T : IZ.b(2,IY.b(1,IX.BX1).BY2).BZ1
```

After goal 3:

```
X = a : i.b(1,d(3).b(2,i.nil).nil).nil     X --1-- Y --2-- Z
Y = a : d(3).b(1,i.nil).b(2,i.nil).nil              |
Z = a : i.b(2,d(3).b(1,i.nil).nil).nil              3
                                                    |
                                                    |
                                                    a
```

From these dependency tags the exact chain of goals through which each variable became instantiated can be obtained - they are its modifying goals.

Alternative solutions

If upon successful execution of a goal alternative solutions are sought, backtracking must take place. The selective backtracking mechanism views the process of backtracking as the need to explore the search space relevently, not as the need to explore it thoroughly. One can view the search for alternative solutions as a user-generated failure of the previous solution. What the user wants is, in fact, to modify the previous solution, i.e. the arguments of the solved top goal.

Just picture replacing <- goal(X) by something like <- goal(X) , user_satisfied(X) .

Now, the goals where the arguments might be modified are precisely all the arguments' modifying goals. Thus, after forgetting any subsisting legacy sets, all the modifying goals for the arguments of the top goal are taken as the backtracking candidates and backtracking is re-instated.

4. SIMPLIFICATIONS

If a combination of some or all simplifications described next is used, selective backtracking can be incorporated as a standard facility without undue overhead.

1) Obtaining the modifying goals. Rather than analysing the failed matches of G with clause heads, one may simply take all the modifying goals of all arguments of a failed G, irrespective of whether they entered in some conflict.

Alternatively, for every G one may take only the modifying goals of the first conflict encountered in each mismatch and remember them for eventual use.

Optional for the first alternative is letting the user state which arguments alone can give rise to failure. (This is a refinement of 'mode declarations'.)

2) **Storing the modifying goals.** Only one slot is needed for each goal variable to store its modifying goals if the next simplification is made. When two free goal variables are bound, store nothing in their slots but mark the goal for backtracking, irrespective of whether it belongs to the modifying set of some future conflict. In case one of the variables is already instantiated, besides marking the goal for backtracking, also copy its slot into the slot of the free variable. In all other cases where a goal variable gets instantiated, store in its slot the goal number. Do nothing otherwise.

3) **Determining strong-determinism.** It is irrealistic to expect the system to evaluate strong-determinism unaided and still be efficient. More expediently, the conditions under which a goal is strongly-deterministic are easily supplied by the user, e.g.

strong_det(append(X,Y,Z)) <- nonvar(X)

In our latest implementation, written in Prolog itself as the others had been (Pereira and Porto, 1979b, 1980a), we use 3) and the second alternative of 1), but not 2). For storing the modifying goals we use the representation shown before. A low level implementation is needed though to make the selective backtracking mechanisms presented truly competitive.

SPECIFICATION AND TRANSFORMATION

PROGRAM TRANSFORMATION
BY DATA STRUCTURE MAPPING

Åke Hansson   Sten-Åke Tärnlund

UPMAIL
Computing Science Department
Uppsala University
Sturegatan 4 A
S-752 23 Uppsala
Sweden

1. INTRODUCTION

Before proceeding to a formal treatment let us get a firmer idea of our problem. Suppose that we have a program P that uses data structure d and we want an isomorphic program P' that, for example, is more efficient than P. A common method is to substitute a new data structure d' for d and to manipulate P so that we get an equivalent program P'. An example of this is the transformation of the heap sort algorithm on binary trees to an algorithm on arrays (see Knuth, 1973).

In logic programs there are two representations of lists that are commonly used. One is simple lists the other is d-lists. Programs on d-lists are usually more efficient but sometimes less transparant than those on simple lists. We shall look at the formal transformation of programs using simple lists into equivalent programs using d-lists. The transformation makes use of a 1-1 function between simple lists and d-lists.

Program transformation can be viewed as a special case of program synthesis from a specification given as a program. It can also be used as an auxiliary method for deriving programs from abstract specifications (e.g., abstract in the sense that no data structure is specified). This point is elaborated on further in (Hansson and Tärnlund, 1979a,b).

Figure 1 depicts the situation where several different programs can be derived from an abstract specification by different derivation paths. So we can derive P' either by a derivation from the specification or by a transformation of P. The transformation is often much shorter. As an example, the derivation of a quick sort program on d-lists takes about 100 steps from an abstract specification using a natural deduction proof (see Hansson, 1980). In contrast, in section 3 we derive the same program from a quick sort program on simple lists in 11 steps by a data structure mapping.

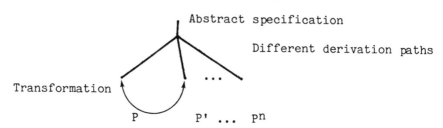

Fig. 1. Development of programs by formal derivations.

The idea of formal program transformation by data structure mapping seems to be due to Burstall and Darlington (1975), who used it for recursion equations. The subject of program development by derivations in first order logic has been taken up by several authors using different methods e.g., (Green, 1969; Clark, 1977; Bibel, 1978; Manna and Waldinger, 1978; Hogger, 1979; Kowalski, 1979b; Hansson and Tärnlund, 1979a,b; Clark and Darlington, 1980).

2. DATA STRUCTURE MAPPING

We illustrate the technique of data structure mappings by using a characterization of a 1-1 mapping between simple lists and d-lists given in definitions 1 and 2 below. The latter are useful data structures. They were first formally defined in (Clark and Tärnlund, 1977) and some operations on d-lists are studied in (Tärnlund, 1978). We shall use the notation x.y for a simple list with x as first element and y as remainder. The drawback of the simple list data structure is the difficulty of appending an element to the back of the list. To do this we must traverse the list from the front. With d-lists, especially most general d-lists, we can add an element to the back without traversing the list. So programs in which lists are concatenated are often more efficient if d-lists are used. A d-list is written as a pair <u,w>, where u and w are simple lists and from some element of u the remainder of u is identical to w. For example, <a.b.c.∅,c.∅> and <a.b.x,x> both denote the list a.b.∅, but the latter is the most general d-list since the variable x stands for any list. In particular <u,u> denotes the empty list.

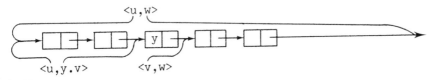

Fig. 2. d-lists

Notice that the result of adding y to the back of the d-list
<u,y.v> is the d-list <u,v>. Before we can write down our 1-1
function between simple lists and d-lists we need the following append program as an auxiliary function. The result of
appending a simple list u to the empty list is u, moreover,
the result of appending a simple list z to a simple list x.y
is a simple list where x is the first element and the rest is
the result of appending z to y. We write this algorithm in a
programming language with identity (see Hansson et al. 1982).

$$\begin{aligned}
&\text{append}(\emptyset,u)=u\\
&\text{append}(x.y,z)=x.\text{append}(y,z)
\end{aligned} \tag{1}$$

For convenience, we omit universal quantifiers in front of an
entire sentence. Using this append relation we can define a
1-1 function between simple lists and d-lists. The function m
maps a simple list, composed of a simple list y.z appended to
the back of a simple list x, to a d-list <u,w> exactly when m
maps the simple list x to the d-list <u,y.v> and the simple
list z to the d-list <v,w>. More precisely:

m : simple list -> d-list

Definition 1.

m(append(x,y.z))=<u,w> <--> m(x)=<u,y.v> & m(z)=<v,w>
m(∅)=<u,u>

The definition formalises the relationship between d-lists
and simple lists.

Let us give the inverse function of m the name m^{-1} .

m^{-1}: d-list -> simple list

Definition 2.

m^{-1}(<u,u>)=∅
m^{-1}(<u,w>)=append(x,y.z) <--> m(append(x,y.z))=<u,w>

We shall take up a program that reverses a simple list. It maps simple lists to simple lists. We shall transform it into a program from lists to d-lists. The result of reversing an empty list is the empty list, and moreover the result of reversing a list x.y is the list x.∅ appended to the back of to the result of reversing the list y.

$$rev(∅)=∅$$
$$rev(x.y)=append(rev(y),x.∅) \tag{2}$$

The weakness of this program when we run it is that an element cannot be appended until the remaining list has been reversed, and then we have to traverse the entire list from the front to the rear. By using d-lists as the output structure we can remove these inefficiencies.

Let us call the reverse function from lists to d-lists, REV. Using rev of (2) and m of definition 1 we can give a simple definition of REV. The REV of a simple list z is a d-list <u,w> if and only if the reverse of a simple list z is a simple list rev(z) which is mapped by m onto <u,w>.

Definition 3.

REV(z)=<u,w> <--> m(rev(z))=<u,w>

Using this definition as a program would be no more efficient than using (2). But we can derive from it two theorems and these will be an efficient program. We use Prawitz's (1965) natural deduction system for the derivations.

```
1. REV(x.y)=<u,w> <--> m(rev(x.y))=<u,w>      ∀ elim. def. 3
2. REV(x.y)=<u,w> <-->
              m(append(rev(y),x.∅))=<u,w>     Identity 1 and (2)
3. m(append(rev(y),x.∅))=<u,w> <-->
              m(rev(y))=<u,x.w> & m(0)=<w,w>  ∀ elim. def. 1
4.*   REV(y)=<u,x.w>                          Hypothesis
5.*   m(rev(y))=<u,x.w>                        -> elim. 4, def. 3
6.*   m(rev(y))=<u,x.w> & m(∅)=<w,w>           & intro 5, def. 1
7.*   m(append(rev(y),x.∅))=<u,w>             -> elim. 3, 6
8.*   REV(x.y)=<u,w>                           -> elim. 7, 2
9. REV(x.y)=<u,w> <- REV(y)=<u,x.w>           -> intro 4, 8
```

The implication of step 9 together with a trivial base case, comprise a more efficient program for reversing a list than the program in (2). The new program appends an element to the rear of the d-list without traversing the entire list.

$$REV(\emptyset)=<u,u>$$
$$REV(x.y)=<u,w> \quad <- \quad REV(y)=<u,x.w> \qquad (3)$$

3. PROGRAM DEVELOPMENT AND DATA STRUCTURE MAPPINGS

Formal program development is a more general subject than data structure mappings as was illustrated in figure 1. However, we have made the point that data structure mappings can be useful for program development. We shall now follow up the point. Formal program development usually starts from a specification that may be abstract in several ways, e.g., no data structure is specified or the specification language is more general than the programming language. For example, suppose that we follow Green (1969b) and specify the idea of sorting as: y is a sorted version of x exactly when y is ordered and a permutation of x. More formally:

$$sort(x)=y \quad <--> \quad ordered(y) \text{ \& } permutation(x,y). \qquad (4)$$

In relation to our problem the definitions of ordered and permutation are not important so we can leave them out.

This specification is abstract in the sense that many different sorting algorithms can be derived from it. This is demonstrated in (Clark and Darlington 1980; Hansson 1980). In the latter paper three different sorting algorithms are obtained using a natural deduction system. But each derivation is quite long, over 100 steps; therefore it would be of interest to have a method that can simplify this work. Fortunately, we can make use of the idea of data structure mapping that gives us a quicksort program on d-lists in 11 derivation steps from a corresponding program on simple lists. Let us first informally describe a quick-sort program. The result of sorting the empty list is the empty list, and the result of sorting a list x.y is to append a compounded list consisting of the element x and a quick-sorted list y" to a quick-sorted list y', where the result of partitioning the list y with respect to x is such that all elements less than x are on y' and those greater than x are on y". Formally

$$q(\emptyset)=\emptyset$$
$$q(x.y)=append(q(y'),x.q(y")) \quad <- \quad part(x,y,y',y") \qquad (5)$$

The program maps simple lists into simple lists. We shall transform it into one that maps simple lists into d-lists. For the transformation we shall not need a definition of part(x,y,y',y"). This is the relation that holds when y' comprises the list of elements on y less than x and y" are those elements on y greater than or equal to x. The new program will be more efficient because there will be no call to append. First, we define the new quicksort function, Q, in terms of m and q from definition 1 and (5) respectively.

Definition 4.

$Q(y)=\langle u,w \rangle \longleftrightarrow m(q(y))=\langle u,w \rangle$

This definition uses the sort program in (5) and thus cannot be more efficient as a program. We arrive at a more efficient quicksort program on d-lists (Q) by the following derivation.

```
1.  Q(x.y)=<u,w>  <-->  m(q(x.y))=<u,w>         ∀ elim. def. 4
2.  Q(y')=<u,x.v>  <-->  m(q(y'))=<u,x.v>       ∀ elim. def. 4
3.  Q(y")=<v,w>  <-->  m(q(y"))=<v,w>           ∀ elim. def. 4
  4.*   Q(y')=<u,x.v> & Q(y")=<v,w>             Hypothesis
  5.*   m(q(y'))=<u,x.v> & m(q(y"))=<v,w>       <--> elim. 2,3,4
  6.*   m(append(q(y'),x.q(y")))=<u,w>          <--> elim. 5 and def.1
    7.**    part(x,y,y',y")                     Hypothesis
    8.**    q(x.y)=append(q(y'),x.q(y"))        --> elim. 7 and (5)
    9.**    m(q(x.y))=<u,w>                     Identity 6 and 8
   10.**    Q(x.y)=<u,w>                        <--> elim. 9 and 1
11. Q(x.y)=<u,w>  <-- Q(y')=<u,x.v> &           --> intro. 4 and 7
              Q(y")=<v,w> & part(x,y,y',y")
```

The base case: $Q(\emptyset)=\langle u,u \rangle$ is trivially derived. Combining the basis and the implication of step 11 yields an efficient quicksort program on d-lists.

$$Q(\emptyset)=\langle u,u \rangle$$
$$Q(x.y)=\langle u,w \rangle \leftarrow Q(y')=\langle u,x.v \rangle \text{ \& } Q(y")=\langle v,w \rangle \text{ \& } part(x,y,y',y") \tag{6}$$

4. CONCLUSION

We have argued that program transformation using data structure mapping is useful for developing logic programs. We have exemplified this using a particular mapping between simple lists and d-lists. In the examples, no derivation was longer than 11 steps, but it is not difficult to find problems that are more complicated and may consist of over 100 steps. Consequently, we would benefit from a derivation editor that allows us to take longer steps, which suggests derivation structures and which takes care of proof administration. Such an editor has been developed by Eriksson and Johansson (1981).

LOGIC PROGRAM SPECIFICATION OF NUMERICAL INTEGRATION

Keith L. Clark   William M. McKeeman   Sharon Sickel

Department of   Wang Institute,   Logical Paradox, Inc.
  Computing   Tyngsboro   26 Moreno Drive,
Imperial College   MA 01879   Santa Cruz
  London SW7   USA   CA 95060.
   England   USA

1. INTRODUCTION

In this paper we develop several different numerical integration algorithms using the notation and concepts of logic programming. We begin with a logic program that is just a relational encoding of two axioms about definite integrals. This program is a specification of the input/output relation of an integration algorithm. It also defines our first, highly non-deterministic, algorithm. We then consider different control strategies for the program to constrain the non-determinism. By pairing the program with each of three different control strategies we define three families of integration algorithms, each member of a family being defined by a tighter control strategy. This is the logic + control (L + C) specification of an algorithm advocated by Kowalski (1979b) and others (Hayes, 1973; Pratt 1977). Step by step, we then transform each L + C specification into a new L' + C' specification in which the logic is elaborated and the control is simplified. At each step we preserve the correctness of the logic, we make sure that our program still comprises a set of true statements about numerical integration. In the final stage of the transformation we tighten the control so as to define a deterministic algorithm. In this way we systematically develop five deterministic integration algorithms. Each is specified by a logic program paired with a sequential control.

2. LOGIC PROGRAMMING NOTATION

We assume familiarity with the concepts of logic programming

as expounded by Kowalski (1974). Our logic programs will be
sets of implications of the form

$$B \text{ <- } A_1,\ldots,A_m \quad m \geq o,$$

where B and each A_i are atomic formulae. The implication is a
procedure for the relation of the atomic formula B. The body
of the procedure comprises a set of preconditions/procedure
calls $A_1,..,A_m$. For readability we shall make free use of
infix notation, e.g. writing e<EPS instead of $\leq$(e,EPS). We
shall also allow arithmetic expressions to appear as argument
terms. That is, as shorthand for an explicit precondition
y=e, which names the relation: y has value of e, we will drop
the equality and replace all other occurences of y by e. So,
instead of

$$I(a,b,f,y,e) \text{ <-} $$
$$I(a,m,f,y_1,e_1), \; I(m,b,f,y_1,e_1), \; y=y_1+y_2, \; e=e_1+e_2$$

we shall write

$$I(a,b,f,e_1+e_2, \; y_1+y_2) \text{ <- } I(a,m,f,y_1,e_1), \; I(m,b,f,y_2,e_2).$$

Logic + Control

An evaluation of a logic program is the computation of output
bindings for the variables of a procedure call B'. In
answering the call any of the program procedures for the
relation of the call may be used. This is one dimension of
the non-determinism of the computation. A rule which selects
for each call <u>exactly</u> one procedure to be used to answer the
call we shall call a <u>choice rule</u>. The other dimension of non-
determinism arises from the fact that the calls $A_1,..,A_m$ of a
procedure can be executed in any order, even coroutined. A
rule which determines for each invoked procedure the evaluation order of its calls, or which gives a criterion for
alternating between the evaluations of some or all the calls,
we shall call a <u>computation rule</u>. A logic program paired with
a choice rule and a computation rule becomes a <u>deterministic
algorithm</u> (deterministic because our choice rule selects
exactly one procedure for each call). It will terminate if
the choice rule selects a successfully terminating evaluation
path from all the possible evaluation paths.

Families of algorithms

A logic program with control unspecified is a non-deterministic algorithm. It is the family of all the deterministic

algorithms that can be obtained by adding specific computation and choice rule control. By partially specifying this control we obtain a new non-deterministic algorithm that is a subfamily of this family of algorithms.

3. REVIEW OF NUMERICAL INTEGRATION

The numerical approximation of integrals goes back to the early Greeks and the approximation of Π. An excellent survey of the problem and modern solution methods is found in (Davis and Robinowitz, 1976).

Ultimately, all numerical approximations take the form

$$\int_b^a f(x)dx = (b-a) \sum_{k=0}^{n-1} w_k f(x_k) \quad \text{where} \quad \sum_{k=0}^{n-1} w_k = 1$$

That is, the approximation is a weighted sum of function values over the interval of integration. The problems are:

1. choosing the sample points (x_k)
2. choosing the weights (w_k)
3. knowing how accurate the result is.

Adaptive algorithms cluster the points within regions where the intergrand is most intractable. The strategies for doing so, and the resulting programs, have tended to become increasingly opaque and complex (Lyness, 1970).

It is usual to present only deterministic numerical algorithms. They vary by the kind of approximation used, the order of applying approximations, and the strategy for termination. If we broaden our view to include non-deterministic algorithms, we can arrange them hierarchically; the lower in the hierarchy, the more deterministic the algorithm. The hierarchy defines families of algorithms and is a natural result of using logic programs as specifications.

4. FORMAL SPECIFICATION OF ADAPTIVE QUADRATURE

The specification is a set of axioms about definite integrals. The first is a formal identity from the calculus.

$$\int_a^b f(x)dx = \int_a^m f(x)dx + \int_m^b f(x)dx$$

From the above, and some elementary number theory, we can derive the following theorem:

$$|\int_a^m f(x)dx - y_1| \leq e_1 \quad |\int_m^b f(x)dx - y_2| \leq e_2, \quad a < m < b \quad (1)$$

$$=> \quad |\int_a^b f(x)dx - (y_1 + y_2)| \leq e_1 + e_2$$

Proof: $|s| \leq x$, $|t| \leq y => |s+t| \leq x+y$

Formula (1) gives the basic step of the adaptive routine, reducing the whole problem to two, presumably simpler, sub-problems. The subdivision process terminates when it is determined that a numerical approximation can be used. There are many ways to make the approximation, each depending upon a pair of formulas, named here quad and err. For example, given the trapezoidal approximation

    trap(f, a, b) = (f(a)+f(b))*(b-a)/2

we may use

    quad(f, a, b) = trap(f, a, (a+b)/2) + trap(f, (a+b)/2, b)
and
    err(f, a, b) = |quad(f, a, b) - trap(f, a, b)|

as the definitions of the quad and err functions. For a suitable class of functions the inequality

$$|\int_a^b f(x)dx - quad(f, a, b)| \leq err(f, a, b) \quad (2)$$

holds. Formulas (1) and (2) are two of the assumptions upon which numerical quadrature routines are based and therefore have the status of axioms here. In other words, we only deal with functions for which (2) holds.

5. FROM SPECIFICATION TO PROGRAM

Given an interval $<A,B>$, a function F, and an error bound EPS, we would like to find a y such that

$$| \int_A^B F(x)dx - y | \leq EPS \qquad (3)$$

Let us introduce the relation $I(a, b, f, e, y)$ via the definition

$$I(a, b, f, y, e) \text{ iff } | \int_a^b f(x)dx-y| \leq e \qquad (4)$$

In logic programming terms, our integration problem (3) is the task of answering the query

$$y: I(A, B, F, y, e), e \leq EPS \qquad (5)$$

(find a y such that $I(A,B,F,y,e)$ for some $e \leq EPS$)

using some logic program for the relation I. Our specification axioms (1) and (2) provide us with such a program. Using definition (4) they can be reformulated as the pair of logic program procedures:

$$I(a,b,f,y_1+y_2,e_1+e_2) <-$$
$$a<m<b,I(a,m,f,y_1,e_1),I(m,b,f,y_2,e_2) \qquad (6)$$

$$I(a,b,f,quad(f,a,b),err(f,a,b)) \qquad (7)$$

Adding the control

The use of this program in answering query (5) is highly non-deterministic. In the very first step we can either use the approximation procedure (7) or the splitting procedure (6), and on each use of the splitting procedure that choice presents itself again for each of the two recursive calls. Too early a use of the approximation rule for a particular interval may lead to a failure to satisfy the $e \leq EPS$ condition on the sum of all the error estimates. Too late a use means redundant computation in satisfying the error limit EPS. There is also non-determinism in the evaluation of the call $a<m<b$ of the splitting procedure. We shall assume that this call is answered with a non-deterministic program that binds m to some value in the interval.

The choice rule controls this non-determinism. It will select a particular evaluation path for the program that answers each a<m<b call. That is, it determines the intermediary point m. It also decides for each call $I(a,b,f,y,e)$ whether to use procedure (6) or (7), i.e. whether to split the interval <a,b> or not. The overall effect of the choice rule is to determine a set of k+1 sub-intervals

$$S = \{<A,m_1>, <m_1, m_2>, \ldots, <m_k, B>\}$$

of the given initial interval <A, B>. Over each sub-interval the approximation is applied. To define a successfully terminating algorithm the choice rule must be such that the sum of the error estimates over these sub-intervals is no greater than EPS.

The other dimension of non-determinism is controlled by the computation rule for the calls of the splitting procedure. The computation rule determines the generation method for the set of intervals S. The most straightforward computation rule is the one which executes the calls sequentially in the order in which they are given. That is, we use the call a<m<b to find the split point and then integrate the intervals one after the other. This corresponds to a left to right traversal of the interval <A,B>, with the set S being generated as a sequence

$$<A, m_1>, \ldots, <m_{i-1}, m_i>,\ldots$$

Each time the choice rule selects the approximation procedure to answer a call $I(m_i, m_{i+1}, f, y, e)$ it is adding a new interval $<m_i, m_{i+1}>$ to the sequence.

By combining the logic program of (6), (7) with particular computation and choice rules we obtain different integration algorithms. By partially determining the computation/choice rule control we define a subfamily of integration algorithms identified by the non-deterministic algorithm that this partial control defines. Let us consider three such families, identified by three non-deterministic algorithms numbered 1, 2, 3.

Algorithm 1.
This uses the sequential computation rule. We must add to this a choice rule that ensures that the sum of all the approximation errors for the intervals in the set S meets the overall limit EPS. To guarantee this we can use a choice rule that uses the base case approximation procedure for the call $I(m_i, m_{i+1}, f,y,e)$, only when the error estimate for the

$<m_i,m_{i+1}>$ interval is less than $EPS(m_{i+1}-m_i)/(B-A)$, a fraction of EPS linearly related to the size of the interval. A choice rule constrained in this way defines a simple non-deterministic integration algorithm. It is non-deterministic since the way in which the choice rule determines the intermediary points on the $a<m<b$ calls is left unspecified.

Algorithm 2.

The above constraint on the choice rule embodies a strict condition for guaranteeing that the overall error limit EPS will be met. A more sophisticated choice rule could take into account the slack that may accrue because the sum e' of the computed error estimates for the intervals $<A,m_1>,..,<m_{i-1},m_i>$ is less than $EPS(m_i-A)/(B-A)$, the proportion of EPS for the span they cover. To obtain this behaviour the choice rule selects the approximation procedure for the call $I(m_i,m_{i+1},f,y,e)$ only if the error estimate for the $<m_i,m_{i+1}>$ interval is less than $(EPS-e')(m_{i+1}-m_i)/(B-m_i)$. This is the fraction of the remaining error limit $(EPS-e')$ distributed linearly over the interval that remains. Algorithm 2 is defined by the sequential computation rule and this partially specified choice rule. Again the method for determining the split point is unspecified.

Algorithm 3.

Algorithm 2 is able to reap the benefit of early approximations that do better than their assigned proportion of the error limit EPS. If the approximations near to A are good, it can do less work in dividing the interval near to B. However, this is a bias towards the left end of the interval. If the approximations near the B end are very good, we do not reap the benefit of this by being able to do less work on the integral near to A.

For symmetry of treatment, we need to have a computation rule that can alternate between the evaluations of the recursive calls of the splitting procedure. Let us imagine a sequence of steps of such a coroutined computation in which the choice rule has always selected the splitting procedure. The general state of such an evaluation is represented by a set of calls of the form

$$S' = \{I(A,m_1,f,e_1,y_1), I(m_1,m_2,f,e_2,y_2), .., I(m_k,B,f,e_k,y_k)\}$$

The computation rule can select any one of these calls. If it selects the call $I(m_i,m_{i+1},f,e_i,y_i)$, and the choice rule again picks the splitting procedure, we are effectively expanding a possible set of approximation intervals

$$S = \{<A,m_1>, \ldots, <m_k,B>\}$$

into an augmented set that includes the two new intervals $<m_i,m>$, $<m,m_{i+1}>$ instead of $<m_i,m_{i+1}>$. Here m is the intermediary point determined by the non-deterministic evaluation of the call $m_i<m<m_{i+1}$ of the splitting procedure. Clearly, the choice rule should only select this evaluation path if the error limit EPS cannot be met by evaluating each of the calls of S' using the approximation procedure. That is, the splitting procedure should be used only if the sum of the error estimates for the set of intervals S is greater than EPS. If we cannot yet meet the error limit we need more splitting of the interval. In selecting the call to evaluate the computation rule is selecting the interval to split. We should choose an interval with the largest error estimate. The computation rule should select $I(m_i,m_{i+1},f,y,e)$ only if $err(m_i,m_{i+1},f)$ is the maximum of the error estimates for intervals in S. These considerations lead us to algorithm 3. The computation rule for this algorithm always evaluates the call a<m<b of the splitting procedure first, but it then coroutines between the recursive calls. At each evaluation step it picks the call with the largest error estimate. The choice rule repeatedly selects the splitting procedure until the sum of the error estimates for all outstanding calls is less than EPS. It then repeatedly selects the approximation procedure. Notice how this algorithm focuses on the trouble spots of the interval. We believe it characterises a new family of integration algorithm.

6. AMALGAMATING LOGIC AND CONTROL

In the preceding section we gave informal descriptions of the control components which gave us our three algorithms. If we want to have executable algorithms we should formalise the control description.

One possibility is to develop a formal notation for describing control. The annotations of IC-PROLOG (Clark et al. 1982) are one such proposal. They are however too weak to express the control concepts that we need. Hayes (1973) has suggested using another logic program to specify the control, and Gallaire and Lasserre's (1982) proposals are a first step in this direction. As a method for formally specifying algorithms we believe this method holds great promise. It remains to be seen whether efficient executors of the dual logic programs can be implemented.

An alternative to direct execution of the logic+control (L+C) description of an algorithm, especially when the control is complex, is a logic transformation. This is the reformulation of the given L+C into a new L'+C' that defines the same algorithm but which has a much simpler, more conventional control. Gregory (1980) applied this method to the L + C given by an annotated IC-PROLOG program. The goal of the transformation was a program that could be executed with the sequential computation rule and a simple choice rule. This is the tactic we shall adopt.

Reformulation of Algorithm 1

Strengthening
In algorithm 1 the choice rule selects the splitting procedure

$$I(a,b,f,y_1+y_2,e_1+e_2)<-a<m<b,I(a,b,f,y_1,e_1),I(m,b,f,y_2,e_2)$$

whenever the call $I(a,b,f,y,e)$ is such that the error estimate $err(f,a,b)$ for the interval $<a,b>$ is greater than its share $EPS(b-a)/(B-A)$ of the overall error limit EPS. When this is not the case, it selects the approximation procedure

$$I(a,b,f,quad(f,a,b),err(f,a,b)).$$

We can absorb this selection condition into each of the procedures by __strengthening__. Strengthening is the adding of an extra call, logically the 'anding' in of an extra pre-condition, to a logic program procedure. This tactic never effects the partial correctness of the program. For if B <- A is a true statement, so is B <- C,A.

Strengthening will give us two new procedures:

$$I(a,b,f,y_1+y_2,e_1+e_2)<- err(f,a,b)\geq EPS(b-a)/(B-A): a<m<b,$$
$$I(a,m,f,y_1,e_1),I(m,b,f,y_2,e_2) \qquad (8)$$

$$I(a,b,f,quad(f,a,b),err(f,a,b))) <-$$
$$err(f,a,b)\leq EPS(b-a)/(B-A): \qquad (9)$$

We can now achieve the effect of our original choice rule by treating the new calls as guards (cf. Dijkstra, 1976). We can use the simpler choice rule: select a procedure with a true guard, the guard being the first call of the procedure. We have placed a ":" after the guard call to indicate its special role.

Generalising

There is a drawback. We have simplified the choice rule at the cost of introducing the constants A, B, EPS into the program. We have a program that works only for the specific query

$$y: I(A,B,F,y,e), \quad e \leq EPS \tag{5}$$

For a new query, with different A, B and EPS, we need to rewrite the program. Previously, A,B, EPS were parameters to the choice rule. To regain our original generality we must replace the guards of (8) and (9) by guards that have the same effect, but which do not refer to A, B or EPS. Firstly, let us note that in an evaluation of query (5) using (8) and (9) the summing of the error estimates to get a value for e is redundant. We can therefore exploit the invertibility (see Kowalski, 1974 or Sickel 1978) property of logic programs and use the error argument e not to return an error estimate but to receive the error limit EPS. Instead of query (5) we can use the query

$$y: I(A,B,F,y,EPS). \tag{10}$$

Let us examine the use of (8) in answering this new query. Remember that the e_1+e_2 in the head is shorthand for

$$I(a,b,f,y_1+y_2,e) <- e=e_1+e_2,....$$

in which an explicit equality appears in the procedure. With e as input, this equality call would be used to split the given error limit into error limits for the recursive calls. An equitable split would be $e_1=e(m-a)/(b-a)$ and $e_2=e(b-m)/(b-a)$. Since these two equalities imply $e=e_1+e_2$, the procedure

$$I(a,b,f,y_1+y_2,e)<- err(f,a,b)>EPS(b-a)/(B-A): \quad a<m<b, \quad (11)$$
$$e_1=e(m-a)/(b-a), \quad e_2=e(b-m)/(b-a),$$
$$I(a,m,f,y_1,e_1), \quad I(m,b,f,y_2,e_2)$$

is just a special case of (8).

Now notice that on first use of the procedure to answer query (10) e=EPS, a=A and b=B. So for the first use the guard can be replaced by the test err(f,a,b)>e. Also, the e_1 and e_2 returned by the calls $e_1=e(m-a)/(b-a)$, $e_2=e(b-m)/(b-a)$ are exactly the right fractions of EPS needed for the guard evaluation for the recursive calls. This property holds whenever e has the correct value on entry to procedure (11). Thus, for an evaluation of query (10), the generalisation,

$$I(a,b,f,y_1+y_2,e) \leftarrow err(f,a,b)>e: a<m<b, \qquad (12)$$
$$e_1=e(m-a)/(b-a), \quad e_2=e(b-m)/(b-a)$$
$$I(a,m,f,y_1,e_1), \quad I(m,b,f,y_2,e_2)$$

of (11) gives exactly the same choice rule behaviour as (11). Moreover, (12) is still a true description of the integration relation defined by (4). Likewise, the generalisation

$$I(a,b,f,quad(f,a,b),e) \leftarrow err(f,a,b)\leq e: \qquad (13)$$

of (9), when used in conjunction with (12), will be choice rule equivalent to procedure (9). It is also still a true statement about our integration relation. The generalised program, comprising procedures (12) and (13), must be used with a query of the form (10). Paired with the sequential computation rule and our new guard check choice rule, it also defines Algorithm 1.

Deterministic instances of Algorithm 1

To obtain a deterministic instance of Algorithm 1 we must constrain the non-deterministic selection of m in the call $a<m<b$. This call guesses an interval $<a,m>$ that will be tested by the guards for the recursive call $I(a,m,f,y_1,e_1)$. If this guess for m does not satisfy the guard $err(f,a,m) \leq e_1$, the splitting procedure is again used and a new call $a<m'<m$ is used to move the intermediary point nearer to a. This narrowing of the interval continues with each recursive call of the splitting procedure. It stops when an interval is reached over which the approximation can be applied. Thus, the choice rule determination of the intermediary point m of each call $a<m<b$, together with the unbounded recursive evaluation of $I(a,m,f,y_1,e_1)$, constitute an algorithm for finding a sub-interval over which the approximation can be applied.

To have both arbitrary selection of the intermediary point m and arbitrary depth of recursion is an unnecessary luxury. We can make do with a choice rule that always returns a fixed intermediary point, say $(a+b)/2$. Alternatively, we can insist that the choice rule for the evaluation of $a<m<b$ returns an m such that $I(a,m,f,y_1,e_1)$ can always be evaluated using the approximation rule. That is, we can fix the choice rule so that it returns an m such that $err(f,a,m) \leq e(m-a)/(b-a)$. The two alternatives give rise to two deterministic instances of Algorithm 1.

Taking the first alternative gives us the logic program:

$$I(a,b,f,y_1+y_2,e) \leftarrow err(f,a,b) > e: \tag{14}$$
$$I(a,(a+b)/2,y_1,e/2), \; I((a+b)/2,b,y_2,e/2)$$

$$I(a,b,f,quad(f,a,b),e) \leftarrow err(f,a,b) \leq e: \tag{15}$$

Taking the second alternative gives us the tail recursive program:

$$I(a,b,f,quad(f,a,m)+y,e) \leftarrow err(f,a,b) > e: \tag{16}$$
$$approx\text{-}point(a,m,b,f,e)$$
$$I(m,b,f,y,e(b-m)/(b-a))$$

$$I(a,b,f,quad(f,a,b),e) \leftarrow err(f,a,b) \leq e: \tag{17}$$

Procedure (16) is obtained from procedure (12) by replacing the call $a<m<b$ by the new call $approx\text{-}point(a,m,b,f,e)$. On the assumption that the evaluation of this call is equivalent to the choice rule evaluation of $a<m<b$ that always gives an m with $err(f,a,m) \leq e(m-a)/(b-a)$, we can pre-evaluate the recursive call $I(a,m,f,y_1,e_1)$ using the approximation procedure. We can do this program transformation since we know that the approximation procedure will always be applied to this call. The following is a program for approx-point with the required property:

$$approx\text{-}point(a,(a+b)/2,b,f,e) \leftarrow err(f,a,b) \leq e/2: \tag{18}$$

$$approx\text{-}point(a,m,b,f,e) \leftarrow err(f,a,b) > e/2: \tag{19}$$
$$approx\text{-}point(a,m,(a+b)/2,f,e/2)$$

Algorithm 4.
This comprises procedures (14), (15), the sequential computation rule and the guard check choice rule.

Algorithm 5.
This comprises procedures (16) to (19), with the same control.

These two deterministic members of the family of algorithms covered by Algorithm 1 both find the first approximation subinterval $<A,m_1>$ of the given interval $<A,B>$ by a sequence of binary chops of $<A,B>$. Algorithm 4 then finds the next sub-interval by binary chopping, if necessary, an interval $<m_1,m>$ of the same size as $<A,m_1>$, this interval having been left in the argument bindings of the second recursive call. In contrast, Algorithm 5 finds the next subinterval by binary chopping of the whole of the remaining interval $<m_1,B>$. Algorithm 5 therefore does more work finding the sequence of approximation subintervals of $<A,B>$. It has the advantage that it is tail recursive, that it is an iterative rather than recursive algorithm.

Reformulation of Algorithm 2

The only difference between Algorithms 1 and 2 was that Algorithm 2 took account of the accumulated error estimate e for the subinterval $<A,M>$ over which approximations had already been applied. The limit to be met by the integal over $<M,B>$ was then taken to be (EPS-e).

We cannot immediately further transform the programs we have for Algorithms 4 and 5 to incorporate this more sophisticated choice rule. This is because they no longer sum the error estimates. What we need is program that both sums the error estimates and divides the error limit. We need a program for the augmented relation I' defined by:

$$I'(a,b,f,y,e,e') \text{ iff } |\int_a^b fdx-y|\leq e\leq e' \qquad (20)$$

The following modifications of (14) and (15), which amalgamate these procedures with the original program procedures (6) and (7), are both true statements about this new relation.

$$I'(a,b,f,y_1+y_2,e_1+e_2,e)<-err(f,a,b)>e: \qquad (21)$$
$$I'(a,(a+b)/2,f,y_1,e_1,e/2),$$
$$I'((a+b)/2,b,f,y_2,e_2,e/2)$$

$$I'(a,b,f,quad(f,a,b), err(f,a,b),e)<- err(f,a,b)\leq e: \qquad (22)$$

Used to answer the query

$$<y,e>: I'(A,B,F,y,e,EPS)$$

(21), (22) define an elaboration of algorithm 4 in which error limit e that is actually met is returned. We can now transform (21) and (22) to get a deterministic instance of Algorithm 2. The transformation is simply the substitution of $e-e_2$ for the e/2 of the second recursive call.

Algorithm 6.

$$I'(a,b,f,y_1+y_2,e_1+e_2,e)<- err(f,a,b)>e: \qquad (23)$$
$$I'(a,(a+b)/2,f,y_1,e_1,e/2),$$
$$I'((a+b)/2,b,f,y_2,e_2,e-e_1)$$

I'(a,b,f,quad(f,a,b), err(f,a,b),e)<- err(f,a,b)$\leq$e: (24)

Here we use the sequential computation rule and guard check choice rule. We ask the reader to check that this last transformation has not affected the property that the procedures are true statements about the relation defined in (20). Moreover, since the error limit set for the second recursive call is $e-e_1$ (which is greater than or equal to e/2), this algorithm incorporates the more sophisticated choice rule of Algorithm 2.

We can apply an exactly analogous transformation to procedures (16) and (17) to get a second deterministic instance of Algorithm 2. Like Algorithm 5 this is iterative.

Algorithm 7

I'(a,b,f,quad(f,a,m)+y,err(f,a,m)+e',e)<- err(f,a,b)>e: (25)
                                        approx-point(a,m,b,f,e),
                                        I'(m,b,f,y,e',e-err(f,a,m)))

I'(a,b,f,quad(f,a,b), err(f,a,b),e)<- err(f,a,b)$\leq$e: (26)

plus the procedures for approx-point and the usual computation and choice rules.

Reformulation of Algorithm 3

The transformation of Algorithm 3 into a logic program that can be executed as a sequential program with only a guard check choice rule requires a much more radical change of logic. At each step, such a sequential program needs to be able to select the right call from the set of outstanding calls of the coroutined evaluation. The set of outstanding calls defines the current candidate set

$$S= \{<A,m_1>, \ldots, <m_k,B>\}$$

of intervals of <A,B>. This suggests that we should look for a new logic program not for the relation I, but for a generalisation I" of the relation in which the pair of arguments a,b is replaced by a set of sub-intervals of <a,b>. This new relation is defined by:

I"(s,f,y,e) iff s=$\{<m_0,m_1>, \ldots, <m_k,m_{k+1}>\}$ (27)

where $m_0<m_1<\ldots<m_{k+1}$ and $|\sum_{i=0}^{k} \int_{m_i}^{m_{i+1}} f dx -y| \leq e$

Algorithm 3 terminated when the sum of the error estimates for the intervals of S was less than the given error limit EPS. Assuming that EPS is given and passed down via the e argument, the procedure:

$$I''(s,f,sumquad(s,f),e)<-sumerr(s,f)\le e \qquad (28)$$

corresponds to this termination condition providing the sumquad and sumerr functions satisfy the specifications:

$$sumquad(s, f) = \sum_{<m,m'> \in s} quad(f, m, m') \qquad (29)$$

and

$$sumerr(s, f) = \sum_{<m,m'> \in s} err(f, m, m') \qquad (30)$$

We leave the reader to check that (28) is a true statement about the relation defined in (27).

When the sum of the error estimates of the intervals in S is greater than the given error limit EPS Algorithm 3 selects the interval with the greatest error estimate and then splits the interval. The following recursive description of I'' is a procedure for this splitting case.

$$I''(s,f,y,e)<-sumerr(s,f)>e: \qquad (31)$$
$$max\text{-}delete(s,i,s'), \; split(f,i,i_1,i_2),$$
$$I''(union(s',i_1,i_2),f,y,e)$$

Here, $split(f,i,i_1,i_2)$ is true when i_1, i_2 is some splitting of the interval i, and max-delete and union satisfy:

$$max\text{-}delete(f,s,<a,b>,s') \text{ iff } <a,b> \in s \; \& \; s'=s-\{<a,b>\} \qquad (32)$$
$$\& \; err(f,a,b)=max\{err(f,m,m')|<m,m'> \in s\}$$

$$union(s',<a,m>,<m,b>)= s' \cup \{<a,m>,<m,b>\} \qquad (33)$$

We now need to find procedures for these auxiliary relations and functions. These will access and manipulate some representation of a set S of interval pairs. As with all algorithms, there is a trade-off between the complexity of the representation and the efficiency with which it is handled. A simple minded representation records the <u>set</u> of intervals by a <u>list</u> of the intervals in the set. The drawback of this representation is that the sumerr function must compute the error for each interval for each guard evaluation, and the max-delete relation must likewise repeatedly compute the errors for each interval.

To avoid recomputation for the guard evaluation we can represent the set of intervals as a pair <L,E>. L is the list of intervals and E is the sum of the error estimates for all the intervals of L. This makes sumerr(s,f) a simple access function. To speed access to the interval with largest error estimate we can order the intervals in L by decreasing value of the error estimate. Adding a new interval to S now means inserting it into L at a position determined by its error estimate. To save recomputation of the error estimate of the intervals in L on an insertion we should store the error estimate with the interval. But computing err(f,a,b) for an interval <a,b> involves finding the values of f(a), f(b) and f((a+b)/2). Since these same values will be needed on termination by the sumquad function, and at least the values of f(a) and f(b) will be needed to compute new error estimates if the interval is split, we should record these values along with the error estimate. This ensures that the function being integrated is evaluated just once at any point in the interval. Each interval <a,b> in S is now represented by the six-tuple (a,f(a), f((a+b)/2), f(b), b, err(f,a,b))) in the list L. L is ordered by decreasing value of the error estimate field. In the overall representation of S as the pair <L,E>, E is the sum of the errors recorded in the tuples in L.

Relative to this representation, the following procedures define the max-delete relation and extend the "=" (has value of) relation to handle errsum, sumquad, and union:

$$e=errsum(<l,e>) \tag{34}$$

$$QUAD(a,fa,fm,fb,b)+sumquad(f,<l,e>)=$$
$$sumquad(f,<(a,fa,fm,fb,b,e'):l,e>) \tag{35}$$

$$0=sumquad(f,<Nil,e>) \tag{36}$$

$$max\text{-}delete(f,<i:l,e>,i,<l,e>) \tag{37}$$

$$<ord\text{-}insert(i_2,ord\text{-}insert(i_1,l)),e>=union(<l,e>,i_1,i_2) \tag{38}$$

Here, QUAD is identical to our earlier quad function except it uses the precomputed function values fa,fm,fb. The function ord-insert inserts an interval (a,fa,fm,fb,b,e) into the list L preserving the ordering on the error estimates. The infix ":" is a list constructor such that i:l is a list with head i and tail l and "Nil" denotes the empty list.

The procedure for "split" must do the work of maintaining the six-tuple representation of intervals. If we always do a binary split this can be done with just two new function evaluations at the new mid-points. We can use:

$$\text{split}(f,(a,fa,fm,fb,b,e),(a,fa,fm_1,fm,m,e_1), \tag{39}$$
$$(m,fm,fm_2,fb,b,e_2))$$

$$\begin{aligned}
&<-m=(b+a)/2,\\
&\quad fm_1=f(a+(b-a)/4),fm_2=f(b-(b-a)/4),\\
&\quad e_1=\text{ERR}(a,fa,fm_1,fm,m),e_2=\text{ERR}(m,fm,fm_2,fb,b)
\end{aligned}$$

ERR is the update of the err function that uses the precomputed values of the function being integrated.

Algorithm 8

This is defined by procedures (34)-(39), the procedures:

$$I''(s,f,\text{sumquad}(s,f),e)<-\text{sumerr}(s,f)\leq e:$$

$$\begin{aligned}
I''(s,f,y,e)<&-\text{sumerr}(s,f)>e:\\
&\text{max-delete}(s,i,s'),\text{split}(f,i,i1,i2),\\
&I''(\text{union}(s',i_1,i_2),f,y,e)
\end{aligned}$$

and the interface procedure:

$$\begin{aligned}
I(a,b,f,y,e)<&-fa=f(a),fb=f(b),fm=f((b+a)/2),\\
&e'=\text{ERR}(a,fa,fm,fb,b),\\
&I''(<(a,fa,fm,fb,e'):\text{Nil},e'>,f,y,e)
\end{aligned}$$

They are executed sequentially with the guard check choice rule. Used to answer the query:

$$y:I(A,B,F,y,EPS)$$

it behaves exactly like a deterministic instance of the family of algorithms covered by Algorithm 3. It uses a clever representation of the set of intervals to minimise evaluations of the function being integrated.

6. CONCLUDING REMARKS

The specification of several different algorithms by giving different control strategies for a fixed logic program offers a new tool for the analysis and comparison of algorithms. The subsequent progressive transformation of the program, to incorporate the control in the logic, also represents a new approach to the systematic development of programs from their specifications. In this paper we have illustrated these ideas in the domain of numerical integration.

RUNNABLE SPECIFICATION AS A DESIGN TOOL

Ruth E. Davis

Electrical Engineering and Computer Science Department
University of Santa Clara,
Santa Clara,
CA 95053
USA

1. INTRODUCTION

There are at least four phases in the development of
"correct" software:
- Understanding the problem. The program designer may work
with intended users of the system to develop an intuitive
understanding of the problem and possible approaches to its
solution.
- Formal specification. Once the designer knows intuitively
how to solve the problem, the solution must be specified
unambiguously.
- Programming. An implementation of the specification is
programmed.
- Verification. The implementation developed in step three is
shown to satisfy the specification of step two.

There is a certain amount of testing and debugging that goes
on at each of these stages until one is satisfied with the
current step and moves on to the next. Several verification
techniques have been developed to assist in accomplishing
step four. However, even after a proof is completed we cannot
claim to have a "correct" program, only one that satisfies
the given specification.

How does one "debug" a specification? We cannot hope to
formally prove that a specification is "correct" with respect
to our intuition, but we can at least test it to see that it
conforms to our intuition in specific cases.

Rather than write a program, being guided by the specifications, and then prove that it satisfies the specifications,

one can automatically generate a program from the specifications that is guaranteed to preserve the semantics (thus
obviating the need for the verification step entirely). Of
course the feasibility of this approach depends upon the kind
of specifications involved. In (Davis, 1979) we show that
programs can be generated automatically given a specification
that includes a Horn Clause description of the desired relationships. Others have studied program synthesis from more
general specifications, such as full first-order logic or
recursion equations (for example, the work of Manna and
Waldinger 1975; Burstall and Darlington 1977; Clark and
Darlington 1980). Although these techniques are not automatic, one can develop a program through transformations that
are guaranteed to preserve the semantics of the original
specification.

The truly creative (and most difficult) step in the development of a program is the construction of an acceptable formal
specification from an intuitive understanding of the problem.
Thus, our efforts should be placed on developing design tools
to help with the construction and testing of the specification.

2. EQUATIONS VERSUS CLAUSES

Guttag and Horning (1980) present an algebraic specification
technique as a design tool. As an example they describe part
of the specification of a high-level interface to a flexible
display and discuss the analysis of the specification. A
salient feature of their approach is the ability to "ask
questions" of the specification, derive answers, and change
the design if the answers are unacceptable. In this way they
hope to test and debug the specification.

I suggest that Horn Clauses provide a much better specification language than do algebraic axioms. The two languages are
closely related; it is a simple matter to translate between
them. The ease of writing a specification in one language
versus the other is undoubtedly a matter of personal taste
and depends largely on one's familiarity with the language.
The same may be said of the readability of a specification.
Horn Clauses, as well as algebraic axioms, can be analyzed
for answers to specific questions and modified accordingly.

The major distinction between the two methods is the manner
in which questions can be handled. With the Guttag-Horning
approach, an informal question is posed and submitted to an

"expert" who reformulates the question, often generalizing it. The questioner must then be convinced that the formal statement developed by the expert does indeed reflect the original question, and an answer to the formal question will provide an answer to the informal one. Finally, an attempt is made to derive an answer from the axioms.

The same approach may be taken with Horn Clauses, but it is not necessary. Since Horn Clauses are executable, if the questioner wants to know what happens in a particular case, it is possible to simply "try it and see". The expert will still be needed to develop the specification and to determine what modifications should be made to the specification to change an unacceptable answer, but the "what if ...?" questions no longer need be formalized. For example, given the Horn Clause specification of a display, and the definitions for the primitives that interface the underlying logic with the commands controlling the appearance of the screen, it is possible to execute logic programs that manipulate the display. Ideally, a "front-end" command language should be provided by the designer(s) that enables the users/testers of the design to make their requests of the system in the same way in which they are expected to interact with the final product.

Once one is satisfied that a Horn Clause specification is a reasonable embodiment of one's intuition, the task of refining the specification into an efficient program can proceed. The ability to run a specification makes the problem of testing and debugging it much more tractable.

3. AN EXAMPLE SPECIFICATION

As an example, I have written the Horn Clause specification of the display specified with algebraic axioms by Guttag and Horning. The fundamental assumption is that a user will want to be able to display several distinct blocks of information on the screen at once. The top level concept is that of a view. A view is a spatial arrangement of pictures; a picture is a block of displayable information. A picture consists of a boundary, a contents, and a coordinate transformation to be applied in viewing its contents. Examples of pictures are the entire display (with implicit boundary), and the interior of a defined area on the display; examples of contents are text, figures, and views. Fig. 1 is an example of a picture (or a view containing a single picture).

Fig. 1.

Fig. 2.

Fig. 2 presents a view containing three pictures, each of which has the same contents; they differ in their boundaries and the coordinate transformation applied in viewing their contents.

The Guttag-Horning specification of picture is as follows:

Operators:

MakePicture: Contents X (Coordinate -> TruthValues)
                        X (Coordinate -> Coordinate) -> Picture
Picture.Appearance: Picture X Coordinate -> Illumination
Picture.In: Picture X Coordinate -> TruthValues

Axioms:

Picture.Appearance(MakePicture(cont, bound, trans), coord)
                = Contents.Appearance(cont, trans(coord))

Picture.In(MakePicture(cont,bound,trans),coord)= bound(coord)

The operators are listed first, giving their functionality, then the axioms defining them are given. MakePicture is not defined further since it is simply the constructor function for the type Picture. The first axiom tells us that the appearance at a given coordinate in a picture is determined by the appearance at a coordinate (the result of applying the transformation to the original coordinate) in the contents of the picture. The second axiom indicates that a coordinate is in a picture if it is within the boundary of the picture as defined by the function bound.

The specification of type Picture using Horn Clauses is given below. We distinguish predicate names by capitalizing the first letter; constants and function symbols appear in bold type; and variables are in lower case. The Horn Clause specification clearly indicates the distinction between constructor functions, such as **make-picture**, and the predicates indicating relationships among their arguments. The type constraints, indicating functionality of the predicates, are given only for the clause(s) defining the type being specified. Type-checking can be included explicitly in each clause; however, we assume the required type is made obvious to the reader by consistent naming of variables and choose to leave it out of the rest of the specification for the sake of readability.

Picture(**make-picture**(cont, bound, trans)) <-
         Contents(cont), Boundary(bound), Translation(trans)

Picture-Appearance(**make-picture**(cont,bound,trans),
                                    coord, illum) <-
    Compute-Position(coord, trans, coord'),
    Contents-Appearance(cont, coord', illum)

Picture-In(**make-picture**(cont, bound, trans), coord, tv) <-
                Lies-In(coord, bound, tv)

In the Guttag-Horning axiomatic specification of the display, a boundary is a function from Coordinate to TruthValues and a translation is a function from Coordinate to Coordinate. Horn Clause syntax does not allow functions as arguments, thus I have treated trans and bound as objects. Compute-Position is a predicate that accomplishes the translation from coord to coord' indicated by the Guttag-Horning trans. Similarly, Lies-In(coord, bound, tv) results in tv being bound to **true** if and only if the coordinate indicated lies within the given boundary, and to **false** if it does not. I would not need the predicates Compute-Position and Lies-In if I had an evaluation predicate that accepts a function and its arguments and applies the function to the arguments, such as the LISP "apply". For this example I have remained within first-order logic and the strict limitations of Horn Clauses. Others have concerned themselves with the problem of moving to second-order, as shown in the "demonstrate" predicate used by Bowen and Kowalski described in this volume.

The specification of type View, given algebraically, is as
follows:
Operators:

View.Empty: -> View
AddPicture: View X Coordinate X PictureId X Picture -> View
View.Appearance: View X Coordinate -> Illumination
View.In: View X Coordinate -> TruthValues
FindPictures: View X Coordinate -> IdList
DeletePicture: View X PictureId -> View

Axioms:

View.Appearance(AddPicture(v, coord', id, p), coord) =
    if Picture.In(p, Minus(coord, coord'))
    then Picture.Appearance(p, Minus(coord, coord'))
    else View.Appearance(v, coord)

View.Appearance(View.Empty, coord)   intentionally left
                                                  unspecified
View.In(View.Empty, coord) = False

View.In(AddPicture(v, coord', id, p), coord) =
        Picture.In(p, Minus(coord, coord')) v
                                      View.In(v, coord)

    FindPictures(View.Empty, coord) = IdList.Empty

FindPictures(AddPicture(v, coord', id, p), coord) =
        if Picture.In(p, Minus(coord, coord'))
        then IdList.Insert(id, FindPictures(v, coord))
        else FindPictures(v, coord)

DeletePicture(View.Empty, id) = View.Empty

DeletePicture(AddPicture(v, coord, id', p), id) =
    if PictureId.Equal(id, id')
    then v
    else AddPicture(DeletePicture(v, id), coord,id',p)

Guttag and Horning use the convention of prefixing a function
name by the type it is operating on and a dot. In this way
they can use the same name for similar functions being
defined over several different types. They chose to use a 0-
ary function, View.Empty, to indicate the empty view, we use
a constant **mt-view**. AddPicture is the constructor function
for type View. Appearance and In are determined by the
components (pictures) making up a view. FindPictures is a
function that constructs a list of names of pictures

containing a given coordinate. DeletePicture deletes a picture, specified by its id, from a view.

Again, using Horn Clauses, we indicate the types of arguments only in the specification of View, and assume the desired types are made apparent by the choice of names for variables.

```
View(mt-view) <-
View(add-picture(v, c, id, p)) <- View(v), Coordinate(c),
                                  PictureId(id), Picture(p)
View-Appearance(mt-view, coord, x) <-
```

As in the algebraic specification, we leave unspecified the appearance of the mt-view at any coordinate. Since we have no if-then-else, the axiom describing View.Appearance corresponds to two Horn Clauses, one for each alternative.

```
View-Appearance(add-picture(v,coord',id, p), coord, illum) <-
        Picture-In(p, minus(coord, coord'), true),
        Picture-Appearance(p, minus(coord, coord'), illum)

View-Appearance(add-picture(v, coord',id,p), coord, illum) <-
        Picture-In(p, minus(coord, coord'), false),
        View-Appearance(v, coord, illum)

View-In(mt-view, coord, false) <-
```

Horn Clauses are not allowed alternative conditions. Thus the second axiom for View.In is handled by the following three Horn Clauses, one for each alternative making the conclusion true, and a third to enable us to derive the fact that a coordinate is not in a view.

```
View-In(add-picture(v, coord', id, p), coord, true) <-
        Picture-In(p, minus(coord, coord'), true)
View-In(add-picture(v, coord', id, p), coord, true) <-
        View-In(v, coord, true)
View-In(add-picture(v, coord', id, p), coord, false) <-
        Picture-In(p, minus(coord, coord'), false),
        View-In(v, coord, false)
FindPictures(mt-view, coord, mt-idlist) <-
FindPictures(add-picture(v, coord', id, p), coord,
                        idlist-insert(id, idl)) <-
        Picture-In(p, minus(coord, coord'), true),
        FindPictures(v, coord, idl)
FindPictures(add-picture(v, coord', id, p), coord, idl) <-
        Picture-In(p, minus(coord, coord'), false),
        FindPictures(v, coord, idl)
```

DeletePicture(**mt-view**, id, **mt-view**) <-
DeletePicture(**add-picture**(v, coord, id, p), id, v) <-
DeletePicture(**add-picture**(v, coord, id',p), id,
                    add-picture(v', coord, id', p)) <-
        PictureIdEqual(id, id', **false**),
        DeletePicture(v, id,v')

FindPictures and DeletePicture present no surprises. Again, an if-then-else in an axiom corresponds to two clauses in the Horn Clause specification.

4. QUERYING THE SPECIFICATION

In analyzing the specification using the algebraic axioms one needs an expert to go between the questioner and the specification. For example, an informal question asked of Guttag and Horning was: "Is it the case that pictures are not transparent or even translucent? I.e., if two pictures overlap does the bottom one have no effect on what one sees through the top one?". The alternatives are pictured in Fig. 3a and 3b.

The question was formalized as:

"Is it true that
  ($\forall$c, c', w, id, v_1, v_2)
  (Picture.In(w, Minus(c, c'))) ->
          ((View.Appearance(AddPicture(v_1, c', id, w), c)
      = View.Appearance(AddPicture(v_2, c', id, w), c)))?"

The formal question is answered affirmatively, following directly from the first alternative in the first axiom of type View.

Fig. 3a.

Fig. 3b.

If we so desired, we could formalize the question to be put to our Horn Clause specification and derive the same answer, using the second clause in the definition of View-Appearance, but there is no need. Since we can run the Horn Clause specification, all the user need do is construct overlapping pictures and look at the result. This is sufficient to answer questions about specific cases. If one is interested in proving general properties, then we must fall back to a formalization of the question and formal derivation of an answer from the specification. In order to accomplish this derivation, we often need the "closed world" assumption, that is, we assume that the specification is complete. For the current example, the question is formalized as:

"Is it true that
  View-Appearance(**add-picture**(v_1, c', id, p), c, illum) <-
    Picture-In(p, **minus**(c, c'), **true**),
    View-Appearance(**add-picture**(v_2, c', id, p), c, illum) ?"

By assuming the "only-if" direction of the first clause in the definition of View-Appearance, which is clearly the intent of the definition, we can derive that Picture-Appearance(p, minus(c, c'), illum). Then using the same clause, exactly as stated, we derive the result.

Using Horn Clauses as a design tool we enjoy all the benefits of the algebraic approach, and gain the advantage that testing is more easily accomplished. An expert is (and should) still be required to develop the design specification and to modify it if necessary, but the analysis of the design can be carried out by people who may be experts in the problem domain but not in the specification language.

METALEVEL INFERENCE

AMALGAMATING LANGUAGE AND METALANGUAGE IN LOGIC PROGRAMMING

Kenneth A. Bowen
School of Computer and Information Science
Syracuse University, Syracuse, NY, 13210, USA

Robert A. Kowalski
Department of Computing
Imperial College of Science and Technology
London SW7 2BZ, England

ABSTRACT

It is argued that present-day logic programming systems exhibit shortcomings which can be overcome by extending the original object language to include that portion of the metalanguage which deals with the object language provability relation. Such a system is sketched, and some of its applications and properties are presented.

Logic programming systems have proven to be a powerful tool for computer science. These systems have been especially congenial for work in artificial intelligence and database management (cf. Gallaire and Minker, 1978; Kowalski, 1979a). Inevitably, as with almost any system, shortcomings have been discovered. Central among these is the problem of managing the system's database of clauses. Simply put, it is this: The conceptual basis of logic programming is deduction from a single fixed theory, while many applications must deal with deduction from varying or alternative theories. Thus in maintenance over time of a simple relational database, tuples are added, deleted, or modified. Addition of a tuple to a relation corresponds to assertion of a simple unit clause. Here only one theory at a time is involved, but it changes over time. Moreover, the problem of maintaining integrity constraints amounts to testing the consistency of the proposed addition with the theory constituting the database.

The need in this example is for an ability to explicitly refer to theories (i.e., collections of clauses) and to discuss derivability from these theories. Our approach is to construct a system which amalgamates an object-level logic system with a portion of a metalanguage suitable for formalizing the derivability relation of the original object language system. We shall argue that the resulting system will have greater expressive and problem-solving power than the original object language system alone. However, we will carry out this amalgamation in such a way as to preserve the standard semantics of logic. Our purpose in this enterprise is primarily practical. However, in the resulting system it is possible to carry through rather direct proofs of incompleteness phenomena of the sort first discovered by Gödel (1931). Our use of metalanguage is similar to that of Weyhrauch (1980), the main difference being that he does not consider systems, such as ours, which completely amalgamate object and metalanguage.

1. PRELIMINARIES

We will collect together here a number of preliminary remarks on notation and terminology. Either Robinson (1979) or Shoenfield (1967) is an excellent source of background material on logic. Introductions to logic programming can be found in Bowen (1979) and Kowalski (1979a).

The subtlety of some of our discussions requires that we make our variable conventions explicit. The object language will ultimately be seen as an amalgamation of some first-order language together with a suitable (formal) metalanguage for it. However, discussion of this amalgam must take place in an informal metalanguage. In this informal metalanguage, we will use A, B, C, and D as metavariables ranging over formulas of the object (amalgamated) language, and s and t will be meta-variables ranging over terms of the object language. Other lower case identifiers (e.g., x, y, proc, pred, etc.) will be used as (concrete) variables of the object (amalgamated) language, while uppercase identifiers (e.g., Nil, Empty-Subst) will be used as constants.

Given a first-order language L together with formulas $A_1, \ldots, A_n$, and B of L, we will specify that B can be derived from $A_1, \ldots, A_n$ by application of a single rule of inference by writing:

$$\frac{A_1, \ldots, A_n,}{B}$$

If T is a theory formulated in L and B can be proved from T we will write $T \vdash_L B$

2. REPRESENTABILITY

Our desired amalgamation of object language and metalanguage uses a construction which is a special case of representing a relation by means of a predicate symbol in the context of a set of sentences. The representation of the append relation for lists by the predicate symbol App in the set of sentences

    A1) App(Nil,y,y) <-
    A2) App(u.x, y, u.z) <- App(x,y,z)

is a simple example of the same general notion. Here on the assumption that Nil names the empty list and Head.Tail names the result of affixing the object named Head in front of the list named Tail, App in A1-A2 represents the append relation in the sense that:

    for all lists x,y, and z, z is the result of appending y
    to x iff   A1-2 ⊢ App(x',y',z'),

where x' names x, y' names y, and z' names z.

In general, a predicate symbol P in the context of a set of sentences S represents a relation R if and only if

    there is a naming relation which pairs individuals i in
    the domain of R with terms i' in such a way that for all
    $i_1, i_2, \ldots i_n$ in the domain of R

    $(i_1, i_2, \ldots, i_n) \in R$ iff S ⊢ $P(i_1', i_2', \ldots, i_n')$.

Representability does not require that ¬ P in S represents the complement of R, i.e, that

    for all $i_1, i_2, \ldots, i_n$ in the the domain of R,
        $(i_1, i_2, \ldots, i_n) \notin R$ iff S ⊢ ¬ $P(i_1', i_2', \ldots, i_n')$.

Suppose now that R is the provability relation ⊢$_L$ of a language L. (In our intended applications L is the full standard form of logic or some subset such as Horn clause logic.) To represent ⊢$_L$ in another language M (possibly identical to L) it is necessary to name sentences, sets of sentences and other linguistic expressions of L by means of terms of M. For example, we might name the atomic formula

    P(x, Bill)

of L by the term: atom(pred(1), var(1).constant(212).Nil)

of M, where atom, pred, var, and constant are function symbols, and 1, 212, and Nil are constants. Let us assume that some such coding is employed and to avoid going into details we shall simply write "P(x, Bill)" to stand for a term of M which names P(x,Bill). In general if A is a linguistic expression or a finite set of expressions of L we shall write either "A" or simply A' to stand for a term of M which names A.

Let Demo be a binary predicate symbol of M. Then in the context of a set Pr of sentences of M, Demo represents $\vdash_L$ iff

for all finite sets of sentences A and single sentences B of L,
A $\vdash_L$ B   iff   Pr $\vdash_M$ Demo(A',B').

Note that representability does not require that $\neg$ Demo in Pr (if it is expressible) represents unprovability. Indeed the undecidability of first-order logic (Church, 1936) means that no representation of provability (in a finitary system) also represents unprovability. We shall see later that the undecidability of provability is closely related to the incompleteness of any formalization of provability.

3. THE REPRESENTATION OF PROVABILITY

The following two clauses D1-2 constitute the top-level of a Horn clause representation of Horn clause provability in resolution logic. (Both the object language L and the meta-language M are Horn clause logic.) By virtue of the procedural interpretation of Horn clauses, D1-2 can be regarded as the top level of an interpreter for Horn clause programs.

D1) Demo(prog,goals) <- Empty(goals)
D2) Demo(prog,goals) <- Select(goals, goal, rest),
                         Member(proc, prog),
                         Rename(proc, goals, variantproc),
                         Parts(variantproc, concl, conds),
                         Match(concl, goal, sub),
                         Apply(conds+rest, sub, newgoals),
                         Demo(prog, newgoals)

D1 states that any program achieves an empty collection of goals. Noting that the term x'+y' names the set $x \cup y$, D2 states that a program achieves a non-empty collection of goals if it achieves the new goals obtained by:

1. selecting a goal,
2. finding a procedure in the program,
3. renaming the variables in the procedure so they are distinct from the variables in the goals,
4. matching the conclusion of the resulting procedure with the selected goal, and
5. applying the matching substitution to the remaining old goals together with the conditions of the applied procedure.

Successful application of D2 requires finding the right object level procedure to apply to the selected goal. However, it is independent of the goal which is selected.

Horn clause interpreters for Horn clause programs have been written in PROLOG for several years by various researchers. In particular, both H. Gallaire and L. Periera have written interpreters incorporating some metalanguage capabilities oriented towards the control of deduction.

It is interesting to note that if the metalanguage M includes negation and Pr is any Horn clause representation (within M) of the provability relation of a language L, then for no program A and collection of goals B do we have

$$Pr \vdash_M \neg Demo(A', B')$$

This is simply because Horn clause derivations cannot yield negative conclusions. However, some unprovability theorems can be proved if D1-2 and all lower level procedures are expressed in "if-and-only-if form", e.g.

    Demo(prog,goals) <->
        Empty(goals) or
        (Select(goals,goal,rest) &...& Demo(prog, newgoals))

Suppose that Demo not only represents $\vdash_L$, but that it simulates the behavior of the proof predicate of L at least to the extent that A $\vdash_L$ B will fail finitely iff Pr $\vdash_M$ Demo(A',B') fails finitely. Then if Pr* consists of the Horn clause representation Pr reexpressed in if-and-only-if form together with the appropriate equality axioms then

    Pr* $\vdash_M \neg$ Demo(A',B') iff
    the attempt to establish A $\vdash_L$ B terminates in failure.

Therefore, the attempt to prove A $\vdash_L$ B goes into a nonterminating loop in just those cases where neither

Pr* ⊢ Demo(A',B') nor Pr* ⊢ ¬ Demo(A',B') is provable. This
is a consequence of Clark's results (1978) on negation as
failure.

4. A DATABASE MANAGEMENT EXAMPLE

Database management requires a combination of object language
and metalanguage. The object language is needed to represent
and query the database, whereas the metalanguage is needed to
update and maintain the database as it changes in time. The
following top level of a simplified database management
system illustrates how the Demo predicate can be used to
interface the object language and metalanguage.

Here the predicate Assimilate(currdb, input, newdb) describes
the relationship which holds when the assimilation of an
input sentence into a current database results in a new
database (possibly identical to the current one). The terms
x'+y' and x'-y' name the sets $x \cup \{y\}$ and $x-\{y\}$ respectively.

A1)   Assimilate(currdb,input,currdb) <- Demo(currdb, input)

A2)   Assimilate(currdb,input, newdb) <- info ∈ currdb,
                interdb = (currdb-info),
                Demo(interdb+input, info),
                Assimilate (interdb, input, newdb)

A3)   Assimilate(currdb,input,currdb) <-
                Demo(currdb+input, False)

A4)   Assimilate(currdb,input,currdb+input) <-
                Independent(currdb, input)

The clauses A1-4 respectively deal with the cases in which
the new information is already implied by the database,
implies information in the database, is inconsistent with the
database, or is independent from the database. Clause A2, in
particular, selects one item of information in the current
database, removes it if it is implied by the rest of the
database together with the input, and recursively assimilates
the input into the smaller database. The constant symbol
False names the empty clause, which denotes contradiction.
Therefore Demo(A', False) expresses that A is inconsistent.

Notice that in conventional PROLOG systems, the effect of the
definitions A1-A4 can be approximated through the extra-

logical addition and deletion of clauses from the system's global database. Instead of the explicit call on the Demo predicate, one makes use of the ability to use variables in the place of procedure calls. Thus, the clause A1 would be replaced by: Assimilate(input) <- input.

Here currdb is identified with the current state of the system's global database. Clauses A2 and A3 can be approximated in present-day PROLOG, but unfortunately, these approximations do not have a direct logical semantics.

The predicate Independent(currdb, input) can be represented in a variety of ways. The clause

A5) Independent(currdb, input) <-
    ¬ Demo(A1-3,"E x Assimilate(currdb,input,x)")

in particular, states that the input is independent[1] from the current database if it cannot be assimilated by any of the preceding procedures A1-3.

Notice that A1-5 can be embedded in a program which processes input streams. Here the predicate

    Process (currdb, inputstream, newdb)

describes the relationship which holds when assimilating a stream of inputs into a current database results in a new database:

P1) Process(currdb, Nil, currdb) <-

P2) Process(currdb, input.restin, newdb) <-
            Assimilate(currdb, input, interdb),
            Process(interdb, restin, newdb).

The clauses P1-2 and A1-5 together with the appropriate lower level clauses and the representation Pr of provability

---

[1]The notion of "independence" expressed explicitly here can be represented implicitly in PROLOG. First the clauses A1-A3 would be modified by adding a slash (/) at the end of each clause. The effect of using A4 could then be achieved simply by using: A4') Assimilate(currdb, input, currdb+input) <- . The addition of the slashes at the end of A1-A3 is necessary to prevent failures of later procedure calls causing unwanted backtracking into alternatives for Assimilate.

constitute a complete, if somewhat simple-minded, database management system. Notice that the use of Pr to solve goals of the form Demo(A',B'), however, means that the system operates entirely at the metalanguage level using Pr to simulate the object language. Later we shall describe the use of linking rules to solve Demo(A',B') by solving A - B directly at the object language level. The use of such linking rules achieves the amalgamation of object language and metalanguage which we desire.

The simplified database management system has several deficiencies. Many of them are due to the simplified version of the Demo predicate which we have employed. A more realistic version would include additional parameters:

- a control parameter which constrains the way the proof procedure searches for proofs, and
- an output parameter which returns results.

The control parameter can be used, in particular, to limit the extent of the search for a proof. In clauses A1-5, for example, it could be used to restrict the amount of resources employed to assimilate new information into the database. Input might be regarded as independent from the database if the attempt to assimilate it by other means (A1-3) exceeded the resources allocated.[1]

The output parameter can provide useful information, both about proofs and about unsuccessful searches for proofs. In the case A3, for example, in which the input is inconsistent with the database, the proof of inconsistency can be returned as output and can be examined to identify the information in the database which contributes to the inconsistency. The identification of such information can then be used in a revision process which might add the new information to the database while abandoning or modifying old information. (Cf. Doyle 1979; Kowalski 1979a, Chapter 13.)

Thus a more sophisticated data management system would employ a four place Demo predicate such that

---

[1] This is essentially a notion of "consistent because a contradiction is too difficult (long)". This is related to notions of Esenin-Volpin (1970) which in turn have been investigated in a formal setting by Parikh (1970).

Pr $\vdash_M$ Demo(A', B', C',D')

given the problem A $\vdash_L$ B and the control C the object language proof procedure returns the "output" D.

Such a four place Demo predicate would more accurately reflect the behavior of practical proof procedures. The representation and application of substitutions is a particular case: Structure-sharing implementations of logic programming do not explicitly apply the substitutions generated by the matching process (cf. D1-D2), but instead carry them along separately. The output which results from solving a goal in the context of a given substitution is itself an augmented substitution. Thus the "output" D we envision here might well incorporate such substitutions as well as other information. For the purpose of simplicity, however, we shall use the two place Demo predicate for most of the rest of this paper.

5. ON THE POWER OF THE METALANGUAGE

The assumption that Demo in Pr adequately represents the provability relation means that the metalanguage can faithfully simulate the object language and, except for a reduction in efficiency, can replace the object language altogether.

But the metalanguage using Pr can perform other functions which the object language may not be able to perform directly for itself. For example, it can generate consequences of object language assumptions:

Pr $\vdash_M$ Ex Demo(A',x)

Moreover, it can generate object language hypotheses from conclusions:

Pr $\vdash_M$ Ex Demo(A'+x, B')

In both cases, instances of x which satisfy the theorem can be extracted from the proof in a manner which is familiar in resolution theorem-proving and in logic programming. Moreover, in the first case, the range of consequences can be constrained by proving theorems of the form

Pr $\vdash_M$ Ex(Demo(A',x) & Interesting(x))

where Pr contains an appropriate characterization of the

predicate Interesting(x). Similarly, hypotheses can be constrained by proving theorems of the form

Pr $\vdash_M$ Ex(Demo(A'+x,B') & MoreReasonable(x, B', A'))

where MoreReasonable(x,y,z) expresses that x is "more reasonable" than y in context z. The characterization of "more reasonable" needs to be included in Pr. To execute such goals in practical systems, one will need to co-routine the behaviour of Demo and the other predicate. For example, in the first case, the test Interesting can be initiated on the partially generated consequence x of the Demo predicate. This makes it possible to reject uninteresting consequences before they are fully constructed.

More important for applications in intelligent systems and mathematical theorem-proving is the use of the metalanguage to compress many object language proofs into one. For example a single metalanguage proof of the theorem[1]

Pr $\vdash_M$ $\forall$n $\forall$A'(Member("P(0)",A') &
$\forall$i(i$\leq$n -> Member("P(i)->P(i+1)", A'))
-> Demo(A' , "P(n+1)")).

replaces infinitely many object level proofs

---

[1]Careful readers will note that the use of the notation "P(i)" is not quite correct. Our earlier convention would require that "P(i)" denote a name of the formula P(i) and this formula contains the free variable i. However, what is required is an expression which denotes a name for the formula obtained from P(i) by replacing all occurrences of i by whatever term i is bound to in the larger context. This could be achieved by using, for example, the term

atom(pred(1),i.Nil)   instead of   atom(pred(1),var(12).Nil)

(where var(12) names the variable i) in place of "P(i)". Because of the simplicity of the examples in the rest of this paper we shall, since there is little likelihood of misunderstanding, use the simpler, slightly abusive notation.

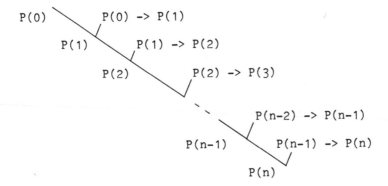

of unbounded length. In this example, of course, Pr would have to include an axiom of induction on the length of proofs. Such a single induction axiom in the metalanguage, moreover, can replace infinitely many induction axioms associated with data structures in the object language. On the other hand, no axioms of induction at all are required for the more modest objective of simply representing the object level proof procedure.

6. THE AMALGAMATION

We have noted that, because object language problems $A \vdash_L B$ can be replaced by metalanguage problems $Pr \vdash_M Demo(A', B')$, the metalanguage can replace the object language altogether. On the other hand, many object language problems can be solved more naturally and more efficiently in the object language than in the metalanguage. Thus it is desirable to combine the directness of the object language with the power of the metalanguage in an amalgamation which facilitates the communication of problems and their solutions between them. Such communication can be accomplished by means of linking rules:

1) $$\frac{Pr \vdash_M Demo(A', B')}{A \vdash_L B}$$ 2) $$\frac{A \vdash_L B}{Pr \vdash_M Demo(A',B')}$$

These rules simply restate the two parts of the definition of representability. The first rule allows the metalanguage to communicate the solutions of object language problems to the object language, whereas the second rule allows the object language to communicate the solutions of its problems to the metalanguage. (Weyhrauch (1980) calls these rules "reflection principles". The use of eval in LISP is also similar to the second of these two rules.)

Notice that the linking rules would be useful in the database
management example. Whereas the database manager executes the
top-level procedures P1-2 and A1-5 in the metalanguage, calls
of the form Demo(currdb,input), for example, can be translated and solved directly in the object language. Just when and
where these rules are to be applied is a (not insignificant)
control problem.

The amalgamation of languages L and M consists of L and M
together with

a) a naming relation which associates with every linguistic
   expression of L at least one variable-free term of M. (A
   single expression of L might have several associated
   names in M. But every name in M is associated with a
   unique expression of L.)
b) a representation of $\vdash_L$ by means of a predicate symbol
   Demo in the context of sentences Pr of M, and
c) the rules (1) and (2).

The amalgamation of L and M is a conservative extension in
the sense that no new theorems are provable in the amalgamation that were not already provable in either L or M. In fact
every proof in the amalgamation can be transformed into a
normal proof in L or M by eliminating application of the
linking rules. Because of the assumption of representability,
each application of linking can be replaced by an equivalent
argument entirely within one of the languages L or M. Application of the first rule can be replaced by an object
language argument, whereas application of the second rule can
be replaced by a metalanguage argument.

The only restriction on the languages L and M imposed by the
amalgamation is that the metalanguage M be adequate for the
representation of the provability relation of L. Horn clause
logic is more than adequate as such a metalanguage. However,
in the sequel we do not restrict the metalanguage M to Horn
clause logic. Notice, moreover, that the amalgamation allows
the case L=M, where the two languages are identical. This
case is of special importance, as it allows the formulation
both of sentences which mix object language and metalanguage
and of self-referential sentences.

Consider, for example, the English sentence

"A person is innocent if he or she cannot be proved guilty".

This can be formulated as:

I)   Innocent(x) <- Person(x),
                     ¬Demo(facts,"Guilty(x)"),
                     Relevant(facts).

Its formalization mixes a metalanguage condition with an object language condition and conclusion. Here "facts" names the relevant facts and assumptions which can be used in the attempt to establish guilt. Notice that a person might be guilty but not provably guilty. In such a case the object level sentence

        Innocent(x) <- Person(x), ¬ Guilty(x)

would not lead to the conclusion that he or she is innocent, whereas the mixed object-metalanguage sentence would. Note that if the relevant "facts" change, then the definition of Relevant(facts) would need to change accordingly. In this way, it would be possible to capture both the dependency of innocence on the relevant "facts" and the dependency of relevant facts on time. Moreover, the process of change itself can be formalized as in the earlier database management example.

The case L=M also allows the formalization of self referential sentences such as

        "This sentence contains five words."
        "The third sentence in this list contains four words."
        "This sentence is provable."
        "This sentence is unprovable."

We shall investigate the construction of such sentences in the last section of this paper.

7. APPLICATIONS TO LOGIC PROGRAMMING

Here we will just touch on topics that bear much fuller investigation. The explicit ability to construct names and to refer to theories in Demo allows us to simulate many useful programming devices. Locality of definition is such a device. One form this might take in logic programs is the definition of predicates purely local to a given clause. For example, one might desire a construct such as:

        P(x) <- Local(aux,"Q(x,y,z)"),R(x,z)

where aux names a set of clauses defining Q. The intent of the first condition in the clause above is that $Q(x,y,z)$ should be demonstrated in that extension of the present theory in which Q is defined by the clauses named by aux. Note that the expression Local(aux,...) is regarded as a single unitary goal. One way to achieve this is to add the following clause to a modified definition of Demo which makes result substitutions explicit. In this definition, we employ a three-place Demo predicate (a simplified variant of the four-place Demo predicate descussed at the end of section 4) such that

> Pr $\vdash_M$ Demo(A', B', S') iff
> given the problem A $\vdash_L$ B the object language proof procedure returns the substitution S.

The additional clause is:
D1.1)   Demo(prog,goals,result-subst) <-
           Select(goals, "Local(aux,subgoals)", rest),
           ExtendAndRename(prog,aux,new-prog),
           Demo(new-prog, subgoals, inter-subst),
           Apply(rest, inter-subst, new-goals),
           Demo(prog,new-goals,result-subst).

Thus the definition specified by aux will hold while the subgoals run, but when the processor returns to the rest of the original goals, the definition aux will no longer be used.

As a second example, consider the definition of a "mapping" predicate (Cf. LISP's mapping functions) All(p,list) in which "p" ranges over predicate symbols of the object language, and "list" ranges over lists of names of argument tuples to the predicate symbol named p. The predicate All(p,list) is intended to hold if and only if the predicate p holds of each of the argument tuples named on "list". It is defined by adding the following clauses to the definition of the three-place Demo:

D1.2)   Demo(prog,goals,result-subst) <-
           Select(goals, "All(p,list)", rest),
           CheckAll(prog,p,list,inter-subst),
           Apply(rest, inter-subst, new-goals),
           Demo(prog,new-goals, result-subst).

D1.2.1) CheckAll(prog,p,Nil, Empty-Subst) <-

D1.2.2) CheckAll(prog, p, h.t, result-subst) <-
                Parts(atm, p, h),
                Demo(prog, atm, inter-subst),
                Apply(t, inter-subst, new-t),
                CheckAll(prog, p, new-t, result-subst)

It appears that a considerable number of useful programming constructs can be obtained by such devices. The utility of this approach is that the amalgamated language obtains all these constructs without requiring separate semantic extensions for each.

8. NON-MONOTONIC LOGIC

The amalgamation of object and metalanguage provides an alternative to the non-monotonic logics (McDermott and Doyle, 1980) and default logics (Reiter, 1980) which have been proposed to formalize common sense reasoning. A simple example, considered by McDermott, Doyle and Reiter, is the assumption that "most birds can fly". Given the additional information that "Fred is a bird", it is natural to conclude by default that "Fred can fly" if there is no information to the contrary. If, however, at a later date we are told "Fred is an ostrich, and no ostrich can fly" then it is natural to avoid contradiction by non-monotonically withdrawing the previous inference that Fred can fly.

It is possible to formalize such non-monotonic reasoning in the manner suggested in the section of this paper which deals with the database management example. In this section, however, we shall consider an alternative formalization based upon mixing object language and metalanguage constructs in the same sentence. We may interpret the assumption "most birds can fly" for example, as expressing that "if x is a bird and it is consistent to assume that x can fly, then assume that x can fly".

This is formalized as follows:

T1)   CanFly(x) <- Bird(x),
                Consistent(theory, "CanFly(x)"),
                Current(theory).
where

T2)   Consistent(u,v) <- ¬ Demo(u, not(v)),

and not(v) names the negation of the sentence named by v.

Here the predicate Current(theory) defines the current assumptions which are relevant to the default rule. The current "theory" might or might not include both T1 and T2.

The sentence T1 is very close to the formulation

    CanFly(x) <- Bird(x), M(CanFly(x))

in non-monotonic logic, where M(A) is interpreted as expressing that A is consistent with the current database. M is regarded as an operator of modal logic and the database of current assumptions is implicit rather than explicit.

The formulation: $\dfrac{\text{Bird}(x),\ \text{M}(\text{CanFly}(x))}{\text{CanFly}(x)}$

in default logic similarly leaves the underlying database implicit. Moreover, the implication is formulated as a rule of inference. M(A) is interpreted as expressing that A is consistent. But it is formalized neither in the object language (modal logic in the case of non-monotonic logic) nor in the metalanguage (as in our case).

A major problem for both non-monotonic and default logic is to identify both the implicit database of current assumptions T as well the logical consequences of T. In our case the database is explicitly stated and the notion of logical consequence coincides with the classical notion for first-order logic as it applies to the amalgamation of object language and metalanguage. The explicit identification of the current database T has the advantage that subtle differences in meaning can be expressed by approprate choice of T. In the preceeding example, for instance, we can choose whether or not to include T1 itself in T.

Amalgamation logic inherits both the semantics and proof theory of classical first-order logic. But, although Demo in Pr represents provability, there exists no complete representation of unprovability and therefore of consistency (as we shall prove in the next section). Different "definitions" Pr differ accordingly in the degree of completeness with which they represent consistency. Thus the provable consequences of a nonmonotonic database formulated in amalgamation logic will depend not only on the identification of T in such sentences as T1 but also on the definition Pr. Moreover, negation can be interpreted either as standard classical negation, or as "negation by failure." In the latter case, we can always re-interpret it as classical negation by using

Clark's results (1978).

The following example (Reiter, 1979) illustrates the difference in semantics between non-monotonic, default and amalgamation logic:

If you don't know where a person lives then it is reasonable to assume she lives where her spouse does. It is also reasonable to assume she lives where her employer is located. In amalgamation logic these assumptions can be formalized, using infix notation, as follows:

T1)   x lives-in y <- spouse(x) lives-in y,
                       Current(theory),
                       Consistent(theory, "x lives-in y").
T2)   x lives-in y <- x works-in y,
                       Current(theory),
                       Consistent(theory, "x lives-in y").
Now suppose that

T3)   Mary works-in Vancouver
T4)   spouse(Mary) lives-in Toronto
T5)   u=v <- x lives-in u, x lives-in v
T6)   ¬ (Vancouver = Toronto).

If the current "theory" mentioned in T1 and T2 consists of T1-T6, then neither of the sentences

T7)   Mary lives-in Vancouver
T8)   Mary lives-in Toronto

is a consequence of the assumptions T1-6 ∪ Pr. However, if the theory consists of T3-6 and ¬ Demo in Pr represents at least finite unprovability, then both T7 and T8 are consequences of T1-6 ∪ Pr and therefore T1-6 ∪ Pr is inconsistent.

The assumptions corresponding to T1-6 in non-monotonic logic imply neither T7 nor T8 but do imply

T9)   Mary works-in Vancouver or Mary works-in Toronto.

In default logic, on the other hand, T7 and T8 are alternative beliefs which hold in alternative extensions of T3-6, sanctioned by the default rules corresponding to T1 and T2.

Notice moveover that in our formulation the "theory" in T1 can differ from the "theory" in T2. In particular, we can

impose a priority on the application of these rules by means
of such variation. For example, let the "theory" of T1
consist solely of T3-T6, but let T2 be modified to:

    x lives-in y <-
            x works-in y,
            Current(theory),
            Consistent(theory+T1, "x lives-in y").

In this case, we can conclude that Mary lives in Toronto, but
not that Mary lives in Vancouver. Thus we have given priority
to T1 in the sense that T2 must respect the consequences of
T1, but not vice versa. (This observation is due to Keith
Clark.)

If amalgamation logic attains greater expressive power by
employing an explicit parameter which names the current
relevant database of assumptions, then it achieves still
greater expressiveness when a four place Demo predicate is
employed with explicit control and result parameters. By
explicitly referring to the amount of deductive processssing
to be employed in testing for consistency, for example, we
can formalize such English sentences as:

Unless you are given explicit information to the contrary,
assume that your salary next year will be the same this year.

Such explicit control over the resources allocated to
attempted demonstrations of consistency reconciles the use of
logic with Winograd's criticism (Mc Dermott, 1980) of logic
for non-monotonic reasoning.

9. THE CONSTRUCTION OF SELF-REFERENTIAL SENTENCES

Let us assume that the system Pr contains a predicate symbol
"Substitute" such that

        Pr ⊢ Substitute(t, v, f, r)

if and only if, when t, v, f, and r are names of Term, Var,
Form, and Result, respectively, Result is obtained by
replacing all (free) occurrences of Var in Form (which are
free for Term) by Term. Moreover, we will assume that
Substitute is functional in its fourth[1] argument. Let n be a

---

[1] We need only assume that if Sb is as defined below, then
Pr $-(\forall x|, z, w)(Sb(x,z) \& Sb(x,w) \rightarrow (Demo("Pr",z) <-> Demo("Pr",w)))$

function symbol such that for any name t, n(t) is a name of the name t. Then define

Sb(x,y) iff Substitute(n(x), "x_0", x, y)

and let $D_0(x_0)$ be the sentence

$(\forall y)(Sb(x_0,y) \rightarrow \neg Demo("Pr",y))$

Let F be a name of $D_0(x_0)$, and let J be the sentence $D_0(F)$. Finally, let D be such that

Pr ⊢ Substitute(n(F), "x_0", F, D).

That is,
        Pr ⊢ Sb(F, D)

Thus D is a name of the sentence J. It is this sentence which is unprovable. Let us verify this claim.

1) First assume that Pr ⊢ J. Then by correct representability of Pr, we have
        Pr ⊢ Demo("Pr", D).

On the other hand, by the definition of J,

Pr ⊢ $(\forall y)(Sb(F,y) \rightarrow \neg Demo("Pr", y))$,

so that by universal instantiation,

Pr ⊢ Sb(F, D) $\rightarrow \neg$ Demo("Pr", D)

But by choice of D, Pr ⊢Sb(F, D), and so

Pr ⊢ $\neg$ Demo("Pr", D)

which is a contradiction.

2) Now assume that Pr ⊢ $\neg$ J. Then by the definition of J,

Pr ⊢ (Ey)(Sb(F,y) & Demo("Pr", y))

However, Pr ⊢ Sb(F,D), and Sb(x,y) is functional in its second argument since Substitute is functional in its fourth argument. Consequently we must have Pr ⊢ Demo("Pr", D) and so by correct representability, we have Pr ⊢ J which is again a contradiction. Thus neither J nor $\neg$ J is derivable from Pr. On the other hand, under the intended interpretation, J is true since it asserts of itself that it is underivable.

ACKNOWLEDGEMENTS

The authors gratefully acknowledge the useful comments made on an earlier draft of this paper by Keith Clark, Ray Reiter, and Alan Frisch. Kowalski also acknowledges support from the British Science Research Council and Syracuse University.

METALEVEL CONTROL FOR LOGIC PROGRAMS

Herve Gallaire   Claudine Lasserre

Laboratoires de Marcoussis   Ecole Nationale Superieure de
   CGE Route de Nozay   l'Aeronautique et de l'Espace
   91460 MARCOUSSIS   BP 4032   31055 TOULOUSE Cedex
       France   France

ABSTRACT

This paper deals with a method for incorporating metaknowledge capabilities in a PROLOG-like Horn clause interpreter,
expressed as a general or specific control strategy. The
paper gives an overview of current approaches and introduces
new means of control. A solution is investigated, consisting
of a metalevel expression of control for a standard interpreter. Actions allowed by the metarules are described and an
interpreter for the extended language is sketched.

1. INTRODUCTION

The problem we address here is that of controlling deduction
in a proof system operating on Horn clauses. However:
- we restrict ourselves to linear strategies, as they are
well founded (Hill, 1974) and can be efficiently implemented.
PROLOG (Roussel, 1973) is such an implementation and we take
this as the basis of our study.
- we shall often discuss the problem in terms of the more
general concepts of logic programming (Kowalski, 1979a).

Controlling a linear deduction on Horn clauses means determining the part of the search tree which is useful to explore, and its expansion order; at each step of the derivation, it has to be decided which literal to solve and which
clause to use to resolve it. In a backtracking regime this
gives rise to the following two types of control decision:
-    during the forward execution process a first decision on
both choices is set and tried;

- during the backtracking process, in case of failure in the forward one, it has to be decided which previous steps have to be erased and which new choices are to be made.

These two sides of the control are of course strongly dependent on each other: we can expect that a complete control of the forward process, by leading to determinism, may eliminate backtracking, while an "intelligent" control of the backtracking process, which avoids further failures, may render unnecessary a "clever" control of the forward process. In fact, as neither extreme is reachable, we would be content with a reasonable control of the forward process to alleviate causes of backtrack, combined with a backtrack intelligent enough to avoid some of the possible failure paths.

In the system we take as a reference, i.e. PROLOG, the choices are the following:
- choose the leftmost literal and the first matching clause (sorted in writing order),
- backtrack to the preceding resolvent in chronological order and choose the next matching clause for this same literal.

These strategies are simple and enable the programmer to control the execution of his program as he would do in a procedural language. However they prove to be uselessly limited compared to the range and quality of controls allowed by other possible solutions.

Our first step is to explore the various ways of modifying this static control (which proves to be efficient in many cases) by expressing in various ways metaknowledge, i.e. knowledge on how to deal with the knowledge itself as con-stituted by the program. Then we shall present a solution we investigated, consisting of using metarules for controlling the forward execution process. This method has been comple-mented by a control method for the backtracking process, described in (Lasserre and Gallaire, 1980); this is not described here as it is superseded by a more recent paper (Bruynooghe and Pereira, 1981).

2. VARIOUS WAYS OF CONTROLLING THE DEDUCTION

Various techniques enable the user to control the forward and backward execution processes. Here we briefly survey other methods that are used or have been proposed.

2.1 Pragmatic Control

This consists of writing a program tailored to the fixed strategy of the interpreter. For example, in PROLOG the programmer orders the literals and clauses so as to obtain the desired algorithm on his data.

It is clear that this approach detracts from the objective of declarative programming which is the separation between "what" and "how", i.e. between logic and control, or between knowledge and metaknowledge. Nevertheless, it improves the efficiency of the system in the search for a solution, and proves to be a very natural way of expressing the control because of procedural programming experience.

The following two alternatives consist of enlarging the range of possible actions of the interpreter and differ in the way of invoking them by means of primitives.

2.2 Explicit Control Incorporated in the Program

It is possible to add to a logic program, under the syntactic form of a literal (so as to preserve the syntax of the clause and the general process of literal selection of the interpreter), specific primitives enabling the control of certain aspects of the derivation process. These primitives express, in terms of interpreter actions, the intended behavior of the program, and generally tend to make the program more deterministic. An example is the PROLOG cut "!". When selected, its evaluation side-effects the control stack and so modifies the subsequent backtracking behavior.

Another possibility is the use of annotations, particularly annotations on variables that define a selection criterion for literals in terms of data flow. As an example of the utility of such a control concept consider the program:

    +GRANDFATHER(x,y)-FATHER(x,z)-FATHER(z,y)
    +FATHER(Paul,Pierre)
    .
    .   set of assertions defining FATHER
    .

(Note that we use in all our examples   x, y, z ... for variables.   We also use the original PROLOG notation of

$$+A-B_1- B_2 \ldots -B_k, \quad k \geq 0$$

for the implication
                A if B and B_2 and ... and B_k.)

If the problem to solve is: -GRANDFATHER(Paul,y) it seems natural to select first the literal -FATHER(Paul,z) of the resolvent -FATHER(Paul,z)-FATHER(z,y). If, instead the problem is: -GRANDFATHER(y,Paul) it is more efficient to select first the second literal of the resolvent -FATHER(x,y)-FATHER(y,Paul), i.e. -FATHER(y,Paul).

The most complete work done on the use of annotations to express such control is the IC-PROLOG system (Clark and McCabe, 1979b). Using variable annotations, one can define different orders of evaluation for different uses of a clause, set up producer-consumer coroutining between the evaluation of different literals, or set up pseudo parallel evaluation. In the coroutining the objects produced and consumed are variable bindings; each new or further instantiation of a variable leads to a transfer of control. By annotating the above clause

$$+GRANDFATHER(x,y)-FATHER(x,z)-FATHER(z,y?)$$

the second literal is made an eager consumer for y. If this variable is bound when the clause is used, it will be selected first, as required. In this case the consumer annotation on y delays the evaluation of -FATHER(x,z) until z is bound.

This idea of delaying the evaluation of a literal until one or more of its variables are bound is implemented in the latest version of PROLOG (Colmerauer et al. 1979), using the evaluable predicate GELER. The literal -GELER(P(x),x) is equivalent to -P(x), but the evaluation of P(x) will be delayed until x is bound. Similar constructs can be found in (Pereira and Porto, 1979a).

The interpreter takes the same advantage of such meta-knowledge information as the interpreter of a data flow language would do. The links between data flow and logic programming are being studied, e.g. by Byrd, (1980). Other possible interpretations of logic programs executions in terms of flow of data are those of actors (Kahn, K. 1980), Kahn and McQueen nets (van Emden and Lucena, 1979), execution by necessity or demand driven (Hansson et al. 1980)

2.3 Explicit Control Separated from the Program

This approach differs from the use of annotations and the use of control literals in that the metaknowledge is made explicit through metarules, i.e. special rules syntactically separated from the rules of the program: the interpreter will

distinguish between these two levels of knowledge and special
interpretation routines will be run according to the actions
specified by these metarules.

It is this approach we advocate especially for the control of
the forward execution process; it will be illustrated in more
detail in section 3. Such a view has already been proposed by
Davis (1977) for problem solving. We first proposed it for
logic programming in (Gallaire and Lasserre, 1979), and were
influenced by Hayes (1973). In (Dincbas, 1980b) the same
approach as ours is investigated.

The interest of separating the program from the control lies
for a great part in the clarity of the program so obtained.
It allows control of the execution of the program without
alteration of the program text. This separation also enables
the programmer to express more elaborate control: for
example, the metarules can name an entire clause and are not
restricted to the expression of control within a clause as in
(Clark and McCabe, 1982) or (Pereira and Porto, 1979a).

The difficulties of this approach are:
- to find adequate means of designating the objects, i.e the
literals and clauses the metaknowledge deals with,
- to choose the useful control strategies whilst avoiding
those that would be too costly to execute.

In section 3 we shall present various metarules and their
interpretation. We have chosen to express the metarules as
Horn clauses. Even though their semantics is not the standard
one, the declarative interpretation still applies. The only
difference is the domain of the objects to which they apply,
a point made some time ago by P. Hayes, (1973). We shall also
suggest various ways to improve the metarule interpretation
process.

2.4 Specific Control (Knowledge Structuring)

Other approaches are followed by all those who use specific
interpreters for their problem e.g. (Bundy et al. 1979;
Dincbas, 1980a). Instead of talking in terms of interpreter
behavior, they talk in terms of levels of perception of the
world (e.g objects, assemblies, equations, heuristics in
Bundy et al. 1979). As no general agreement has yet been
reached on a world structuring language, they are led to
build their own language and interpreter.

2.5 Automatic Control

Some strategies expected to be common to all the problems to solve need not be expressed as metarules. To accelerate their interpretation, they can be included in the interpreter and invoked at the right moment without any intervention of the programmer. Backtracking mechanisms can very well accomodate such an approach.

3. A LANGUAGE OF METARULES FOR THE FORWARD EXECUTION CONTROL

The metalanguage presented here extends that of Gallaire and Lasserre, (1979) both in its syntax and its semantics; this presentation is based on Fahmi (1979). We shall see examples of general strategies, much in the spirit of Minker (1977), as well as problem related ones. We hope to demonstrate the versatility of the approach.

3.1 Syntax of the Metarules

The syntax allows one to express meaningful actions related to the derivation process and to have several ways of indicating which objects (i.e. clauses or literals) are involved in the metarules.

a) The general form of a metarule is:

$$+\text{Action} -\text{Condition}_1 \ \ldots\ -\text{Condition}_k$$

The predicate of Action is a metapredicate expressing an action on the derivation process and is implemented by a system predicate. Condition is a literal which is either system-defined or user-defined in a program.

A metarule describes an action to be undertaken by the interpreter whenever the interpreter focuses its attention on an object involved in the metarule. The set of objects involved in a metarule is obtained from a combination of direct and-or indirect selection through the Action and Condition arguments according to the following rules:

- a literal P or a clause +P-Q is directly designated by a literal P' if P=P's for some substitution s. Of course, P' is a term in the metarule.

- an indirect designation of a clause may be either position-directed or content-directed as exemplified below:

* example of position-directed invocation:
    +OPORDER(P(x,y),n_1.n_2....NIL)-C_1-C_2..-C_k

will select clauses numbered n_1, n_2, .. in that order for resolution of literals which are instantiations of P(x,y), provided the conditions C_i are verified.

* example of content-directed invocation:
    +OPBEFORE(R(x,A),t_1,t_2)-CLAUSE(t_1,z,P(x,y).NIL)
                            -CLAUSE(t_2,r,Q(x,y).NIL)

will select for the resolution of literals of the form R(x,A), clauses containing literal P(x,y) before clauses containing Q(x,y). The condition CLAUSE(1, name, litlist) holds when 1 belongs to the subset of clauses named by name that contain the literals of litlist. In this example, in both uses of CLAUSE, the clauses are named by variables. Hence this metarule would apply to all clauses with head matching R(x,a). We can restrict its scope by replacing z and r by terms that name specific clauses. There is a second form for the CLAUSE metapredicate, namely CLAUSE(1,name,n). This makes 1 belong to the sublist of the clauses named by name whose bodies contain n literals (see 3.2).

- an indirect designation of a literal is given by:
    LITERAL(x,name,list-of-properties)
This selects a literal x named by name that satisfies each of list-of-properties. This is a list of pairs $(P_i:V_i)$. The properties P are to be taken from a set of predefined symbols: ANCESTOR, FATHER, DEPTH, SOLVED,..
As an example, consider:
    +BEFORE(t_1,t_2)-LITERAL(t_1,x,DEPTH:n_1)
                     -LITERAL(t_2,y,DEPTH:n_2)-LESS(n_1,n_2)

This program will impose a breadth-first strategy for the interpreter; further restictions on x and y would impose such a strategy only to the named literals.

b) Remarks. The syntax illustrated above is flexible enough to express any reasonable designation of a clause or literal that the user would want. As for the set of available properties P_i, more experience must be gained before finalizing it. We must stress again the possibility for the user to express very general metarules by using variables to name literals, or conversely to express very specific metarules using very specific names and selection conditions.

3.2 Semantics of Metarules

Metapredicates are provided for clause and literal selection. By selection we mean either electing a candidate among others, or eliminating a candidate. Of course, we shall have default evaluation rules, namely that of PROLOG.

a) <u>Clause   selection</u>. Let S be the set of clauses that could be used to resolve the active, i.e selected, literal. A metarule can express the following control:

-ordering between clauses in S. This can be specified by using OPORDER which gives an exact order of clauses in S, by using OPFIRST which points to the clause to be used first, and by using OPBEFORE which gives relative orders to the clauses.
Example:
$+OPBEFORE(t,t_2,t_3)-CLAUSE(t_2,x,n)-CLAUSE(t_3,y,m)-LESS(n,m)$

Such a metarule expresses the "shortest clauses first" heuristic, a control outside of the scope of the other approaches discussed in section 2.

-inhibition of clauses in S, mutual exclusion of clauses taken from S, etc. A set of such clause selection metapredicates has been precisely defined in (Fahmi, 1979).

b) <u>Literal selection</u>. These metarules are used to select the next literal to solve; they provide for the following:
- turning off metarule control during the proof of a literal; this is an essential characteristic in a realistic environment
- priority of one literal over another (BEFORE)
- restricting the attention of the interpreter to the selected literal and to its descendents until it is proved (FINISH)
- recovering the space of a literal's proof
- unsolvability of a literal
- determinism
- recursion level limitation
- inhibition of a literal on backtracking (generalizing the "cut" by giving conditions under which backtracking is either permitted or supressed)
- necessary and sufficient conditions for a literal to be selected..

The semantics of these metarules is rather straightforward (see Fahmi, 1979). Here, we shall briefly explain the meta predicates for literal selection. They are related to the producer-consumer primitives of IC-PROLOG. NEED says that a literal must have a resource available before it can be selected. READY says that, if certain resources are available, the literal must be selected as soon as possible. Thus, READY is related to the eager consumer of IC-PROLOG when the resource is the binding x/t of some variable x. But it does not have the inheriting property of an eager consumer - variables in the binding term t do not automatically become needed resources for the descendants of the eager consumer. Example:

$$NEED(P(x,y,z))-INST(x)$$

says that literal $P(x,y,z)$ can be selected only if its variable x is bound. There is also a way of expressing a producer relationship by using a NEEDBY metapredicate:

$$+NEEDBY(t_1,t_2)-Condition$$

says that t_1 needs resources expressed by Condition, which, if lacking, will be produced by t_2; thus it requires selection of t_2 to generate the resource.

c) <u>Interpretation process</u>. The interpreter is basically a literal selection - clause selection loop (see Dincbas, 1980b; Bowen and Kowalski, 1982). The basic loop of an interpreter looks like:

$$+Goal(R_i) - Select\ literal(R_i,L_j)$$
$$- Select\ clause(L_j,C_j)$$
$$- Substitute(R_i,L_j,C_j,R_{i+1})$$
$$- Goal(R_{i+1})$$

At each step in the loop, metarules of the appropriate type (literal or clause selection) are activated. Their selection is driven by literals or clauses they name; this means that if we had a resolvent $-P-A-B$ and two metarules (in that order)

$$+BEFORE(B,P)$$
$$+BEFORE(A,P)$$

then A will be selected rather than B or P.

Although many metarules express a global control, in many cases it is possible to eliminate the overhead incured by this global control by compiling into a new program; or it is possible to compile links between literals and metarules which might name them, thus accelerating the process.

4. EXAMPLES OF METARULE PROGRAMMING

(i) Consider the following metarules:
    +OPORDER(P(x),1.2.3.NIL)-Cond$_1$(x)
    +OPORDER(P(x),1.3.2.NIL)-Cond$_2$(x)
    +OPORDER(P(x),3.1.NIL)-Cond$_3$(x)

They heuristically guide the search for the proof of literals
of the form -P(x). For different conditions on the argument x
they specify a different try order for the clauses numbered
1,2, 3 that have P(x) as head.

(ii) The grandfather example above would be solved by:
    +GF(x,y)-F(x,z)-F(z,y)
    +NEED(F(u,v))-OR(INST(u),INST(v))
where OR is defined as logical OR, and INST is true when its
parameter is bound.

(iii) The eight queens problem is easily solved through
coroutining:

    +QUEEN-Q(x$_1$)-.....-Q(x$_8$)
        -PASS((1.x$_1$)....(8.x$_8$).(NIL.NIL))
    +Q(1)
    .
    .
    .
    +Q(8)
    +PASS((t$_1$.x$_1$).(t$_2$.x$_2$).r)-TEST((t$_1$.x$_1$),(t$_2$.x$_2$).r)
                        -PASS((t$_2$.x$_2$).r)
    +PASS((t$_8$.x$_8$).(NIL.NIL))
    +TEST((t$_1$.x$_1$),(t$_2$.x$_2$).r)-POSSIBLE((t$_1$.x$_1$),(t$_2$.x$_2$))
                        -TEST((t$_1$.x$_1$),r)
    +TEST((t$_1$.x$_1$),(NIL.NIL))
    +POSSIBLE ....: program testing whether two queens
                    attack each other

In order to get a reasonable behavior, each time a new queen
is assigned a position, that position is tested against all
previous ones and work is done so as to see later that it
passes all future tests; this is done as follows:

    +READY(PASS(y$_1$.y$_2$.r))-CONST(y$_1$)-CONST(y$_2$)
    +READY(TEST(y$_1$,y$_2$.r))-CONST(y$_2$)
    +READY-FINISH(POSSIBLE(t$_1$,t$_2$))

where CONST tests whether its argument is a constant; note
the use of FINISH.

(iv) Another example is the Sieve of Eratosthenes algorithm
for computing prime numbers:

```
+PRIME(x)-INTEGER(2.y)-ERA(2.y,x)
+INTEGER(p.q.r)-SUCC(p,q)-INTEGER(q.r)
+ERA(p.in,p.pr)-FILTER(p,in,new)-ERA(new,pr)
+FILTER(p,q.in,out)-MULT(p,q)-FILTER(p,in,out)
+FILTER(p,q.in,q.out)-FILTER(p,in,out)
```

where MULT and SUCC are the multiplication and successor
predicates. This program loops; we get a natural coroutining
process by adding the following metarules:

```
+NEED(INTEGER(x,y))-INST(y)
+NEED(FILTER(x,y,z))-INST(y)
+NEED(ERA(x,y))-INST(x)
```

The first metarule insures that INTEGER will always be
blocked unless everything else is. An equivalent behavior
could be obtained with:

```
+READY(FILTER(x,y,z))-INST(y)
+READY(ERA(x,y))-INST(x)
```

the first predicate INTEGER will only get to run when y is
not instantiated in all FILTER predicates already generated
and if x is free in ERA. One could also write a more local
control:

```
+NEED(t)-LITERAL(t,FILTER(x,y,z),FATHER:ERA(v,w).NIL)
          -INST(x)
```

(v) A further class of applications is illustrated in the
next example which shows how one implements content-directed
invocation as defined by Davis (1977): in order to make sure
we select a clause which "mentions" some predicate in its
body, directly or indirectly, one writes:

```
+OPBEFORE(x,t1,t2)-CLAUSE(t1,z,r)-MENTIONS(z,r,P(u))
+MENTIONS(z,b,p)-IN(b,p)
+MENTIONS(z,b,p)-IN(b,p1)-CLAUSE(u,p1,z)-MENTIONS(p1,z,p)
```

where IN(b,p) holds if p is in the list b. Recall that in the
condition CLAUSE(t1,z,r) z is the head of a clause and r is
its body.

(vi) The classical sameleaves example can be expressed in
either of two ways:

$+SAME(x,y)-L(x,s)-L(y,s)$

Let us assume that $L(x,s)$, which is the relation: s is the leaf profile of tree x, is recursively defined on the structure of the tree.

$+READY(L(x,s))-INST(s)$ or $+NEED(L(x,s))-INST(s)$

will set up coroutining between the two calls of the clause.

(vii) This example deals with a type of global control, unreachable in any of the other approaches described earlier. It is nevertheless quite real as shown by Warren (1981). Given a query in a deductive database, it can be seen as a resolvent to prove; the database contains both unit clauses (the data) and non unit clauses (the general rules); a PROLOG interpreter can be used to deal with such databases. In (Warren, 1981) several rules have been incorporated to the interpreter to re-order literals so as to lower the overall access cost of the query evaluation. Our approach allows one to express and modify very easily such ordering rules; no local control can attain such a result. We give two simple examples:

$+BEFORE(t_1,t_2)-LITERAL(t_1,x,y)-LITERAL(t_2,u,v)$
$-COST(x,n_1)-COST(u,n_2)-LESS(n_1,n_2)$

where COST can be defined by the user as in (Warren, 1981). A different and less general control can be expressed:

$+NEEDBY(BORDER(x,y),COUNTRY(x))-INSTOR(x,y)$
$+INSTOR(x,y)-INST(x)$
$+INSTOR(x,y)-INST(y)$

this says that literal BORDER has cost inferior to that of COUNTRY provided at least one of its arguments is instantiated.

5. CONCLUSION

We have presented means for controlling the forward execution process via a metarule mechanism; we now need to exercise it so as to feel where and when the metarule evaluation really reduces the cost of resolution of a resolvent. We expect this to be the case at some but not all of the abstraction levels we go through during programming, and to be the case at least for coroutining primitives. The interpreter must also be improved, in the direction of precompiling information given by (some of) the metarules or by links to the metarules.

The control so expressed is characterized as being global to the whole program; in fact it can be as much local or as much global as one wants it to be, depending on the user's precisions in the various parts of the metarule (parameters, conditions ..). Some of the effects we get in real life examples are truly important. We stress that the use of such metarules keeps us inside the logic programming frame. Again we mention control of the backtracking process and that a merging of both controls is highly desirable. Why not generalize the metarule approach to the backtracking process?

In any case, logic appears, among all procedural approaches to be outstanding for experiments in facing these very important problems in all problem solving situations. Meta-language facilities are certainly to be used in more ways than the ones we chose here (Bowen and Kowalski, 1982).

ACKNOWLEDGMENTS

We want to thank Keith Clark for helping us improve the syntax and the semantics of the paper, and Sten-Åke Tärnlund and Alain Grumbach for their editorial help.

Part of this research was financed by CNRS under ATP4270 when both authors were at ENSAE - CERT.

CONTROL ISSUES

PREDICATE LOGIC AS A LANGUAGE
FOR PARALLEL PROGRAMMING

M.H. van Emden

G.J. de Lucena Filho

Department of Computer Science
University of Waterloo
Waterloo, Ontario
N2L 3G1 CANADA

Departamento de Sistemas e
Computacao
Universidade Federal da Paraiba
Campina Grande, Paraiba, BRAZIL

ABSTRACT

We describe the formulation, execution, semanticization, and verification within first-order predicate logic of programs in Kahn's model of computation. The relations computed by process activations are defined in logic. The state of a network of communicating parallel processes is specified as a single statement of logic which is about the concisest possible textual representation of such a network.

1. INTRODUCTION

Kahn has proposed (1974) an attractive model of computation, together with a mathematical semantics for it. In a subsequent paper (Kahn and McQueen, 1977) an implementation of the model was described and illustrated by examples which show that the model is conducive to elegant and easy-to-verify solutions to interesting programming problems.

We introduce a description of Kahn's model of computation by a simple programming problem. The problem is to perform "balanced addition" on a sequence of reals. Usually numbers are added as in

$$((((((a_1 + a_2) + a_3) + a_4) + a_5) + a_6) + a_7) + a_8$$

With respect to rounding errors it is preferable to add them as in

$$((a_1 + a_2) + (a_3 + a_4)) + ((a_5 + a_6) + (a_7 + a_8))$$

which is an example of <u>balanced addition</u>. The programming problem requires this to be done in a single pass over a sequence of reals which has to be sequentially accessed. The length of the sequence is not known in advance.

A Parallel program (we use the capitalized "Parallel" to denote something specific to Kahn's model of computation) consists of a network of processes connected by channels which transmit data. In order to perform balanced addition on the eight numbers of our example we use a network of three processes which all perform the same computation (called "add") of getting two successive numbers out of their input channel and putting the sum into their output channel.

The above network is of course not a satisfactory solution. The number of add-processes in the network should depend on how many reals have to be added. So instead of the above <u>static</u> network, which does not change its configuration, we need a <u>dynamic</u> network, which does. We define a process called "sigma" with an input channel only.

When it has read two numbers x and y, it changes the network to

Sigma is an example of a dynamic process. The effect is to generate exactly as many activations of the add-process as are necessary to perform balanced addition on a sequence of reals of which the length is initially unknown. As soon as sigma reads eof, it prints the number previously read, if present, otherwise it prints 0.

2. LOGIC SPECIFICATION OF RELATIONS COMPUTED BY PROCESSES

The distinguishing feature of networks of process activations is that control of the sequencing of the activations of the processes is of no concern to the programmer: it is implicit in the way processes are connected by channels in the net-work. The primitive operations on channels in Kahn's model are get, put and test for eof. They are such that the programmer can regard each process as computing a relation between the histories of the channels to which the process is connected.

We represent histories by terms. As variables we use u, v, w, x, y, z, possibly with postscripts. In our examples the constants are numbers or the symbol "eof" which stands for a special kind of history. The only thing we need to assume about eof is that it contains no data to be processed. More typically, a history is a term of the form x:y, where x is a number and y is a history and is that part of x:y that comes after x.

The relation computed by the ADD process is defined as the least model of the following set of clauses:

$$\{ \ add(eof,eof)$$
$$, \ add(x{:}eof,x{:}eof) \tag{2.1}$$
$$, \ add(x_{12}{:}y,x_1{:}x_2{:}x) \ \text{<-} \ sum(x_1,x_2,x_{12}) \ \& \ add(y,x) \}$$

where sum is a "built-in" relation. The clause set is considered to contain the clause "sum(a,b,c)" for all numbers a,b, and c such that a+b=c.

3. THE PROCESS INTERPRETATION OF HORN CLAUSE LOGIC

In Kowalski's procedural interpretation of Horn clause logic (1974) a goal statement is interpreted as the stack of a single sequential computation. In the process interpretation, a goal statement must represent the state of a network of sequential computations. As a result, in the process inter-pretation, a goal statement is interpreted as a network of stacks connected by channels with contents given by terms of the goal statement.

When the body of a process definition contains only a single stack, it causes a process activation to be replaced by a single process activation and hence does not change the net-work. An example of such a definition is the one for "add". A body may also have more than one stack; in that case its definition is dynamic as it will cause the network to change; "sigma" is an example. Apparently we need a notation to demarcate the stacks in a goal statement or in a definition. We do this by putting extra parentheses around a stack's constituent atomic formulas.

We will give rules for reading off from the goal statement

which activations are connected by a channel, what its direction is, and what its contents are. We first show an example of a logic derivation representing the successive states of a network of processes performing balanced addition on the sequence of numbers 5, 4, 3, 2, 1.

The relations computed by the processes are given by

$$\{add(eof,eof),add(x{:}eof,x{:}eof)$$
$$,add(x_{12}{:}y,x_1{:}x_2{:}x) \leftarrow (sum(x_1,x_2,x_{12}) \; \& \; add(y,x)) \qquad (3.1)$$
$$,sigma(0,eof),sigma(x,x{:}eof)$$
$$,sigma(z,x_1{:}x_2{:}x) \leftarrow (sum(x_1,x_2,x_{12}) \; \& \; sigma(z,x_{12}{:}y))$$
$$\& \; (add(y,x))$$
$$\}$$

The first goal statement of the derivation is:

$$\leftarrow (sigma(z,5{:}4{:}3{:}2{:}1{:}eof))$$

The corresponding network is:

We now continue to list goal statements of the derivation with comments explaining their process interpretation. Matching the last clause for sigma gives:

$$\leftarrow (sum(5,4,x_{12}) \; \& \; sigma(z,x_{12}{:}y)) \; \& \; (add(y,3{:}2{:}1{:}eof))$$

There are now two process activations, connected in a network as follows

The fact that there are two stacks of goals to be executed in parallel, is copied from the premiss of the third clause for sigma. The connection between the two follows from the fact that the input history of sigma is x_{12} (which is going to be 5+4) followed by the output history of add. By the definition of history of a channel as the sequence of all data items that are ever contained in the channel, it follows that <u>there is a channel directed from add to sigma containing 5+4 in the present state.</u>

The goals sum and add can now be replaced in either order or simultaneously, giving

$\leftarrow$ (sigma(z,9:x_{12}:y)) & (sum(3,2,x_{12}) & add(y,1:eof))

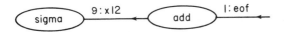

Both processes now have sufficient input to execute. We also execute the goal sum(3,2,x_{12}) which belongs to the sequential code of add. After executing sum and sigma in any order, we obtain

$\leftarrow$ (sum(9,5,x_{12}) & sigma(z,x_{12}:y_1)) & (add(y_1,y))
      & (add(y,1:eof))

This is interpreted as the network:

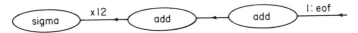

Only the rightmost process has enough input. Hence

$\leftarrow$ (sigma(z,14:y_1)) & (add(y_1,1:eof))

with network

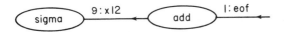

Notice that in our formulation a stopped process vanishes. Again only the rightmost has enough input:

$\leftarrow$ (sigma(z,14:1:eof))

with network

$\leftarrow$ (sum(14,1,x_{12}) & sigma(z,x_{12}:y)) & (add(y,eof))

has network

$\leftarrow$ (sigma(z,15:eof))

Now the second clause for sigma derives the empty goal statement and hence finishes the derivation/computation. The resulting substitution for z in this goal statement, and also in the initial goal statement, is 15.

After having seen examples of all its features, it is now time to give the process interpretation of logic.

a) Cyclical processes are defined as relations among histories, which need not be finite. The definition is inductive where the induction step refers only to finite subsequences of the histories involved. The induction step in the definition corresponds to one cycle in the execution of the cyclical process. If the histories are finite, then the inductive definition has a basis.

b) For the purpose of the process interpretation, the premisses of the logic definitions are partitioned into stacks. Each stack corresponds to a sequential computation. Hence, in the definition of a static process, where the body is a single sequential computation, there is only one stack. In the definition of a dynamic process, when the body specifies parallel execution of process activations, there is more than one stack; one for each process activation.

c) The goals of a goal statement consist of a number of stacks, one for each process activation in the corresponding network. If two stacks share a variable, then the corresponding activations share a channel. In one of the stacks the term containing the shared variable consists of that variable only, say u. This stack is the activation of the producer process. In the other stack the term containing the shared variable has the form $t_1:\ldots:t_n:u$. This stack is the activation of the consumer process. The terms $t_1,\ldots,t_n$ are the contents of the channel; t_1 is received first, t_2 next, and so on. In case n=0 the channel is empty and there is no way to tell in which direction the data flow.

d) In Parallel computation, any activation is eligible for execution except those which are blocked in an input operation on an empty channel. In logic, any goal of a goal statement may be selected when performing a derivation step. For only certain selections can such a derivation step be interpreted as a parallel computation step: the goal must be in an activation which is eligible for execution. Once the activation has been determined, the selected goal is also determined as the leftmost. Because in logic there are no explicit "get" operations, the rule which determines whether a process activation is ready for execution varies from case to case. For example, unless the next item is eof, always two items must be present before the cycle of an "add" or "sigma" process activation can be initiated.

We have seen that every computation step of a Parallel program is a derivation step, but it is not so the other way around: the process interpretation disallows in general the selection of most of the goals of a goal statement. However, from the logical point of view the same result is obtained whatever goal is selected at each particular derivation step. Some selections, although disallowed by the process inter-pretation, are instructive variants of Kahn's model of computation.

For instance, take in the above example the goal statement

<- sigma(z,14:y_1) & add(y_1,1:eof)

with network

Sigma is not eligible for execution as it requires two items in the input channel. Suppose it would nevertheless be selected. Then the next goal statement would be

<- (sum(14,x_2,x_{12}) & sigma(z,x_{12}:y)) & (add(y:x))
  & (add(x_2:x,1:eof))

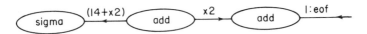

With selections admissable under the process interpreation, the second argument of add is always input and the first is always output. However, now (according to rule (c) above) the situation has been reversed in the channel between the two activations of add: x_2 has been sent from left to right. x_2 is a variable, not a data item, which also occurs elsewhere, for example in the input channel of sigma. Next time the rightmost activation of add sends an item it is not communi-cated in the usual way: the variable x_2 will be instantiated with the item wherever the variable occurs. We see this by now executing the rightmost add:

<- (sum(14,1,x_{12}) & sigma(z,x_{12}:y)) & (add(y,eof))

The resulting state is now one which also occurs in the previous example. Apparently, process activation can be allowed (in logic) to run ahead of their input. The missing items appear as variables in the internal computations and are also sent as variables to where they should have come from. When the missing items are eventually produced, the variables are instantiated with the items and everything ends up in the situation which would also be obtained according to the rules of Parallel computation.

4. CORRECTNESS FOR TERMINATING PARALLEL COMPUTATIONS

For verification of parallel programs expressed in logic we can use the method of consequence verification proposed and demonstrated by Clark (1977). According to this method the definitions used for computation are proved as theorems from specifications in first-order predicate logic. Unlike the definitions, the specifications are not necessarily in clausal form. The type of verification obtained is partial correctness: if the computation terminates, the instance of the relation derived by the computation is also an instance of the relation defined by the specification.

As an example, the following axioms are a specification of the sigma and add relations of example 3.1.

The universal quantifier is written as $\forall$; the existential quantifier as E.

$$sigma(0,eof) \hspace{7.5cm} (4.1)$$
$$\forall x,y,z. \; sigma(z,x{:}y) \; <\text{-}> \; Ez_1.sigma(z_1,y) \; \& \; sum(x,z_1,z) \hspace{0.5cm} (4.2)$$
$$\forall x,y. \; add(x,y) \; <\text{-}> \; Es.sigma(s,x) \; \& \; sigma(s,y) \hspace{1.8cm} (4.3)$$

According to the specification, the sum sigma is obtained in the normal way. We can verify the program by deriving each of the clauses of (3.1) as a theorem. We can use some general arithmetical knowledge, such as the properties of "sum". We prove in effect that, for associative addition of reals (it is this property that rounding errors typically invalidate), balanced addition is equivalent to naive addition. We leave the reader to check that each clause can be so derived.

5. CORRECTNESS FOR NONTERMINATING PARALLEL COMPUTATION

Let us briefly review the main features of the fixpoint semantics for logic programs as developed in (van Emden and

Kowalski, 1976). With a set P of definite clauses there is associated a monotone mapping T from interpretations to interpretations such that I is a Herbrand model of P iff I contains T(I). Hence the least fixpoint of T is the set of all variable-free atomic formulas which are true in all Herbrand models of P and it is also the set of all possible results of derivations (and hence finite computations) from P. The least fixpoint semantics of van Emden and Kowalski, (1976) is adequate for terminating computation.

Consider the following network consisting of a single process Incr which continues reading a number, writing it, incrementing it by one, and placing the result on its output channel, which is also the input channel. This channel contains initially a single number 0.

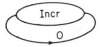

The definition of the relation computed by Incr is:

$$Incr(x_1:y,x:z) <- sum(x,1,x_1) \ \& \ Incr(y,z)$$

The network is specified by the goal statement <-Incr(x,0:x). This goal statement initiates an infinite computation, which substitutes for x successively 1:...:n:x_n for n=1,2,... .

Let us see what the sentence

$$P = \{Incr(x_1:y,x:z) <- sum(x,1,x_1) \ \& \ Incr(y,z)$$
$$,Omega(0:x) <- Incr(x,0:x)$$
$$\}$$

says about the result 0:1:2:... of the computation starting with <- Omega(x). The result certainly is not in the denotation of Omega in the least fixpoint of T, the transformation associated with P, which is empty. One reason why we cannot expect otherwise is that the underlying domain, the Herbrand universe, contians only finite terms. In fact, with this domain, the denotation of Omega in any fixpoint of T is empty. Thus, if we are to find a semantics for infinite computations we must consider infinitary Herbrand universes containing all terms of the usual Herbrand universe plus the infinite trees that are the limits of monotone sequences of finite terms.

Now, the denotation of Omega in the least fixpoint of T, when taken in the infinitary Herbrand universe, is also empty. This time, however, the denotation of Omega in the greatest

fixpoint of T is exactly what we want, namely the sequence
0:1:2:... of all natural numbers.

The results in (Andreka et al.) can be used to verify P. In
the first place, if we can show that no derivation from P
exists with <- Omega(X) as first goal statement and X some
variable-free term not equal to the omega sequence, it would
follow (Apt and van Emden, 1982) that any such Omega(X) is
false in all models of

$$P' = \{ Incr(x_1:y,x:z) \rightarrow sum(x,1,x_1) \ \& \ Incr(y,z)$$
$$,Omega(0:x) \rightarrow Incr(x,0:x)$$
$$\}$$

which is the converse of P. If we can show that all derivations from P starting from <- Omega(0:1:2:...) are infinite
then it would follow that Omega(0:1:2:...) is true in the
greatest model of P', provided that the infinitary Herbrand
universe is the underlying domain.

6. RELATED WORK

Kowalski (1974, 1979a) introduced the procedural interpretation and discussed the possibility of coroutining among
goals. Clark and his colleagues have pursued this coroutining
much further. They arrive at a model of computation of great
generality, having among others as special cases Kahn's model
and lazy evaluation (Clark et al. 1982).

Another logic programming language in which Kahn style communicating processes can be represented is that of Hansson et
al. (1982). Using equations, they can define infinite data
structures and terminating computations over them. They use
the classical semantics of predicate logic for a domain that
contains the infinite structures. The language of Bellia et
al. (1982) incorporates the idea of lazy, coroutined evaluation. They give the language a least fixed point semantics
for a Herbrand universe extended with undefined objects.

This paper, and the above approaches, have in common that
coroutining computations are obtained by a suitable choice of
selected atom. Another approach is taken by Pereira and
Monteneiro (1981) who assume that, for efficiency reasons,
the leftmost goal is always the selected atom. They obtain
the equivalent of parallel execution by a systematic and very
elegantly conceived transformation of the logic definition.

CONCURRENT LOGIC PROGRAMMING

C.J. Hogger

Department of Civil Engineering
Imperial College
London SW7
ENGLAND

ABSTRACT

Some concurrent algorithms are represented using the logic programming formalism and some general principles are extracted from the formulation. The treatment is shown to be semantically pure and compatible with current approaches to logic program development. The principal contribution of the paper is to show that algorithms which depend upon communication between concurrent processes can be described satisfactorily by pure logic programs controlled by selective data-flow annotations of the kind already available in the IC-PROLOG Implementation. Some indication is also given of how those programs can be derived from logic describing non-concurrent algorithms for the same problems.

1. INTRODUCTION

Studies in logic programming have usually assumed program execution to be the responsibility of a single processor. This assumption makes it easy to explain conventional PROLOG-like programs using ideas prevalent in other programming formalisms, in particular the idea of interpreting procedure calls as tasks to be completed one at a time by the processor. More recently, significant advances have been made in diversifying the means of specifying control, that is to say, in providing program annotation schemes which indicate control preferences supplementing the usual default strategy. A notable scheme of this kind has been developed by Clark and McCabe (1979b) and provides elegant facilities for coroutining and pseudo-parallelism in IC-PROLOG. This allows one to

write logically lucid programs whose behaviour is explicitly
prescribed in terms of the nature of the data flow through
specially annotated variables; the annotations enable call
evaluations, by a single processor, to be temporally
interleaved, allowing a finer grain of interaction between
them than if the annotations were absent. Formerly,
comparable behaviour could only have been achieved by
executing programs of greater logical intricacy.

Despite the benefits obtained from such elaborations of the
control mechanism, there remain numerous simple problems
which could be solved yet more efficiently if multi-processor
hardware were available. Indeed, Clark and McCabe (1979b)
find an example of this in their discussion of coroutined
programs for the eight-queens problem. The present paper
arose from the author's attempt to formulate in logic the
essence of a classic problem chosen by Owicki and Gries
(1976) to demonstrate verification of concurrent ALGOL-like
programs. The ideas presented here are somewhat tentative and
are chiefly intended to stimulate interest in this and
similar problems, rather than to constitute a comprehensive
proposal for implementing concurrency. The reader is expected
to be familiar with logic programming; this has been
comprehensively described by its originator Robert Kowalski
(1979).

2. ASSUMPTIONS AND NOTATION

Programs are presented here using the standard arrow notation
for Horn clause goals and procedures. Variables are
distinguished from constants by denoting the former by
identifiers beginning with lower-case letters.

Assume that several processors $P_1,...,P_n$ are available for
solving a collection of calls. Then a goal <- A, B can be
executed using P_1 and P_2 to execute (evaluate) the two
respective subgoals, the evaluations proceeding concurrently.
For a simple model, imagine that P_1 and P_2 operate as
distinct interpreters sharing access to a single set of
procedure definitions. A desire to execute the goal in this
way can be expressed by writing it as <- A//B where // is
interpreted logically as conjunction but operationally as a
prescription for concurrent execution of A and B. This use of
the // symbol is therefore referred to as **conjunctive**
concurrency.

Further annotations can be devised to declare which

processors are to deal with which calls, if this is
prescribable, or else processor allocation can be decided
dynamically by the implementation. The details of such
arrangements are not relevant to what follows and so are not
discussed further.

We can also permit expression of concurrency within procedure
bodies. An example of this is seen in the problem of
comparing the frontiers of two binary trees. Derivation of a
program for this problem is shown by Hogger (1979), in which
a tree with frontier (A,B,C,D,E,F) like

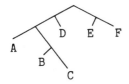

is represented by a term
$t(t(t(l(A),t(l(B),l(C))),l(D)),t(l(E),l(F)))$. Then a concurrent program which seeks to show that two trees T_1 and T_2
represented by such terms have the same frontier is:

```
<- same(T₁,T₂)
   same(x,x) <-
   same(x,y) <- split(u',x",x)//split(u',y',y),same(x',y')
   split(u',x',t(l(u'),x')) <-
   split(u',x',t(t(x₁,x₂),x₃)) <- split(u',x',t(x₁,t(x₂,x₃)))
```

Observe that the executions which decompose the frontiers of
x and y spend most of their time restructuring the trees
until they become ready to compare the frontiers' first
labels. This restructuring is best performed concurrently as
indicated in the second procedure.

Although concurrent executions are easiest to conceive and
control when they do not manipulate shared data, no
limitations are imposed here upon the argument structures of
calls conjoinable by //. Thus to express the problem of
deciding whether a given element E belongs to given sets A
and B, construct a goal whose concurrent subgoals can be
executed independently:

$$<- m(E,A) // m(E,B) .$$

Similarly, to find an element u common to A and B, construct
the goal:
$$<- m(u,A) // m(u,B) .$$

It will be assumed that concurrent executions share access to a common vector of goal variables, so that in the example just shown there will exist one 'slot' u associated with the two subgoals. Thus if either execution assigns data to u, the other execution is instantly sensitive to this event irrespective of its own current progress. To prevent the possibility of binding conflicts it is sufficient to arrange that unification steps are always mutually exclusive. Unification is therefore the indivisible (or critical) event for our concurrent formalism.

We shall insist that substitution of a parallel connective (//) for any serial connective (,) in a program shall not alter the set of logically computable solutions. In the case of standard PROLOG, the left-to-right selection of calls embodied in the so-called 'computation rule' has the effect of confining search to some subspace of the total space of logically admissible computations; different orderings of calls in the input program determine different subspaces. However, when one or more serial connectives are replaced by // the execution of the program then traverses a more arbitrary region of the total space, this region being determined wholly by the relative speeds of the concurent processors. The solution set nevertheless remains unaltered.

The sharing of variables between concurrent executions potentially complicates the implementation of backtracking. For instance, suppose execution of the P subgoal in <- P(x,y),Q(y,z) binds data to y and subsequently fails. Meanwhile, the execution of the Q subgoal has proceeded to some extent after inheriting that data. Then in the course of backtracking P's execution, repealing the binding to y, it will normally be necessary also to backtrack Q's execution to the point where it inherited the binding. An implementation would therefore need to be capable of coordinating the management of the separate stacks associated with the concurrent executions.

3. PROGRAMMING STYLES FOR CONCURRENT ALGORITHMS

In general it is preferable to arrange that as little detail as possible regarding run-time control is programmed into the logic of procedure definitions, for various methodological reasons which are well documented in the logic programming literature. Nevertheless there must exist practical limits upon the complexity of extralogical control annotations. Consider, for instance, how algorithmically intricate such annotations would have to be in order to instruct an interpreter to elicit Dantzig's 'Simplex' algorithm from naive procedures expressing the meaning of linear optimization; they would assume the character of computer programs in their own right and would be more difficult to compose and verify than the procedures they were intended to control. Therefore in practice it is only realistic to expect 'cleverness' in implemented algorithms to derive mainly from the logical content of their procedures. This applies particularly to concurrent algorithms because their efficacy often depends upon carefully contrived communication between the various executions, whilst the control of this communication depends upon subtle, problem-specific logical relationships holding over the evolving data structures which those executions mutually compute and consult. So it is useful to find out what kind of logical constructions can help the programmer to arrange for efficient cooperation between concurrent executions. Some insight into this comes from investigation of a simple problem which is now examined in detail.

4. A CONCURRENT ALGORITHM

An algorithm is required to decide whether a given element E belongs to either of two given sets A and B, and is to achieve this by searching A and B concurrently. One simple way of doing this is to use a program like

```
<- /^/ belongs(E,A,B)
        belongs(u,x,y) <- u in x
        belongs(u,x,y) <- u in y
```

where the new annotation /^/ labels a call in order to indicate that all procedures responding to it are to be tried concurrently (so that the derived subgoals <- E in A and <- E in B would be assigned to distinct processors). Successful termination of any one of the ensuing executions would signal successful execution of the annotated call and simultaneously abandon any other unfinished executions instigated by it. Such an arrangement could be called disjunctive concurrency, since it is tantamount to solving the goal <- (E in A v E in B) by investigating its disjuncts concurrently. However, although such an annotation might have a useful role to play in the concurrent, quasi-breadth-first exploration of alternatives, it brings us no nearer to an understanding of how to arrange for concurrent executions to access and react to detailed knowledge about each other's progress. We shall therefore develop an alternative solution which does.

Instead of using a predicate like belongs, which needs to refer to both sets, introduce a predicate $m(u,x,a)$ which deals with just one set x. The specification of m is as follows:

$m(u,x,a) <--> (u$ in x, $a=YES) v (u$ in x, $a=NO)$

so that its third argument a acts as an explicit 'answer' to the question of whether u belongs to x. Using terms to represent sets, together with an appropriate definition of in, compose a straight-forward procedure set for m:

$$m(u,Nil,a) <- a=NO$$
$$m(u,v:x,a) <- u=v, a=YES$$
$$m(u,v:x,a) <- u{\neq}v, m(u,x,a) .$$

Now consider an execution X_1, running on a processor P_1, of a call $m(E,A,a_1)$ where E and A are well-formed input data. Suppose that a concurrent execution X_2, running on a processor P_2, is dealing with a call $m(E,B,a_2)$ and binds YES to a_2. If X_1 were somehow 'told' that YES had been bound to a_2, it could sensibly abandon its attempt to decide E in A, record an arbitrary answer DONTKNOW for a_1 and then terminate successfully. This suggests the use of an alternative predicate $m^*(u,x,a_1,a_2)$ which allows the answer a_1 computed for the question u in x to be contingent upon the state of a_2. Its specification just extends that for m in order to admit the alternative answer for a_1:

$m^*(u,x,a_1,a_2) <--> m(u,x,a_1) v (a_2=YES, a_1=DONTKNOW) .$

Procedures for m^* then follow by trivial transformation of those for m above:

$$C1: m^*(u,Nil,a_1,a_2) <- a_1=NO$$
$$C2: m^*(u,v:x,a_1,a_2) <- u=v, a_1=YES$$
$$C3: m^*(u,v:x,a_1,a_2) <- u{\neq}v, m^*(u,x,a_1,a_2)$$
$$C4: m^*(u,x,a_1,a_2) <- a_2=YES, a_1=DONTKNOW .$$

Procedures C1-C4 can now be used to solve the following goal whose two subgoals are to be dealt with by concurrent processors P_1 and P_2 respectively:

$$<- m^*(E,A,a_1,a_2) // m^*(E,B,a_2,a_1)$$

Observe that C_1-C_4 compute logically correct answers a_1 and

a_2 to this goal whether execution of the subgoals is concurrent or sequential. Note also that it is logically impossible to compute $a_1=a_2=$DONTKNOW but logically possible to compute $a_1=a_2=$YES. For efficiency's sake we wish to control execution in such a way as to prevent the latter case from being computed.

Once again suppose that X_2 confirms E in B and assigns YES to a_2. Meanwhile, X_1 is at the point of evaluating some derived subgoal $m*(E,A',a_1,a_2)$ where A' is the subset of A remaining to be searched for E. As soon as X_2 instantiates a_2 with YES we want X_1 to select C4 and terminate rather than select C1-C3; prior to this, X_1 should have been selecting C1-C3 in preference to C4. These control preferences, which are motivated towards the earliest possible termination, require some modifications to C1-C4, because they cannot be implemented merely by changing the procedures' input ordering or by decorating their heading arguments with selective data-flow annotations like those provided in IC-PROLOG.

As a first step towards achieving the desired behaviour, insert some checks $a_2 \neq$YES to obtain

$$C1': m*(u,Nil,a_1,a_2) <- a_2 \neq YES, a_1=NO$$
$$C2': m*(u,v:x,a_1,a_2) <- a_2 \neq YES, u=v, a_1=YES$$
$$C3': m*(u,v:x,a_1,a_2) <- a_2 \neq YES, u=v, m*(u,x,a_1,a_2)$$
$$C4=C4': m*(u,x,a_1,a_2) <- a_2=YES, a_1=DONTKNOW .$$

This does not affect (partial) correctness, since C1'-C4' are logically implied by C1-C4. The checks ensure that when a_2 has been instantiated by YES, searching with C1'-C3' is discontinued and termination by C4' follows immediately. However, these checks must not become operative until a_2 is instantiated, as they would otherwise cause nondeterministic behaviour. To guard against this we can exploit the annotations of IC-PROLOG which enable the selection of procedures to be controlled according to the states of the arguments in the invoking calls. This scheme works as follows. If any variable in some procedure's heading is suffixed by ? then that procedure can be invoked only if that variable would become bound to a non-variable term during the invocation step. Contrariwise, if any variable in the heading is suffixed by ^ then the procedure can be invoked only if that variable would not become bound to a non-variable during the invocation step. In each case, the procedure's invokability depends upon the actual arguments transmitted from the call in a more selective manner than that determined by unifiability alone.

Applying these ideas to the present example, we label the a_2
heading arguments of procedures C1-C3 and C1'-C4' and combine
the results as follows:

```
C1 : m*(u,Nil,a1,a2^) <- a1=NO
C1': m*(u,Nil,a1,a2?) <- a2≠YES, a1=NO
C2 : m*(u,v:x,a1,a2^) <- u=v, a1=YES
C2': m*(u,v:x,a1,a2?) <- a2≠YES, u=v, a1=YES
C3 : m*(u,v:x,a1,a2^) <- u=v, m*(u,x,a1,a2)
C3': m*(u,v:x,a1,a2?) <- a2≠YES, u=v, m*(u,x,a1,a2)
C4 : m*(u,x,a1,a2?) <- a2=YES, a1=DONTKNOW .
```

Now, for as long as the goal variable a_2 remains unbound,
only procedures C1-C3 are invokable, these being used to
compute a_1. If a_2 becomes bound, then only C1'-C4' are
invokable; these then compute a_1 according to the value of
a_2. This is the behaviour obtained when, as assumed
throughout this discussion, X_2 computes a_2 before X_1 has
terminated. The exact complement of this behaviour occurs, as
desired, if X_1 should instead compute a_1 before X_2 has
terminated.

The solutions for the goal variables (a_1,a_2) which are
logically computable from these procedures are (NO,NO),
(NO,YES),   (YES,YES),   (YES,NO),   (YES,DONTKNOW)   and
(DONTKNOW,YES); but when execution is constrained by the
given control annotations, the unwanted answer (YES,YES) is
not computable.

Finally, note that an alternative program can be derived by
extending rather than modifying C1-C4:

```
C1 : m*(u,Nil,a1,a2^) <- a1=NO
C2 : m*(u,v:x,a1,a2^) <- u=v, a1=YES
C3 : m*(u,v:x,a1,a2^) <- u≠v, m*(u,x,a1,a2)
C4 : m*(u,x,a1,a2?) <- a2=YES, a1=DONTKNOW
C5 : m*(u,x,a1,a2?) <- a2≠YES, m(u,x,a1)
```

together with the three given procedures for m.

This formulation arises by deriving a new m* procedure

```
m*(u,x,a1,a2) <- m(u,x,a1)
```

then inserting a check a_2 ≠YES and then annotating C1-C5
appropriately. It gives much the same behaviour but slightly
clearer logic.

5. THE GENERAL PRINCIPLES

The principles underlying the treatment above are as follows:
(1) Suppose that the problem to be solved has been formulated as a program intended for sequential call execution using a single processor - in other words, as a standard non-concurrent logic program.

Further suppose that the program's goal contains some call $P(t_1,...,t_r)$. Usually it will be possible to solve the problem more efficiently by simply arranging that one or more other calls are executed concurrently with this call to P. However, even greater improvement may be possible when that call is replaced by

$$p*(t_1,...,t_r,x_{r+1},...,x_n)$$

where the x_i variables are shared with the other concurrent calls. In effect, this replacement anticipates that useful data from concurrent executions will be transmitted to the x_i variables whilst the call P* is being executed, and thereby makes the goal more efficiently solvable than the original one which called P instead.

In the example, the goal for the non-concurrent formulation would have been <- $m(E,A,a_1)$, $m(E,B,a_2)$. This can be solved more efficiently by concurrent processing:
<- $m(E,A,a_1)$ // $m(E,B,a_2)$ and more efficiently by sharing the variables a_1 and a_2 between calls:
<- $m*(E,A,a_1,a_2)$ // $m*(E,B,a_2,a_1)$.

So here the transformation process outlined above has been applied to two calls in the goal. In this example the improvement in efficiency lies in the fact that new kinds of answers like (a_1,a_2) = (DONTKNOW,YES) will be accepted as solutions to the problem, and moreover will be more efficiently computable than (YES,YES).

(2) Compose procedures for P* capable of solving any activated call to P* which has only variables in its argument positions r+1 to n. In the example these procedures are C1-C4. They are the procedures which, in the final program, will be invoked in response to P* calls until such time as concurrent executions transmit data through the shared variables.

(3) Now freely insert into these procedures any number of arbitrary calls whose inspection of the arguments in positions r+1 to n of the invoking call, communicating data

from concurrent executions, improves efficiency. <u>This step</u>
<u>inevitably   preserves   partial   correctness</u>. Usually the
inserted calls are devised by considering how to obtain
optimal behaviour and may not simply arise as a natural
result of deriving sufficient P* procedures to deal with all
cases logically admitted by the P* specification.

In the example the insertions produced C1'-C4'. They are the
procedures which, in the final program, will be invoked in
response to P* calls after data computed by concurrent
executions has been transmitted to the shared variables.

(4) Combine the procedures from steps (2) and (3) and adorn
them with control annotations - these determine which
procedures to invoke in response to P* calls, according to
the instantaneous states (bound or unbound) of the shared
variables.

6. ANOTHER EXAMPLE

Owicki and Gries (1976) give a detailed account of an
algorithm proposed by Rosen (1974) which, given an input list
L of arbitrary numbers $L(1),\ldots,L(N)$, computes $i*$ as the
least i, if any, satisfying $L(i)>0$. If no such i exists then
$i*$ is computed as N+1. The algorithm pursues two concurrent
searches, one inspecting $L(i)$ for even i and the other
inspecting $L(i)$ for odd i. The former search computes j as
the least even i satisfying $L(i)>0$ if this exists, but
otherwise computes j=N+1. The latter search computes k
analogously for the odd-indexed members. Finally $i*$ is
computed as the least of j and k. The chief virtue of the
algorithm is that if one execution X_1 finds some $L(i)>0$ then
the other execution X_2 can respond either by setting its
answer to N+1 and terminating or else by continuing its own
search - depending on whether or not X_2 has yet searched
through L beyond $L(i)$. The usefulness of this consultation
between the searches derives from properties of the ordering
relation over list indices. It is therefore problem-specific,
and this is reflected in the logical structure of the
following formulation:

```
<- find*(L,N,2,j,k) // find*(L,N,1,k,j), least(j,k,i*)
   find*(x,n,i,j,k^) <- i<n, x(i)<0, find*(x,n,i+2,j,k)
   find*(x,n,i,j,k?) <- i<n, i<k, x(i)<0, find*(x,n,i+2,j,k)
   find*(x,n,i,j,k^) <- i<n, x(i)>0, j=i
   find*(x,n,i,j,k?) <- i<n, i<k, x(i)>0, j=i
   find*(x,n,i,j,k?) <- i>k, j=n+1
   find*(x,n,i,j,k)  <- i>n, j=n+1 .
```

These procedures can be derived quite easily according to the
principles already enunciated, beginning with a simple
program in which the two searches proceed sequentially and
independently:

```
<- find(L,N,2,j), find(L,N,1,k), least(j,k,i*)
   find(x,n,i,j) <- i≤n, x(i)≤0, find(x,n,i+2,j)
   find(x,n,i,j) <- i≤n, x(i)>0, j=i
   find(x,n,i,j) <- i>n, j=n+1 .
```

Here   find(x,n,i,j)   holds when   j   is the least $\hat{\imath}$ in
i,i+2,...,n   satisfying   x(i)>0,   if   any; otherwise j=n+1.
Then find is elaborated to find* and find* procedures are
composed satisfying the specification

$$\text{find*}(x,n,i,j,k) \longleftrightarrow \text{find}(x,n,i,j) \lor (i \geq k, j=n+1) .$$

Efficient control of these procedures, governed by the data-
flow through k, is then imposed using the annotations shown.

7. DISCUSSION

The treatment illustrated here is consistent with the usual
incremental approach to logic program development.
Disregarding concurrent capability, a suitable goal and
procedure set are composed which would execute correctly
under IC-PROLOG, with no restrictions imposed on the use of
the available control mechanisms. By reasoning about the
program's behaviour we decide how to obtain a more efficient
execution were concurrent processing available. If this
improvement requires no communication between concurrent
executions then it is obtainable by simply writing selected
conjuctions as //. Otherwise, new predicates are defined
which introduce shared variables as the vehicle of
communication, and the program is reformulated such as to
compute solutions consulting those variables' states.
Correctness-preserving modifications - typically insertion of
calls to manipulate the shared variables - are next applied
together with any further necessary control annotations. None
of these steps violate the formalism's first-order semantics.

The examples given here indicate that for logic programming
the introduction of concurrency does not require departure
from our usual way (see Hogger, 1981) of establishing partial
correctness (by deriving procedures from specification).
(However, termination proofs may become more tedious, though
no different in principle, through having to examine the

constraints imposed by control annotations.) In particular we can easily satisfy the 'non-interference' criterion proposed by Owicki and Gries (1976): namely that if a correctness proof for each concurrent execution, acting in isolation, is not invalidated by the addition of logical assertions about what the others compute, then the composite execution also proceeds correctly. For if, for each subgoal, we construct a separate verification of the logic procedures which it invokes, and if the entire goal is executed (concurrently or sequentially) such as to comply with its logical interpretation, then the union of these verifications is a verification for the complete goal. This is just a consequence of our being able to specify concurrency in the program text without altering its logical meaning.

There are several other aspects of concurrent logic programming which need to be properly researched. For example, it may be necessary to devise ways of specifying temporal coordination. In our examples neither execution needed to wait for results from the other, but in other cases waiting might be necessary; the existing coroutining facilities may not be able to express all such requirements in sufficient detail. At present we could assume a simple default strategy - that if, in response to a call, all logically responding procedures were blocked by data-flow restrictions, then the call would just suspend (rather than, as at present, register a control error) until data became available from other executions. A possible effect of such arrangements is deadlock - the relevance of this to logic programming makes an interesting research topic.

Also, logic programs can accomodate at least two kinds of concurrency (conjunctive and disjunctive) having differing logical associations (nondeterministic call activation and nondeterministic procedure invocation). Some descriptions of other formalisms do not seems to provide clear relationships between their notions of concurrency and nondeterminism, and it may be that clarification could be obtained by comparison with the various nondeterministic features of logic.

Finally, there are other ways in which executions can communicate besides through shared variables. An interesting alternative is the use of global assertions regarded as data structures, supported by mechanisms for enabling concurrent executions to update and interrogate them communally. For both modes of communication it will be useful to discover their practical limitations in order to understand better why the originators of other formalisms, such as Hoare's CSP

(1978) and Brinch Hansen's Concurrent PASCAL (1975) have considered it necessary to rely upon intermediate devices like specialized input-output regimes and monitor processes in preference to global data sharing.

8. RELATED WORK

Examples of concurrent logic programs requiring temporal coordination have been studied by Winterstein et al. (1980). They have also resorted to labelling variables in procedure headings as a means of controlling procedure invocation according to data-flow through global variables, but with the difference that their method decides whether calls either invoke the labelled procedures or suspend in a 'wait' state. They deal successfully with examples such as the classic consumer-producer problem. Their approach is also semantically pure despite their expressed doubts to the contrary.

Pseudo-parallel programs intended for monoprocessing have been studied by Pereira and Monteiro (1978). They define, in logic, the properties of various interpreters whose own executions elicit serial, pseudo-parallel or coroutined behaviour from logic programs submitted as data. Formal proofs are given of certain completeness and equivalence properties of the interpreters. They also consider how to specify true parallelism within logic programs, introducing a number of special evaluable predicates for interrogating the states of variables and for implementing suspension of calls. These devices appear to be more cumbersome than ours although they serve much the same purpose. However, they do not clearly demarcate the respective contributions of logic and control to their concurrent algorithm formulations.

Other researchers who have discussed concurrent logic programs include Tärnlund (1975), who has examined parallel unification algorithms, and Clark and McCabe (1980), who have implemented pseudo-parallelism in IC-PROLOG.

ACKNOWLEDGEMENT

This paper revises that presented to the Logic Programming Workshop held in Debrecen, Hungary in July 1980. The original paper benefited from earlier discussions with members of the Theory of Computing Research Group at Imperial College, in particular Keith Clark and Robert Kowalski.

INTERMISSION — ACTORS IN PROLOG

Kenneth M. Kahn

UPMAIL, Uppsala University
Computing Science Department
S-750 02 Uppsala, Sweden

ABSTRACT

Prolog as a computer language offers simplicity, power, and a declarative interpretation of programs. Computer languages based upon computational entities called "actors" offer modularity, parallelism, full extensibility and a simple but powerful computational semantics. Prolog is not well-suited for controlling computation, for defining new data types, or for writing programs that are independent of the physical representation of their data. This paper introduces the concept and motivation for actors and then describes a system called "Intermission" which implements actors in Prolog. The thesis presented is that a hybrid of actors and logic programming is a strong alternative to a language based upon either concept alone.

1. INTRODUCTION AND MOTIVATION

During the last ten years there has been much research on a new kind of computational entity, variously known as "actors", "objects", and "abstract objects". An actor combines both procedure and data into a single object. Actors perform computation via "message passing". Various computer languages have been built upon actors, among them are Smalltalk (Goldberg, 1976; Kay, 1977), Act 1 (a descendant of Plasma) (Hewitt, 1977; Lieberman, 1981) and Director (Kahn, K., 1978; 1979).

Among the advantages of building systems in such languages are increased modularity and extensibility. Actors are also very well-suited for describing parallel processing. On highly parallel hardware it is anticipated that actor programs will be simplier and more efficient than the traditional alternatives.

Prolog (Coelho et al. 1980; Warren, 1977) is a programming language that has the unique feature that programs written in it can be viewed either procedurally or declaratively as logical statements. However, as a high-level programming language it has certain deficiencies. It is difficult to write programs that are not dependent upon the representation of the data. A typical sort program, for example, works only upon lists as they are provided by Prolog and a different version is needed for difference lists or other kinds of lists. It is also quite awkward in Prolog to handle "virtual data objects", such as the list of successive natural numbers whose parts are computed as needed. In general it is difficult to delay computations until they are needed. The ability to construct new kinds of data structures in Prolog is limited to those that can be represented by terms and list structures. These very general data structures are on occasion extremely inefficient in comparison with more specialized structures such as arrays or bit strings. Other more general data structures are often more convenient than those whose parts are accessed by their position in the structure. The "packagers" of Act 1 which support named subcomponents and partial descriptions are an example of such. As I hope to show, many of these deficiencies of Prolog can be remedied by the inclusion of actors.

This report describes an implementation in Prolog of actors modeled after the Act 1 language. The implementation is called Intermission.

There is another motivation for implementing actors in Prolog besides the alleviation of the above mentioned deficiencies: that is that it may lead to a better or different actor semantics. The logical view of Prolog programs applies to Prolog programs that implement actors. Certain unusual features of Prolog carry over to the actors implemented in Prolog. The possibility of reversing the normal "input" and "output" variables of a Prolog relation, for example, changes the normal semantics of actor computations. The ability to use the same program in many different ways is very attractive and adds new dimensions to actor programs.

2. WHAT IS AN ACTOR

An actor is a computational entity that combines in a single unit both program and data. Actors therefore subsume both procedures, functions, and all kinds of data structures. Computation is performed only by sending messages. It is not possible to reach inside an actor or change an actor without sending that actor a message requesting such an operation. This guarantees the integrity of the objects of computation. The programs written in an actor language depend only upon the behavior of modules and not upon their physical representation.

An actor consists of two parts: a "script" which decides what should be done with incoming messages and a set of "acquaintances" which are the other actors that the actor knows. The acquaintances play the role of local data for the actor. An actor can only send a message to someone it knows, i.e. either to one of its acquaintances or to someone referred to in the incoming message.

Actors can represent a data type in many different ways and the programs that use them need not know which representation it is dealing with. For example, one can define matrices as two-dimensional arrays, or as pairs of indices and values (perhaps stored in a hash table), or as a procedure that computes the values as needed. The first alternative is the traditional way of representing matrices and exploits the way memory is addressed in conventional computers. The second one provides great savings of space and time if the matrix is large and sparse. The third alternative is ideal for special matrices such as identity matrices.

Since programs depend only upon the behavior of the "data" there is no difficulty defining infinite objects such as the list of prime numbers. Lists are actors that accept messages asking for their first and rest components, for printing, for determining equality with other lists, and for matching against other lists. Some lists accept other messages such as those asking for its length or to append another list to itself. There are no constraints that such lists must be explicitly represented or finite.

In a totally consistent actor system, it is relatively easy to add actors that represent computations yet to be done or that are being done in parallel (perhaps even on another processor). The actor can be passed around, inserted in lists, and the like and only when its value is needed must the computation involved finish. Again the dependence upon the behavior, as opposed to the physical implementation of a data structure, makes this possible.

3. HOW TO PUT ACTORS INTO PROLOG

If one were adding actors to Prolog to produce a better practical computer language then they would have to be incorporated at a low level of implementation. They would have the same status as functors, symbols and numbers have in current implementations of Prolog. However, this report describes an incorporation of actors in Prolog whose purpose is to clarify and explore the issues and ideas involved. As a consequence, the actors are added to Prolog in a very clean, general, and flexible manner that is unfortunately extremely inefficient. The implementation has proved adequate for running simple programs like quick sort or the sieve of Eratosthenes and for implementing six or seven different types of lists. We implement "bi-directional" message passing with the relation "sent" between a TARGET, a MESSAGE, and the RESULT of the transmitting the MESSAGE to the TARGET.

Let us consider a simple implementation of lists to illustrate the relation. Of course, since Prolog already has lists this is meant solely as an illustration of the basic ideas. It turns out we will represent actors as Prolog lists, so this clearly will not make Prolog more powerful - later examples are for that. Actors are represented as lists whose first element is their type which plays the role of the "script" and the rest of the list are the "acquaintances" of the actor.

First we define the message "first" which returns the first element of the actor list, and the message "rest" which returns the rest of the list. (Lower case words are literals; upper case are variables.)

```
sent((list,FIRST,REST),first,FIRST).
sent((list,FIRST,REST),rest,REST).
```

For example, to find the rest of the list (A B) we type the following to Intermission.

```
sent((list,A,(list,B,(empty-list))),rest,R).
/* and the system responds */
R = (list,B,(empty-list))
```

Next we define a means of making lists by adding new elements in front (i.e. "cons" in Lisp).

```
sent((list,FIRST,REST),(add-element,NEW-ELEMENT),
               (list,NEW-ELEMENT,(list,FIRST,REST))).
```

To get started we need the empty list, which we will represent as an actor without any acquaintances.

```
sent((empty-list),(add-element,NEW-ELEMENT),
               (list,NEW-ELEMENT,(empty-list))).
```

Now suppose we want our lists to respond to "length" messages. We could define this as follows:

```
sent((list,FIRST,REST),length,N) :-  /* the length is N if */
  sent(REST,length,M),   /* the length of its rest is M and */
  sent(M,(+,1),N).       /* N = M + 1
                          (numbers are described below) */
sent((empty-list),length,0).  /* the empty list is 0 long */
```

To extend our lists so that they can respond to messages asking if they are equal to another list, we have the following:

```
sent((list,FIRST,REST),(equal,ANOTHER-LIST),true) :-
  sent(ANOTHER-LIST,(are-you-a,list),true),   /* is other
                                                 a list */
  sent(ANOTHER-LIST,first,OTHERS-FIRST),/* is other's first */
  sent(FIRST,(equal,OTHERS-FIRST),true),   /* equal to mine */
  sent(ANOTHER-LIST,rest,OTHERS-REST),      /* and his rest */
  sent(REST,(equal,OTHERS-REST),true).   /* equal to mine */
```

We define empty lists to equal themselves.

```
sent((empty-list),(equal,(empty-list)),true).
```

We introduced a new message of general usefulness that verifies the type of the actor. We need both lists and the empty list to answer yes to the question "are you a list".

```
sent((empty-list),(are-you-a,list),true).
sent((list,FIRST,REST),(are-you-a,list),true).
```

There remains a problem at this point. Suppose we have the list (A B C) and we ask it are you equal to (Z B C) then it will ask A if it is equal to Z. But A and Z are Prolog symbols not actors. The solution to this problem that we take

is similar to that taken by Act 1 in handling "rock bottom"
actors. We represent numbers and symbols specially but they
still behave just like full-fledged actors. The representation we choose is Prolog's. For example, to enable Prolog
symbols to answer "equal" message we do the following:

```
sent(SYMBOL,(equal,SYMBOL),true) :- atomic(SYMBOL).
```

4. A LIST OF INTEGERS

The actor lists we just defined have no advantages over
Prolog lists and are more complex and awkward. An example
that points to some of the advantages of the actor approach
is a list of integers. We can represent a large class of them
simply by an actor with three acquaintances: the first
element, the last element, and the difference between
successive elements. We can define "first" and "rest"
messages for such lists as follows:

```
sent((nlist,BEGIN,END,INCREMENT),first,BEGIN).
sent((nlist,BEGIN,END,INCREMENT),
     rest,
     (nlist,NEW-BEGIN,END,INCREMENT)) :-
          /* add INCREMENT to BEGIN to get the NEW-BEGIN */
   sent(BEGIN,(+,INCREMENT),NEW-BEGIN).
```

The "rest" message can be read as "if a list of numbers is
asked for the rest of its elements it answers with a list of
numbers just like itself except that the first element is the
old first element plus the increment." Notice that the
addition is performed by actors; the first number is sent the
message "add the value of increment" to yourself. Numbers are
able to take messages like this because they are "rock
bottom" actors with message handlers such as the following:

```
sent(NUMBER,(+,ANOTHER),RESULT) :-
   integer(NUMBER),
   integer(ANOTHER),                /* if they are both numbers */
   RESULT is ANOTHER + NUMBER.          /* then add them */
```

We could go on and define "equal", "length", "are-you-a", and
"print" messages for these new kinds of lists but some of it
will be a repetition of the previous clauses. Other kinds of
lists will be defined and some will have even more in common
with the behavior of our actor lists. The solution to this
problem in Act 1 and Director is "message delegation". When
an actor does not know how to handle a particular message it

"delegates" it to someone it thinks can handle it for him. This actor which delegates is called the "client" and it delegates to its "proxy". Delegation is implemented by having the following two clauses be the last ones of "sent".

```
sent(ANYONE,MESSAGE,RESULT) :-          /* if an actor can't
                    handle a message we ask it for its proxy */
    sent(ANYONE,proxy,PROXY),           /* and send the PROXY a
                    message to handle this for the actor */
    sent(PROXY,(handle-for,ANYONE,MESSAGE),RESULT).

sent(ANYONE,(handle-for,CLIENT,MESSAGE),RESULT) :-
    /* and if a proxy cannot handle the problem passed to him,
                    he passes it on along to his proxy */
    sent(ANYONE,proxy,PROXY),
    sent(PROXY,(handle-for,CLIENT,MESSAGE),RESULT).
```

This simple scheme greatly increases the power of the actor system by facilitating the sharing of knowledge. The programmer now can place knowledge at as high a level of abstraction as desired. For example, we can define a "print" message for all kinds of lists as follows:

```
sent(list,(handle-for,LIST,print)) :-
    write('('),                         /* print an open parenthesis */
    sent(LIST,print-elements),/*print the elements of the list*/
    write(' )').                        /* print a close parenthesis */

sent(list,(handle-for,LIST,print-elements)) :-
    write(' '),
    sent(LIST,first,FIRST),
    sent(FIRST,print),      /* send "print" to the first element */
    sent(LIST,rest,REST),
    sent(REST,print-elements)./* "print elements" to the rest */
```

Now if we declare that our number lists have the generic "list" actor as a "proxy" as follows:

```
sent(nlist,proxy,list).
```

then we can print "nlists" without difficulty. For example,

```
sent((nlist,1,15,2),print).
/* the previous command causes the following to be printed */
( 1 3 5 7 9 11 13 15 )
```

This is fine but how should a list like "(nlist,1,1000000,1)" be printed? The delegation mechanism provides only a default behavior, we can override it in this case as follows:

```
sent(nlist,(handle-for,LIST,print-elements)) :-        /* nlist
        picks up "handle for" messages so it can be a proxy */
    sent(LIST,length,LENGTH),    /* find the length of the list */
    sent(LENGTH,(>,5),true),          /* and its greater then 5 */
    sent(LIST,print-elements-with-dots)./* print it specially */

sent(nlist,(handle-for,LIST,print-elements-with-dots)) :-
    write(' '),
    sent(LIST,first,FIRST),
    sent(FIRST,print),                    /* print the first element */
    write(' '),
    sent(LIST,2,SECOND),        /* Lists can respond to numbers
                                      with their Nth element */
    sent(SECOND,print),            /* print the second element */
    write(' '),
    sent(LIST,3,THIRD),
    sent(THIRD,print),                 /* print the third element */
    write(' ... '),                        /* print three dots */
    sent(LIST,last,END), /* ask the list for its last element */
    sent(END,print).           /* and print the last element */
```

Our change has not affected lists of numbers with less than 6
elements. However if we try to print the first million
integers, the list behaves sensibly as follows:

```
sent((nlist,1,1000000,1),print).
( 1 2 3 ...  1000000 )
```

Notice that our print method asks the list for its length.
This could be quite expensive considering that the general
method for length keeps sending "rest" messages until the
list is empty. (One part of our "nlist" actor that has been
omitted here are the clauses that determine if an "nlist" is
empty.) We can fix this by adding a method which simply finds
the difference between the first and last element and divides
by the increment when asked for the length. Alternatively, we
can extend lists to accept "are you longer than n" messages.
A similar problem exists with the "last" element message.
This one is trivial for "nlist" to handle and quite expensive
if the general method in "list" handles it. As it turns out,
we have defined "nlists" in such a way that they can
represent infinite lists. For example, the list of all the
positive odd integers is just "(nlist,1,(infinity),2)".
"Infinity" is just a number actor which has clauses such as
the following:

```
sent((infinity),proxy,number).          /* infinity delegates
                                                    to number */
sent((infinity),(+,ANYONE),infinity). /* infinity+x =
                                                   infinity */
sent((infinity),(>,ANYONE),true)./*infinity is the greatest*/
```

Properly all the clauses of "infinity" should be modified to make sure that the other number which it is being compared with is not itself infinity. The list of odd integers can be added to, taken apart, printed, asked its length, and so on. For example,

```
sent((nlist,1,(infinity),2),print).
(1 3 5 ... infinity)

sent((nlist,1,(infinity),2),length,L).
L=(infinity).
```

5. DELAYED COMPUTATIONS

Sometimes it is easy to describe what each object or process in a computation should be or do but the parts depend upon each other in such complex ways that it is difficult to order the events. One would like to have each process run in parallel and wait when they need some value that has yet to be computed. Actor systems are well-suited for describing parallel processing because of message passing and the internalization and localization of state descriptions. However, since achieving concurrency within Prolog would require major changes to the interpreter the actor primitives for parallelism were not implemented. A primitive for delaying computations until the value is needed has, however, been implemented. It is especially useful for computing with infinite objects. The default behavior for "delay" messages could be defined as follows:

```
sent(actor,(handle-for,CLIENT,(delay,MESSAGE)),
           (delayed-transmission,CLIENT,MESSAGE,VALUE)).
```

If any actor receives a message beginning with "delay" followed by a message it "returns" an actor that is a delayed transmission whose acquaintances are the original recipient of the message, the delayed message, and a variable representing the to-be-computed result of sending the message to the actor. The next problem is to define delayed transmissions as actors that when they get a message finally do the delayed action and then send the message on along to the result.

```
sent((delayed-transmission,TARGET,DELAYED-MESSAGE,VALUE),
     MESSAGE,RESULT) :-
  sent(TARGET,DELAYED-MESSAGE,VALUE),        /* do delayed
                                                computation */
  sent(VALUE,MESSAGE,RESULT).              /* and send MESSAGE
                                              to the RESULT */
```

The difficulty with this solution is that the actor will recompute its delayed computation every time it is sent a message. We would like it to compute it the first time only and from then on have it behave as the result. To avoid this we take advantage of Prolog's ability to compute with partially instantiated structures. The first time the computation is performed "value" is instantiated. To take advantage of this we add the following:

```
sent((delayed-transmission,TARGET,DELAYED-MESSAGE,VALUE),
     MESSAGE,RESULT) :-
  nonvar(VALUE),/* If the VALUE is instantiated, then use it*/
  sent(VALUE,MESSAGE,RESULT)./*and send MESSAGE to the VALUE*/
```

One use of this "delay" message is to construct the lists of integers by extending our "list" actor as follows:

```
sent(list,(integers-beginning,N),RESULT) :-
  sent(N,(+,1),N-PLUS-ONE),
  sent(list,(delay,
          (integers-beginning,N-PLUS-ONE)),DELAYED-REST),
  sent(list,(add-element,N,DELAYED-REST),RESULT).
```

The result of sending a "integers beginning 1" message to "list" is the list of natural numbers. "Result" is bound to "(list,1,DELAYED-REST)" where "delayed-rest" is a delayed transmission of sending "integers beginning 2" to "list". An example of using such a list is in implementing a very old algorithm for computing prime numbers called the "sieve of Eratosthenes". The idea is simple. You repeatedly take the first element of a list, add it to the list of primes, and delete all multiples of it from the list. The list is initially the integers beginning with 2. With actors and "delay" messages there are no difficulties dealing with these infinite objects and computations. We can define the list of primes as follows:

```
sent(list,create-primes,THE-PRIMES) :-
  sent(list,(integers-beginning,2),NUMBERS),
  sent(NUMBERS,sift,THE-PRIMES).
```

```
sent(list,(handle-for,LIST,sift),RESULT):-
sent(LIST,first,FIRST),
sent(LIST,rest,REST),
                /* now we perform the delayed computation */
sent(REST,(cross-out-those-divisible-by,FIRST),THOSE-LEFT),
sent(THOSE-LEFT,(delay,sift),PRIMES),
sent(list,(add-element,FIRST,PRIMES),RESULT).

sent(list,(handle-for,LIST,(cross-out-those-divisible-by,N)),
    RESULT) :-
sent(LIST,first,FIRST),
sent(LIST,rest,REST),
sent(FIRST,(mod,N),MOD),
cross-out-helper(FIRST,REST,MOD,N,RESULT).

cross-out-helper(FIRST,REST,0,N,RESULT) :-
        /* mod is 0 means that this one is a multiple of N */
sent(REST,(delay,(cross-out-those-divisible-by,N)),RESULT).

cross-out-helper(FIRST,REST,-,N,RESULT) :-         /* is not a
            multiple of N so keep it and delay the recursion */
sent(REST,(delay,
            (cross-out-those-divisible-by,N)),THOSE-LEFT),
sent(list,(add-element,FIRST,THOSE-LEFT),RESULT).
                                        /* the commands: */
sent(list,create-primes,P), sent(P,print).
                /* results in the following being typed */
( 2 3 5 7 11 13 17       /* until we interrupt the program */
```

6. DATA REPRESENTATION FREE PROGRAMMING

The original instigation of this research was reading two
Prolog programs: one for quick sorting an ordinary list and
another for difference lists (Hansson and Tärnlund, 1979;
Hansson, 1980). Using Intermission's message passing we can
write a quick sort that works for any sort of list as
follows:

```
sent(list,(handle-for,LIST,(quick-sort,RELATION)),LIST) :-
        /* the sorted version of any empty list is itself */
sent(LIST,empty,true).
```

```
sent(list,
    (handle-for,LIST,(quick-sort,RELATION)),SORTED-LIST) :-
  sent(LIST,first,FIRST),
  sent(LIST,rest,REST),
      /* Partition the list into two parts - those which are
  RELATION (e.g. less than) of FIRST and those that are not */
  sent(REST,(partition-by,(RELATION,FIRST)),TRUES,FALSES),
                        /* sort the two smaller lists */
  sent(TRUES,(quick-sort,RELATION),FIRST-PART-SORTED),
  sent(FALSES,(quick-sort,RELATION),REST-SORTED),
                    /* put the sorted lists together */
  sent(REST-SORTED,(add-element,FIRST),NEW-REST-SORTED),
  sent(FIRST-PART-SORTED,(append,NEW-REST-SORTED),SORTED-LIST).

sent(list,(handle-for,LIST,
                  (partition-by,PREDICATE)),LIST,LIST)
        /* If a list is empty it partitions into itself */
  :- sent(LIST,empty,true).

sent(list,(handle-for,LIST,(partition-by,PREDICATE)),
      TRUES,FALSES) :-
  /* partition LIST by whether the PREDICATE is true or not */
  sent(LIST,first,FIRST),
  sent(LIST,rest,REST),
  sent(FIRST,PREDICATE,true),
  sent(REST,(partition-by,PREDICATE),REST-TRUES,FALSES),
  sent(REST-TRUES,(add-element,FIRST),TRUES).

sent(list,(handle-for,LIST,(partition-by,PREDICATE)),
      TRUES,FALSES) :-
      /* this handles the case where the Predicate is false */
  sent(LIST,first,FIRST),
  sent(LIST,rest,REST),
  sent(FIRST,PREDICATE,false),
  sent(REST,(partition-by,PREDICATE),TRUES,REST-FALSES),
  sent(REST-FALSES,(add-element,FIRST),FALSES).
```

Notice that this quick sort procedure works for any kind of
list and any partial ordering of elements. For example, it
works on Intermission's ordinary lists, lists of integers
(finite ones only), difference lists, lists of lists (an
implementation of lists which behaves as if all the sub-lists
were appended together) and others. One somewhat silly test
which shows off some of the features of Intermission is one
in which a list of all different sorts of lists is sorted by
their length. Some of the elements are infinite lists. All
that was required for this test was to extend lists to answer
messages asking if they are longer than another list.

7. OTHER WAYS THE FEATURES OF INTERMISSION MIGHT BE PROVIDED

We have shown how by replacing the data types of Prolog with actors we have increased the expressive power of the language. Certain kinds of data structures that were difficult to express in Prolog (such as infinite lists) are not difficult in Intermission. Intermission also provides more control over the computation as exemplified by the "delay" message. Intermission programs are by their very nature independent of the representation of the data. One question that needs to be answered is whether these advantages of Intermission could not have been achieved easily in Prolog. We need to emphasize the word "easily" in our question since we are dealing with Universal Computers that are Turing equivalent. For example, suppose instead of sending messages, we have Prolog relations for dealing with all data structures.

```
sent((list,FIRST,REST),first,FIRST). /* Intermission's way */
first((FIRST,REST),FIRST).           /* Prolog's way */
```

This scheme is admittedly simpler and a less drastic departure from ordinary usage of Prolog but is much more limited than the message passing actor system in Intermission since it represents the message as relation. The scheme gets more awkward when the message is a list structure (e.g. "partition-by predicate"). Operations such as delegation and delay which apply to all kinds of messages are very difficult to express in this setup. Also, Prolog provides little support for this form of restricted representation-independent programming such as convenient syntax or efficient compilation.

8. PROBLEMS WITH INTERMISSION

There are many problems with Intermission of course. The syntax is very awkward and verbose. This is not a consequence of the use of actors or message passing but of how Intermission was built upon Prolog. Delegation, for example, requires handlers for "handle for ..." messages. With the proper defaulting this level of detail would not appear in any user's program as is the case in most actor languages. The worst problem with the syntax of Intermission compared to Prolog is the use of explicit constructors and selectors instead of pattern matching. This is ironic since in most other actor languages pattern matching is an essential part of the language. Intermission can only partially make use of

Prolog's pattern matching because it is representation
dependent. Two behaviorly equivalent, but syntactically
different, terms are not unifiable. What is needed in Intermission is a pattern like "(Head,..Tail)" which will match
any kind of list while binding "Head" and "Tail" to the
result of sending a "first" and a "rest" message, respectively, to the list. These syntactic problems with Intermission could be overcome by placing a "front end" parser
between Intermission programs and Prolog or by changing the
Prolog interpreter.

Certain deficiencies with Prolog have been inherited by
Intermission. For example, in the presence of backtracking it
is difficult to describe default behavior. The delegation
mechanism is intended to take over only when the actor in
question cannot handle the current message. One cannot
describe a pattern for all the messages that an actor cannot
handle directly and instead one is forced to rely upon the
search order of Prolog's theorem prover so that the
delegation clauses are tried only after all the others have.

Debugging in Prolog is very difficult compared to an actor or
Lisp-like language. The major difficulty is the lack of a
distinction between failures and errors. Both cause backtracking, however in the case where the program has a "bug"
this leads to bizarre behavior (e.g. message delegation in an
inappropriate situation) and often the program will not
terminate.

The most serious short-coming of Intermission as a practical
programming language is that it is terribly slow and
inefficient. This is a consequence of the way in which actors
will built on top of Prolog instead of being incorporated at
a much lower level. Much of the inefficiency is also due to
the lack of control over Prolog's search behavior.

There is no reason to believe that the use of actors and
message passing necessarily entails computational inefficiencies. Experience with Act 1, Director, and Smalltalk
indicate that much (if not all) of the "overhead" of actors
and message passing can be compiled out without any loss of
flexibility. Many researchers anticipate actor compilers that
will be more efficient than those of conventional languages
because the programs being compiled rely only upon the
behavior of the objects involved leaving the compiler great
freedom in performing optimizations.

Also there has been much research that suggests that the

actor model of computation leads to programs that can fully exploit the parallel processors of the not-too-distant future.

9. POSSIBLE CONTRIBUTIONS TO THE ACTOR MODEL OF COMPUTATION

This research was performed with two goals: to improve Prolog by adding actors and to improve actors by implementing them in Prolog in such a way so as to preserve some of its unusual features. One beneficial side-effect of this research is that Intermission seems to be a good way of introducing actors and message passing concepts to a community familiar with Logic Programming.

One very appealing feature of Prolog is the ability to use the same program in many ways. For example, the Prolog definition of "append" can be used not only to compute the result of appending two lists together but can also be used as a predicate to verify if the result of appending two lists is a third list, as a generator of pairs of lists that append to a particular list, as a way of finding the difference between two lists, and as a generator of triples of lists such that the first two appended form the third.

This feature of Prolog has only partially been preserved in Intermission. The problem is that when sending a message to an uninstantiated actor Prolog often never terminates while it creates more and more examples of the wrong kind of actor. The difficulty is primarily the inability to control Prolog's search. Prologs with control primitives such as IC-Prolog might alleviate these problems. (Clark et al. 1982).

One of the most important features of Prolog is that the programs have both a declarative logical interpretation and a procedural one. Because of the way Intermission was built upon Prolog, programs written in Intermission also have these two interpretations. This is important for several reasons. Sometimes the declarative interpretation is simpler and thus it is easier to write and debug programs in such cases. The task of implementing programs that understand themselves is eased by the ability to reason about the code as logical statements. Verification of programs is made easier by taking a logical interpretation of the code. There is also the possibility that theorem provers could derive programs from specifications (Hansson and Tärnlund, 1979; Hansson, 1980).

10. FUTURE RESEARCH

Experience is needed using Intermission for more than "toy" programs. Before this can be done a more efficient and practical implementation needs to be made. The big problem here is how to accomplish this while preserving the features of Prolog, especially the declarative interpretation of programs. One view of this research is that it is an attempt to generalize the "procedural" interpretation of Prolog programs without losing the declarative.

Another avenue of research is to implement a Prolog-like language in an actor language such as Act 1. This would help clarify the relationship between the two languages and would provide many of Act 1's features to Prolog. The idea here is similar to that behind QLOG (Komorowski, 1979) which provides Interlisp features to Prolog. An implementation of a Prolog-like language in Act 1 was attempted by the author. It lead to a new language called "Uniform" (implemented in Lisp for pragmatic reasons) which extends unification to such an extent that no other mechanism is needed. (Kahn, K., 1981).

ACKNOWLEDGMENTS

I would like to thank Sten-Åke Tärnlund for his help and encouragement with this research. I am also indebted to Carl Hewitt for most of the ideas about actors incorporated in Intermission and to Henry Lieberman whose actor language Act 1 was the model for Intermission.

LOGIC PROGRAMMING LANGUAGES

PROLOG AND INFINITE TREES

Alain Colmerauer

Groupe Intelligence Artificielle
Faculté des Sciences de Luminy
Université Aix-Marseille II
13288 Marseille cedex 2, France

ABSTRACT

The paper deals with the manipulation of infinite trees in the context of the programming language Prolog. With this purpose a novel and concise model of Prolog is presented. The model does not explicity involve the first order logic. The problem of unifying two terms is replaced by that of determining whether or not a system of equations has at least one solution. Several examples of the use of infinite trees are also given.

1. FOREWORD

Prolog is a programming language that has been developed in Marseille, mainly by Roussel and Colmerauer in (Battani, 1973; Colmerauer et al. 1973; Roussel, 1975). The name "Prolog" was given by Roussel for "Pro(gramming) in log(ic)". Originally, it was a theorem prover based on the resolution principle of Robinson (1965), with strong restrictions to reduce the search space: linear proof, unification applying only on the first literal of each clause, etc... Credit is given to van Emden and Kowalski (1976) for having proposed a very simple theoretical model, the Horn clauses, which explains our restrictions and specifies exactly what Prolog tries to compute (minimal Herbrand interpretation).

However, there is a basic difference between most Prolog interpreters and the theoretical model: for efficiency purposes the interpreters utilize a simplified variant of the unification algorithm. The simplification consists of

suppressing the "occur check", that is, to allow the unification of a variable with a term already containing this
variable. This simplification may be unsafe but the
efficiency gains are considerable. For example, with the
"occur check", the concatenation of two lists requires (at
least) a time proportional to the square of the size of the
first list. If the "occur check" is eliminated the time
becomes linear. This is the case even when considering the
fastest unification algorithms available (Baxter, 1976;
Martelli and Montanari, 1976; Paterson and Wegman, 1976).

The objective of this paper is to describe a novel theoretical model of Prolog involving infinite trees. This model
corresponds to the Prolog interpreters which do not perform
the "occur check". However, the unification algorithm for
these interpreters must be modified so as to assure termination. The best way to achieve this termination is an open
problem which is not discussed here.

The availability of elaborate data structures such as as
infinite trees allow novel solutions to programming problems.
Several examples of these solutions are given. The examples
were tested using a recent Prolog system developed by
Colmerauer et al. (1981) and which incorporates the ideas
proposed herein.

2. RATIONAL TREES

In Prolog each variable represents a finite tree which is
constructed over a set F of functional symbols. To unify the
variable x with the term f(a,x), means that x is also allowed
to represent the infinite tree in (1).

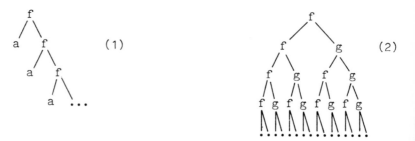

An infinite tree is a tree with an infinite set of nodes. We
need only consider a special class of infinite trees: the
"rational" trees.

DEFINITION: a "rational" tree is a tree which has a finite set of subtrees.

The tree in (1) is rational because it contains only the two subtrees: itself and the one node tree a. The tree in (2) is also rational, because it contains only two subtrees. However, the tree:

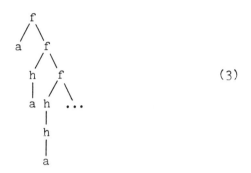

(3)

is not rational since the set of its subtrees is not finite.

A rational tree may be transformed into a finite diagram by "merging" all the nodes from which the same subtrees start. For the two previous rational trees we obtain respectively:

(4)   (5)

These diagrams are the "minimal representations" of the two infinite trees. The number of nodes in each diagram equals the number of subtrees of the tree. Notice that even the minimal representation of a finite tree may contain fewer nodes than the tree itself. For example:

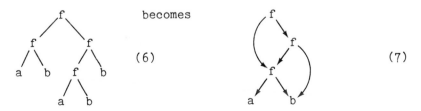

becomes

(6)   (7)

3. SYSTEM OF EQUATIONS

In addition to the set F of functional symbols, we introduce an infinite set V of variables which allows us to construct terms over $F_U V$.

A "tree-assignment" X is a finite set of ordered pairs of the form:

$$X = \{x_1 := r_1, \ x_2 := r_2, \ \ldots, \ x_n := r_n\}$$

where the r_i's are (possibly infinite) trees and the x_i's are distinct variables. If a given term t contains no variables other than the x_i's in X, then t/X denotes the tree defined by:

if t = x_i then   t/X = r_i
if t = $ft_1 \ldots t_m$ then   t/X = f (the one node tree f when m=o)
                                       /\
                              $t_1/X \ldots t_m/X$

An "equation" is an ordered pair of terms (s,t) written as s=t and a tree-assignment X is a "tree-solution" of this equation iff s/X= t/X.

By systems of equations we mean only finite sets of equations. A tree-assignment X is a tree-solution of a system E of equations iff X is a subset of a tree-assignement which is a tree-solution of every equation in E.

Let us consider a system of equations of the form:
$\{x_1=u_1, \ \ldots, \ x_n=u_n\}$, where the x_i's are distinct variables and each u_i contains exactly one functional symbol and no variables other than the x_i's.

It can be shown that such a system has exactly one tree-solution of the form $\{x_1 := r_1, \ \ldots, \ x_n := r_n\}$ and that the r_i's are rational trees. The proof of this property is beyond the scope of this paper.

For example, to the system: $\{x_1=f(x_2,x_1), \ x_2=a\}$ corresponds diagram (8) which gives the tree-solution in (9).

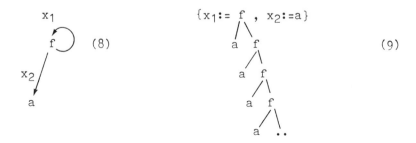

This leads to the first result:

SOLVABLE FORM: A system of equations of the following form has at least one tree-solution: $\{x_1 = t_1, \ldots, x_n = t_n\}$, where the x_i's are distinct variables and the t_i's are any terms.

The second result is obvious:

UNSOLVABLE FORM: A system of equations containing an equation of the following form has no tree-solution:

$fs_1 \ldots s_n = gt_1 \ldots t_m$, where f,g are distinct functional symbols.

We now introduce five transformations on systems of equations:

COMPACTION (C): Eliminate any equation of the form x=x where x is a variable.

VARIABLE ELIMINATION (VE): If x,y are distinct variables, x=y is in the system and x has other occurrences in that system then replace these other occurrences of x by occurrences of y.

VARIABLE ANTEPOSITION (VA): If x is a variable and t is not a variable then replace t=x by x=t.

CONFRONTATION (CO): If x is a variable and t_1, t_2 are not variables and $|t_1| \leq |t_2|$ then replace $\{x = t_1, x = t_2\}$ by $x = t_1, t_1 = t_2$. By $|t|$ we denote the size of t, i.e. the number of occurrences of elements of $F_U V$.

SPLITTING (S): Replace $\{fs_1 .. s_1 = ft_1 .. t_n\}$ by $\{s_1 = t_1, .., s_n = t_n\}$

These transformations have interesting properties:
- They preserve equivalence. Two systems are equivalent iff they have the same tree-solutions.
- Every repeated application of these transformations, on an initial system, leads, after a finite number of steps, to a dead end where no transformation can be applied. The system thus obtained is a "simplified form" of the initial system.
- A simplified form has a tree-solution iff each of its equations is of the form x=t, where x is a variable.

The first property is obvious, the second will be proved at the end of this chapter and the third is a direct consequence of our solvable and unsolvable forms.

For example, let x,y be variables, h a unary functional symbol and k a 0-ary functional symbol.

The system: $\{x=hhx,\ hhk=x\}$ has no tree-solution because of the transformations in (10).

The system: $\{x=y,\ x=hhx,\ y=hhhy\}$ has a tree-solution because of the transformations in (11).

$\{x=hhx,\ hhk=x\}$	(VA)		$\{x=y,\ x=hhx,\ y=hhhy\}$	(VE)
$\{x=hhx,\ x=hhk\}$	(CO)		$\{x=y,\ y=hhy,\ y=hhhy\}$	(CO)
$\{x=hhx,\ hhx=hhk\}$	(S)	(10)	$\{x=y,\ y=hhy,\ hhy=hhhy\}$	(S) (11)
$\{x=hhx,\ hx=hk\}$	(S)		$\{x=y,\ y=hhy,\ hy=hhy\}$	(S)
$\{x=hhx,\ x=k\}$	(C)		$\{x=y,\ y=hhy,\ y=hy\}$	(CO)
$\{k=hhx,\ x=k\}$			$\{x=y,\ hy=hhy,\ y=hy\}$	(S)
			$\{x=y,\ y=hy\}$	

Note that the test in the confrontation is necessary: The following loop results from eliminating the test in the second confrontation of the last example:

$\{x=y,\ y=hhy,\ y=hy\}$	(CO, without test)
$\{x=y,\ y=hhy,\ hhy=hy\}$	(S) (12)
$\{x=y,\ y=hhy,\ hy=y\}$	(VA)
$\{x=y,\ y=hhy,\ y=hy\}$	(CO, without test)

By introducing intermediate variables so that every term contains no more than one functional symbol the check for a greatest term is no longer necessary. The entire simplification process becomes similar to the efficient unification algorithm on general trees proposed by Huet (1976). The intermediate variables correspond to the pointers needed to represent a term in a computer. In our Prolog implementation we avoid the test in another way. We order the equations and then apply the transformations under certain conditions depending on the ordering. Unfortunately we have not been able to obtain a proof of the termination of this algorithm, but it has never failed in any of the programs we have run.

We now give the outline of the proof that it is impossible to construct an infinite sequence of systems E_i of equations:

$$E_0,\ E_1,\ \ldots,\ E_i,\ E_{i+1},\ \ldots$$

where E_{i+1} is obtained by applying one of our five transformations to E_i.

First we prove that such a sequence has to be finite if we do not apply the splitting transformation. Let us consider the initial system E_0. Let N be the number of equations of the form x=x or x=y and let M be the number of equations of the form x=t or t=x. The number of compactions and the number of variable eliminations cannot be greater than N. The number of variable antepositions and the number of confrontations cannot be greater than M.

Secondly, we consider the sequence of positive integers:

defined by: $\|E_0\|$, $\|E_1\|$, $\ldots$, $\|E_i\|$, $\|E_{i+1}\|$, $\ldots$

$$\|\{ s_1=t_1, \ldots, s_n=t_n\}\| =$$

$$k^{\max\{ |s_1| , |t_1| \}} + \ldots + k^{\max\{ |s_n| , |t_n| \}}$$

where k is the greatest n-arity of functional symbols occurring in E_0. From the definition of the transformations, it is possible to show that:

$\|E_i\| \geq \|E_{i+1}\|$ for all the transformations, and
$\|E_i\| > \|E_{i+1}\|$ in the case of a splitting transformation.

Our first result proved that the existence of an infinite sequence of E_i's implies an infinite number of applications of the splitting transformation. From the above inequalities it follows that this infinite sequence is impossible because the integers $\|E_i\|$ would become negative.

4. RECURSIVE DEFINITION OF ASSERTIONS

Let F be a set of functional symbols and let V be an infinite enumerable set of variables. A Prolog program is basically a recursive definition of a subset A of the (possibly infinite) trees over F. The elements of this subset are called "assertions". This recursive definition has to be elaborated by means of set of rule schemas, each being of the form:

t -> $t_1 \ldots t_n$ in which n can be equal to 0 and $t, t_1, \ldots, t_n$ are terms over $F \cup V$.

These rule schemas induce a set of rules: $t/X \to t_1/X \ldots t_n/X$ obtained by considering all the possible tree-assignments X to the variables.

Each of these rules: r -> $r_1 \ldots r_n$
can be interpreted in two different ways:

1. As the "rewriting rule":
   r can be rewritten in the sequence $r_1 \ldots r_n$
   and thus, when n=o, as: r can be erased.

2. As the "logical implication" dealing with the subset A of
   trees:
   r_1 element of A and ... and r_n element of A implies r
   element of A.
   For n=0, this becomes: r element of A.

Depending on whether we use the first or the second interpretation, the "assertions" are defined by:

DEFINITION 1: The "assertions" are the trees which can be
erased in a finite number of steps, using the "rewriting
rules".

DEFINITION 2: The "assertions" are the smallest subset A of
trees which satisfy the "logical implications".

It is shown in (Colmerauer, 1979b) that the two definitions
are equivalent. The second has the advantage of being more
abstract and related to logic. The first definition is more
akin to the way the Prolog interpreter works.

Consider for example the well known Prolog program consisting
of the two schemas:

```
plus(suc(x),y,suc(z)) -> plus(x,y,z)
plus(zero,x,x) ->
```

in which x,y,z are variables and zero,suc,plus are functional
symbols of n-arity 0,1,3 respectively. These schemas induce,
among others, the two rules:

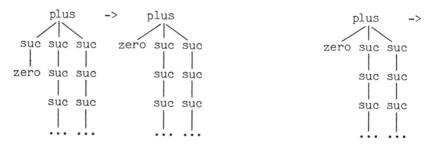

According to the first definition the rational tree:

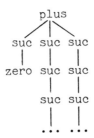

is an assertion, because it can be erased in two steps using
the two preceding rules as rewriting rules. According to the
second definition the above tree is also an assertion,
because any set E which satisfies the logical implications of
these two rules must contain this tree. Note that this tree
being an assertion can be viewed as the existence of an x
such that 1+x=x. If this is to be avoided one should give a
more precise definition of plus(x,y,z), that is:

    plus(suc(x),y,suc(z)) -> plus(x,y,z)
    plus(zero,x,x) -> integer(x)

    integer(zero) ->
    integer(suc(x)) -> integer(x)

5. COMPUTATION OF SUBSETS OF ASSERTIONS

We have just explained what a Prolog program means, but not
what it does. When the Prolog interpreter is invoked, it
tries to solve the following problem:
- given a program, which is a recursive definition of a set
of assertions A,
- given a set of terms $\{t_1, t_2, \ldots, t_n\}$ which acts like a
"window" over the assertions, and given the set of variables
$\{x_1, \ldots, x_m\}$ which occur in it,
- find all the assertions which can be "seen" through this
window, i.e.: compute all the tree-assignments of the form
$X = \{x_1 := r_1, \ldots, x_n := r_n\}$ such that $\{t_1/X, \ldots, t_n/X\}$ becomes a
subset of A.

To do so we will work on pairs of the form:

$(t_1 \ldots t_n, E)$ where $t_1 \ldots t_n$ is a (possibly empty) sequence
              of terms, and E a system of equations.

DEFINITION OF "=>": We introduce the following binary relation between the above pairs:

$$(s_0 s_1 \ldots s_m, \; E) \; \Rightarrow \; (t_1 \ldots t_n s_1 \ldots s_m, \; E_U\{s_0 = t\}) \qquad \text{iff}$$

$t \rightarrow t_1 \ldots t_n$ is obtained by renaming the variables of a
schema in such a way that its variables are dis-
joint from those of $s_0 \ldots s_m$ and those of E, and
$E_U\{s_0 = t\}$ is a system of equation which has at least one
tree-solution.

We write $x \Rightarrow^* y$ iff there exist a finite sequence of u_i's
such that $x = u_0$, $u_0 \Rightarrow u_1$, $u_1 \Rightarrow u_2, \ldots u_n = y$.

The following is the main result on which the Prolog interpreter is based:

WINDOW PRINCIPLE: let $\{t_1, \ldots, t_n\}$ be a set of terms, let
$\{x_1, \ldots, x_m\}$ be the set of its variables, and let X be a tree-
assignement of the form $X = \{x_1 := r_1, \ldots, x_m := r_m\}$:

$\{t_1/X_1, \ldots, t_n/X\}$ is a subset of the set A of assertions   iff
X is a tree-solution of a system E of equation such that:
$(t_1 \ldots t_n, \{\;\}) \Rightarrow^* (\text{empty}, \; E)$

The proof of a similar result is found in (Colmerauer,
1979b). A more precise explanation of the Prolog interpreter
is now given.   Let S_0 be the sequence of terms in the window
and E_0 the empty system.   The interpreter enumerates all the
sequences of pairs (S_i, E_i) which are such that:

$$(S_0, E_0) \; \Rightarrow \; (S_1, E_1) \; \Rightarrow \; (S_2, E_2) \; \Rightarrow \; \ldots$$

The interpreter expects all these sequences to be finite (It
is up to the programmer to assure that this is the case). The
ability of printing, at any time, a tree satisfying the
current set of equations E_i, is one of the multiple features
which have to be added to the theoretical model of Prolog to
render it usable as a programming language.

Let us consider again the rules schemas:

    plus(zero,w,w) ->
    plus(suc(x),y,suc(z)) -> plus(x,y,z)

Assume that we wish to compute all the tree-assignements:

    $X = \{u := r_1, \; v := r_2\}$ such that the set:

    $\{\text{plus(suc(zero),u,v)}/X, \; \text{plus(suc(zero),v,u))}/X\}$

becomes a subset of the assertions. Then the pairs (S_i, E_i) become successively (E_i' is a simplified form of E_i):

S_0 = plus(suc(zero),u,v) plus(suc(zero),v,u)
E_0 = { }
E_0' = { }

S_1 = plus(x,y,z) plus(suc(zero),v,u)
E_1 = E_0 ∪ {plus(suc(zero),u,v)=plus(suc(x),y,suc(z))}
E_1' = {u=y,v=suc(z),x=zero}

S_2 = plus(suc(zero),v,u)
E_2 = E_1 ∪ {plus(x,y,z)=plus(zero,w,w)}
E_2' = {u=w=y=z,v=suc(z),x=zero}

S_3 = plus(x',y',z')
E_3 = E_2 ∪ {plus(suc(zero),v,u)=plus(suc(x'),y',suc(z'))}
E_3 = {u=w=y=z=suc(z'),v=y'=suc(z),x=zero,x'=zero}

S_4 = empty
E_4 = E_3 ∪ {plus(x',y',z')=plus(zero,w',w')}
E_4' = {u=w=y=z=suc(z'),v=w'=y'=z'=suc(z),x=zero,x'=zero}

It follows that the only solution is:

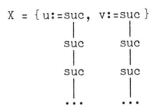

X = { u::=suc, v::=suc }

6. EXAMPLE USE OF INFINITE TREES

6.1 Grammars

Consider the following context-free grammar:

    S -> N   non-terminals: {S,N }
    S -> aSb   initial non-terminal: S
    N -> c
    N -> cN   terminals: {a,b,c}

If we trace the rules of this grammar, starting from S, we obtain the infinite and-or tree which enumerates the generated strings ("and" is to be understood as "followed-by"):

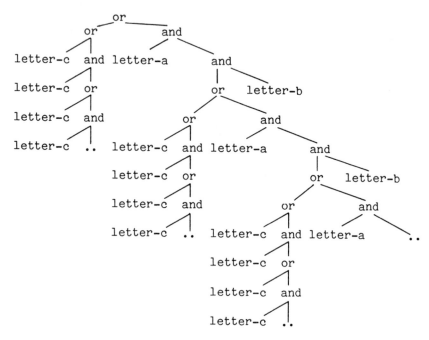

The above is a rational tree whose minimal representation is:

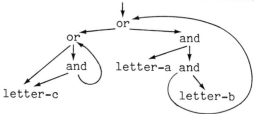

Let us assume that variables are represented by one-letter identifiers. The program to define the grammar is:

```
grammar(s) ->
    equal(s,or(n,and(letter-a,and(s,letter-b))))
    equal(n,or(letter-c,and(letter-c,n)))

equal(x,x) ->
```

Terminal strings are defined by:
```
  terminal-string(nil) ->
  terminal-string(and(a,x)) -> terminal(a) terminal-string(x)

  terminal(letter-a) -/
  terminal(letter-b) ->
  terminal(letter-c) ->
```

Examples of terminal strings are:

```
string-1(and(letter-a,and(letter-c,and(letter-b,nil)))) ->
string-2(and(letter-a,and(letter-b,and(letter-b,nil)))) ->
```

Consider the term produces(p,x) with:

produces(p,x)	iff	p becomes a grammar and
becomes an		x becomes a terminal string and
assertion		x can be generated by p.

It can be defined by:

```
produces(p,x) -> gives(p,x,nil)

gives(or(p,q),x,y) -> gives(p,x,y)
gives(or(p,q),x,y) -> gives(q,x,y)
gives(and(p,q),x,z) -> gives(p,x,y) gives(q,y,z)
gives(a,and(a,x),x) -> terminal(a)
```

The reader will have guessed that:

gives(p,x,y)	iff	p becomes a grammar and
becomes an		x becomes a tree of the form:
assertion		$and(a_1,and(a_2,...and(a_n,y)...))$
		and $a_1a_2...a_n$ can be generated by p.

To check if the strings acb and abb belong to the considered
language, we start (respectively) from:

```
grammar(p) string-1(x) produces(p,x)
grammar(p) string-2(x) produces(p,x)
```

It is also possible to use produce(p,x) to enumerate (inde-
finitely) all the strings x of the language defined by p. It
is even possible, under certain conditions, to enumerate all
the grammars p which generate x! Similary we can program
produces-not(p,x) which means:

produces-not(p,x)	iff	p becomes a grammar and
becomes an		x becomes a terminal string and
assertion		x cannot be generated by p.

The program is:

```
produces-not(p,x) -> terminal-string(x) gives-not(p,x,nil)

gives-not(or(p,q),x,y) -> gives-not(p,x,y) gives-not(q,x,y)
gives-not(and(p,q),x,z) -> each-cut-fails(and(p,q),x,x,z)
gives-not(a,x,x) -> terminal(a)
gives-not(a,and(b,x),x) -> different-terminals(a,b)
gives-not(a,and(b,x),y) -> terminal(a) ends(y,x)

each-cut-fails(p,x,and(a,z),z) ->
each-cut-fails(p,x,and(a,y),z) ->
   ends(z,y) cut-fails(p,x,y,z) each-cut-fails(p,x,y,z)

cut-fails(and(p,q),x,y,z) -> gives-not(p,x,y)
cut-fails(and(p,q),x,y,z) -> gives-not(q,y,z)

ends(x,and(a,x)) ->
ends(x,and(a,y)) -> ends(x,y)
```

with of course, in this case:
```
   different-terminals(letter-a,letter-b) ->
   different-terminals(letter-a,letter-c) ->
   different-terminals(letter-b,letter-a) ->
   different-terminals(letter-b,letter-c) ->
   different-terminals(letter-c,letter-a) ->
   different-terminals(letter-c,letter-b) ->
```

6.2. Back to the Finite

Let us now introduce some general programs to manipulate
rational trees. A rational tree has a finite set of subtrees,
so it is possible to compute their list. Let us define:

subtrees(p,x)	iff	p becomes the tree r_1,
becomes an		$r_1, r_2, \ldots, r_n$ are the subtrees of r_1,
assertion		x becomes a tree of the form:

$$\text{list(is}(n, r_n),$$
$$\vdots$$
$$\text{list(is}(2, r_2),$$
$$\text{list(is}(1, r_1), \text{nil}))\ldots)$$

We have:
```
   subtrees(p,x) -> union-subtrees(nil,p,x)

   union-subtrees(x,p,x) -> in(is(n,p),x)
   union-subtrees(x,p,y) ->
    dominates(p,u) new-integer(x,n) unions(list(is(n,p),x),u,y)

   unions(x,nil,x) ->
   unions(x,list(p,u),z) -> union-subtrees(x,p,y) unions(y,u,z)
```

```
in(a,list(a,x)) ->
in(a,list(b,x)) -> in(a,x)

new-integer(nil,n) -> first-integer(n)
new-integer(list(is(n,p),x),m) -> next-integer(n,m)
```

where, for the previous grammar trees:
```
  dominates(a,nil) -> terminal(a)
  dominates(or(p,q),list(p,list(q,nil))) ->
  dominates(and(p,q),list(p,list(q,nil))) ->
```

We must also introduce:
```
  first-integer(1) ->

  next-integer(1,2) ->
  next-integer(2,3) ->
         :
```

From the subtrees of a tree we can compute a system of equations which define it. Consider:

equations(p,s) iff   p becomes a tree with $r_1,\ldots,r_n$
becomes an   as subtrees,
assertion   s becomes a system having
                         $\{x_1:=r_1,\ldots,x_n:=r_n\}$ as solution
                       the variables $x_1,\ldots,x_n$ are
                       represented by $1,\ldots,n$,
                       s is represented by the tree:
                         $list(equal(n,f_n(i_{n1},i_{n2},\ldots,i_{nk_n}))$,
                              :
                         $list(equal(2,f_2(i_{21},i_{22},\ldots,i_{2k_2}))$,
                         $list(equal(1,f_1(i_{11},i_{12},\ldots,i_{1k_1}))$,
                                                    $nil))\ldots)$

The program is:

```
    equations(p,s) -> subtrees(p,x) into(x,s,x)

    into(nil,nil,x) ->
    into(list(is(n,p),x),list(equal(n,q),s),y) ->
       similar(p,q) dominates(p,u) dominates(q,v)
       into-bis(u,v,y) into(x,s,y)

    into-bis(nil,nil,x) ->
    into-bis(list(p,u),list(n,v),x) ->
                        in(is(n,p),x) into-bis(u,v,x)
```

with (in the case of our grammar tree):

```
similar(a,a) -> terminal(a)
similar(or(p,q),or(x,y)) ->
similar(and(p,q),and(x,y)) ->
```

This program allows us to compute the equations which correspond to the minimal representation of a rational tree. For example, if we consider the previous grammar and we start from:

```
        grammar(p) equations(p,x)
```

x becomes as first solution as shown in (13), which gives the already mentioned minimal representation of the grammar as shown in (14).

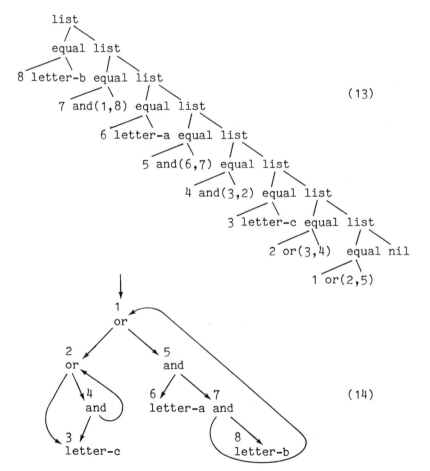

```
list
/ \
equal list
 \   / \
8 letter-b equal list                                    (13)
         \   / \
        7 and(1,8) equal list
               \   / \
              6 letter-a equal list
                      \   / \
                     5 and(6,7) equal list
                            \   / \
                           4 and(3,2) equal list
                                  \   / \
                                 3 letter-c equal list
                                         \   / \
                                        2 or(3,4)  equal nil
                                              \
                                             1 or(2,5)
```

```
        1
        or

2           5
or          and
  4       6     7                                        (14)
  and   letter-a and

3               8
letter-c        letter-b
```

The program which defines equations(p,x) is a fundamental one. One can also use it to output infinite trees in a finite way. For this purpose there is a simpler program which transforms any rational tree p into a finite pseudo-term q, which, in case of infinity, contains pointers to upper level nodes.

```
into-pseudo-term(p,q) -> changes(p,q,nil)

changes(p,to(n),x) -> in(is(n,p),x)
changes(p,q,x) ->
    similar(p,q) dominates(p,u) dominates(q,v)
    new-integer(x,n) change(u,v,list(is(n,p),x))

change(nil,nil,x) ->
change(list(p,u),list(q,v),x) -> changes(p,q,x) change(u,v,x)
```

If one runs the program starting from:

```
grammar(p) into-pseudo-term(p,q)
```

then q becomes:

```
level 1...............or......................
                     /      \
level 2........or.............and.............
             /    \          /    \
level 3..letter-c..and.....letter-a..and........
                  /    \            /    \
level 4..letter-c.....to(2)......to(1)..letter-b
```

6.3. Finite Automatons

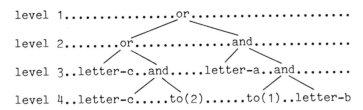

(15)

(16)

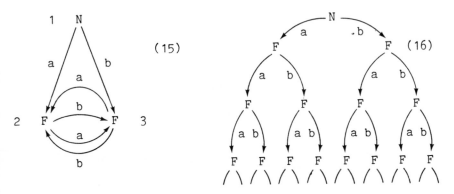

A finite state automaton consists of:
- An input vocabulary. We will limit ourselves to {a,b}.
- A non-empty finite set of states which will be the nodes of a graph. There are two kinds of states: final and non-final

states (respectively labeled by F and N).
- A selected state called the initial state.
- A set of arrows connecting the states. Each arrow is labeled by an input symbol. We will only consider automata which are complete and deterministic, that is: for each node and for each input symbol there is exactly one arrow which exits the node and which is labeled by the symbol.

Our first automaton in (15) can be programmed by:

```
automaton-1(s1) -> non-final-state(s1)
                final-state(s2)
                final-state(s3)
                arrow(s1,letter-a,s2) arrow(s1,letter-b,s3)
                arrow(s2,letter-a,s3) arrow(s2,letter-b,s3)
                arrow(s3,letter-a,s2) arrow(s3,letter-b,s2)
```

where final, non-final, and arrow will be specified later.

An automaton accepts (otherwise rejects) a string of input symbols a_1 a_2 ... an iff there exists a path of the form

$$--a_1--> --a_2--> \ldots --a_n-->$$

which starts from the initial state and ends on a final (otherwise not final) state.

Acceptance can be programmed as:

```
accepts(s,nil,true) -> final-state(s)
accepts(s,nil,false) -> non-final-state(s)
accepts(r,list(a,x),v) -> arrow(r,a,s) accepts(s,x,v)
```

From the point of view of string acceptance, our first automaton in (15) can be represented by the infinite graph in (16) which can be coded as the rational tree:

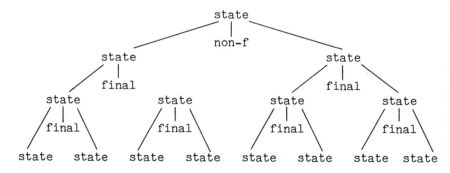

We can now define:

```
final-state(state(x,final,y)) ->

non-final-state(state(x,non-f,y)) ->

arrow(state(x,f,y),letter-a,x) ->
arrow(state(x,f,y),letter-b,y) ->
```

Consider the problem: compute the automaton which has the smallest number of states and which, from the point of view of acceptance, is equivalent to a given automaton. The solution to the problem is to compute the minimal representation of the rational tree which corresponds to the automaton. As we have already seen the program which defines equation(p,s), does this task. To properly execute it we need, however, to add the two rules:

```
dominates(state(x,f,y),list(x,list(y,nil))) ->
similar(state(p,f,q),state(x,f,y)) ->
```

If we invoke the program, starting from :
    automaton-1(s) equations(s,x)
x becomes as first solution:

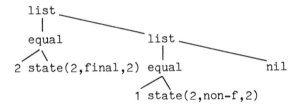

that is the automaton in (17).

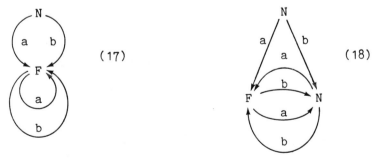

Therefore our first automaton in (15) was not minimal. Consider the second automaton in (18).

```
automaton-2(s₁) -> non-final-state(s₁)
                   final-state(s₂)
                   non-final-state(s₃)
                   arrow(s₁,letter-a,s₂) arrow(s₁,letter-b,s₃)
                   arrow(s₂,letter-a,s₃) arrow(s₂,letter-b,s₃)
                   arrow(s₃,letter-a,s₂) arrow(s₃,letter-b,s₂)
By starting from:
    automaton-2(s) equations(s,x)
```

x becomes now:

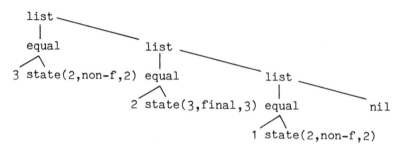

which proves that the second automaton is already minimal.

Consider now the set of "good" input strings: {ab, ba}
and the set of "bad" input strings: {a, b, aa, bb, aab, bba}.
The problem is to compute the automata which have no more
than three states and which accept the good strings and
reject the bad ones. We write:

```
    solution(x) -> automaton-3(s) equations(s,x)

    automaton-3(s) -> good-1(x₁) accepts(s,x₁,true)
                      good-2(x₂) accepts(s,x₂,true)
                      bad-1(y₁) accepts(s,y₁,false)
                      bad-2(y₂) accepts(s,y₂,false)
                      bad-3(y₃) accepts(s,y₃,false)
                      bad-4(y₄) accepts(s,y₄,false)
                      bad-5(y₅) accepts(s,y₅,false)
                      bad-6(y₆) accepts(s,y₆,false)

good-1(list(letter-a,list(letter-b,nil))) ->
good-2(list(letter-b,list(letter-a,nil))) ->
bad-1(list(letter-a,nil)) ->
bad-2(list(letter-b,nil)) ->
bad-3(list(letter-a,list(letter-a,nil))) ->
bad-4(list(letter-b,list(letter-b,nil))) ->
bad-5(list(letter-a,list(letter-a,list(letter-b,nil)))) ->
bad-6(list(letter-b,list(letter-b,list(letter-a,nil)))) ->
```

The limit on the number of states is introduced by reducing the definition of next-integer to:

    next-integer(1,2) ->
    next-integer(2,3) ->

By starting from solution(x), x becomes:

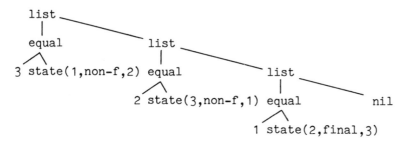

which is the automaton in (19).

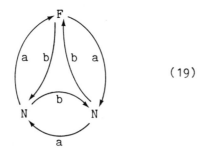

(19)

The strings accepted by this automaton are those whose number of occurrences of a's is the same as the number of occurrences of b's, modulo 3. The reader famliar with Prolog will notice the small number of non-deterministic situations this program will confront.

ACKNOWLEDGEMENTS

Thanks are given: to A. Porto for the numerous comments he made on this paper, to M. Van Caneghem for making available the first Prolog interpreter that allowed me to test examples on infinite trees, and finally to J. Cohen for the help provided in giving the final touches to the manuscript. This work was sponsored by the CNRS grant "ATP Informatique 1978".

IC–PROLOG LANGUAGE FEATURES

K.L. Clark   F.G. McCabe   S. Gregory

Imperial College of Science and Technology,
Department of Computing,
180 Queen's Gate, London, SW7 2BZ

ABSTRACT

In this short paper we introduce the principal features of
IC-PROLOG mainly through examples. IC-PROLOG differs from
PROLOG in not providing extra logical primitives such as the
slash ("/") and "isvar", nor does it allow the addition and
deletion of clauses during a query evaluation. On the plus
side, negation and set expressions are primitives of the
language, and there is a rich set of control facilities. For
example, a programmer can:
(1) make the evaluation order of the calls of a procedure
dependent upon its mode of use,
(2) initiate the (pseudo) parallel evaluation of a set of
calls in which shared variables are one way communication
channels.
The control is specified by annotations which have no effect
on the declarative semantics of the program. The evaluation
of an IC-PROLOG program is genuinely a controlled deduction.

1. PROCEDURES AND QUERIES

An IC-PROLOG <u>procedure</u> is an implication of the form:

$$B <- L_1 \& .. \& L_k, \quad k \geq 0$$

where B is an atomic formula and each L_i is a literal, i.e.
an atomic formula or its negation. Atoms are of the form
$R(t_1,..,t_n)$ where R is a relation name and each t_i is a term.

As in DEC-10 PROLOG (Pereira et al. 1978) the syntax can be modified by declaring operators. This enables one to use infix form for binary relations, using r R t' instead of R(t,t').

The declarative reading of the procedure is as an implication universally quantified with respect to all the variables of the procedure[1]. The procedures describe a set of relations over terms which are the data structures of the program.

A _query_ is of one of the three forms:

(i)	: $L_1\&..\&L_k$
(ii)	t: $L_1\&..\&L_k$
(iii)	$\{t: L_1\&..\&L_k\}$

in which t is a term and each L_i is a literal. Let $x_1,...,x_n$ be all the variables of the conjunction $L_1\&..\&L_k$ and let $y_1,..,y_k$ be the subset of these that do not appear in t. The queries are read:

(i)   For some $x_1,..,x_n$, $L_1\&..\&L_k$

(ii) A t such that for some $y_1,..,y_k$, $L_1\&...\&L_k$

(iii) All the t's such that for some $y_1,..,y_k$, $L_1\&..\&L_k$

Query Evaluation.   Both queries and procedures can be annotated in ways that will shortly be exemplified in order to control the query evaluation process. The default evaluation of a completely unannotated program and query is that of standard PROLOG. Literals (calls) of the query are selected one at a time in left to right order. Failure to prove the literal L_i with the variable bindings generated by the preceding calls $L_1\&..\&L_{i-1}$ causes backtracking. Set queries of the form (iii) are answered by backtracking after each successful evaluation until there are no untried proof paths. The before/after order of the program procedures is the order in which they will be tried during backtracking.

Negated Atoms. Negated atoms are evaluated using the negation as failure proof rule. That is, -A is assumed true if all attempts to prove A fail. The call -A fails (i.e. is assumed false) only if there is a proof of A that does not bind any variable of the atom. If A can only be proved with some variable bound, the evaluation terminates with an error message. As explained in (Clark, 1978), this proof rule is

---

[1]There is an exception to this rule if the procedure contains set equalities. See section 2.

sound on the assumption that the relation R of atom A, and any auxiliary relations used to describe R, are relations that are completely defined by the procedures of the program. The programmer implicitly declares that this is the case by using a negation involving R.

Example Use of Negation.   Suppose that we want to find unmarried children of Bill. We need to pose the query:

All the x such that Bill is the father of x and it is not the case that, for some y, x is married to y.

The only way we can express this in IC-PROLOG is to introduce the auxiliary relation, married(x), whose definition is the condition

"for some y, x is married to y"

that we wish to negate. We therefore add the procedure:

    married(x) <- x married-to y .

We can now pose the query as:

    {x: Bill father-of x & -married(x)}

2. PRIMITIVE RELATIONS

IC-PROLOG has primitive relations for natural number arithmetic, for reading and writing files, and for constructing a list of all the solutions of a query. The reading and writing of files we shall describe in section 4. Here we illustrate the use of the arithmetic relations and the set expression.

Arithmetic Relations TIMES, PLUS, LESS.   The arithmetic relations are unusual in that there are no input/output restrictions on their use. For example, the primitive TIMES relation can be used to multiply, to divide, to find all the pairs of divisors of a number, even to generate all the tuples of natural numbers which lie in the relation. This generality of use allows one to write elegant arithmetic programs that are just the obvious definitions of the relations they compute.

Abstractly, the arithmetic primitives can be viewed as though defined by a data base of assertions that gives all the

instances of each relation. The natural number arguments can
be denoted by successor terms or the usual decimal numerals.
Thus "s(s(0))" and "2" are synonymous, and the term "s(s(x))"
denotes any number greater than 1. The query:

  {<s(s(x)), y>:TIMES(s(s(x)),y,36) & LESS(s(x),y)}

returns the set: {<2,18>,<3,12>,<4,9>,<6,6>}.

  even(y) <- TIMES(x,2,y)

defines the property of being even. It can be used for
testing or generating.

  x divides z <- TIMES(x, y, z)

defines the divides relation. It can be used for testing, for
finding divisors, or for finding multipliers.

  has-divisor(z) <- s(s(x)) divides z & -s(s(x))=z

defines the property of having a proper divisor. Used for
generating, as in the query:

  {z: has-divisor(z)}

it will generate the infinite set of properly divisible
natural numbers: {4, 6, 8, 9, 10,....}. (More exactly, it
generates the set until the query evaluation is interrupted
or the numbers exceed the range handled by the host
computer.)

Finally,

  prime(z) <- LESS(1, z) & - has-divisor(z)

defines the property of being a prime and

  x prime-divisor-of z <- x divides z & prime(x)

defines the prime divisor relation. The query:

  {u: prime(u)}

gives all the primes, and the query:

  {u: u prime-divisor-of 100}

gives all its prime factors of 100. The definitions of "prime" and "prime-divisor-of" are really specifications of these relations. IC-PROLOG enables these specifications to be used, somewhat inefficiently, for computing instances of the relations.

Set Constructor.   The set constructor is an equality of the form:

$$x = \{t: A\}, \quad t \text{ a term, } A \text{ an atom} \tag{1}$$

Used in a query or procedure it is logically equivalent to the non-atomic condition:

$$\forall u(u \text{ in } x <-> Ey_1,..,y_k(u=t\&A)). \tag{2}$$

where $y_1,..,y_k$ are 'local' variables that only appear in t:A. As an example, the procedure:

p mother-of-children l <- female(p) & l = q:q child-of p

is equivalent to:

p mother-of-children l <- female(p) & $\forall$u(u in l <->
                                             Eq(u=q & q child-of p))

The p is not existentially quantified since it appears in another condition of the query. It is not 'local' to the set expression. Universally quantified equivalences such as that above can be expressed directly in the logic language of Hansson et al. (1982).

The set constructor (1) is used to generate a binding for x. This is its only use. It cannot be used to generate a binding for any other free variable of the equivalence (2), or to test that some list satisfies the condition.

Every member of the list generated for x is an instance ts of the term t. Here, s is a set of bindings for the local variables $y_1,..,y_k$ such that As is true. The list constructed by finding all the solutions to the query t:A . Each solution instance ts becomes an element on the list x. As with negation as failure, the evaluation method is sound on the assumption that the relation of A is completely described by the program. However the evaluation method does not necessarily generate the smallest list x that satisfies condition (2). This is because different evaluation paths of the query t:A may give rise to the same answer instance t' of

t. In this case more than one copy of t' appears on the list binding for x.

Example use

(a)   { <s, l>: student(s) & l = {u: s takes u} }

This finds all the pairs <student, list of courses the student takes>. Using the expansion rule given above, it is equivalent to:

{<s, l>: student(s) & ∀u(u in l <-> s takes u)}

(b) l is-list-of-prime-factors-of x <-
                             l = u:{u prime-divisor-of x}

This defines the relation that holds between a number x and the list l of its prime divisors. It is equivalent to:

l is-a-list-of-prime-factors-of x
                     <- ∀u(u in l <-> u prime-divisor-of x)

Because of the restrictions on the use of the set constructor the procedure can only be used for finding the list of prime factors of a given number x.

3. LINKING CONTROL WITH USE

As we have already mentioned, the default control of IC-PROLOG is left to right evaluation of the conjunction of conditions of a query. This rule also applies to the preconditions/calls of a procedure. Unfortunately it is not always possible to find an ordering of the preconditions that is appropriate for every use.

As an example, consider the following definition of the "has-descendant" relation:

x has-descendant y <- x parent-of y
x has-descendant y <- x parent-of z & z parent-of y
x has-descendant y <- x parent-of z & z has-descendant w
                           & w parent-of y

Used to find descendants, in a query such as

{y: Tom has-descendant y},

the ordering of the three procedures and their preconditions results in a backtracking search which starts with the given "Tom". The first procedure finds all the children of "Tom". The second procedure generates the grandchildren of "Tom" by finding the children of his children. Finally, the last procedure will find all other descendants by finding each child of a descendant of one of his children.

Used to find ancestors, in a query such as:

   { x: x has-descendant Bill},

the ordering of the preconditions results in a very inefficient search. Thus, the second procedure will generate the grandparents of Bill not by finding the parents of his parents, but by searching through all the parent-child pairs until a parent of Bill is found. The more efficient search would require the preconditions of the procedure to be in the reverse order. The last procedure also requires a reverse order of its preconditions if its use to find ancestors is to be an efficient search.

In standard PROLOG, one way round the problem is to define the complement relation, has-ancestor, with the ordering of preconditions appropriate to the finding of ancestors. Then this relation is used instead of the has-descendant relation for calls intended to generate ancestors. But this involves introducing a logically redundant relation, and it detracts from the invertibility property that is unique to logic programming. Another solution, again in standard PROLOG, is to use the meta-level primitive isvar which tests whether a variable is bound. The second procedure for the has-descendant relation is then expanded to the two procedures:

```
x has-descendant y <-
             isvar(y) & x parent-of z & z parent-of y
x has-descendant y <-
             -isvar(y) & z parent-of y & x parent-of z.
```

The major drawback of this solution, as with the use of the other meta-level primitives of PROLOG, is that it affects the declarative reading of the procedures. The procedures are no longer implications that can be read as simple definitions of relations.

In IC-PROLOG, no such pollution of the declarative semantics is allowed. Meta-level conditions, such as isvar(y), and all other issues of control are expressed in a separate language of program annotations. The above pair of procedures become the annotated control alternatives:

    [x has-descendant y^ <- x parent-of z & z parent-of y,
     x has-descendant y? <- z parent-of y & x parent-of z]

The "^" on the y of the first procedure expresses the control condition that y must be unbound on entry to the procedure. The "?" annotation of the second procedure is the control condition that it should be bound to a non-variable. These are the exact equivalents of isvar(y) and -isvar(y) conditions. Finally, the bracketing together of the procedures tells the evaluator that they are control alternatives, not logical alternatives. A similar pair of control alternatives can be given for the last has-descendant procedure. The program will then result in reasonably efficient search for all modes of use.

For further discussion of control alternatives, and for a description of the semantics of the head annotations, we refer the reader to (Clark and McCabe, 1979b). Head annotations are similar to the mode declarations of Dec-10 PROLOG (Pereira et al. 1978). However the annotations allow the expression of more complex input/output modes, and unlike Dec-10 PROLOG, the mode declaration for a procedure is translated into a runtime test. In the logic programming language proposed by (Hansson et al. 1982), different orders of evaluation of the preconditions of a procedure are generated automatically for different modes, the ordering being based on a topological sort in which calls which contain input arguments have priority. This removes the responsibility from the programmer, but does not necessarily result in the most efficient order of evaluation. It also does not cover the case when the control for different modes is not just a different order of sequential evaluation, but is a different mix of sequential/non-sequential evaluation.

4. NON-SEQUENTIAL EVALUATION

Various forms of non-sequential evaluation can be specified in IC-PROLOG. We shall exemplify them by considering the classic illustration of the benefit of non-sequential evaluation, the problem of checking that two binary trees have the same leaf profile.

The following procedures are a logic program that is essentially a specification of the "sameleaves" relation on trees. The different trees:

have the same leaf profile. We use "t(x,y)" to denote a tree
with subtrees x and y and "l(u)" for a tree with just the
label u. The term "u.x" denotes the list with head u and tail
x, "Nil" is the empty list.

sameleaves(x,y) <- w profile-of x & w profile-of y

u.Nil profile-of l(u)
u.z profile-of t(l(u),y) <- z profile-of y
w profile-of t(t(x,y),z) <- w profile-of t(x,t(y,z))

Let us now consider the test use of the program. A sequential
execution of the "sameleaves" procedure means that the
profile of the tree x is generated first and this is then
tested against the profile of y. (So we have both a generate
and test use of the procedures defining "profile-of".) If the
trees have the same profile, both trees need to be traversed,
and a sequential execution is as good as any. But if not, it
is wasteful to generate the leaf profile of x beyond the
point at which they differ. We need to specify a control that
will ensure this early cut-off.

First, let us notice that the evaluation of the call
w profile-of x will generate the output binding for w as a
series of partial approximations. Thus, suppose that x is the
tree t(l(A),t(l(B),l(C))). The second procedure for "profile-
of" is the only one that applies to the call "w profile-of
t(l(A),t(l(B),l(C)))" and its use will bind w to A.z. Here z
is the profile of t(l(B),l(C)) yet to be generated. The next
step in the evaluation will actually bind z to B.z', which
implicitly binds w to the next approximation A.B.z'. Thus,
the generation of the profile of the tree is such that each
leaf label is 'made available', through the binding of w, as
soon as the leaf is visited. There are three evaluation
strategies for the sameleaves procedure that can exploit this
label by label generation of the output binding for w.

Unsynchronised Parallel Evaluation. The simplest strategy is
to execute the two "profile-of" calls in parallel. This is
specified in IC-PROLOG by replacing the "&" by "//".

sameleaves(x,y) <- w profile-of x // w profile-of y

The effect of the "//", which has the declarative reading "and", is to fork the evaluation of any procedure in which it appears into separate processes. These are placed on a process queue and the evaluator time shares between the processes by rotating the queue. In each time slice the process at the head of the queue, if not suspended for some reason (see below), is given a time slice sufficient for at least one resolution step. Notice that this means that only one process can bind a variable. It is never the case that two processes try to bind the same variable at the same time. After a process has bound a variable, all other processes must read and agree with that binding.

In our example, this means that the first "profile-of" process to bind w is the one which has the tree with the shortest path to the leftmost label. Thereafter, the other process must 'read' this binding. The evaluations proceed with labels added to and read from w in an order determined by the shapes of the trees. As soon as both processes reach a mismatched label, the parallel evaluation fails.

Parallelism with Directed Communication. We can restrict the parallel evaluation so that only one process is allowed to generate the binding for the shared variable w. We do this by either annotating the occurrence of w in the producer process with a "^", or by annotating it in the consumer process with a "?". Thus,

sameleaves(x,y) <- w profile-of x // w^ profile-of y

makes the second call the producer of the leaf profile. In the parallel evaluation, the first consumer call becomes suspended if it tries to add a label to w. It becomes a read-only process on the binding of w. Each time the second process finds a new leaf, the first process is reactivated in order to check the label.

Data Triggered Coroutining. The above direction of communication constraint on w prevents the consumer process from doing unnecessary work visiting labels that occur after the mismatch. It does not prevent the producer generating extra labels. To prevent this, we need to specify a control in which the producer process is suspended wherever it finds a new label, and is only reactivated when the consumer process is resuspended because it needs the next label. This is specified by retaining the producer annotation on the variable, but by reverting back to the "&" connective.

sameleaves(x,y) <- w profile-of x & w^ profile-of y

Because we have "&" rather than "//", there is no forking. Only one process is active at any one time, but there is an alternation between the evaluations of the two calls. The "^" annotation makes the second call a lazy producer of the binding for the shared variable w.

The above example has served to illustrate three kinds of non-sequential control that one can specify using the annotations of IC-PROLOG. The unconstrained parallel control is the simplest. It simulates a parallel evaluation of conjunctive conditions in which the only constraint is that only one process is allowed to bind a variable. This is the form of parallelism discussed by Hogger (1982). Parallelism with designated producer processes for shared variables enables one to simulate networks of parallel processes with one way communication channels. This is the parallelism of the Kahn and McQueen model (1977). It is also treated in the logic programming context by van Emden and de Lucena (1982) and by Hansson et al. (1982). Finally, coroutining with a designated producer corresponds to lazy evaluation in a functional language (Friedman and Wise 1976).

Non-Sequential Control with Backtracking.   Because the different forms of non-sequential control are specified explicitly with annotations they can be mixed. Coupled with backtracking search, this allows a rich variety of control strategies to be specified.

As an example we give the top level procedures of a solution to the eight queens problem. This is a slight modification of a purely coroutining solution to the problem given in (Clark and McCabe, 1979b). The procedures that complete the program are given in that paper. The candidate solutions to the problem are permutations of the list of the numbers 1 to 8, the i'th number in the permutation being the column position of the queen in the i'th row.

Queens-sol(x)<- Safe(x) & x^ perm-of 1.2....8.Nil
Safe(u.x)<- u cannot-take-any-of x // Safe(x)

The "^" annotation in the "perm-of" call makes this a lazy producer of the permutation. The relation can be defined so that the permutation is generated as a stream of partial approximations, as with the leaf profile of a tree. Each new number placed on x is a new queen that is immediately checked by the Safe(x) condition. The evaluation of this is a forking parallel computation. For each queen placed on the board there is a new process generated to check that it cannot take any of the queens yet to be placed. Failure of any of these checks on the new queen results in backtracking to find a different placing. Thus, each candidate partial solution becomes a phalanx of parallel processes which grows and shrinks with the backtracking evaluation of the "perm-of" call. This sophisticated algorithmic behaviour results from simple control annotations attached to a program that is close to a specification of the problem that it solves.

Other Control Annotations. There are two other ways of controlling a parallel evaluation. There is a delay primitive which is a "!" immediately following a variable in a call of a procedure. If a process invokes the procedure, and its evaluation reaches the "!" annotated call, the process will be suspended until the variable is bound by some other process. The annotation is ignored if every other process is suspended. The following example is an annotated version of a program given in (Kowalski, 1979a). It defines an admissible list of pairs of numbers as one in which the second number of each pair is double the first, and in which the first number of the next pair is three times the second number of the preceding pair.

```
Admissible(1) <- Double(1)//Triple(1)
Double(Nil)
Double(<x,y>.1) <- TIMES(x!,2,y) & Double(1)
Triple(<x,y>.Nil)
Triple(<x,y>.<z,w>.1) <- TIMES(y!,3,z) & Triple(<z,w>.1)
```

The program will test or generate a list of admissible pairs by a parallel evaluation of the two conditions that it must satisfy. One generate use is particularly efficient. This is for calls of the form "Admissible(<N,x>.1)" in which the N is given. The delays on the "TIMES" calls of the "Double", "Triple" procedures mean that the remaining numbers on the list will be generated by a deterministic sequence of multiplications of the seed N.

The last control annotation is ":". This can be used to make the evaluation of the first call of a procedure act as a guard (cf. Dijkstra, 1976) on its use. The effect of the ":" in a procedure

$$B \leftarrow G: A_1 \&...\& A_m$$

is to make the unification with head B and the evaluation of the guard atom G an indivisible unit during a parallel or coroutined evaluation. It is most commonly used to delay the communication of variable bindings that result from the unification with B until after the successful evaluation of the guard. If the guard fails, the binding is not transmitted to the other processes. Guards are similar to the constraints of Bellia et al. (1982). The difference is that in IC-PROLOG a successful guard evaluation does not mean that the procedure is the only one that can be used for the call. It does not exclude the possibility that other procedures will unify with the call and have true guards.

5. STREAM I/O

Another unique feature of IC-PROLOG is stream I/O. The primitive READ(x) binds its argument variable not to a single character or term, but to the entire stream of characters that will be typed at the terminal. The programmer processes this stream as though it were a list of characters. The list is lazily produced by the evaluation of the READ(x) call. Thus, in a query of the form

   y: READ(x) & P(x,y)

"P" must be a relation from a list of characters to the output y. Characters are read from the terminal as unifications in the evaluation of "P(x,y)" demand more of the list x. Because x is the list of all the characters typed there is no problem with backtracking. As characters are read in they are explicitly stored in the list binding for x that READ(x) is lazily producing. After backtracking, evaluation steps of the "P(x,y)" call get characters from this partially recorded list. Only when this is exhausted will new characters be read from the terminal. This processing of streams generated at the terminal is handled by a modified unification algorithm that 'knows' about special values that are pointers to the terminal buffer.

The primitive WRITE(y) will display the list binding for y at the terminal. As with the lists produced by READ(x), special constants are used to denote invisible characters. Thus the constant "LINE" will be 'displayed' by generating a carriage return.

WRITE(y) can also be used with its argument generated as a stream. Consider a query of the form

: READ(x) & WRITE(y) & R(x,y^),

in which "R" is a relation over lists of characters that generates the output binding for y as a stream as it consumes x. The evaluation of the query will interleave lines of output with lines of input. Each carriage return that is typed is a signal that allows the display of the next segment of y that ends with the "LINE" constant.

6. CONCLUDING REMARKS

IC-PROLOG is a pure logic based language that enables one to illustrate a wide variety of programming concepts. Using the set constructor and control alternatives one can develop general purpose deductive data bases. Using stream I/O and data triggered coroutining one can illustrate the idea of lazy evaluation. Finally, the parallel evaluation and the various ways of controlling it correspond to current ideas in the area of communicating processes. IC-PROLOG is therefore an ideal language for teaching these programming concepts. It has been used in this way at Imperial College and at Syracuse University with some success.

ACKNOWLEDGEMENTS

The research on IC-PROLOG was supported by the British Science & Engineering Research Council.

PROPERTIES OF A LOGIC PROGRAMMING LANGUAGE

A. Hansson   S. Haridi*   S-A. Tärnlund

UPMAIL
Computing Science Department,
Uppsala University, Uppsala, Sweden

*Department of Computer Systems,
The Royal Institute of Technology, Stockholm, Sweden

ABSTRACT

We have developed a logic programming system based on natural
deduction. It consists of a class of statements which is a
superclass of Horn clauses. We can run as programs logical
statements that formerly have been considered specifications.
For example, the language contains the logical constants
negation, equivalence, universal quantifier and identity. We
can define functions, as well as relations, infinite data
structures and virtual classes. Computation rules provide
control information. A demand driven computation rule results
in computations on infinite data structures that terminate.

1. INTRODUCTION

Logic programming as in the Prolog systems (see Colmerauer et
al. 1972; Pereira et al. 1978) is based on Horn clauses and a
procedural reading of relations (see Kowalski, 1974). The
logical system is resolution (Robinson, 1965). In contrast,
our language is based on a natural deduction system (see
Prawitz, 1965). Our procedures are special cases of co-
operating agents. The language is first order and has the
following features in common with Prolog: (1) general tree-
like data structures, (2) non-determinate programs treated by
automatic backtracking, (3) no distinction between input and
output, (4) logical variables that enable programs to
manipulate partially specified data structures, (5) tail
recursion optimization.

Its additional features are: (1) truth functional semantics

for all statements in the language, (2) functions defined by equalities or conditional equalities, (3) equivalence definition of relations, (4) negation, (5) virtual classes, (6) infinite data structures, (7) a partial evaluation computation rule such that the execution order of the goals of a statement depends on the instantiation pattern of variables in the head of the statement, (8) a demand driven computation rule that enables us to write programs which behave operationally as a network of co-operating agents (processes) communicating through streams; the networks may be static or dynamically evolving, cyclic or acyclic, the streams may be finite or infinite and the agents may be determinate (functions) or nondeterminate (relations), (9) method for terminating programs operating on infinite data structures.

2. SYNTAX OF THE PROGRAMMING LANGUAGE

Let us outline the syntax of our language mainly by simple examples that also illustrate some concepts of the language.

Different properties of finite and infinite data structures lead us to have a two sorted language. There are canonical variables that range over finite data structures and non-canonical variables that range over finite or infinite data structures. A canonical object has its name as value (cf. Martin-Löf, 1979). They are our data structures. In contrast to ordinary programming languages logic languages can have data structures that are unspecified or partially specified e.g., the list A.x whose tail is an unspecified list. This property and the notion of identity may lead to conceptually infinite data structures that can be represented cyclically. For example the equation x=A.A.x has a solution only if the variable x is allowed to denote a conceptually infinite list A.A... .

The programming language is built up from six disjoint syntactic categories.

(1) <u>Constants</u>. A constant is written as an upper-case letter followed by a string of letters and digits, but a number is written in the usual way. Constants are canonical objects.
(2) <u>Data structures</u>.   A data structure is a composite term e.g., Tree(Nil,A,z). For convenience some data structures are written in infix form, e.g. the list A.B.x . They are canonical objects.
(3) <u>Variables</u>.   They are either canonical or noncanonical.

A canonical variable is written as a string of letters and digits prefixed by a dollar ($) sign, e.g. $x1. A noncanonical variable is written as a lower-case letter followed by a string of letters and digits, e.g. xx.
(4) <u>Functions</u>. A function is defined using identity e.g., conc(x.y,z)=x.conc(y,z).
(5) <u>Relations</u>. These are defined by implications and equivalences e.g., rev(x.y,w) <-- rev(y,z) & conc(z,x.Nil,w).
(6) <u>Logical constants</u>. ⊥ (absurdity or falsity), --> (implication), & (and), <--> (equivalence), v (or), ∀ , E (universal and existential quantifiers), = (identity), - (negation).

A program is a collection of sentences. A sentence is of the form: 'A', 'A <-- B' or 'A <--> B'. The symbol A stands for a literal, i.e., an atomic formula or its negation. The atomic formula may be an equality. The symbol B stands for an arbitrary logical formula.

3. COMPUTATIONS

We have two types of computation rules for controlling the construction of derivations (computations).

The first type controls sequential computation. Here, given two conditions (procedure calls) the derivation tree of one of them is completely constructed (the call is terminated) before the other condition is treated (the other call is invoked).

The second type controls co-operating agents communicating through channels. For example, given two literals the derivation trees of these literals are built up in a pseudo-parallel way. The alternation is dependent on the instantiations made on their common variables.

For sequential processing the evaluation order can be determined at compile time or at runtime. The default is compile time fixed order of evaluation. Dynamic runtime ordering has to be explicitly requested by the programmer. For an entirely relational statement the evaluation order is the left to right order as in Prolog. For statements involving functions we use an applicative order rule that the following examples illustrate.

Example 1

The following program defines the list concatenation function.

conc(Nil,u)=u   (1)
conc(x.y,u)=x.conc(y,u)

We can use this to define quick-sort.

Example 2

quick-sort(Nil)=Nil   (2)
quick-sort(x.y)=conc(quick-sort(y_1),x.quick-sort(y_2)) <--
                                        partition(x,y,y_1,y_2)

The following figure gives the evaluation order for calls of the recursive statement.

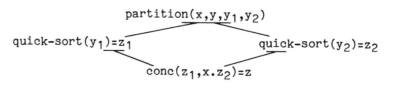

Fig. 1. Partial evaluation order of the quick-sort statement.

Partial evaluation rule

If dynamic ordering is requested, the ordering of the calls is based on the instantiation pattern of certain variables in the head of a statement. This pattern induces a partial evaluation order on the calls. Different invocations of the same statement may result in different partial orderings due to different patterns of instantiation. In our compiler, the dynamic ordering algorithm is applied to a statement only if a meta rule of pattern instantiation is associated with the statement. In this rule, we specify which variables in the head of the statement that are of interest. The ordering algorithm then generates different partial orderings to cover the various combinations of instantiated and uninstantiated variables. Though this rule requires a runtime check, it is useful in programs operating on data bases. A rule similar to this exists in IC-Prolog, where the programmer, however, specifies explicitly the various orders of evaluations (see Clark and McCabe, 1979b).

Example 3

We illustrate this idea further by a data base example of Pereira and Porto given in Coelho et al. (1980).

$$
\begin{aligned}
\text{query(student,professor)} \;\texttt{<--}\; &\text{takes(student,}course_1) \;\&\; \quad (3)\\
&\text{course-at(}course_1,day_1,\text{room)} \;\&\;\\
&\text{prof-teaches(professor,}course_1) \;\&\;\\
&\text{takes(student,}course_2) \;\&\;\\
&\text{course-at(}course_2,day_2,\text{room)} \;\&\;\\
&\text{prof-teaches(professor,}course_2) \;\&\;\\
&course_1 \neq course_2,
\end{aligned}
$$

where the computation rule is pattern instantiation on professor.

The above statement answers the query: "is there a student such that a professor teaches him two different courses in the same room?", from a data base of students who take courses, of professors who teach courses, and of courses held on certain weekdays and rooms. Our compiler produces two execution orderings based on whether the variable 'professor' is instantiated or not. Now, suppose that we want to find a student x such that query(x,Pereira) is satisfied, we get an execution order extracted from the partial order depicted in the following figure.

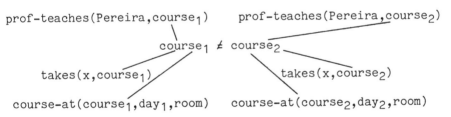

Fig. 2. The partial order according to the instantiation pattern of query(x,Pereira).

Demand driven rule

We also have a demand driven computation rule. Operationally, a statement to be executed using this rule defines a network of agents communicating through unbounded buffers. These networks are related to the streams of Kahn and McQueen (1977), to those of Landin (1965), and to data flow computation of Dennis (1971). Assuming a single processor the agents will behave like coroutines. The following statement:

$$n(x)=y \gets p(x)=z \ \& \ c(z)=y \qquad\qquad\qquad (4)$$

when executed in a demand driven mode, specifies a simple network of two agents, p and c, communicating through a channel z. When n is invoked, two agent instances for p and c will be created with variable z used as a communication link. The variable z is called a channel variable, agent p is called a producer for z and agent c is called a consumer of z. In every such network there is an agent (here c) that is called the initial demander and drives the whole network. The computation proceeds as follows: c runs until it needs a further specification of z, the control is then transferred to p until it produces such a specification of z, whereupon the control is returned to c at the point of suspension. In a statement whose execution is governed by the demand driven rule, the initial demander will start the execution of the body of the statement. If the network is cycle-free any nonproducing consumer can be the initial demander. In a cyclic network with one cycle or a number of overlapping cycles, any agent in such cycles can be the initial demander. If the network is composed of disjoint cycles with one cycle acting as a producer to one or more cycles, then there must be at least one cycle that acts as a nonproducing consumer. Any agent in such a cycle can be the initial demander. The only restriction we have is that there can only be one designated producer for a variable. This seems reasonable since a problem would arise in deciding which producer should grant a demand.

In an acyclic network, when the agents are functions, a demand driven computation reduces to an equivalent form of lazy evaluation (see Hendersson and Morris, 1976), and in a cyclic network it is equivalent to computations expressed in the stream processing language of Kahn and McQueen (1977). Streams in the context of logic programming have also been treated by Clark and McCabe (1979b) and by Bellia et al. (1982). Coroutining has also been studied by the former and by Gallaire and Lasserre (1982).

It is worth noting that our agents may also be nondeterministic relations, something that may be useful for specifying problems in concurrent programming. As an example we show how to specify and run "the bounded buffer problem". This illustrates that we can use logic to specify a concurrent programming problem and, furthermore run the specification to observe its behavior.

Example 4

Let us assume a bounded buffer of size N. This buffer may be viewed as an agent that accepts two sequences, (1) a write sequence of the form "Write(x_1).Write(x_2)...." (denoted by ws), (2) a read sequence of the form "Read.Read...." (denoted by rs). It produces an answer sequence (denoted by as) corresponding to the read command sequence. Now we can formalize the bounded buffer as follows:

$$bounded\text{-}buffer(ws,rs,as) \longleftrightarrow bmerge(ws,rs,0,s_1) \ \& \qquad (5)$$
$$buffer(s_1,<\$u,\$u>)=as$$

where the computation is assumed to be demand driven with s_1 as a channel variable. Here, the "bounded-buffer" is composed of two agents, "bmerge" which merges the write and read sequences, and "buffer" which responds to the read and write operations. Moreover, "bmerge" is a relation which accepts the write sequence, the read sequence and a number indicating the number of items in the buffer, and it outputs an interleaved sequence of reads and writes. This relation is characterized by the following two statements:

$$bmerge(Write(x).ws,rs,i,Write(x).as) \longleftrightarrow i<N \ \& \qquad (6)$$
$$bmerge(ws,rs,i+1,as)$$
$$bemerge(ws,Read.rs,i,Read.as) \longleftrightarrow i>0 \ \&$$
$$bmerge(ws,rs,i-1,as).$$

"buffer" is a function which accepts a sequence of reads and writes. It responds to Write(x) by storing the item x at the rear of an internal queue (represented by a difference-list, (see Clark and Tärnlund, 1977). It responds to Read by fetching an item from the front of the queue and outputting the item:

$$buffer(Write(x).s,<\$v,x.\$w>)=buffer(s,<\$v,\$w>) \qquad (7)$$
$$buffer(Read.s,<x.\$v,\$w>)=x.buffer(s,<\$v,\$w>).$$

We observe from this example that we get non-deterministic sequences produced by "bmerge".

Infinite data structures

The notion of infinite data structures can simplify writing a program, but there is a problem to treat them computationally. A noncanonical term may denote a conceptually infinite data structure. It cannot be tranformed into canonical terms, the transformation would need infinite time.

But we can transform a noncanonical term into a noncanonical term containing a greater canonical subpart which can be used in a computation.

Example 5

We can define an infinite list of integers starting with 2:

$$intfrom2()=inc(2) \tag{8}$$
$$inc(x)=x.inc(x+1)$$

It follows that $intfrom2()=2.3.inc(4)$, where this infinite list is built up by a canonical part 2.3 followed by a noncanonical term $inc(4)$. We can select the first n positive numbers starting with 2

$$\text{n-integers}(n)=y \text{ <-- } intfrom2()=x \text{ \& } select(n,x)=y \tag{9}$$

where

$$select(0,z)=Nil \tag{10}$$
$$select(n,x.y)=x.select(n-1,y) \text{ <-- } n>0$$

A call n-integers(2)=y gives y=2.3.Nil provided we use the demand driven computation rule on sentence (9). Moreover the computation can be terminated when there is no more demand from any consumer. This rule has a proof theoretical justification in our system as we shall see in section 4.

When we prefer to think of a computation as an agent operating on an infinite data structure (a stream), on which no agent can give a complete result, demand driven computation gives satisfying partial results. We illustrate this point further by a more complicated example from Kahn and McQueen (1977). The program computes the prime numbers according to Eratosthenes' sieve on a stream of positive integers. The example shows how a network evolves dynamically during a computation.

Example 6

```
prime()=sift(intfrom2())                                    (11)
            where the prime statement is demand driven
            and sift is the initial demander
sift(x.y)=x.sift(filter(x,y))
            where the sift statement is demand driven
            and sift is the initial demander
filter(x,y.z)=y.filter(x,z) <-- mod(y,x)≠0
filter(x,y.z)=filter(x,z) <-- mod(y,x)=0
```

Our goal is to compute the stream of primes, i.e. prime()=z, this computation will never stop. The demanding agent sift will successively demand an integer that will be filtered if not a prime. Every activation of the sift agent gives rise to a new filter agent for the currently recognized prime number. Here, sift is an example of a network evolving dynamically during a computation. The following figure gives a snapshot of a few computation steps illustrating this point. A channel variable is pictured as a solid line directed from the producer agent to the consumer, the argument position of a channel variable in the consuming agent is replaced by a dot.

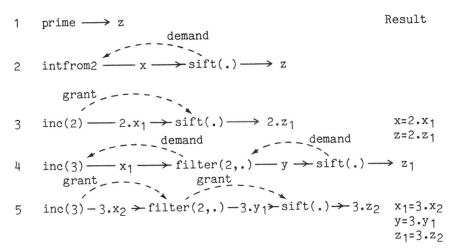

Fig. 3. The evolution of the net for the first prime numbers. The output stream is $z=2.3.z_2$.

Example 7

We illustrate a cyclic network of agents by an example from Dijkstra (1976), where a stream is generated having elements of the form $2^a*3^b*5^c$, where a,b and c are positive integers, and moreover, the elements shall appear in increasing order without omission or repetition. An abstract idea of the solution is that every generated element (the first element is 1) of the stream is multiplied by 2, 3 and 5 respectively, and the results are put into three sets of potential elements respectively, and the least element from these sets will be picked as the next generated element. In the program the elements of these sets will only be created on demands. We have:

```
p()=1.y <-- merge(mul(2,1.y),merge(mul(3,1.y),mul(5,1.y)))=y
          where the p() statement is demand driven
      merge(x.y,u.v)=x.merge(y,u.v) <-- x<u                    (12)
      merge(x.y,u.v)=u.merge(x.y,v) <-- x>u
      merge(x.y,u.v)=x.merge(y,v) <-- x=u
      mul(x,y.z)=x*y.mul(x,z)
```

Here, "merge" selects the least element from two increasing
streams of elements; and "mul" multiplies the first element
of a stream by a number. Our goal is to compute the stream
p()=z. The cyclic network defined by the p() statement will
successively pick the least element from three substreams
generated by the three "mul" agents on demands from the
"merge" agents. This network can be illustrated by the
following figure.

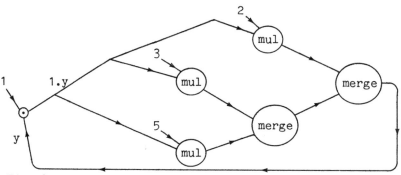

Fig. 4. A cyclic network representing the p() statement.

4. TERMINATION

In this section we show how termination can be obtained, in
demand driven mode, of programs operating on an infinite data
structure. For demand driven computation we have the rule: if
the producer p for a channel variable x is a function or is
reduced to a function and all consumers of x have been terminated then terminate p. This rule has a proof theoretical
justification that we now shall explain. Let us return to
example 5. To derive n-integers(2)=y we need two derivations,
of intfrom2()=x and of select(2,x)=y. The latter derivation
is obtained as usual. The former derivation can be obtained
in the following way.

```
                                   inc(3)=3.inc(4)  z=3.w inc(4)=w
                                   -------------------------------
               inc(2)=2.inc(3)  x=2.z                inc(3)=z
               ------------------------------------------------
intfrom2()=inc(2)                       inc(2)=x
--------------------------------------------------
                    intfrom2()=x
```

The derivation is dependent on the assumptions on x, z and w, but we can readily obtain a derivation independent of the assumptions. We substitute inc(4) for w, 3.inc(4) for z and 2.3.inc(4) for x and obtain a derivation dependent only on the statements of (8), where intfrom2()=2.3.inc(4) and select(2,x)=y is now select(2,2.3.inc(4))=y. This independence follows from the identity axiom.

Identity gives a slightly simpler treatment of termination in comparison with having relations e.g., suppose that we have a relation inc(n,w) instead of inc(n)=w, then we also need an axiom $\forall x \exists w inc(x,w)$ to terminate the computation. For an infinite data structure e.g., x=A.x we would also need the axiom $\exists x(x=A.x)$.

Example 8

The execution of prime() in example 6 will never stop, but we can use prime() to write a prime generator that generates all prime numbers up to an integer n.

```
primegen(n)=y <-- prime()=x & until(n,x)=y
  where primegen is demand driven and x is a channel variable,
    and until is the initial demander;
until(n,x.plist)=NIL <-- x > n
until(n,x.plist)=x.until(n,plist) <-- x ≤ n
```

From primegen(2)=y we get the following sequence of statements:

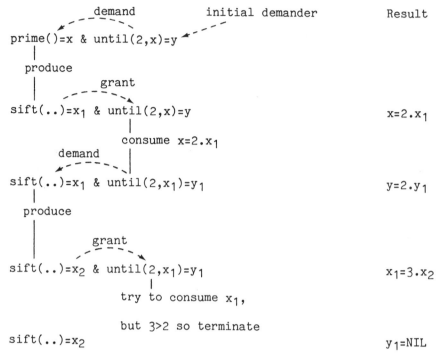

Fig. 5. Primes until 2 are generated where y=2.NIL.

All the consumers of x_2 have terminated so we can also terminate the producer.

5. NEGATION

A negated predicate A is defined as

   -A if and only if A --> ⊥   (13)

As pointed out by Prawitz (1965), to derive -A we have to find a proof of absurdity (⊥) from an assumption A and then use introduction of implication. It should be noted that the assumption A can contain free variables that may be bound during a derivation and in this way we find objects that satisfy a negated statement.

To derive a negation -A we often make use of definitions by equivalence. We shall take up an example from Clark (1978) and give a definition of a maths-major, but we make this definition conditional and say that a maths-major has to be a student. In this way we exclude non-students from the definition.

$$student(x) \rightarrow \qquad\qquad (14)$$
$$(maths\text{-}major(x) \leftrightarrow \forall y(maths\text{-}course(y) \rightarrow takes(x,y)))$$

Suppose that we want to show -maths-major(x) for some instance of x. Then we assume maths-major(x) and try to derive absurdity from that assumption. But before we can make use of definition (14) of a maths-major we have to pick a student from the data base of students e.g., defined by student(x) <-- x=Brown v x=Smith. Let us assume x=Brown. Then we have access to the equivalence of definition (14) and in particular the only-if part. If we succeed in making the definiens false we have derived absurdity. So we try to make maths-course(y) true for some instance of y and takes(Brown,y) false for this instance. Notice that the takes relation has to be defined by equivalence so the false instances of this relation can be recognized.

This treatment of negation differs logically from Prolog which strictly speaking does not have negation, and also from IC-Prolog which treats negation as failure to prove and does not have conditional equivalences (see Clark et al. 1982).

6. VIRTUAL CLASSES

It seems desirable to have sets in a programming language, and both IC-Prolog and Prolog have built in primitives for treating 'sets'. We shall introduce a notion virtual classes that is weaker than the notion of sets, but it has the advantage that we can define it in the language.

$$p\text{-}class(l) \leftrightarrow \forall x(p(x) \leftrightarrow memb(x,l)) \qquad (15)$$
where
$$-memb(u,Nil) \qquad\qquad (16)$$
$$memb(u,x.y) \leftrightarrow u=x \ v \ memb(u,y)$$

The drawback of a p-class is that we have to write a new definition for each p.

Example 9

We define a class of employees of a department

$$employee\text{-}class(d,l) \leftrightarrow \forall x(employee(d,x) \leftrightarrow memb(x,l)) (17)$$

furthermore, we define the employee relation

$$employee(d,x) \longleftrightarrow (d{=}CS \;\&\; (x{=}John \;v\; x{=}Bill)) \;v \qquad (18)$$
$$(d{=}EE \;\&\; (x{=}Mary \;v\; x{=}Jim))$$

A query employee-class(CS,l) gives l=John.Bill.Nil.

7. FINAL REMARKS

We have a compiler which translates our language to the instructions of a virtual logic machine. The compiler is written in the language C and we make use of the compiler generator YACC. The prototype implementation is for the PDP-11/UNIX and VAX/UNIX systems. The language is quite extensive in comparison with Prolog, so the structure of the generated code and the instructions of our logic machine are partly different and partly extensions of the Prolog machine described by Warren (1977).

Different aspects of this project have been reported formerly in (Hansson et al. 1980; Hansson and Haridi, 1981; Haridi, 1981; Tärnlund, 1981).

ACKNOWLEDGEMENT

We wish to thank Keith Clark for helping us to improve the presentation.

This work has been supported by the National Swedish Board for Technical Development (STU).

THE CALL BY NAME SEMANTICS OF
A CLAUSE LANGUAGE WITH FUNCTIONS

Marco Bellia   Pierpaolo Degano   Giorgio Levi

Istituto di Scienze dell'Informazione
Università di Pisa,
Corso Italia, 40
I56100 Pisa, ITALY

1. INTRODUCTION

In the last few years, languages based on first order logic have become very popular. The main features of such languages are:
- They have a clear mathematical basis, which allows the definition of a straightforward formal semantics and which provides a natural environment for proving properties of programs;
- They are examples of applicative languages, languages whose semantics are not based on state transitions. As such they lead to a hierarchically structured "non-von Neumann" programming style (Backus, 1978);
- Last but not least, today's technology allows the design of efficient implementations (Warren, 1977; Roussel, 1975; McCabe, 1978; Roberts, 1977; Szeredi, 1977).

Predicate logic programming languages can be classified according to the kind of procedures they allow. In the first class (relational languages) procedures define relations. The first example of a relational language is PLANNER (Hewitt, 1972). Kowalski's language (1974) is a milestone within this family, because of the formal definition of procedures as sets of Horn clauses, and its clean mathematical semantics (van Emden and Kowalski, 1976). On Kowalski's footsteps, PROLOG (Warren, 1977; Roussel, 1975; McCabe, 1978; Roberts, 1977; Szeredi, 1977; Warren et al. 1977; Colmerauer, 1975) and other similar languages (Tärnlund, 1977; Hansson and Haridi, 1981; Sickel, 1979) have been proposed. Relational languages have been extensively used in such fields as Problem Solving (Bundy et al. 1979) and Data Base (Futo et al. 1978a; Tärnlund, 1978), where invertibility of programs, intelligent backtracking, and the highly declarative style they provide are crucial. Furthermore, the efficiency and the expressive power of relational languages have been improved by allowing an explicit control (Kowalski, 1979b) over the non-deterministic features of the interpreters (Clark and McCabe, 1980a; Gallaire and Lasserre, 1980; Pereira and Porto, 1979a).

In the second class of languages (functional languages) procedures are sets of functional equations. Languages within such a class have been motivated by several different problems, namely proving program properties in formal systems (Levi and Sirovich, 1975; Burstall, 1976; Aubin, 1977; Boyer and Moore, 1977; Cartwright and McCarthy, 1979) and abstract data type specification (Burstall and Goguen, 1977; Goguen and Tardo, 1977; Guttag et al. 1978; Musser, 1979). In fact, properties of programs and data abstractions (i.e. lemmas and theorems to be used in proving programs correct) can easily and fruitfully be expressed in the functional language approach. Moreover, efficient evaluation rules can be adopted to define interpreters which are quite similar to those used for standard programming languages.

The language described in this paper was designed as an extension of the functional language TEL (Levi and Sirovich, 1975). The extensions we provide are conditional equations and multi-output functions (described by a relational syntax).

Note that even though we use a relational notation, our language defines (deterministic) functions only. A set of procedures is represented by a set of Horn clauses, where input and output parameters are explicitly specified. The result is a language quite different from relational languages. However, the relational framework allows us to take van Emden and Kowalski's semantics (1976) as the basis to define a fixed-point semantics. Our language, however, being an extension of TEL, has a call-by-name semantics and allows the definition of non-strict functions and non-terminating procedures having infinite data structures (streams) as inputs and/or outputs. A non-trivial extension to van Emden and Kowalski's semantics is needed to cope with such features.

2. THE SYNTAX OF FPL

The Functional plus Predicate Logic (FPL) programming language is a many sorted first order language, whose programs are equations defined according to first order logic over the alphabet $A = \{S, C, D, V, F, R\}$, where:

S is a set of identifiers. Given S, we define a <u>sort</u> s which
   is: i)   simple if s belongs to S,
       ii) functional if s belongs to $S^* \text{-->} S$,
       iii) relational if s belongs to $S^* \text{-->} S^*$.
C is a family of sets of constant symbols indexed by simple sorts.
D is a family of sets of data constructor symbols indexed by functional sorts.
V is a family of denumerable sets of variable symbols indexed by simple sorts.
F is a family of sets of function symbols indexed by functional sorts.
R is a family of sets of predicate symbols indexed by relational sorts.

Families are defined in the language by <u>declarations</u>, which assign a specific simple or functional or relational sort to each object. Examples are:

   0: -->NAT; succ: NAT-->NAT.
   nil: -->NLIST; cons: NAT x NLIST-->NLIST.
   +: NAT x NAT-->NAT.   eqn: NAT x NAT-->BOOL.
   ndiv: NAT x NAT-->NAT x NAT.

A FPL program is a set of declarations and equations. Each symbol occurring in an equation must be declared.

The syntax of equations is based on the standard concepts of term and atomic formula.

A <u>term</u> is either a data term or a functional term.
A <u>data term</u> of sort s (s belonging to S) is:
   i)   a constant symbol of sort s,
   ii) a variable symbol of sort s,
   iii) a data constructor application $d(t_1, \ldots, t_n)$ such that $t_1, \ldots, t_n$ are data terms of sorts $s_1, \ldots, s_n$ and d, belonging to D, has sort $s_1 \text{ x } \ldots \text{ x } s_n \text{-->} s$.
A <u>functional term</u> of sort s (s belonging to S) is a function application $f(t_1, \ldots, t_n)$, such that $t_1, \ldots, t_n$ are data terms of sorts $s_1, \ldots, s_n$ and f, belonging to F, has sort $s_1 \text{ x } \ldots \text{ x } s_n \text{-->} s$.

An <u>atomic formula</u> is either:
   i) a functional atomic formula of the form $t=d$, where d is
      a data term of sort s and t is a term of the same sort,
      or
   ii) a relational atomic formula of the form $r(\underline{in}:t_1,\ldots,t_m;$
      $\underline{out}:t_p,\ldots,t_n)$, such that $t_1,\ldots,t_m,t_p,\ldots,t_n$ are data
      terms of sorts $s_1,\ldots,s_m,s_p,\ldots,s_n$ and r, belonging to
      R, has sort s_1 x...x s_m-->s_p x...x s_n.

<u>Equations</u> are formulas of the form l , c <-- r , where l
(left part) is an atomic formula, c (constraint) and r (right
part) are (possibly empty) lists of atomic formulas. The
equation is functional or relational, according to the type
of its left part.

Example:
1. true:-->BOOL   2. false:-->BOOL
3. 0:-->NAT   4. s: NAT-->NAT
5. minus: NAT x NAT-->NAT   6. lt: NAT x NAT-->BOOL
7. ndiv: NAT x NAT-->NAT x NAT
e1. minus(x,0)=x<--   e2. minus(s(x),s(y))=z<--minus(x,y)=z
e3. lt(0,s(x)=true<--   e4. lt(x,0)=false<--
e5. lt(s(x),s(y))=z<--lt(x,y)=z
e6. ndiv($\underline{in}$:x,y;$\underline{out}$:0,x),lt(x,y)=true<--
e7. ndiv($\underline{in}$:x,y;$\underline{out}$:s(q),r),lt(x,y)=false<--
               ndiv($\underline{in}$:z,y;$\underline{out}$:q,r),minus(x,y)=z
e8. isfact(x,y)=false,ndiv($\underline{in}$:y,x;$\underline{out}$:z,s(r))<--
e9. isfact(x,y)=true,ndiv($\underline{in}$:y,x;$\underline{out}$:z,0)<--

Declarations 1-3, 4, 5-6, 7 are constant, data constructor,
function and relation declarations, respectively. The example
is completed with the functional equations e1-e5, e8-e9 and
the relational equations e6-e7. The above example defines
some standard arithmetic functions (minus, lt), the integer
division (ndiv) and a predicate (isfact) which checks if its
first parameter is a factor of its second parameter. All the
functions are defined over the sort NAT, defined by the
constant 0 and the constructor s (successor). A non-empty
constraint appears in equations e6, e7, e8 and e9.

Equations are used as reduction rules. Let a: $f(t_1,..,t_n)=v$
$(r(\underline{in}:t_1,..,t_n;\underline{out}:v_1,..,v_m)$) be an atomic formula to be
reduced and let e be an equation l,c<--r . a can be rewritten
by e if
   i)   a and l have the same function (or predicate) symbol.
       Let l be the atomic formula $f(u_1,..,u_n)=w$
       $(r(\underline{in}:u_1,..,u_n;\underline{out}:w_1,..,w_m))$.
   ii) There exists an instantiation L of variable symbols to
       terms, such that $(u_i)L = t_i$, i=1,..,n.

iii) The constraint (c)L, obtained by applying L to the variable symbols occurring in c, is satisfied (i.e. it can be successfully reduced).

If all the above conditions are satisfied, the atomic formula a is reduced to the list of atomic formulas obtained by applying L to the right part r of the equation.

We will restate the definition of reduction in more precise terms in the next section. The above definition was introduced to give a flavour of the operational semantics and to allow us to use a simple example to show the meaning of our syntactic constructs.

Our equations are conditional rewrite rules. Conditional rewriting was extensively used in several reduction systems (see, for example, Griesmer and Jenks, 1971; Hearn, 1971). Conditions (constraints in our language) allow one to express complex preconditions for the application of a reduction. In our language, constraints are introduced so as to guarantee deterministic reductions. As an example, assume

$$ndiv(\underline{in}:s(s(0)),s(0);\underline{out}:u,v)$$

is the atomic formula to be reduced. Equations e6 and e7 are candidate reduction rules. Both equations satisfy conditions i) and ii). However, they have different constraints. Once we apply the instantiation, the two constraints are, respectively,

$$lt(s(s(0)),s(0))=true \quad and \quad lt(s(s(0)),s(0))=false$$

which are reduced by e5 to

$$lt(s(0),0)=true \quad and \quad lt(s(0),0)=false$$

Only the second constraint is reduced successfully by e4. Hence only equation e7 can be applied resulting in the list of atomic formulas

$$ndiv(\underline{in}:z,s(0);\underline{out}:s(q),v),minus(s(s(0)),s(0))=z.$$

Determinism could be achieved by assuming that the set of equations has some order, or by using a conditional on the right part of the equation, which would lead to a LISP-like language where a function is defined by a single conditional equation. Our solution does not require specific conditional primitives or orders, which would affect the mathematical semantics as well.

To guarantee deterministic evaluation the definition of
equation must be tightened to the definition of well-formed
equation. Well-formedness is a set of (statically verifiable)
conditions, which will not be precisely defined here see
(Bellia, et al. 1980) for a complete formal definition).

The first set of conditions for well-formedness is concerned
with relations among atomic formulas in a right part or in a
constraint. Their goal is to ensure that each atomic formula
has the relevant input information and that each output is
supplied by just one atomic formula.

Some examples of non well-formed equations will give a
general idea of the problem.

$$r(\underline{in}:x;\underline{out}:y,z) \; <-- \; g(w)=y,f(x)=w,q(\underline{in}:x;\underline{out}:w,z)$$

Output variable w is computed by two different atomic
formulas

$$p(\underline{in}:x,y;\underline{out}:z) \; <-- \; h_1(t,w)=z,h_2(x,y)=w$$

Input variable t to the atomic formula $h_1(t,w)=z$ is unbound.

The above problems arise from our choice of a relational
syntax, which was adopted i) to allow the definiton of
multiple output functions, and ii) to allow the output
computed by a function to be provided as input to more than
one function.

For example, in the equation

$$f(x)=y \; <-- \; r(\underline{in}:x;\underline{out}:w_1,z),h_1(z)=w_2,h_2(z)=w_3,g(w_1,w_2,w_3)=y$$

the predicate r models a two-output function, whose second
output (z) is input both to h_1 and h_2. A different syntax for
the equation (following the style of NPL, Burstall, 1976),
could be

$$f(x)=g(w_1,h_1(z),h_2(z)) \; \underline{where} \; r'(x)=<w_1,z>.$$

Such a notation, however, requires some primitive notion of
tuple to model multiple output functions (no specific primitive is needed in our relational framework). Our notation,
any way, has to be considered the abstract syntax, on which
both the interpreter and the fixed-point semantics are
defined. A NPL-like notation can naturally be taken as
concrete syntax.

The second set of conditions is concerned with well-formed-

ness of sets of equations. A <u>set of equations</u> should denote
sets of procedures. Since our aim is to restrict sets of
equations so as to define (deterministic) procedures by
disjunct cases, we are forced to introduce specific conditions, which are concerned with the non superposition property
on the equations left parts and are based on (first order)
unification (see Bellia et al. 1980). Roughly speaking, the
non superposition test guarantees that, given any "closed"
program atomic formula (i.e. a formula whose inputs are non
variable data terms), it can be rewritten by at most one
equation in the set.

Let us finally note that the functional and relational
aspects of FPL can be separated leading to two different
subsets of the language. The language obtained by ruling out
relational atomic formulas and left part constraints, is a
subset of the functional language TEL (Levi and Sirovich,
1975). It is a subset since it does not allow the expression
of properties of programs. Ruling out functional atomic
formulas and left part constraints, we obtain a specific
class of Horn clauses, characterized by input-output separation. Because of this case, we lose the full expressive power
of Horn clauses, which allows to define relations and leads
to program invertibility. On the other hand, we are able to
define a deterministic interpreter.

3. OPERATIONAL SEMANTICS

FPL has several semantic aspects which are worth detailing
before going into the description of the interpreter. Some of
these aspects are concerned with the operational semantics
only, while a few of them affect the fixed-point semantics as
well.

a) The language has an external evaluation rule, hence
defined procedures are allowed to be non-strict.
b) The language leads naturally to a call by need (Wadsworth,
1971; Vuillemin, 1974) interpreter, i.e. an interpreter based
on call by name and structure sharing. In fact, our language
allows the expression of structure sharing thus making it
something more than a mere implementation aspect.
c) Our interpreter is based on a lazy evaluation rule
(Henderson and Morris, 1976; Friedman and Wise, 1976) i.e. it
allows data structure incremental evaluation. Lazy evaluation
is achieved by letting the data constructors to be non-strict
(at least in some of their arguments). Our data constructors
are intrinsically lazy in all of their arguments. As a

consequence of lazy constructors, data are not forced to be ground data terms (i.e. terms not containing any variable symbol), but are allowed to be suspensions, i.e. partially evaluated data structures.
d) Lazy constructors allow us to cope with infinite data structures (streams) and with nonterminating procedures having streams as inputs and/or outputs.

We will give an informal definition of the interpreter. A complete formalization of the operational semantics is too tedious and lengthy to be given here and is essentially the same as the semantics given in (Bellia et al. 1980). The interpreter is used to reduce a program, which consists of a set of atomic formulas satisfying well-formedness conditions similar to those for equations. More specifically, the interpreter's goal is to compute the outputs of the program. Therefore, an attempt is made to rewrite a formula f which produces some output of the program.

Rewriting requires the formula to be matched against the left part of an equation e (whose variable symbols are consistently renamed). Matching is based on
- unification with the left part of e, possibly resulting in an instantiation L,
- successful reduction of the constraint of e (if nonempty).

Unification may require the instantiation of some input variable in f (which must also appear in the outputs of some other formula in the program). This situation mirrors the fact that on some input of f there is not yet sufficient information. Hence the interpreter recursively attempts to reduce the formula which has that variable as output. Such a formula is reduced to the point where its outputs meet the requirements of the unification with f.

Both the lazy evaluation rule and the possibility of handling streams are based on the above mechanism. Note also that the reduction of a constraint might cause new reductions and refine the instantiation to be applied to the equation right part.

If the matching process succeeds (remember that a unique successful matching can exist, because of the non superposition property), the instantiation L is applied to the right part of e, which replaces the formula f in the program. This follows a final unification process, which is needed to bind the output variables of f to the outputs of the left part of e.

Note that, if matching f against the left part of e fails, a is matched against another equation in the set. However, all those reductions that were possibly performed in the previous attempt need not to be performed again. Note also that, when the non superposition property is satisfied, we don't need unrestricted backtracking, i.e. backtracking to a choice point which had already succeeded. In fact, if the matching process (including constraint reduction) succeeds, no other successfully matching equation exists. If matching fails, we only need to kill the current attempt.

The behaviour of the interpreter can be better understood through an example. Let the set of equations be the set defined in Section 2 extended with the following declarations and equations.

8. cons: NAT x STREAM-OF-NAT --> STREAM-OF-NAT
9. integer: NAT --> STREAM-OF-NAT
10. prime: --> STREAM-OF-NAT
11. $prime_1$: STREAM-OF-NAT --> STREAM-OF-NAT
12. filter: NAT x STREAM-OF-NAT --> STREAM-OF-NAT
13. select: NAT x STREAM-OF-NAT --> NAT
e10. integer(x)=cons(x,y) <-- integer(s(x))=y
e11. prime()=x <-- $prime_1$(y)=x, integer(s(s(0)))=y
e12. $prime_1$(cons(x,y))=cons(x,z)<--$prime_1$(w)=z,filter(x,y)=w
e13. filter(x,cons(y,z))=w,isfact(x,y)=true<--filter(x,z)=w
e14. filter(x,cons(y,z))=cons(y,v),isfact(x,y)=false<--
                    filter(x,z)=v
e15. select(0,cons(y,z))=y<--
e16. select(s(x),cons(y,z))=w <-- select(x,z)=w

The function prime generates a stream (infinite list) of all the prime numbers and is based on the Eratosthenes sieve algorithm. Integer generates the stream of all the natural numbers starting from the value of its parameter. Filter removes from a stream all the numbers which are a multiple of its first parameter. Select returns the (i+1)th element of the stream if i is its first parameter.

Assume that we want to compute the third prime number. Then the program should be

$$select(s(s(0)),y)=x,prime()=y$$

In the sequel we will show the reduction of the program, by describing the sequence of rewritings. Underlined formulas are the formulas under rewriting and the corresponding matching equation is associated to each reduced program. For the sake of simplicity, we will not consider the reduction of the function isfact, which will be considered a primitive operation.

(e11) select(s(s(0)),y)=x,<u>prime()=y</u>
(e10) select(s(s(0)),y)=x,prime$_1$(y$_1$)=y,<u>integer(s(s(0)))=y$_1$</u>
(e12) select(s(s(0)),y)=x,<u>prime$_1$(cons(s(s(0)),y$_2$)=y,</u>
               integer(s(s(s(0))))=y$_2$
(e16) <u>select(s(s(0)),cons(s(s(0)),z$_1$))=x</u>,prime$_1$(w$_1$)=z$_1$,
         filter(s(s(0)),y$_2$)=w$_1$,integer(s(s(s(0))))=y$_2$
(e10) select(s(0),z$_1$)=x,prime$_1$(w$_1$)=z$_1$,filter(s(s(0)),y$_2$)=w$_1$,
     <u>integer(s(s(s(0))))=y$_2$</u>
(e14) select(s(0),z$_1$)=x,prime$_1$(w$_1$)=z$_1$,integer(s(s(s(s(0)))))=y$_3$,
     <u>filter(s(s(0)),cons(s(s(s(0))),y$_3$))=w$_1$</u>
(e12) select(s(0),z$_1$)=x,<u>prime$_1$(cons(s(s(s(0))),v$_1$))=z$_1$</u>,
     integer(s(s(s(0))))=y$_3$,filter(s(s(0)),y$_3$)=v$_1$
(e16) <u>select(s(0),cons(s(s(s(0))),z$_2$))=x</u>,prime$_1$(w$_2$)=z$_2$,
  filter(s(s(0)),v$_1$)=w$_2$,filter(s(s(0)),y$_3$)=v$_1$,
  integer(s(s(s(0))))=y$_3$
(e10) select(0,z$_2$)=x,prime$_1$(w$_2$)=z$_2$,filter(s(s(s(0))),v$_1$)=w$_2$,
    filter(s(s(0)),y$_3$)=v$_1$,<u>integer(s(s(s(s(0)))))=y$_3$</u>
(e13) select(0,z$_2$)=x,prime$_1$(w$_2$)=z$_2$,filter(s(s(s(0))),v$_1$)=w$_2$,
    <u>filter(s(s(0)),cons(s(s(s(s(0)))),y$_4$))=v$_1$</u>
     ,integer(s(s(s(s(0)))))=y$_4$
(e10) select(0,z$_2$)=x,prime$_1$(w$_2$)=z$_2$,filter(s(s(s(0))),v$_1$)=w$_2$,
    filter(s(s(0)),y$_4$)=v$_1$,<u>integer(s(s(s(s(0)))))=y$_4$</u>
(e14) select(0,z$_2$)=x,prime$_1$(w$_2$)=z$_2$,filter(s(s(s(0))),v$_1$)=w$_2$,
    <u>filter(s(s(0)),cons(s(s(s(s(0)))),y$_5$))=v$_1$</u>
     ,integer(s(s(s(s(s(0))))))=y$_5$
(e14) select(0,z$_2$)=x,prime$_1$(w$_2$)=z$_2$,
    <u>filter(s(s(s(0))),cons(s(s(s(s(s(0))))),v$_2$))=w$_2$</u>,
    filter(s(s(0)),y$_5$)=v$_2$,integer(s(s(s(s(s(0))))))=y$_5$
(e12) select(0,z$_2$)=x,
    <u>prime$_1$(cons(s(s(s(s(s(0))))),v$_3$))=z$_2$</u>,
    filter(s(s(s(0))),v$_2$)=v$_3$,filter(s(s(0)),y$_5$)=v$_2$,
    integer(s(s(s(s(s(0))))))=y$_5$
(e15) <u>select(0,cons(s(s(s(s(s(0))))),z$_3$))=x</u>,
    prime$_1$(w$_3$)=z$_3$,filter(s(s(s(s(s(0))))),v$_3$)=w$_3$,
    filter(s(s(s(0))),v$_2$)=v$_3$,filter(s(s(0)),y$_5$)=v$_2$,
    integer(s(s(s(s(s(0))))))=y$_5$

The last rewriting binds the output variable x to s(s(s(s(s(0))))), thus terminating the reduction (even if the current program is not empty).

4. FIXED-POINT SEMANTICS

In this Section, we will describe the fixed-point semantics of a set of equations $E=\{e_i\}$.

From the fixed-point semantics viewpoint, an equation can be considered a Horn clause, obtained by moving all the formulas occurring in the constraint to the right part. Let the equation have the form

and let

1.   P,Q <-- R,S

2.   P   <-- R,S,Q

be the transformed equation. Equations 1 and 2 might have different operational semantics. In fact, Q could never be evaluated with equation 2, resulting in a different semantics when the reduction of Q does not terminate. However, this situation may arise only if equation 2 is not well-formed (Bellia et al. 1980). If the reduction of Q terminates and equation 2 is well-formed, then the two equations have the same semantics. In any case, the fixed-point semantics of equation 2 is equivalent to the operational semantics of equation 1 (Bellia et al. 1980).

The semantics we will give in this Section is strongly related to the fixed point semantics given in (van Emden and Kowalski, 1976) for Horn clauses. However, a non trivial extension is needed to cope with the call by name semantics and lazy constructors (Levi and Pegna, 1982).

The fixed-point semantics of a set of equations $E=\{e_i\}$ is a model of E, obtained as the fixed-point of a transformation PHI(E) on interpretations. Our semantics is a call by name semantics, hence the sets of constants symbols in C are extended to contain, for each simple sort s, a distinct constant symbol $\perp_s$, which stands for undefined.

Interpretations are defined on an abstract domain A, which is a family of sets A_s, each set being indexed by a sort s occurring in E. Each A_s is defined as follows:
  i) $\perp_s$ belongs to A_s.
  ii) All the constant symbols of sort s, occurring in E, are in A_s.
  iii) For each data constructor symbol d of sort
       $s_1 \times ... \times s_m \rightarrow s$, A_s contains all the terms
       $d(t_1,...,t_m)$, such that $t_1,...,t_m$ belong to
       $A_{s_1},...,A_{s_m}$, respectively.

The domain A contains the standard many-sorted Herbrand universe as a proper subset, i.e. the set of all the terms in which none of the $\bot s$ occurs. In addition, A contains suspensions, i.e. terms in which both normal and undefined constant symbols occur. Suspensions are data not completely evaluated. Unevaluated data components are denoted by undefined constants. Finally, A contains fully undefined terms, i.e. terms in which only undefined constant symbols occur. The abstract domain A is partially ordered by the relation $\leq$ defined as follows:

1) for each constant symbol c_i of sort s, $c_i \leq c_i$ and $\bot s \leq c_i$
2) for each data constructor symbol d of sort
    $s_1 \times \ldots \times s_m \longrightarrow s$
    i) $\bot s \leq d(t_1, \ldots, t_m)$ and $d(t_1, \ldots, t_m) \leq \bot s$
       if $t_i \leq \bot s_i$ and $\bot s_i \leq t_i$, $i=1, \ldots, m$;
    ii) $d(t_1, \ldots, t_m) \leq d(t_1', \ldots, t_m')$ if $t_i \leq t_i'$, $i=1, \ldots, m$.

The partial ordering relation $\leq$ on the abstract domain A, is related to the intuitive notion of suspension approximation as introduced by the lazy constructors. As an example, the relation $cons(1, \bot) \leq cons(1, cons(2, \bot))$ mirrors the fact that $cons(1, cons(2, \bot))$ is a refinement of $cons(1, \bot)$.

Interpretations are defined as subsets of the interpretation base B. <u>The interpretation base</u> B is a set of atomic formulas defined as follows:
i)   For each function symbol f (occurring in E) of sort
    $s_1 \times \ldots \times s_m \longrightarrow s$, B contains all the formulas
    $f(t_1, \ldots, t_m) = t$ such that $t_1, \ldots, t_m$ and t have sorts
    $s_1, \ldots, s_m, s$ respectively, and $t \leq \bot s$ does not hold.
ii) For each predicate symbol r (occurring in E) of sort
    $s_1 \times \ldots \times s_m \longrightarrow s_p \times \ldots \times s_n$, B contains all the
    formulas $r(\underline{in}:t_1, \ldots, t_m; \underline{out}:t_p, \ldots, t_n)$, such that
    $t_1, \ldots, t_m, t_p, \ldots, t_n$ have sorts $s_1, \ldots, s_m, s_p, \ldots, s_n$
    respectively, and there exists at least one of the terms
    t_i, $i=p, \ldots, n$, such that $t_i \leq \bot s_i$ does not hold.

The interpretation base B is the set of all the ground atomic formulas, i.e. formulas not containing variable symbols. Each formula in B assigns specific ground output terms for the application of function (or predicate) symbols to ground input terms. Since our language is deterministic, the semantics of a set of equations cannot contain <u>colliding atomic formulas</u>, i.e. formulas assigning different output terms to the same function or predicate application.

B is partially ordered by the relation $\leq^*$, such that $f_i \leq^* f_j$

if and only if f_i and f_j are colliding, and for each pair of output terms (t_{ik}, t_{jk}) of f_i and f_j, $t_{ik} \leq t_{jk}$. Intuitively, $f_i \leq^* f_j$ reflects that at least one of the outputs of f_j is a refinement of the corresponding output of f_i.

An **interpretation** is any subset of B not containing colliding atomic formulas.

The set of interpretations $\{J_i\}$ can be partially ordered by the relation $\leq.$, defined as follows: $J_i \leq. J_j$, if and only if for each formula f_{ik} in J_i, there exists a formula f_{jh} in J_j, such that $f_{ik} \leq^* f_{jh}$.

Roughly speaking, an interpretation assigns output values to applications of functions and relations to ground input values. All the other applications have only undefined outputs. Note that the partial ordering relation $\leq.$ on interpretations corresponds to an intuitive notion of better approximation. In fact, if $J_i \leq. J_j$, then either J_j assigns output values to some applications that in J_i had only undefined outputs, or J_j refines some output value of J_i.

Let J_i anofJ_j be interpretations a J_i' be the set of all the formulas of J_i colliding with formulas of J_j. If $J_i' \leq. J_j$, the operation § on ordered interpretation pairs is defined as follows:

$$J_i \S J_j = f_k, \text{ such that } f_k \text{ belongs either to } J_j \text{ or to } \{(J_i - J_i')\}.$$

Note that $J_i \S J_j$ is an interpretation, such that $J_i \leq. J_i \S J_j$, and $J_j \leq. J_i \S J_j$.

We will now introduce the transformation PHI(E) which maps interpretations onto interpretations and will be used to define the semantics of a set of equations E.

Let J_i be any interpretation and e_k: $H(e_k) \leftarrow G(e_k)$ be an equation of E. The equation e_k defines a transformation PHI_k which maps J_i onto the interpretation $J_{ik} = PHI_k(J_i) = J_i \S J_{ik}'$, where J_{ik}' is defined as follows. For each instantiation L of variables to terms of A, the formula $(H(e_k))L$ belongs to J_{ik}',
1) if at least one output variable of $(H(e_k))L$ is not undefined, and
2) if for each atomic formula a_j in $G(e_k)$ either
   2.1) $(a_j)L$ belongs to J_i, or
   2.2) all the output variables of $(a_j)L$ are undefined.

Note that L must instantiate a variable v of sort s to a term belonging to A_s, and that if $G(e_k)$ is empty, Condition 2 is satisfied for any instantiation L.

Note also that J_{ik}' is an interpretation, since with a single equation we cannot derive colliding atomic formulas. Furthermore, J_{ik} is always defined, since for each formula f_r in J_i such that there exists a colliding formula f_q in J_{ik}', $f_r \leq^* f_q$, as a consequence of the non superposition condition (Bellia et al. 1980). Hence J_{ik} is an interpretation such that $J_i \leq. J_{ik}$.

The transformation PHI(E) is the transformation defined by all the equations of E according to the above definition.

It can be proven that transformation PHI(E) on the set of interpretations partially ordered by $\leq.$ is monotonic and continuous. Hence, there exists the least fixed-point interpretation J^* such that $J^*=PHI(E)(J^*)$, which can be obtained by iteratively applying PHI(E), starting with the empty subset of B, which is the bottom element of the partially ordered set of interpretations.

Let us consider a simple example which should show the behaviour of the transformation applied to an equation which defines a nonterminating function. Let e_k be the equation

$$integer(x)=cons(x,y) \; \longleftarrow \; integer(s(x))=y,$$

and let $\perp s_n$ denote the undefined constant symbol of sort STREAM-OF-NAT. The sequence of interpretations generated by the transformation PHI_k is the following (we will not consider here the undefined values of sort NAT, because they are not relevant to our example).

$J_0= \{ \}$
$J_1= \{ integer(0)=cons(0,\perp s_n), integer(s(0))=cons(s(0),\perp s_n),....\}$
$J_2= \{ integer(0)=cons(0,cons(s(0),\perp s_n)),$
$\quad\quad integer(s(0))=cons(s(0),cons(s(s(0)),\perp s_n)),...\}$
$\vdots$

The semantics of e_k is the limit of the above sequence.

The equivalence between the fixed-point semantics and the operational semantics defined in Section 3 is related to the completness of first order logic. In fact, if the fixed-point interpretation of a set of equations E contains a ground atomic formula $f(t_1,...,t_m)=t$ $(r(\underline{in}:t_1,...,t_m;\underline{out}:t_p,...,t_n))$ then the interpreter, given the program $\overline{f(t_1,...,t_m)}=x$ $(r(\underline{in}:t_1,...,t_m;\underline{out}:x_1,...,x_n))$ produces $t(t_p,...,t_n)$.

A formal proof of the equivalence can be obtained by a straightforward extension of the proof of a similar result (Levi and Pegna, 1982).

5. CONCLUSION

We have described a new first order language, which enriches the functional language TEL with some appealing features of the relational logic languages. This approach allows the language to express both functions and procedures, whilst preserving the possibility of using lazy evaluation to sequence the computation. These extensions to TEL give a language close to that independently developed at Uppsala (Hansson et al. 1980). The paper presents both a mathematical and an operational semantics of the language. The former is obtained by extending the standard model theoretical approach to cast the extensions in. The latter is based on a call by need computation rule, thus it is a close model to efficient implementations.

The improved expressive power of the language is due to the presence of both the function and the procedure constructs and to the left part constraints which provide the full power of a built-in conditional, while saving the first order logic axiomatic flavour. One more interesting feature of FPL is its ability to describe non-strict functions. Non strict functions, as the if-then-else, can easily and naturally be defined in FPL, just because of its external evaluation rule.

We have almost completed an experimental FPL interpreter, which is written in LISP, is based on structure sharing and relies on the LISP garbage collector. Future work on FPL will include relaxing some of the conditions so as to allow the definition of parallel programs and program properties. The first extension is rather straightforward, since our lazy evaluation mechanism is a natural and powerful communication tool. The ability to express and use theorems requires a non trivial extension of the convergence test defined for term rewriting systems, since the non superposition property does not hold. Our final goal is the creation of a programming environment providing tools for editing, proving and executing FPL programs.

LOGIC IN LISP

LOGLISP: MOTIVATION, DESIGN AND IMPLEMENTATION

J.A. Robinson   E.E. Sibert

School of Computer and Information Science
Syracuse University
Syracuse, NY 13210, USA

1. MOTIVATION.

LOGLISP is an implementation of logic programming within LISP. Our motivation in extending LISP in this way was in part to provide ourselves and other LISP users with the equivalent of PROLOG without the need to venture outside the rich, highly convenient and (to us) familiar LISP programming environment. We also believed that a LISP thus enhanced might well be an effective device for helping to persuade diehard LISP adherents that after all - thanks to Kowalski, Colmerauer, van Emden, Clark and other pioneers - something both useful and beautiful has risen from the old resolution theorem-proving ashes.

In part also we wanted to rescue a distinction which seemed to be rapidly ceasing to exist - that between logic programming as described by Kowalski, and the particular implementation of it found in PROLOG. We gladly acknowledge that the rapid growth of interest in logic programming would have been impossible without the various PROLOG implementations, and we share the universal admiration for Warren's marvellous Edinburgh PROLOG system for the DEC-10. However, the procedural interpretation of Horn clauses within a LUSH-resolution theorem-prover permits, but by no means requires, a backtracking process for the exploration of alternative computations. These computations can (as in LOGLISP) be developed in quasi-parallel, thereby avoiding the impression that logic programming is (like PLANNER) about advancing and retreating, trying, failing and trying again, and now and then succeeding.

In LOGLISP the logic programmer has (we hope) instead the
impression of writing down collections of sufficient
conditions for certain predicates to hold of certain tuples
of things. Given such a collection D (a "knowledge base") one
then computes one or more (possibly all) of the environments
(i.e., sets of bindings of terms to variables) E in which a
given conjunction Q of atomic sentences can be shown (using
only D and LUSH-resolution) to hold.

LOGLISP consists of LISP together with a set of logic-
programming primitives which we refer to collectively as
LOGIC. Let us review very briefly the chief conventions and
notations of LISP.

2. LISP

There are only two data types in LISP - atoms and dotted
pairs. Atoms are identifiers, strings and numerals. For any
two data objects A and B there is a dotted pair, written A.B,
whose **head** is A and whose **tail** is B. If X is A.B we write

$$A = hX , B = tX .$$

The atom NIL - also written () - is known as the **empty list.**
In general a list is either () or else a dotted pair whose
tail is a list.

Dotted pairs of the form $A_1.(A_2. \ ... \ (A_n.A_{n+1}) \ ... \ )$ may be
written in the "dotted list notation": $(A_1 \ ... \ A_n \ . \ A_{n+1})$
When A_{n+1} is NIL this may be further elided to: $(A_1 \ ... \ A_n)$
which is "list notation".

3. LOGIC

In LOGIC we represent assertions, queries and all other logic
programming constructs as LISP data-objects. Logical
variables are represented by identifiers beginning with a
lowercase letter. Proper names (i.e., predicates, operators
and individual constants) are represented as identifiers
beginning with an uppercase letter or with a special character such as +, §, $, %, !, =, >, <, *, : or ?. In addition,
numerals and strings (a string is a sequence of characters
enclosed in double quotation marks, as for example "..this is
a string..") can be used as individual constants (but not as
predicates or operators). We refer to proper names which are
not numerals or strings as **proper identifiers.**

We have reversed the Edinburgh convention (that variables begin with uppercase letters and constants with lowercase) in order to follow the one well-established in the predicate calculus (where one would write, e.g., R(x,y) rather than r(X,Y)); on the other hand our convention for operators requires us to write them with uppercase rather than the more traditional lowercase letters. Furthermore, we follow LISP usage in bracketing predicate (or operator) along with its argument(s) as e.g. (R x (F x y)) rather than R(x,F(x,y)), usually omitting commas although LISP permits them if desired.

A term is either a logical variable, a constant, or a list of terms. A predication (= atomic sentence) is a list of terms whose head is a proper identifier. We call sentences of the form:

if each member of A is true then B is true

assertions. In general the conclusion B is a predication and the hypothesis A is a list of predications. An assertion with an empty hypothesis is unconditional, and one whose hypothesis is nonempty is conditional. An assertion containing one or more logical variables is called a rule, while one containing no logical variables is called a datum.

3.1 Assertions

We follow Kowalski's notation in writing the conditional assertion

if each member of $(A_1 \ldots A_n)$ is true then B is true

in the "reverse arrow" form: $B \leftarrow A_1 \ldots A_n$
but the LOGLISP user enters this assertion into the machine by typing the LISP procedure call: $(:- B\ A_1 \ldots A_n)$
which invokes the "assert" function :- . The assert function stores the assertion internally under the primary index P, where P is the predicate of the conclusion B. If P happens to be a "data predicate" (i.e., one for which all assertions are data) then the assertion is also "secondarily indexed" by each proper identifier which occurs in its conclusion. A knowledge base is a set of assertions. It is customary to think of a knowledge base as partitioned into procedures, each procedure corresponding to some predicate P and consisting of all the assertions in the knowledge base whose conclusion has P as its head. The name of the procedure is then by convention taken to be P.

Assertions may also be given their own individual names at

the option of the user. In displaying explanations (=
deductions) it is convenient to be able to refer to an
assertion by its name instead of displaying the entire
assertion.

3.2 Queries

A query is essentially a description

$$((x_1 \ldots x_t) : C_1 \& \ldots \& C_n)$$

of the set of all t-tuples which satisfy some constraint
expressed as a conjunction of predications C_i, i=1, ..., n.
In LOGIC such a query is written

$$(ALL \ (x_1 \ldots x_t) \ C_1 \ldots C_n)$$

and is in fact a LISP procedure call on the procedure ALL
(which is a FEXPR, that is, which does not evaluate its
arguments). The query returns as its (LISP) value a list of
all the tuples which satisfy the given constraint. This list
is called the answer to the query. Its component tuples are
obtained by means of the basic deduction cycle, explained
below, which is the heart of LOGIC and which is invoked by
every query.

Other forms of the basic query are

$$(ANY \ K \ (x_1 \ldots x_t) \ C_1 \ldots C_n) \ ,$$

which returns no more than K of the tuples satisfying the
constraint, and

$$(THE \ (x_1 \ldots x_t) \ C_1 \ldots C_n) \ ,$$

which returns the sole member of the list

$$(ANY \ 1 \ (x_1 \ldots x_t) \ C_1 \ldots C_n) \ ,$$

(rather than the list itself), and

$$(SETOF \ K \ X \ C) \ .$$

Here SETOF is the EXPR function underlying the FEXPRS ALL,
ANY and THE (EXPR functions do evaluate their arguments).
SETOF takes three arguments: K, which should evaluate to a
nonnegative integer or to the atom ALL; X, which should
evaluate to an "answer template" $(x_1 \ldots x_t)$; and C, which

should evaluate to a "constraint list" $(C_1 \ldots C_n)$. It is particularly to be noted that the answer to a query is a LISP data object, and can thus be subjected under program control to internal analysis and manipulation, as well as being displayed at the terminal.

4. THE DEDUCTION CYCLE

The basic process of the LOGIC system is that carried out in the <u>deduction cycle</u> to compute the answer to a query.

4.1 Implicit Expressions

For the sake of both clarity and efficiency the representation of constraints during the deduction cycle is done by the Boyer-Moore technique. This calls for an expression C to be represented by a pair (Q E) called an <u>implicit expression</u>, in which Q is an expression known as the <u>skeleton part</u> and E is a set of variable-bindings known as the <u>environment part</u> of the implicit expression. The idea is that the implicit expression (Q E) represents the expression which is the result of installing throughout Q the bindings given in E.

4.2 Bindings and Environments

In general a <u>binding</u> is a dotted pair whose head is a logical variable, while an <u>environment</u> is a list of bindings no two of which have the same head.

The following account of the deduction cycle is a somewhat abstract one in which concrete details of our implementation have been suppressed in the interests of intelligibility. Despite appearances at this level, access to bindings of variables within environments is not in fact accomplished by searching the environment-list, but by more direct array-like methods which allow us to achieve much faster lookups. As the reader will soon become aware, our non-backtracking approach raises for us a delicate problem of reconciling the space economies of Boyer-Moore structure sharing with the need for essentially direct (= bounded by constant time) access to variable bindings during unification. We postpone further discussion of this problem and our solution to it until after we have explained the deduction cycle.

4.3 Immediate and Ultimate Associates

If the environment E contains the dotted pair A.B we say that

A is defined in E and we write: (DEF A E).   We also say that
B is the immediate associate of A in E   and write:
B=(IMM A E). As was observed above, the computation of B,
given A and E, is done in an essentially direct fashion in
our implementation. Note that if the expression A is defined
in the environment E then A is a logical variable. When (DEF
A E) = false, A may or may not be a logical variable.

The immediate associate of A in E might turn out to be a
variable which is itself also defined in E. When this is the
case we often wish to follow the trail of bindings to its end
and thereby obtain the ultimate associate of A in E, written
(ULT A E), which is the earliest expression in the series

        A, (IMM A E), (IMM(IMM A E) E), ...,

which is not defined in E. So we have:

   (ULT A E) = if (DEF A E) then (ULT(IMM A E) E) else A

Note that (ULT A E) is defined for all expressions A, not
just for logical variables.

4.4 Recursive Realizations

We can now say more precisely how an expression is
represented implicitly by a skeleton-environment pair. The
"recursive realization" (RECREAL X Y) of an expression X in
an environment Y is the expression defined by:

(RECREAL X Y) =if X is U.V then (RECREAL U Y).(RECREAL V Y)
            else if (DEF X Y) then (RECREAL (ULT X Y) Y)
            else X

The skeleton-environment pair (Q E) then represents the
expression: (RECREAL Q E).

4.5 Unification

The deduction cycle calls for repeated application of the
operation of LUSH-resolution (Hill, 1974), which in turn
involves the unification process.

Given two expressions A and B together with an environment E,
we say that A unifies with B in E if and only if there is an
extension E' of E (that is, an environment containing all the
bindings in E and possibly others as well) such that

(RECREAL A E') = (RECREAL B E') .

We then define the function UNIFY in such a way that if A unifies with B in E then the environment (UNIFY A B E) is the most general extension E' of E satisfying the above equation. If A does not unify with B in E then (UNIFY A B E) is the message "IMPOSSIBLE".

The definition of UNIFY is given by:

```
(UNIFY A B E) =  if E is "IMPOSSIBLE" then "IMPOSSIBLE"
                 else (EQUATE (ULT A E) (ULT B E) E)
where
(EQUATE A B E) = if  A is B            then  E            else
                 if  A is a variable then  (A.B).E       else
                 if  B is a variable then  (B.A).E       else
                 if  A is an atom     then  "IMPOSSIBLE" else
                 if  B is an atom     then  "IMPOSSIBLE" else

                 (UNIFY tA tB (UNIFY hA hB E)) .
```

4.6 LUSH Resolution

Now suppose that we have a knowledge base D and a constraint represented by the skeleton-environment pair (Q E).

Let (VARIANT Q E D) be a variant of D having no variables in common with Q or with E. (A variant of D is an object exactly like D with the possible exception that different identifiers are used for some or all of its logical variables.)

Let (SELECT Q E D) be a positive integer no larger than the length of the list Q. SELECT is assumed to be able to use the content and structure of Q, E and D, if need be, to help in determining its result.

Finally, given a nonempty list X and a positive integer K no larger than the length of X, we speak of splitting X with respect to its Kth component, and we define (SPLIT X K) to be the triple (L A R) such that A is the Kth component of X and X is L*(A)*R.

(The concatenation of lists L and M is denoted by L*M, and * is of course associative.)

Thus if (L A R) is (SPLIT X K) then L is the list of the first K-1 components of X and R is the list of the last ((LENGTH X) - K) components of X. In particular, when K = 1,

we have: L = () ,
            A = hX ,
            R = tX .

We are now ready to define the LUSH-resolvents of an implicit constraint (Q E) with respect to a knowledge base D. They are all of the implicit constraints of the form

                (L*H*R(UNIFY A C E))

such that:

(1)   H is the hypothesis, and C the conclusion,
      of an assertion in (VARIANT Q E D) ;
(2)   (L A R) is (SPLIT Q (SELECT Q E D)) ;
(3)   A unifies with C in E .

At present our implementation uses (SELECT Q E D) = 1 for all Q, E and D. More general selection criteria permitted by the theory of LUSH-resolution are currently under study and future versions of LOGLISP may adopt a more complex SELECT.

The "separation of variables" accomplished by taking (VARIANT Q E D) instead of D is managed quite efficiently in LOGLISP as indeed in all of the PROLOG implementations known to us. It is theoretically necessary to take variants in order to preserve the completeness of the resolution inference principle. It was Boyer and Moore who first showed how to represent variants cheaply by means of indexing. Details will be given later.

In LOGLISP the set of LUSH-resolvents of (Q E) with respect to D is returned as a list (RES Q E D) which shares much of its structure, in the Boyer-Moore manner, with (Q E) itself.

In computing (RES Q E D) one often can avoid searching the entire procedure whose predicate is the same as that of the selected predication. It is of course sufficient to search only this procedure (rather than the whole knowledge base!) but in practice one often has conditions under which a relatively small subset of the procedure can be shown to suffice. For example, it may happen that no assertion in the procedure has a conclusion containing any logical variables (as would be the case with a "data procedure" all of whose assertions were unconditional data). In such a case, it is enough to try just those assertions in the procedure whose conclusion actually contains every proper identifier which appears in the selected predication. These assertions are readily retrieved via the secondary indexing system mentioned earlier.

4.7 The Deduction Cycle

We are now ready to define the deduction cycle. If the knowledge base is D, then the answer to the query (SETOF K X P) is the result of the following algorithm:

IN: let SOLVED be the empty set and
     let WAITING be the set containing only (P ())

RUN: while WAITING is nonempty
        and SOLVED has fewer than K members

     do 1 remove some implicit constraint C from
           WAITING and let (Q E) be (SIMPLER C D)

        2 if   Q is ()
           then add E to SOLVED
           else add the members of (RES Q E D)
                to WAITING

OUT: return (SIMPSET X SOLVED)

Remarks on the deduction cycle algorithm

(1) The functions SIMPLER and SIMPSET are discussed below in the section dealing with LISP-simplification.

(2) If K is "ALL" then the test in RUN depends only on its first conjunct.

(3) The queries

$$(\text{ALL } X \ P_1 \ ... \ P_n), \quad (\text{ANY } K \ X \ P_1 \ ... \ P_n), \quad (\text{THE } X \ P_1 \ ... \ P_n)$$

are the same, respectively, as the queries

    (SETOF (QUOTE ALL) (QUOTE X) (QUOTE (P_1 ... P_n))),
    (SETOF K (QUOTE X) (QUOTE (P_1 ... P_n))),
    h(SETOF 1 (QUOTE X) (QUOTE (P_1 ... P_n))) .

(4) The "answer template" X in a query can be a logical variable, or a proper name, or a list of expressions (in particular, a list of logical variables).

(5) (RES Q E D) can be empty. In this case the net effect is just to drop the constraint C from WAITING and to add nothing to SOLVED. C is thus an "immediate failure" (see below).

(6) The selection of C from WAITING is made from among those constraints whose estimated "solution cost" is least. This estimate is a linear combination of the length of C's skeleton part and the length of the deduction which produced C.

4.8 The Deduction Tree. Immediate and Ultimate Failures

Examination of the deduction cycle algorithm reveals that it grows a tree (the "deduction tree") whose nodes are implicit constraints. The root of the deduction tree is the constraint of the original query, implicitly represented, trivially, with empty environment part. The immediate successors, if any, of each node in the deduction tree are its LUSH-resolvents with respect to the given knowledge base.

During the growth process the "fringe" of the growing deduction tree consists of the nodes in WAITING together with those whose environment parts have been added to SOLVED.

The tips of the completed deduction tree fall into two classes. Those whose skeleton part is the empty list are successes, and their environment parts will have been added to the (now also complete) collection SOLVED. Those whose skeleton part is not empty are immediate failures, and they will have contributed nothing to SOLVED. An immediate failure, in other words, is a node whose selected predication will not unify with the conclusion of any assertion in the knowledge base.

An ultimate failure, on the other hand, is a node which, while not itself an immediate failure, nevertheless has no descendants which are successes. It is the root of a subtree all of whose tips are immediate failures. It would be splendid to be able to detect an ultimate failure by means other than that of developing this entire subtree - and in certain cases this is precisely what can be done because of the LISP-simplification process, which we now go on to explain.

4.9 LISP-simplification. The Functions SIMPLER, SIMPSET

In the deduction cycle algorithm the functions SIMPLER and SIMPSET are called in order to activate the LISP-simplification process which gives LOGLISP one of its most characteristic properties. It is here that we find the interface between LOGIC and LISP.

Intuitively, what the LISP-simplification process does is to replace an expression by its reduction (if it has one)

according to the LISP meanings (if any) which it and its
subexpressions may have. For example, the expression (+ 3 4)
can be reduced to the expression 7, and the expression
(LESSP (ADD1 5) (TIMES 2 8)) can be reduced (in three steps)
to T. The reduction of an expression is the result of per-
sistently replacing its subexpressions by their definitional
equivalents, in the manner of computation, until no further
replacements are possible. Reduction is often, but not
always, the same as evaluation. For example, (+ a (+ 2 2))
reduces to (+ a 4). Nor can every expression be reduced -
some are irreducible.   So we speak in general of the LISP-
simplification of an expression, and define this to be the
expression itself, if it is irreducible, or else to be the
(irreducible) expression which results from reducing it as
far as possible (perhaps all the way to a "value", such as T
or a number).

Now (SIMPSET X SOLVED) is just the set (represented as a
list) of all expressions which are the LISP-simplifications
of (RECREAL X E), for some E in SOLVED.

The function SIMPLER transforms the implicit constraint C
selected in step 1 of the RUN loop in the deduction cycle
algorithm. Remember that if C is (Q E) we are "really"
dealing with the list P = (RECREAL Q E) which C implicitly
represents.

SIMPLER's job, intuitively, is to replace the
(SELECT Q E D)th predication in P by its LISP-simplification.
Sometimes the (SELECT Q E D)th predication in P reduces to T,
and in this case SIMPLER deletes it from P (since P
represents the logical conjunction of its components, the
resulting list P' is equivalent to P). If Q' is the result of
deleting the (SELECT Q E D)th component of Q from Q, we will
then have that P' is (RECREAL Q' E). SIMPLER then repeats the
whole process, reducing the (SELECT Q' E D)th predication in
P', and so on, until either the list of predications is empty
or the selected predication does not reduce to T. The output
of SIMPLER is then the implicit constraint representing (with
environment part E) this final list of predications.

Note that one possibility is that the selected predication
might reduce to NIL (= false). Since this will mean that it
will not unify with any conclusion in the knowledge base the
effect will then be to turn a possible ultimate failure into
an immediate one.

The practical consequence of the inclusion of this SIMPLER

transformation of the selected predication is to allow the user to invoke very nearly the full power of LISP <u>from within the hypotheses of LOGIC assertions</u>.

An immediate advantage of this feature is that LOGIC queries - which after all are simply LISP calls on the functions ALL, ANY, THE, or SETOF - can be processed (as terms intended for LISP-simplification) within deductions going on at higher levels. Queries can thus contain sub-queries, and so on, to any depth.

A simple illustration of this is the assertion endowing NOT (which of course is <u>also</u> a LISP primitive) with the extra significance of the "negation as failure" postulate. We do not regard this as part of the meaning of NOT but as something the user may assert about NOT, if he wishes to. The assertion is:

$$(NOT\ p) <- (NULL\ (ANY\ 1\ T\ p))$$

and it says that in order to establish a predication of the form (NOT p) it is sufficient to run the query (ANY 1 T p) and to find that it returns the empty list as its answer. Note that the only possible answers to (ANY 1 T p) are () and (T). The answer (T) would mean that at least one way exists of proving p - and that therefore (NOT p) should be taken as false. The answer () would mean that not even one way of proving p was found, despite a complete search.

Thus a user who is willing to assume of his knowledge base that inability to prove a predication is tantamount to the ability to prove its negation may well wish to add to it the above assertion.

4.10 Infinite Searches. The Deduction Window

Since in general there may be infinitely many components in the answer to a query, some way must be provided of gracefully truncating, after only finitely many components have been found, the otherwise nonterminating process of computing such an answer.

In LOGIC a set of parameters is provided (whose values may be set by the user or left at their default settings) which bound the size of the deduction tree in various ways. For example, the total number of nodes may be bounded, as may the maximum branch length, and the maximum length of any constraint list within a node. It is also possible to limit the number of times in any one branch that rules are applied, and the number of times in any one branch that data are applied.

The set of these bounds is called <u>the deduction window</u>.

It is worth pointing out that the deduction window can be set up for each activation of the deduction cycle simply by annotating the query appropriately. For example, the unadorned query

$$(\text{ALL } X \; P_1 \; \ldots \; P_n)$$

would be run with the default window, but the same query, annotated as

$$(\text{ALL } X \; P_1 \; \ldots \; P_n \; \text{RULES: } 5 \; \text{TREESIZE: } 1000)$$

would be run with bounds of 5 and 1000, respectively, in place of the default bounds.

In addition to controlling the shape and extent of the deduction tree the user may also specify the coefficients to be used in computing the "estimated solution cost" of each constraint added to WAITING during the deduction cycle. Since the constraint selected from WAITING in step 1 of RUN is always one of those whose estimated solution cost is least, this gives the user some control over the manner in which the deduction tree is grown.

It is also possible to specify that the tree be grown in strictly PROLOG style, that is, depth-first and with assertions taken in the exact order in which the user first entered them.

5. EFFICIENCY OF THE IMPLEMENTATION

The running times of LOGIC in answering queries are not as impressive as those of, say, Edinburgh PROLOG using compiled assertions (which has been clocked at something like 20,000 nodes per second). Edinburgh PROLOG achieves something like 1,000 nodes per second when the assertions are run "interpretively", i.e., uncompiled, and we take this rate as a rough benchmark for comparison with LOGLISP, which is also an interpreter.

We find that with our present version of LOGLISP we manage about 150 nodes per second - one sixth the speed of the Edinburgh interpreter.

We aspire to a somewhat larger fraction than this, and are currently refining our techniques in various ways in order to improve our running times. The following account of our present methods may be of interest.

We have to explain, in somewhat more detail, just how environments are represented so that variants can be formed readily and bindings accessed quickly. The technique used is, as already mentioned, a specialization of Boyer-Moore structure-sharing. The implicit representation of an expression is in fact a triple (I Q E) in which I is a non-negative integer "index" which is to be ascribed to every variable occurring in Q. The environment E has, for each index at which bindings have been introduced, a list of bindings for that index, each binding having the form (A J . B), which means that the variable A is bound to the term B, with the index J ascribed to the variables occurring in B.

A query is given the index 0. When computing a resolvent of a constraint with a rule, the rule is given an index one greater than the largest index used in deducing the constraint, thus "instantly" forming a variant of the rule whose variables are distinct from any appearing in the constraint. No new index is introduced when resolving against a datum.

The environment in current use is represented by an array ENV whose i-th entry is a list of bindings for variables with index i. Since the variables bound in one of these lists all come from a single assertion, the lists are never very long. In practice the number of bindings in one list hardly ever exceeds six, and the average is usually less.

Environments other than the one of current interest (i.e. the one stored in ENV) are represented as lists whose entries are the association lists which were formerly entries of ENV. When a new constraint is selected from WAITING, its environment must be "loaded" into the array. Similarly, new environments must be "unloaded" from the array by constructing a list of the array entries. In either case, the time required is at worst proportional to the maximum index for which bindings appear, and is independent of the number of variables bound. Thus loading and unloading can introduce in the overall running time a component which is essentially quadratic in the depth of the deduction.

To reduce the potential seriousness of this effect, the present implementation records the extent to which (some tail of) an earlier list represents the current contents of the array ENV. When unloading the array, the new list shares as much as possible of the earlier list. The same information is used to cut short the loading of the array when it can be seen that some portion of it already has the desired bindings. By these techniques the quadratic component of the running time is considerably reduced, and in some instances entirely eliminated.

6. CONCLUDING REMARKS

Our experience with LOGLISP indicates that it does indeed provide the rich setting for logic programming that our early encounters with PROLOG led us to seek. In particular we find it most convenient to be able to invoke LOGIC from LISP and vice versa. It is very useful to have the answer to a query be delivered as a LISP data object and to be able to subject it to arbitrary computational analysis and manipulation. The LOGIC programmer need not rely upon the system builder to "build in" functions and predicates - he can very easily write his own in LISP and then invoke them from LOGIC.

Nothing in our general design philosophy seems to preclude a much faster deduction cycle algorithm than our current version of it. We believe that by (among other recourses) borrowing Warren's compilation techniques we shall be able to speed things up by at least a factor of 10, and this is one of our present concerns.

ACKNOWLEDGEMENT

The work on LOGLISP was sponsored by USAF Systems Command Rome Air Development Center, Griffiss Air Force Base NY 13441 under contract F30602-77-C-0235.

QLOG — THE PROGRAMMING ENVIRONMENT FOR PROLOG IN LISP

H. Jan Komorowski

Software Systems Research Center
Linköping University
S-581 83 Linköping, Sweden

ABSTRACT

An experimental programming environment for Prolog in Lisp is presented with a special emphasis on the Interlisp version. It is shown that at a very low cost a sophisticated Lisp environment can be inherited by Prolog if the implementation is functionally embedded. A number of regular Lisp facilities as well as ones designed for Prolog are briefly discussed.

1. FOREWORD

Since the pioneering work of (Kowalski, 1974; Roussel, 1975; van Emden and Kowalski, 1976), and others there have been several implementations of the Prolog programming language. It soon appeared that implementing an interpreter for Prolog is not a difficult task. However, providing a good programming environment is not that easy and most of the implementations do not quite succeed in this aspect. There are two reasons for this. One is the difficulty of making correct design decisions concerning a PE, the other the large programming effort required to implement a PE. By a good PE we understand a system which is (1) incremental, i.e., procedures can be added, modified and immediately executed; (2) has error detection, error repair support facilities, and continuation from errors; (3) supports implementing embedded languages, e.g., Qlisp (Sacerdoti et al. 1976); (4) has an editor which updates a program's structure not its text; (5) supports experiments with a program by providing undo and redo facilities and a history of the session in a form understandable by the system.

Each of such facilities requires a lot of code to be written.
In PE's like Interlisp or Maclisp the ratio of the interpreter code to the system code is roughly 1:100. For this reason
no existing Prolog implementation can match any advanced Lisp
PE.

By embedding PROLOG in LISP one could perhaps transfer most
of the LISP PE to PROLOG. The goal of my research was to
investigate to what extent such an embedding is possible, how
Lisp tools fit the requirements of Prolog, what new
facilities should be provided. A secondary goal was to
provide a transportable version of the interpreter which
could be tailored to a particular Lisp environment without
any major redesign of the system's kernel. The efficiency of
the implementation in terms of computing speed was given a
minor attention. On the other hand, I also felt that it would
be desirable to have a set of Prolog primitives within Lisp.
Thus by embedding Prolog in Lisp both languages should
mutually benefit - Lisp would contribute with its most
sophisticated and advanced PE, Prolog - with pattern-directed
invocation, associative data base with richer structure than
the raw property lists, specification oriented programming
methodology, etc.

2. PROLOG IN THE LISP ENVIRONMENT

In implementing one language in another there is a spectrum
of possible choices, from an embedded sublanguage to a freestanding one. As it is characterized in (Komorowski and
Goodwin, 1981) "the conventional implementation of a sublanguage in a host language is freestanding: the new language
processor is written in the host language, but is regarded as
completely separate. The control structures of the new
language are implemented with the help of those of the host
language but are distinct from them. Utilities, such as
formatters or flow analyzers and many more, must in general
be written anew, since they are designed to work on the
syntactic and semantic structures of the host language, not
those of the new language."

The strategy of "maximal embedding" takes over as much as
possible from Lisp and never builds anew without good reason.
I chose the embedded solution since it gives many major components of the Lisp environment almost for free. For example,
the procedure call mechanism is inherited from Lisp by making
Qlog procedures Lisp procedures (cf. FEXPR's). This way we
are provided with utilities like break at minimal cost. I

chose Interlisp (Teitelman, 1979) as my host Lisp system.

The limit case of embedding is to implement the new capability as a set of subroutines in the host language. This maximizes inheritance but permits no departures from the host language semantics. If the subroutines conceal such departures internally, for instance by having backtrack stacks or by treating certain data structures as essentially new data types, then to that extent I would characterize the design as freestanding.

3. THE IMPLEMENTATION STRATEGY

Data types are very easy. No special finesse is required to implement Prolog terms in Lisp S-expressions. This way - virtually for free - Qlog obtained allocators, a garbage collector, READ and PRINT and the respective macros facilities, a list structure editor, etc.

Prolog control structure and variable binding are harder. The control structure of Prolog and the variable binding mechanism required freestanding choices since they are quite different from that of Lisp. The backtrack control structure of Prolog usually demands the retention of procedure activation frames, even after a successful matching of the goal with a head and execution of the body. This required a special control stack for Qlog procedures with pointers to the evaluation environments for their arguments. Similarly, Prolog's variable binding mechanism required a separate stack structure. Also, the sequencing of nested calls is different from Lisp and requested special care.

The procedure call mechanism is functionally embedded. Usually, forms of a new language are not given functional (or procedural) meaning of a host language interpreter. They are rather input parameters to an interpreter build over the host language. In the functionally embedded solution Qlog procedures are Lisp procedures, not purely syntactical data objects. For example, the Prolog APPND procedure written on the left is represented in the Qlog procedure on the right:

```
appnd(nil,:x,:x)                         (APPND
appnd((:kar.:x),:y,(:kar.:z))              (NLAMBDA L
   <= appnd(:x,:y,:z)                        (+GOAL+ L
                                    '( ((APPND  NIL:X:X))
                                      ((APPND(:KAR.:X):Y(:KAR.:Z))
                                        (APPND:X:Y:Z))) )))
```

The APPND Interlisp procedure is a FEXPR (NLAMBDA) with an arbitrary number of arguments L . At the moment of a call to APPND L is bound to a list of the actual parameters and passed to +GOAL+, ie. to the Qlog interpreter.

This encapsulation of a call to the Qlog interpreter provides the functional embedding, since every Qlog procedure is first seen by the regular Lisp interpreter. Moreover, such a procedure is also considered to be an ordinary function object by other book-keeping utilities. Thus, the access to the entire set of function oriented facilities like break, file librarian, history package, etc. is provided.

The Interlisp top loop accepts Qlog forms (since they are just Lisp forms), evaluates them and annotates on the history list. Only a small recording routine is necessary to save Prolog computation multiple results on this list (instead of the standard saving of a single Lisp result).

Breakpoints and procedure traces may be placed on any Qlog procedure using the standard Lisp facilities. Breakpoints work perfectly as they are. Tracing works, but prints the Lisp arguments and bindings instead of the Qlog quantities. Another small interface function is necessary to make the trace print the right things.

Interlisp spelling corrector works fine. An attempt to call an undefined Qlog procedure will be trapped and will be either automatically corrected or will enter into a dialog with the user.

The regular Interlisp editor is called on Qlog procedures through a special EDITQ function (of 5 lines) which fetches the definition of a Qlog procedure and annotates the file librarian if necessary.

The file librarian in Interlisp knows about all structures in working store that need to be saved due to changes. It knows which parts of which files must be updated, and it will ask you where to keep newly defined material. These facilities all work without modifications.

Since the lack of space prohibits me from extending this list I shall limit myself here only to my "worst cases". Because the Interlisp pretty printer does not understand the Qlog procedure structure, a dedicated pretty printer consisting of 36 lines was written anew. Further, although Lisp backtraces i.e. the functions displaying the current content of the

stack with or without variables work, they are not very
useful since they display the interpreter functions and Lisp
variables rather than the Qlog material. There was a clear
need to provide specialized backtraces which would display
the AND/OR tree structure of Prolog computation. Also, there
are new functions which are used to introduce new Qlog
definitions; they notify the file librarian, too.

The reader might ask, why not also use the embedded approach
for the variable mechanism binding? It is in principle
possible, using the Interlisp spaghetti stack. It might seem
that one would inherit Lisp's commands for stack display too.
I admit I was tempted to try that solution and I implemented
it. But the portability was sacrificed, the implementation
became clumsy, and the context switching costs became
unreasonable.

4. THE RESULT OF THE IMPLEMENTATION

The total interface to Interlisp took 20 pages of pretty
printed code. As a rough estimate, the Lisp code for the
parts of the Interlisp PE which this interface adapts to
Prolog use is about 50 times larger.

The resulting PE was named Qlog (read q-log). The interpreter
is 10 pages of pretty printed code (about 20 Lisp functions).
This result is common for system programming - the kernel of
the system is much smaller than the code that interfaces it
to the rest of its environment. Since I did not use any
special features of Interlisp which do not appear in other
Lisps the code is fairly easy to carry across. In fact it has
been moved by Mats Carlsson to Fortran Lisp F3 (Nordström,
1978), by Martin Nilsson to Stanford Lisp 1.6 (Quam et al.
undated) by a group at the University of Pennsylvania in
Philadelphia to Franz Lisp on VAX/780, by a group at the
Josef Stefan Institute at Ljubljana to CDC Lisp, and by
myself to Lisp Machine Lisp (Weinreb and Moon, 1978) at MIT.
The experience from the last implementation will be described
elsewhere.

The speed of execution was not my primary concern; it was
more important to get the best possible PE. To my pleasant
surprise the resulting interpreter runs comparable with the
Prolog DEC10 interpreter. In a benchmark program resulting in
270 function calls Qlog runs 380 milliseconds against Prolog
DEC10's 410 ms. In the worst case (reversing a list) where a
lot of cons cells are done Qlog does no worse then 2 times

slower. This result was obtained despite the fact that the interpreter was designed to optimize portability, not speed of execution.

New Break Commands and Trace Facilities. Since Prolog computation has a different structure there was a clear need for commands which display the AND/OR computation tree. Another useful facility is the "spy" package (Byrd, 1980). The idea was first implemented for Qlisp (Sacerdoti et al. 1976) and significantly improved at Linköping by Emanuelson (1978).

Incremental Indexing. The Prolog DEC10 on-line compiler uses a method of indexing assertion entries by their first argument. The method is similar to a (partial) discrimination net. Unfortunately, it can only be used with a compiled code and it forces a recompilation if an assertion is to be added to a compiled procedure. I developed an "on-line" indexer for an interpreted code which incrementally discriminates the asserted entry.

Compiling. Since Qlog procedures are Lisp procedures, one can run the regular Lisp compiler on them, but the computation is vacuous. The Lisp compiler does not know anything about Qlog code, and sees Qlog procedure as merely a simple function call (to the Qlog interpreter) with a quoted argument (the Prolog assertion). What is needed is a true pattern match compiler. However, if a Qlog system is run on a DEC10 or DEC20 computer a partial solution is possible: the Prolog DEC10 compiler will do the compilation provided a simple syntactical interface is supplied.

Extensions and Improvements. Instead of a special representation for lists Qlog uses the regular Lisp dot notation. In this notation functional symbols may have a variable arity.

There is a provision to write Qlog procedures with variable predicate names. At the moment of the call, however, they must be instantiated to a predicate name, otherwise an error occurs.

The semantics of Qlog is better defined than the semantics of other Prologs, because it is not total. Namely, a call to an undefined procedure does not result in a pattern-match failure and thus in an uncontrolable continuation of the execution, but causes a break and leaves the decision to the user.

5. CONCLUSIONS

Lisp lets me implement Prolog procedures as Lisp procedures, while still retaining my own variable scoping and control mechanism. It is very likely that no other language could do. This maximized the degree of inheritance.

Qlog inherits most of the major components of the Lisp PE with little or no additional code, and obtains a high quality PE. Interfacing the existing Interlisp facilities to the new language required 30 to 50 times less code than the Lisp facilities require themselves. These facilities are rather unique and not found in any other Prolog system. Also some new tools specific for Prolog were developed; not many of them are found in other Prolog programming systems.

Lisp itself has been complemented with pattern directed invocation of functions, associative data base with richer structure than property lists, etc., all that for less than 30 pages of pretty printed Lisp code. The user of Qlog has a free choice. He can use Lisp without ever noticing that Prolog is around, or he can choose to run only Prolog with all the advantages of a modern PE, or he can freely mix Prolog with Lisp. The first option is quite plausible since there is not any change in the Lisp interpreter and thus the only cost of having Qlog in the working space is that of some extra storage, and not of the execution speed. The second option has Lisp as an implementation language (e.g. Assembler or Fortran in other implementations) and never steps down to it. However, should a need arise (e.g. interfacing an existing built-in Lisp function to Qlog, or experimental changes in the Qlog interpreter, or implementing embedded languages in Prolog), there are no obstacles to do so. The third option is provided for those users who are aware of the differences between the languages. However, in contrast to LOGLISP (Robinson and Sibert, 1980), I provided an explicit interface. The LISP function must be called from a Prolog program to initiate a Lisp computation, and vice versa the QLOG function from a Lisp program. It was believed that an extra cautiousness must be taken if Lisp and Prolog codes are to be intermingled.

6. COMPARISON TO OTHER WORKS

Chester (1980a,b) has also implemented a Horn clause interpreter in Lisp. It is close to the idea of Qlog, except that he chose almost a freestanding method, e.g. his Horn not Lisp functions. Thus it is not possible to use the break package nor other function oriented tools. Nevertheless it is still possible to use READ and PRINT, the editor, etc. It is clearly a less embedded solution. Also, the implementation seems to be less efficient since it is at least 4 times slower than the Prolog DEC10 interpreter.

Another implementation of similar ideas is the LOGLISP system developed at the Syracuse University by Robinson and Sibert (1980). Their goal was, however, somewhat different: to provide a logic programming Lisp-like PE which offers logic and Lisp. The goal is clearly more ambitious than mine but it has also resulted in a lesser degree of embedding and much worse efficiency. The efficiency of pure Lisp code is also affected in the LOGLISP environment. A major feature of LOG-LISP is that the user can program the control strategy.

ACKNOWLEDGEMENT

Many scholars contributed to the present shape of the Qlog system. My cooperation with Jim Goodwin was the most fruitful. He patiently assisted me during the Interlisp implementation and contributed with several ideas about the strategy and tactics of embedding languages in Interlisp in order to obtain maximum support at minimum cost: what we have begun to call "the law of maximal embedding".

Several comments from the implementors of other Qlog systems suggested improvements to the kernel of the system.

I had many interesting discussions about the implementation of Qlog with Sten-Åke Tärnlund. He has also encouraged me to write this article.

I am also very indebted to Erik Sandewall for his tireless supervision which generated many new ideas and made my work possible in the first place.

This research has been sponsored by the Swedish Board for Technical Development under contract 77-4380b.

HORN CLAUSE COMPUTABILITY

HORN CLAUSE PROGRAMS FOR RECURSIVE FUNCTIONS

Jan Šebelík

Petr Štěpánek

Institute for Application of
Computing Technique in Control
Prague 1, Husova 8
Czechoslovakia

Department of Cybernetics
and Operational Research
Charles University
Prague 1
Malostranske namesti 25
Czechoslovakia

1. INTRODUCTION

We shall introduce the concept of stratifiable Horn clause
programs and we shall compare these programs with the binary
Horn clause programs introduced by Tärnlund (1975). Stratifiable programs are suggested by a natural hierarchy of
partial recursive functions, starting with some basic
functions at the bottom and generating new computable
functions by the operations of composition, primitive
recursion and minimization. We shall construct a Horn clause
program for every computable function by induction on
recursive functions. These programs have certain syntactic
features in common, that we shall call stratifiable.

We shall show that every Horn clause program constructed by
induction on recursive functions can be transformed into a
binary Horn clause program computing the same function and
that the transformation does not increase the complexity of a
computation. We shall show that the length of a computation
of the resulting binary program does not exceed the length of
a computation of the original program. The computations of
both types of programs are deterministic in a natural way.

On the other hand, we shall show that every binary Horn
clause program can be transformed into a stratifiable Horn
clause program. Moreover, the transformation does not depend
on the first-order language of the original program.

In his paper Tärnlund (1977) used binary Horn clause programs
to simulate the behavior of a Universal Turing machine.

Stratifiable and binary Horn clause programs are suggested by a different formalism for computable functions, but they are close to each other.

Throughout the paper, we shall use standard concepts and notation of Horn logic. We refer the reader to (Kowalski, 1979a; Tärnlund, 1977) for a more detailed exposition. We shall deal mostly with first-order languages without equality containing two function symbols O and S, where we interpret the constant O as zero and the unary function symbol S as the successor function $Sx = x+1$. Hence the terms $O, SO, SSO,...$ can be identified with natural numbers $0, 1, 2,...$.

A clause is a disjunction of literals, i.e. a disjunction of atomic formulas and of negations of atomic formulas. A Horn clause is a clause with at most one positive literal, a binary Horn clause is a Horn clause with at most one negative literal. We call every set consisting of Horn clauses with exactly one positive literal a Horn clause program. The resolution principle with unification as a pattern matching algorithm is the only inference rule of so called Horn logic.

Suppose P is a set of Horn clauses (a program) and C_0 is a negated conjunction of atoms, i.e. $<- L_1,...,L_k$ (a goal clause). A sequence $C_0,...,C_n$ of goal clauses, where $C_n = \emptyset$ is then a deduction (computation) of C', where C' is an instance of the negation of C_0, i.e. $C' = (L_1,...,L_k)\theta$, provided that for every $i<n$, C_{i+1} is a resolvent of C_i and D, where $D \in P$.

If $i<j<n$, we write $P,C_i \vdash C_j$ to say that the goal C_j is deducible from C_i and P. We write $P \vdash C'$ instead of $P,C_0 \vdash \emptyset$, for a derivation of C' from a set of hypotheses P.

The following easy lemma is used quite often in our proofs.

Lemma 1. Let P be a Horn clause program and A a ground atom. Let
$$A' <- B_1,...,B_n$$

be the only clause in P such that A and A' can be unified by a most general unifier θ.

Then $P \vdash A$ iff there is a substitution η such that $P \vdash B\theta\eta$ holds for every $i \leq n$, all $B_i\theta\eta$ being ground atoms.

2. PROGRAMS FOR RECURSIVE FUNCTIONS

We shall describe programs for all partial recursive functions by induction on the complexity of their definitions. We start with basic functions and then we shall construct programs for functions obtained by composition, primitive recursion and minimization. The corresponding programs are naturally motivated and, as we shall see later, they admit a certain stratification.

Now we shall show that for every partial recursive function f of n variables, there is an (n+1)-ary predicate symbol F_f and a Horn clause program P such that:

> for every sequence of natural numbers $\bar{a}$,c $f(\bar{a})$ (1)
> is defined and equal to c iff $P \vdash F_f(\bar{a})$

In fact, assuming P, the predicate F_f represents the function f in such way that c is the only natural number satisfying the right-hand side of (1) whenever $f(\bar{a})=c$, and there is no such c provided that $f(\bar{a})$ is undefined.

In what follows, we shall omit the subscript f of the predicate F. We shall consider the following cases:

a) If f is one of the basic functions, then P consists of one assertion, namely, P is
    (i)   F(x,0) <-
provided that f is the zero function, f(x)=0 for every x
    (ii) F(x,Sx) <-
whenever f is the successor function, f(x) = x+1, and
    (iii) $F(x_1,...,x_n,x_i)$ <-
whenever $f(x_1,...,x_n) = x_i$ for some i, where $1 \leq i \leq n$.

b)(i) f is $f(\bar{x}) = h(g_1(\bar{x}),...,g_k(\bar{x}))$, which is the result of composition, where $\bar{x} = (x_1,...,x_n)$, and g_i for i = 1,...,k is a function of n variables. Now, let H, $G_1,...,G_k$ be predicate symbols corresponding to h, $g_1,...,g_k$, and P_o a program computing h, and let P_i for i=1,...,k be programs computing g_i respectively. By the induction hypothesis, we may conclude that the programs P_i have the above property, i.e.

$g_i(\bar{a}) = b_i$ iff $P_i \vdash G_i(\bar{a},b_i)$ for   i≤k
$h(\bar{b}) = c$ iff $P_o \vdash H(\bar{b},c)$,

for every n-tuple $\bar{a}$ and $\bar{b}$ of natural numbers. We may assume that two programs P_i, P_j have no predicate symbol in common.

Let F be a new (n+1)-ary predicate symbol and $\bar{x}$, $\bar{y}$ and z be new variables. If we add the clause

$$F(\bar{x},z) \leftarrow G_1(\bar{x},y_1),G_2(\bar{x},y_2),\ldots,G_k(\bar{x},y_k)H(\bar{y},z) \qquad (2)$$

to the union of sentences P_0, $P_1,\ldots,P_k$, we obtain a program P for f satisfying (1).

(ii)   Let f be obtained from the functions g and h by primitive recursion, i.e.

$$f(0,x_2,\ldots,x_n) = g(x_2,\ldots,x_n)$$
$$f(Sx_1,x_2,\ldots,x_n) = h(x_1,\ldots,x_n,f(x_1,\ldots,x_n))$$

holds for every $x_1,\ldots,x_n$. Let G, H be predicate symbols corresponding to g and h and let P_1, P_2 be the programs for g and h. We assume that both programs do not share any predicate symbol. Let F be a new (n+1)-ary predicate symbol. The Horn clause program P which is obtained by adding clauses

$$F(0,x_2,\ldots,x_n,z) \leftarrow G(x_2,\ldots,x_n,z)$$
$$F(Sx_1,x_2,\ldots,x_n,z) \leftarrow F(x_1,\ldots,x_n,y), H(x_1,\ldots,x_n,y,z) \qquad (3)$$

together with the union of P_1, P_2 satisfies (1).

(iii) Let f be obtained by minimization from a computable function g, i.e. let

$$f(\bar{x}) = \mu y(g(\bar{x},y)=0) ,$$

Let G be the (n+2)-ary predicate symbol corresponding to g and assume that we already have constructed a program P_0 for g. Let R, F be (n+3)-ary and (n+1)-ary predicate symbols and let P be the program obtained from P_0 by adding the following clauses

$$\begin{aligned} &F(\bar{x},z) \leftarrow G(\bar{x},0,y),R(\bar{x},0,y,z) \\ &R(\bar{x},u,0,u) \leftarrow \\ &R(x,u,Sv,z) \leftarrow G(\bar{x},Su,y),R(\bar{x},Su,y,z) \quad , \end{aligned} \qquad (4)$$

where $\bar{x} = (x_1,\ldots,x_n)$, u,v,y,z are new variables.

Note that for all natural numbers $\bar{a}= (a_1,\ldots,a_n)$, b,c we have

$$\begin{aligned} &P \vdash R(\bar{a},0,0,c) &&\text{iff}& &c=0 \quad , \text{ and} \\ &P \vdash R(a,0,Sb,c) &&\text{iff}& &0<c \text{ and } g(\bar{a},c)=0, \text{ and moreover} \\ & & & & &(\forall i)(0<i<c \rightarrow g(\bar{a},i)>0) \quad . \end{aligned} \qquad (5)$$

The first statement is obvious, the second can be proved by induction on c. To show that P satisfies (1), use the first clause of (4) and Lemma 1, and (5). A computation of a minimization is shown by example 3 at the end of Section 2.

We would like to turn attention to some syntactic properties of programs constructed by induction.

(i) except for the auxiliary symbol R used in minimization, every predicate represents a partial recursive function,

(ii) in every clause

$$G(\ldots) \leftarrow H_1(\ldots), \ldots ,H_k(\ldots) \quad , \tag{6}$$

the predicate symbols H_i, $i \leq k$ are different from each other.

(iii) the above programs for the basic functions and the programs for composition and primitive recursion can be stratified in the following way; it is possible to assign a natural number $n(G)$ to every predicate symbol G occurring in the program in such a way that $n(F_f)=0$ and for every clause (6), $n(H_i) = n(G)+1$ provided that H_i is different from G.

Note that the clauses (4) used in the program for minimization do not admit the above stratification. But the first clause of (4) is used only once in the computation of $f(\overline{x})$, so we can remove this difficulty.

If G' is a new (n+2)-ary predicate symbol corresponding to g and P_1 is obtained from P_0 by replacing G everywhere by G' and by renaming all predicate symbols in P_0 properly, then the program P' obtained from $P_0 \cup P_1$ by adding the clauses

$$F(\overline{x},z) \leftarrow G'(\overline{x},0,y),R(\overline{x},0,y,z)$$
$$R(\underline{x},u,0,u) \leftarrow \tag{4'}$$
$$R(\overline{x},u,Sv,z) \leftarrow G(\overline{x},Su,y),R(\overline{x},Su,y,z)$$

is stratifiable. Hence, every partial recursive function is computed by a Horn clause program stratifiable.

Property (iii) shows that the programs reflect the step by step construction of computable functions. Every partial recursive function can be assigned a rank number according to the level of hierarchy on which it first appears. Usually, the basic functions have rank zero. Hence the stratifying function n from (iii) assign natural numbers to predicate symbols in the reverse order to ranks of the corresponding functions. This motivates the following definition.

Let P be a Horn clause program and A be a predicate symbol which occurs in P. We say that P admits stratification with respect to A iff there is a mapping n that assigns a natural number to every predicate symbol in P such that $n(A)=0$, and for every clause (6) of P the predicate symbols H_i, are pairwise different and for every $i<k$ we have $n(H_i)=n(G)+1$ provided that H_i is not G.

We say that a program is stratifiable if it admits stratification with respect to one of its predicate symbols. A program is left stratifiable if it is stratifiable and for every clause (6), the predicate symbol G can appear only in the leftmost atom on the right hand side.

We say that a computation $C_1, C_2, \ldots, C_n$ of a program P is deterministic if the leftmost atom of every goal C_i, $i<n$ can be unified with the head of exactly one clause in P and C_n may be empty.

It can be shown that for every partial recursive function f and every appropriate tuple $\bar{a}$ of natural numbers, the computation of the corresponding (stratifiable) program P for f starting from the goal $<- F_f(\bar{a},z)$ is deterministic.

We may conclude this section by stating that every computable function on natural numbers is computed deterministically by a stratifiable Horn clause program. This is an analogue of the well-known fact that every computable function is computable by a deterministic Turing machine. Note that this need not be true for all Horn clause programs.

Example 1. Let $f(\bar{x}) = \mu y(g(\bar{x},y)=0)$ and P_0 be a program for $(n+1)$- ary function g. Let F and P be new $(n+1)$-ary predicate symbols and let P be obtained from P_0 by adding the clauses

$$P(\bar{x},0) <-$$
$$P(\bar{x},Sy) <- P(\bar{x},y),G(\bar{x},y,Sz)$$
$$F(x,y) <- P(x,y),G(x,y,0) \quad ,$$

where $\bar{x},y,z$ are new variables. It can be shown by induction on c that for every n-tuple $\bar{a}$ of natural numbers, we have

$$P \vdash P(\bar{a},c) \quad \text{iff} \quad (\forall y<c)(g(\bar{a},y) \text{ is defined as nonzero}).$$

Hence P is a natural program for f but it computes f in a non-deterministic way.

3. BINARY HORN CLAUSE PROGRAMS

We shall show that every program constructed in Section 1 can be transformed into a binary Horn clause program computing the same function. The transformation does not increase the length of a computation. In fact, we can show that for every partial recursive function and every input, the length of a computation of the transformed binary program does not exceed the length of a computation of the original program for f. We shall also show that the computations of the original programs and of the resulting binary programs are deterministic in a natural sense. We shall discuss the relationship between the transformed binary programs and original programs and we shall illustrate it by two examples.

Theorem 1

For every partial recursive function, the corresponding program constructed as in Section 1 can be transformed into a binary Horn clause program computing the same function.

Moreover, for every input, the length of the computation of the resulting binary program does not exceed the length of the computation of the original program.

Sketch of proof

We shall proceed by induction on recursive functions and describe the steps to transform the corresponding stratifiable program to a binary program.

a) If f is one of the basic functions, then the programs described in a(i)-(iii) of Section 1 are already binary.

b) (i) Let f be obtained by composition. As in the case B(i) of the previous Section, we shall assume that G_i, i=1,...,k are (n+1)-ary predicate symbols corresponding to functions g_i and that T_i is a binary program for g_i. Let H be the (k+1)-ary predicate symbol corresponding to h and let T_0 be a binary program for h. We may assume that any two programs have no predicate symbol in common. To avoid the clause (2) which is not binary, we have to modify programs T_i.

Let $\bar{x}, \bar{y}, z$ be new variables which do not occur in any program T_i. We shall add these variables to all atoms in programs T_i for i=1,...,k and we shall convert all assertions of these programs into suitable procedure declarations to establish ties between the resulting programs. For every i=1,...,k-1, let P_i be a binary program obtained from T_i as follows:

Every clause $R(\bar{t})$ <- $Q(\bar{u})$ of T_i is replaced by

$$\bar{R}(\bar{t},\bar{x},\bar{y},z) \text{ <- } \bar{Q}(\bar{u},\bar{x},\bar{y},z) \quad , \tag{7}$$

where $\bar{R},\bar{Q}$ are new predicate symbols.

Every assertion $R(\bar{t})$ <- of T_i is replaced by

$$\bar{R}(\bar{t},\bar{x},\bar{y},z) \text{ <- } \bar{G}_{i+1}(\bar{x},y_{i+1},\bar{x},\bar{y},z) \tag{8}$$

where $\bar{R}$ is as above and $\bar{G}_{i+1}$ is a new $(n+1+n+k+1)$-ary predicate symbol corresponding to G_{i+1}.

For $i=k$, we apply $(\underline{7})$ and every assertion $R(\bar{t})$ <- is replaced by $\bar{R}(\bar{t},\bar{x},\bar{y},z)$ <- $H(\bar{y},z)$.

Let P_i be the resulting programs. Now, we can state the following fact. For every ground atom $P(...)$ and appropriate tuples of natural numbers a,b,c we have

$$T_i \vdash P(...) \quad \text{iff} \quad \text{<-} \ \bar{P}(...,\bar{a},\bar{b},c) \vdash_{P_i} \text{<-} \ \bar{G}(\bar{a},b_{i+1},\bar{a},\bar{b},c)$$

holds for every $i \leq k-1$, and $\tag{9}$

$$T_k \vdash P(...) \quad \text{iff} \quad \text{<-} \ \bar{P}(...,\bar{a},\bar{b},c) \vdash_{P_k} \text{<-} \ H(\bar{b},c).$$

The length of deductions on both sides are the same.

This fact can be proved by induction on the length of the deduction. If we add the clause

$$F(\bar{x},z) \text{ <- } G(\bar{x},y_1,\bar{x},\bar{y},z) \quad ,$$

where $\bar{x},\bar{y}$ are appropriate tuples of variables, to the union of programs $P_1,...,P_k,T_0$, we obtain a binary program P for f. If T is the program obtained by adding (2) to the union of T_i's, it is not hard to prove from (9) and Lemma 1 that the computations of T and P have the same length for every input.

(ii) Let f be obtained by primitive recursion, i.e.

$$f(0,x_2,...,x_n) = g(x_2,...,x_n)$$
$$f(Sx_1,x_2,...,x_n) = h(x_1,..,x_n,f(x_1,...,x_n)).$$

Let G, H be the predicates corresponding to functions g, h respectively, let T_0, T_1 be the respective binary programs. Let T be the program obtained from T_0, T_1 by adding the clauses (3). We shall modify the programs T_0, T_1 to P_1:

every clause $R(...) \leftarrow Q(...)$ of $T_0 \cup T_1$ is replaced by

$$\overline{R}(...,x_1,w,x_2,...,x_n,y,z) \leftarrow \overline{Q}(...,x_1,w,x_2,...,x_n,y,z),$$

every assertion $R(...) \leftarrow$ is replaced by the pair

$$\begin{aligned}
&\overline{R}(...,x_0,w,x_2,...,x_n,y,z) \leftarrow \qquad \text{and} \qquad (10)\\
&\overline{R}(...,Sx_1,w,x,...,x_n,y,z) \leftarrow \\
&\qquad \overline{H}(Sw,x_2,...,x_n,y,v,x_1,Sw,x_2,...,x_n,v,z),
\end{aligned}$$

where $\overline{R},\overline{Q},\overline{H}$ are new predicate symbols (corresponding to R,Q,H respectively) and $x_1,...,x_n,y,v,w,z$ are new variables not occurring in T_0, T_1.

The resulting program P consists of P_1 and the clause

$$F(x_1,...,x_n) \leftarrow \overline{G}(x_2,...,x_n,y,x_1,0,x_2,...,x_n,y,z). \qquad (11)$$

This construction is illustrated by example 2.

It is possible to show by induction on a that for all natural numbers $\overline{a},c$, we have

$$T \vdash F(\overline{a},c) \qquad \text{iff} \qquad P \vdash F(\overline{a},c)$$

and the length of computation on the right-hand side does not exceed the length of computation on the left-hand side.

(iii) Let f be obtained from a function g of (n+1) variables $\overline{x},y$ by minimization, i.e.

$$f(\overline{x}) = \mu y(g(\overline{x},y) = 0) \quad,$$

let G be the (n+2)-ary predicate symbol corresponding to g and T_0 be a binary program computing g. Let T be the program obtained from T_0 by adding the clauses (4), and let P_0 be obtained from T_0 by the following transformation

every clause $P(...) \leftarrow Q(...)$ is replaced by the clause

$$\overline{P}(...,\overline{x},w,y,z) \leftarrow \overline{Q}(...,\overline{x},w,y,z) \qquad \text{and}$$

every assertion $P(...) \leftarrow$ from T_0 is replaced (12) by the following two clauses: the assertion

$$\begin{aligned}
&\overline{P}(...,\overline{x},z,0,z) \leftarrow \qquad \text{and the clause}\\
&\overline{P}(...,\overline{x},w,Sy,z) \leftarrow G(\overline{x},Sw,v,\overline{x},Sw,v,z) \quad,
\end{aligned}$$

where $\bar{x},y,v,w,z$ are new variables not occurring in T_0 and P,Q,G are new predicate symbols of appropriate arity. Let P be obtained from P_0 by adding the clause

$$F(\bar{x},z) \leftarrow \bar{G}(\bar{x},0,y,\bar{x},0,y,z) .$$ (13)

It is possible to show that P satisfies (1), hence we have

$$T \vdash F(\bar{a},c) \quad \text{iff} \quad P \vdash F(\bar{a},c)$$

for all natural numbers $\bar{a}=(a_1,\ldots,a_n),c$, and by the induction on the length of a computation of T it is possible to show that for every computation of T, there is the computation of P on the same input so its length does not exceed the length of a computation of T. This completes the proof of Theorem 1.

Remark. It should be noted that for every appropriate tuple $\bar{a}$ of natural numbers the computations of the above binary programs starting from the goal $\leftarrow F(\bar{a},z)$ are deterministic. Hence we succeded to transform the program of Section 1 to binary programs with deterministic computations of the values of the corresponding functions.

We shall illustrate the proof of Theorem 1 by examples.

Example 2. Let f be defined by primitive recursion as follows

$$f(0)=g=1, \quad f(x+1)=(x+1)+f(x).$$

A stratifiable program T for f consists of the clauses

```
G(SO) <-
PLUS(0,u,u) <-
PLUS(St,u,Sv) <- PLUS(t,u,v)

F(0,z) <- G(z)
F(Sx,z) <- F(x,y), PLUS(Sx,y,z) .
```

Using (10), (11), we can write the binary program P for f.

```
F(x,z) <- Ḡ(y,x,0,y,z)
Ḡ(SO,0,w,z,z) <-
Ḡ(SO,Sx,w,y,z) <- P(Sw,y,v,x,Sw,v,z)

P(0,u,u,0,w,z,z) <-
P(0,u,u,Sx,w,y,z) <- P(Sw,y,v,x,Sw,v,z)

P(St,u,sv,x,w,y,z) <- P(t,u,v,x,w,y,z)
```

We can compare the computations of T and P for <- F(SSO,z).

```
<-F(SSO,z)                              <-F(SSO,z)
<-F(SO,y),PLUS(SSO,y,z)
<-F(O,y'),PLUS(SO,y',y),PLUS(SSO,y,z)_
<-G(y'),PLUS(SO,y',y),PLUS(SSO,y,z)<-G̅(y,SSO,O,y,z)
<-PLUS(SO,SO,y),PLUS(SSO,y,z)         <-P(SO,SO,v,SO,SO,v,z)
<-PLUS(O,SO,y'),PLUS(SSO,Sy',z)       <-P(O,SO,v',SO,SO,Sv',z)
<-PLUS(SSO,SSO,z)       z <- Sz'      <-P(SSO,SSO,t,O,SSO,t,z)
<-PLUS(SO,SSO,z')       z'<- Sz"      <-P(SO,SSO,t',O,SSO,St',z)
<-PLUS(O,SSO,z")        z"<- SSO      <-P(O,SSO,t",O,SSO,SSt",z)
                                                 t"<- SSO, z <-SSt"
     ∅                                      ∅
```

Example 3. Let f be obtained by minimization,

$$f(x) = \mu\, z(x<z)\ .$$

The following program computes the characteristic function of the relation < .

```
    LESS(O,Su,O)  <-
    LESS(u,O,SO)  <-                                        (14)
    LESS(Su,Sv,t) <- LESS(u,v,t)
```

According to (12),(13), we obtain the following binary program P for the function f.

```
    L(O,Su,O,x,z,O,z)  <-
    L(O,Su,O,x,w,Sy,z) <-  L(x,Sw,v,x,Sw,v,z)

    L(u,O,SO,x,z,O,z)  <-
    L(u,O,SO,x,w,Sy,z) <-  L(x,Sw,v,x,Sw,v,z)

    L(Su,Sv,t,x,w,y,z) <-  L(u,v,t,x,w,y,z)
```

Let T be the program obtained from (14) by adding the clauses (4). We can compare the computations of T and P starting from the clause <- F(SSO,z).

```
<-F(SSO,z)                               <-F(SSO,z)
<-LESS(SSO,O,y),R(SSO,O,y,z)             <-L(SSO,O,y,SSO,O,y,z)
<-R(SSO,O,SO,z)
<-LESS(SSO,SO,y),R(SSO,SO,y,z)           <-L(SSO,SO,y,SSO,SO,y,z)
<-LESS(SO,O,y),R(SSO,SO,y,z)             <-L(SO,O,y,SSO,SO,y,z)
<-R(SSO,SO,SO,z)
<-LESS(SSO,SSO,y),R(SSO,SSO,y,z)         <-L(SSO,SSO,y,SSO,SSO,y,z)
<-LESS(SO,SO,y),R(SSO,SSO,y,z)           <-L(SO,SO,y,SSO,SSO,y,z)
<-LESS(O,O,y),R(SSO,SSO,y,z)             <-L(O,O,y,SSO,SSO,y,z)
<-R(SSO,SSO,SO,z)
<-LESS(SSO,SSSO,y),R(SSO,SSSO,y,z)<-L(SSO,SSSO,y,SSO,SSSO,y,z)
<-LESS(SO,SSO,y),R(SSO,SSSO,y,z)         <-L(SO,SSO,y,SSO,SSSO,y,z)
<-LESS(O,SO,y),R(SSO,SSSO,y,z)           <-L(O,SO,y,SSO,SSSO,y,z)
<-R(SSO,SSSO,O,z)
             z <- SSSO                        y <- O, z <- SSSO
   Ø                                     Ø
```

4. BINARY AND STRATIFIABLE PROGRAMS

We shall show that every binary Horn clause program can be
transformed to a stratifiable program computing the same
function. The result is proved by induction on the heigth of
the computation tree corresponding to the binary program and
does not depend on the first-order language of Horn logic.

We shall introduce the concept of a computation tree.

Let P be a Horn clause program, A a predicate symbol
occurring in P. An AND/OR-tree T is called a computation tree
for P and A provided that it has the following properties:

(i)   The OR-nodes of T are labelled by predicate symbols from
      P or by the empty clause and the AND-nodes of T are
      labelled by clauses from P.
(ii) The root of T is an OR-node labelled by A.
(iii) If n is an OR-node of T labelled by a predicate symbol
      Q, the successors of n are AND-nodes labelled by all
      clauses whose head contains Q.
(iv) If n is an AND-node of T labelled by a clause C, the
      successors of n are OR-nodes labelled by the predicates
      occurring in the body of C. If C is an assertion, the
      only successor of n is an OR-node labelled by the empty
      clause.

Given a program P and a predicate symbol A, the computation
tree T for P and A can be infinite. A reduced computation
tree for P and A is the maximal subtree T' of T such that the

root of T' coincides with the root of T and no branch of T'
contains a pair of AND-nodes labelled by the same clause.

Note that both the computation tree and the reduced computation tree for P and A characterize completely the computations of atoms containing A. As P consists of finitely many
Horn clauses, the reduced computation tree is finite.

We say that a reduced computation tree is simple if no two
AND-nodes are labelled by the same clause.

Lemma 2. For every Horn clause program P and predicate symbol
A occurring in P, there is a Horn clause program P' such that

$$P \vdash A' \quad \text{iff} \quad P' \vdash A'$$

holds for every ground atom A' containing A and the computation tree for P' and A is simple.

Sketch of proof.   Let n, n' be two AND nodes of the reduced
computation tree for P and A labelled by the same clause.
Then n,n' are on different branches and it follows from the
labelling of the tree that there are two different OR-nodes
m,m' labelled by the same predicate symbol Q such that n,n'
are in turn the successors of m and m'. Let Q' be a new
predicate symbol of the same arity as Q. We replace by Q' the
label Q of m' and of every OR-node labelled by Q below m'. At
the same time, we replace Q by Q' in all clauses labelling
the related AND-nodes. If the resulting tree is not simple,
the same process is repeated. Eventually, we obtain a simple
reduced computation tree T', the program P' being reconstruc-
ted from T'. Note that the transformation preserves stratifiability and that the programs are binary.

Theorem 2. For every binary Horn clause program P and every
predicate symbol A occurring in P, there is a stratifiable
program P* such that

$$P \vdash A' \quad \text{iff} \quad P* \vdash A'$$

holds for every (ground) atom A' containing A.

Sketch of proof. Let A be an n-ary predicate symbol occurring
in P. According to the preceeding lemma, we may assume that
the reduced computation tree T for P and A is simple. The
proof goes by induction on the height of T. If the heigth of
T is one, then the subset of P described by T is stratifiable, we may take it for P*.

Let the heigth of T be m+1 and let the theorem holds for all programs and predicate symbols whose reduced computation tree has heigth at most m. The program P can be partitionned into five disjoint sets P_i, $i \leq 5$ of clauses. The set P_1 consists of all clauses A(..) <- A(..) and of all assertions A(..) <- . If P and Q stand for arbitrary predicate symbols distinct from A, P_2 consists of all clauses A(..) <- Q(..), P_3 consists of all clauses P(..) <- Q(..), P_4 consists of all clauses Q(..) <- A(..) and P_5 consists of all clauses Q(..) <-.

Let $\bar{x}$ be an n-tuple of new variables, $\bar{s}, \bar{u}$ be appropriate tuples of terms.

Let P_2' be obtained from P_2 by replacing every clause $A(\bar{s})$ <- $Q(\bar{u})$ by the clause $A(\bar{s})$ <- $\bar{Q}(\bar{u},\bar{x}), A(\bar{x})$ where $\bar{Q}$ is a new predicate symbol of appropriate arity corresponding to Q.

Similarly, let P_3' be obtained from P_3 by replacing every clause $P(\bar{s})$ <- $Q(\bar{u})$ by $\bar{P}(\bar{s},\bar{x})$ <- $\bar{Q}(\bar{u},\bar{x})$.

Let P_4' be obtained from P_4 by replacing every clause $Q(\bar{u})$ <- $A(\bar{s})$ by the assertion $\bar{Q}(\bar{u},\bar{s})$ <- , where $\bar{P}, \bar{Q}$ are new predicate symbols corresponding to P, Q and only one new predicate symbol $\bar{Q}$ is used corresponding to Q in P_i', i=2,3,4 for each Q in P.

Let P' be the union of P_1, P_2, P_3, P_5, P_2', P_3', P_4'. Note that the clauses of P_4 rejecting stratifiability of P are removed from P' and the atom $A(\bar{x})$ is copied everywhere by P_2', P_3' to get eventually the appropriate values of variables from P_4'.

Hence, the computations of an arbitrary atom $A(\bar{a})$ by P and P' have the following forms

$$A(\bar{a}) \vdash_{P_1} A(\bar{s}) \vdash_{P_2} P(\bar{t}) \vdash_{P_3} Q(\bar{u}) \vdash_{P_4} A(\bar{s}') - \dots\dots\dots\dots \vdash \emptyset$$

$$\text{(15)}$$

$$A(\bar{a}) \vdash_{P_1} A(\bar{s}) \vdash_{P_2'} \bar{P}(\bar{t},\bar{x}), A(\bar{x}) \vdash_{P_3'} \bar{Q}(\bar{u},\bar{x}), A(\bar{x}) \vdash_{P_4'} A(\bar{s}') - \dots \vdash \emptyset .$$

where $\bar{a}, \bar{s}, \bar{s}', \bar{t}, \bar{u}$ are appropriate tuples of terms.

The reduced computation tree for P' and A has the form

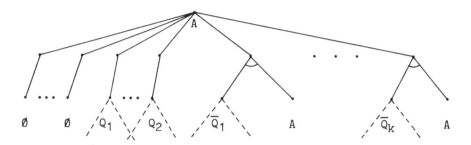

The reduced computation trees for P' and $Q_i, \bar{Q}_i$, i=1,...,k are of the height at most m and do not contain the predicate symbol A. These subtrees correspond to binary programs R_i , R_i', i=1,...,k respectively. It follows from the simplicity of the reduced computation tree for P and A that any of these programs have no predicate symbol in common. By induction hypothesis, there are stratifiable programs $S_1,...,S_k$, $S_1',...,S_k'$ such that

$$\begin{array}{llll} R_i & \vdash Q_i(...) & \text{iff} & S_i \vdash Q_i(...) \\ R_i' & \vdash \bar{Q}_i(...) & \text{iff} & S_i' \vdash \bar{Q}_i(...) \end{array} \qquad (16)$$

holds for every i<k. If n_i, n_i' are the stratifying functions for programs S_i, S_i', i=1,...,k respectively, we can define the stratifying function n for the program

$$P^* = P_1 \cup P_2 \cup P_2' \cup S_1 \cup \cdots \cup S_k \cup S_1' \cup \cdots \cup S_k'$$

as follows:

$$n(A) = 0 \ ,$$

$$n(P) = n_i(P) + 1 \quad \text{if P occurs in } S_i \text{ for some i } ,$$

$$n(\bar{P}) = n_i'(P) + 1 \quad \text{if } \bar{P} \text{ occurs in } S_i' \text{ for some i } .$$

It follows from (15) and (16) that P* satisfies Theorem 2.

5. CONCLUDING REMARKS

The result of Theorem 1 and 2 indicate that there is a strong relationship between binary and stratifiable programs, at least in the case of the resolution arithmetic. In the previous version (Šebelík and Štěpánek, 1980) of the paper, a stronger form of Theorems 1 and 2 was stated, replacing

stratifiability by left stratifiability. These results can be
proved by a little more complicated proofs, but our opinion
is that the left stratifiable programs are less natural than
the stratifiable programs. Moreover, left stratifiable
programs tend to have non deterministic computations. Hence,
we preferred determinism to left stratifiability.

There are some open problems left. We have shown that certain
stratifiable programs in the language of arithmetic can be
transformed into binary programs.

Problem 1.   Is it possible to transform every stratifiable
Horn clause program into a binary Horn clause program
computing the same function?

It is clear that every Horn clause program computing a
partial recursive function has a stratifiable couterpart
computing the same function. Generalizing Theorem 2 to the
case of arbitrary Horn clause programs, one encounters more
complex AND/OR-trees instead of simple computation trees for
binary programs. It seems that one of the possible ways to
attack the problem is coding information about branching of
the tree in natural numbers.

Problem 2.   Is it possible to transform every Horn clause
program to a stratifiable program computing the same
function?

There is still one natural question. We have shown that
certain stratifiable Horn clause programs can be transformed
to binary programs computing the same function and vice
versa.

Problem 3.   Is the resulting program of Theorems 1 and 2
equivalent to the original programs in all the ways it can be
used? How can this equivalence be formulated?

BIBLIOGRAPHY

Abelson, R. (see Schank, R. and -)

Andreka, H. and Nemeti, I. (1976). The Generalized Completeness of Horn Predicate Logic as a Programming Language. DAI Report, No.21., Univ. of Edinburgh.

Andreka, H., van Emden, M.H., Nemeti, I. and Tyurin, J. Infinite-Tree Semantics for Logic Programs. In preparation.

Apt, K. and van Emden, M.H. (1982). Contributions to the theory of logic programming. To appear in Journal of the ACM.

Aubin, R. (1977). Strategies for mechanizing structural induction. Proc. 5th IJCAI, Cambridge, pp. 363-369.

Backus, J. (1978). Can programming be liberated from the von Neumann style? A functional style and its algebra of programs. Comm ACM 21, 613-641.

Balogh, K. (also see Bendl, J. and - , Szeredi, P. and -).

Balogh, K. (1979). On a Logical Method Serving the Proof of the Semantic Features of Programs. (Hungarian) Ph.D. Thesis, Eotvos Lorand University, Budapest.

Balogh, K. (1981). On an interactive program verifier for PROLOG programs. Proc. of Coll. on Math. Logic in Programming, Salgotarjan, Hungary, pp. 111-142. North Holland.

Balogh, K. and Labadi, K. (1975). Software applications of the mathematical logic. (Hungarian) Proc. of the Conference Programming Systems'75, Szeged, Hungary, pp. 26-44.

Balogh, K., Futo, I. and Labadi, K. (1977). The Documentation of a PROLOG Program Verification System. NIM IGUSZI report. (Hungarian).

Balogh, K., Farkas, Z., Futo, I., Garami, P., Herenyi, I. Santane-Toth, E., Szeredi, J., Szeredi, P. and Visnyovszky, J. (1978). The Application of the PROLOG Language to the Design of Software and Hardware Objects. 1-6. (Hungarian) NIM IGUSZI and SZKI reports. SOFTTECH D21-D25, D27, SZAMKI.

Balogh, K., Santane-Toth, E. and Szeredi, P. (1979). Logic based program design. (Hungarian) Proc. of First National Conf. of von Neumann Computer Science Society, Szeged, Hungary, pp. 36-45.

Ban, P., Kohegyi, J., Suhai, Gy., Veszpremi, A. and Zsako, L.
(1979). Some Questions of the Information System of ANSWER.
(Hungarian) ELTE report. SOFTTECH D38, SZAMKI.

Barath, E. (see Futo, I. and -).

Bartha, F. (see Kofalusi, V. and -).

Battani, G. and Meloni, H. (1973). Interpreteur du Langage
de Programmation PROLOG. Groupe Intelligence Artificielle
Université Aix-Marseille II.

Baxter, L.D. (1976). A Practically Linear Algorithm. Technical report CS-76-13, Applied Analysis and Computer Science
Departement, University of Waterloo.

Beaugrande, R. De. (1980).   Text, Discourse, and Process,
Ablex, New Jersey.

Bellia, M., Degano, P. and Levi, G. (1980). A functional plus
predicate logic programming language. In (Tärnlund, 1980).
pp. 334-347.

Bellia, M., Degano, P. and Levi, G. (1982). The call by name
semantics of a clause language with functions. This volume.

Bendl, J. (see also Darvas, F. and -).

Bendl, J., Varga, K., Kosa, M. and Balogh, K. (1978). The
Specification of an Interpreter of a Modular PROLOG.
(Hungarian) NIM IGUSZI report. SOFTTECH D20, SZAMKI.

Bendl, J., Lugosi, Gy. and Markusz, Z. (1979a). An interactive system for checking air pollution - the information
system. (Hungarian) Informacio-Elektronika, XIV. No. 1, 55-
58.

Bendl, J., Boda, J., Bogdanfy, G., Kosa, M., Naszvadi, L. and
Visnyovszky, J. (1979b). A Users' Documentation of the
MPROLOG System. (Hungarian) NIM IGUSZI report.

Bendl, J., Koves, P. and Szeredi, P. (1980a).   The MPROLOG
system. In (Tärnlund, 1980), pp. 201-210.

Bendl, J., Kosa, M. and Szeredi, P. (1980b).   A Rough System
Description of the MPROLOG Compiler for IBM like Architectures. (Hungarian) NIM IGUSZI - SZKI report.

Bergman, M. and Kanoui, H. (1973). Application of mechanical
theorem proving to symbolic calculus.   Third International
Symposium on Advanced Computing Methods in Theoretical Phy-
sics, C.N.R.S., Marseille.

Bibel, W. (1978). On strategies for the synthesis of algorithms. Proc. of the AISB Conference on Artificial Intelligence, Hamburg, July.

Bobrow, D. et al. (1977). Experience with KRL 0. One cycle of
knowledge representation language. Proc. IJCAI 5.

Boda, J. (see Bendl, J. and -).

Bogdanfy, G. (see Bendl, J. and -).

Bowen, K. (1979). PROLOG. Proc. of the 1979 Annual Conference
Association for Computing Machinery, New York, pp. 14-23.

Bowen, K. and Kowalski, R.A. (1982).Amalgamating language and metalanguage in logic programming. In this volume.

Boyer, R.S. and Moore, J.S. (1972). The sharing of structure in theorem proving programs. In "Machine Intelligence" 7, Edinburgh University Press.

Boyer, R.S. and Moore, J.S. (1977). A lemma driven automatic theorem prover for recursive function theory. Proc. 5th IJCAI, Cambridge, pp. 511-519.

Brinch Hansen, P. (1975). The programming language concurrent Pascal. IEE Trans. on Software Engineering. SE-1, No. 2.

Bruynooghe, M. (1976).   An Interpreter for Predicate Logic Programs. Part I. Report CW 10, Applied Mathematics and Programming Division, Katholieke Universiteit, Leuven, Belgium.

Bruynooghe, M. (1978). Intelligent backtracking for an interpreter of Horn clause logic programs. Colloqium on Mathematical Logic in Programming, Salgotarjan, Hungary. (Eds Domolki, B. and Gergely, T.). North Holland 1981. pp. 215-258.

Bruynooghe, M. (1979).   Naar een Betere Beheersing van de Uitvoering van Programma's in de Logika der Hornuitdrukkingen. (In Dutch) Doctoral Dissertation, Afdeling Toegepaste Wiskunde en Programmatie, K.U.Leuven, Belgium.

Bruynooghe, M. (1980).   Analysis of dependencies to improve the behaviour of logic programs. 5th Conference on Automated Deduction. (Eds Bibel, W. and Kowalski, R.A.). Springer Lecture Notes in Computer Science. pp. 293-305.

Bruynooghe, M. (1981). Solving combinatorial search problems by intelligent backtracking. In "Information Processing Letters". 12, no 1, pp. 36-39.

Bruynooghe, M. (1982). The memory management of PROLOG implementations. In this volume.

Bruynooghe, M. and Pereira, L.M. (1981). Revision of Top-Down Logical Reasoning through Intelligent Backtracking. Report CW23, Department of Computer Science, Katholieke Universiteit Leuven, Belgium. Also CIUNL-8/81, Centro de Informática, Universidade Nova de Lisboa, Portugal.   Submitted to European Conference on Artificial Intelligence 1982, Orsay, France.

Bundy, A., Byrd, L., Luger, G., Mellish, C. and Palmer, M. (1979). Solving mechanics problems using meta-level inference. Proc. 6th IJCAI Tokyo, Japan. pp. 1017-1027.

Bundy, A. et al. (1979b). MECHO: A Program to Solve Mechanics Problems. DAI Working Paper No. 50.   University of Edinburgh.

Burstall, R.M. (1976). Recursive programs: Proof, transformation and synthesis. In "Rivista di Informatica". 7. pp. 25-42.

Burstall, R.M. (1977). Design considerations for a functional programming language. Proc. of Infotech State of the Art Conference, Copenhagen. pp. 45-57.

Burstall, R.M., Collins, J. and Poppelstone, R. (1971). "Programming in POP-2". Edinburgh University Press.

Burstall, R.M. and Darlington, J. (1975). Some transformations for developing recursive programs. Proc. Int. Conf. Reliable Software, Los Angeles, California. pp. 465-472.

Burstall, R.M. and Darlington, J. (1977). A transformation system for developing recursive programs. Journal of the ACM 24, No. 1, 46-67.

Burstall, R.M. and Goguen, J.A. (1977). Putting theories toghether to make specifications. Proc. 5th IJCAI, Cambridge. pp. 1045-1058.

Byrd, L. (see also Bundy, A. and -).

Byrd, L. (1980). Prolog debugging facilities. In (Tärnlund, 1980).

Byrd, L. (1980b). Understanding the control flow of PROLOG programs. In (Tärnlund, 1980). pp. 127-138.

Cartwright, R. and McCarthy, J. (1979). First order programming logic. Proc. of 6th POPL, San Antonio. pp. 68-80.

Chang, C.L. and Lee, R.T.C. (1971). "Symbolic Logic and Mechanical Theorem Proving". Academic Press, New York.

Chester, D. (see also Simmons, R.F. and -).

Chester, D. (1980a). A logic program interpreter in LISP. Proc. AAAI 1980, mss. Univ of Texas, Dept. Comp. Sci., Austin.

Chester, D. (1980b). HCPRVR: An interpreter for logic programs. Proc. of The First Annual National Conference on Artificial Intelligence, Stanford University.

Cholnoky, E. (see Futo, I. and -).

Church, A. (1936). An unsolvable problem of elementary number theory. Amer. J. Mathematics 58.

Clark, K.L. (1977). Verification and Synthesis of Logic Programs. Research report, Department of Computing, Imperial College.

Clark, K.L. (1978). Negation as failure. In ."Logic and Data Bases". (Eds Gallaire, H. and Minker, J.). Plenum Press, New York. pp. 293-322.

Clark, K.L. and Darlington, J. (1980). Algorithm classification through synthesis. The Computer Journal 23, no 1.

Clark, K.L. and Gregory, S. (1981). A relational language for parallel programming. In "Functional Programming Languages and Computer Architecture". ACM, New York.

Clark, K.L. and McCabe, F. (1979a). Programmers' Guide to IC-PROLOG. CCD Report 79/7, Imperial College, University of London.

Clark, K.L. and McCabe, F. (1979b). The control facilities of IC-PROLOG. In "Expert Systems in the Micro-Electronic Age" (Ed. Michie, D.), Edinburgh University Press.

Clark, K.L. and McCabe, F. (1980a).IC-Prolog: language features. In (Tärnlund, 1980). pp. 45-52.

Clark, K.L. and McCabe, F. (1982). PROLOG: A Language for Implementing Expert Systems. In "Machine Intelligence" 10. (Eds Hayes, J. and Michie, D.J) Ellis and Horwood.

Clark, K.L., McCabe, F. and Gregory, S. (1982). IC-PROLOG language features. This volume.

Clark, K.L. and Sickel, S. (1977). Predicate logic: A calculus for deriving programs. Proc. 5th Int. Joint Conf. on Art. Intell. Cambridge, Mass.

Clark, K.L. and Tärnlund, S-A. (1977). A first order theory of data and programs. PROC. 77, IFIP, North Holland, pp. 939-944.

Codd, E.F. (1972). Relational completeness of data base sublanguages. In "Data Base Systems" (Ed. Rustin, R.). Prentice-Hall, Englewood Cliffs, New Jersey. pp. 65-98.

Coelho, H. (1979). A Program Conversing In Portuguese Providing a Library Service. Ph.D. Thesis. University of Edinburgh. December.

Coelho H., Cotta J.C. and Pereira L.M. (1980). How to Solve it with Prolog. 2nd edition. Laboratorio Nacional de Engenharia Civil, Lisbon Portugal.

Cohen, J. (1979). Non-deterministic algorithms. ACM Computing Surveys 11, No. 2. 79-94.

Collins, J. (see Burstall, R. and -).

Colmerauer, A. (1975). Les Grammaires de Métamorphose. Groupe Intelligence Artificielle. Université Aix-Marseille II.

Colmerauer, A. (1978). Metamorphosis grammars. In "Natural Language Communication with Computers" no 63, Lectures Notes in Computer Science, (Ed. Bolc L.). Springer Verlag. pp. 133-189.

Colmerauer, A. (1979a). Un sous-ensemble interessant du francais. RAIRO Informatique Theorique 13, no 14. pp. 309-336.

Colmerauer, A. (1979b). Sur les bases théoriques de Prolog. Groupe Programmation et Langages AFCET, division théorique et technique de l'informatique, no 9.

Colmerauer, A., Kanoui, H., Pasero, R. and Roussel, P. (1973). Un Système de Communication Homme-machine en Francais. Research report. Groupe Intelligence Artificielle, Université Aix-Marseille II.

Colmerauer, A., Kanoui, H. and van Caneghem, M. (1979). Etude et réalisation d'un système PROLOG. Internal report. Groupe Intelligence Artificielle. Université Aix-Marseille II.

Colmerauer, A., Kanoui, H. and van Caneghem, M. (1981). Last steps toward an ultimate Prolog. Proc. 7th IJCAI Vancouver.

Colmerauer, A. and Pique, J.F. (1981). About natural logic. In "Advances in Data Base Theory" 1. (Eds Gallaire, H. Minker, J. and Nicolas, J.M.). Plenum Press. pp. 343-365.

Cotta, J.C. (see Coelho, H. and -).

Coursaget-Colmerauer, C. (1975). Etude des Structures du Type Nom de Nom. These de doctorat, Université de Montreal.

Cox, P. (1977). Reduction Plans: A Graphical Proof Procedure for the First Order Predicate Calculus. Report CS 77-28. Department of Computer Science, University of Waterloo.

Cross, M. (see Mellish, C.S. and -).

Dahl, V. (1977). Un Systeme Déductif d'Interrogation de Banques de Donnees en Espagnol. These de 3eme cycle, Groupe Intelligence Artificielle, Université Aix-Marseille II.

Dahl, V. (1979). Quantification in a three-valued Logic for Natural Language Question-Answering Systems. Proc. 6th IJCAI, Tokyo. pp. 182-187.

Darlington, J. (see Burstall, R. and - , Clark, K.L. and -).

Darvas, F. (see also Futo, I. and - , Matrai, G. and -).

Darvas, F. (1978). Computer analysis of the relationship between the biological effect and the chemical structure. (Hungarian) In "Kemiai Kozlemenyek" 50. pp. 97-116.

Darvas, F. (1980). Logic programming in chemical information handling and drug design. In (Tärnlund, 1980). pp. 261.

Darvas, F., Futo, I. and Szeredi, P. (1976). A program for the automatic filtering of drug interactions. (Hungarian) Proc. of the Coll. on the Application of Computing in Medicine and Biology (Ed. Muszka, D.), Szeged (Hungary), pp. 413-422.

Darvas, F., Futo, I. and Szeredi, P. (1978a). Some application of theorem proving based machine intelligence in QSAR: automatic calculation of molecular properties and automatic interpretation of quantitative structure-activity relationships. Proc. of the Symposium on Chemical Structure - Biological Activity: Quantitative Approaches, Suhl, GDR, Akademie Verlag, Berlin, pp. 251-257.

Darvas, F., Futo, I., Szeredi, J., Bendl, J. and Koves, P. (1978b). A PROLOG-based drug design system. (Hungarian) Proc. of Conf. Programming Systems'78, Szeged (Hungary), pp. 119-126.

Darvas, F., Futo, I. and Szeredi, P. (1978c). A logic-based program system for predicting drug interactions. International Journal of Biomedical Computing 9, 259-271.

Darvas, F., Futo, I., Szeredi, J. and Redei, J. (1979a). A logic based chemical information system - theoretical considerations and experiences. (Hungarian). Proc. of First National Conf. of von Neumann Computer Science Society, Szeged (Hungary), pp. 92-96.

Darvas, F., Futo, I. and Szeredi, P. (1979b). Expected interactions of spirololactions: predictions by computer. Proc. of the Conf. on Pathogenesis of Hyperaldosteronism (Ed. Glaz, E.). pp.219-220.

Darvas, F., Lopata, A. and Matrai, Gy. (1980). A specific QSAR model for peptides. In "Quantitative Structure Activity Analysis" (Ed. Darvas, F.). Akademiai Kiado, Budapest, pp. 265-278.

Dausmann, M. (see Winterstein, G. and -).

Davis, P.J. and Rabinowitz, P. (1976). "Numerical Integration", Blaisdell Publishing Co., Waltham Mass.

Davis, R. (1977). Generalized procedure calling and content-directed invocation. Proc. Symposium on Artificial intelligence and Programming languages. Rochester.

Davis, R. (1979). Generation of Correct Programs from Logic Specifications. Ph.D. Thesis, Board of Information Sciences, University of California, Santa Cruz.

Degano, P. (see Bellia, M. and -).

Deliyanni, A. and Kowalski, R. (1979). Logic and semantic networks. Comm. ACM 22, No. 3, 184-192.

Dennis, J. (1971). On the Design and Specification of a common base language. In "Computers and Automata". Brooklyn Polytechnic Institute.

Dijkstra, E.W. (1976). "A Discipline of Programming". Prentice-Hall, Englewood Cliffs, New Jersey.

Dincbas, M. (1980a). A knowledge based expert system for automatic analysis and synthesis in CAD. IFIP congress Tokyo.

Dincbas, M. (1980b). The METALOG problem solving system, an informal presentation. In (Tärnlund, 1980). pp. 80-91.

Doyle, J. (see also McDermott, D. and -).

Doyle, J. (1979). A truth maintenance system. Artificial Intelligence 12, 231-272.

Doyle, J. (1980). A Model for Deliberation, Action and Introspection. MIT AI lab, AI-TR-581.

Dwiggins, D. (see Silva, G. and -).

Eriksson, A. and Johansson, A-L. (1981). NATDED a Derivation Editor. UPMAIL, Computing Science Department, Uppsala University.

Essenin-Volpin, A. (1970). The ultra-intuitionistic criticism and the antitraditional program for the foundations of mathematics. In "Intuitionism and Proof Theory". North-Holland, Amsterdam.

Fahmi, A. (1979). Controle de Systemes de Deduction Automatique Fondes sur la Logique. These de docteur-ingenieur ENSAE-CERT.

Farkas, Z. (see Balogh, K. and - , Szeredi, P. and -).

Friedman, D. and Wise, D. (1976). CONS should not evaluate its arguments. In "Automata, Languages and Programming" (Ed. Michaelson, S.) Edinburgh Univ. Press, pp. 256-284.

Futo, I. (see also Balogh, K. and - , Darvas, F. and - , Szeredi, P. and -).

Futo, I., Darvas, F. and Cholnoky, E. (1977). Practical applications of an AI language (PROLOG). Second Hungarian Computer Science Conference, Budapest, pp. 388-399.

Futo, I. and Szeredi, P. (1977). AI languages - the PROLOG language. (Hungarian) Informacio-Elektronika, XII. No. 2-3, 108-113 and 146-152.

Futo, I., Darvas, F. and Szeredi, P. (1978a). The application of PROLOG to the development of QA and DBM systems. In "Logic and Data Bases" (Eds Gallaire, H. and Minker, J.). Plenum Press, New York and London, pp. 347-376.

Futo, I. and Keresztely, M. (1979). On a Program System Generating COBOL Programs Complying with the COLAMI Standards. Users' Manual. (Hungarian) SZKI report.

Futo, I., Szeredi, J. and Redei, J. (1978b). A Very High Level Language Supplied with Facilities for Parallel Programming. (Hungarian) SZKI report.

Futo, I., Szeredi, J. and Redei, J. (1979a). PAPLAN - Users' Reference Manual. (Hungarian) SZKI report.

Futo, I., Szeredi, J. and Redei, J. (1979b). The very high level language PROPHET and its application. (Hungarian) Proc. of First National Conf. of von Neumann Computer Science Society, Szeged (Hungary), pp. 146-157.

Futo, I., Szeredi, J. and Redei, J. (1979c). The Very High Level Language PROPHET. (Hungarian) SZKI report.

Futo, I. and Szeredi, J. (1980a). PAPLAN - an AI language for parallel problem solving. Proc. of International Conf. on Artificial Intelligence and Information-Control Systems of Robots, Smolenice Castle, Czechoslovakia, pp. 74-76.

Futo, I., Szeredi, J. and Szenes, K. (1980b). A modelling tool based on mathematical logic - T-PROLOG. To appear in Computational Linguistics and Computer Languages.

Futo, I., Szeredi, J., Barath, E. and Szalo, P. (1980c). Using T-PROLOG for a long range regional planning problem. In (Tärnlund, 1980) pp. 172-176.

Futo, I., and Szeredi, J. (1981). A very high level simulation language based on logic: T-PROLOG. To appear in Proc. of 12th Simulation and Modelling Conf. Univ. of Pittsburgh, Pennsylvania, USA.

Gallaire, H. (see also Lasserre, C. and -).

Gallaire, H. and Lasserre, C. (1979). Controlling knowledge deduction in a declarative approach. Proc. IJCAI 6, Tokyo.

Gallaire, H. and Lasserre, C. (1980). A control metalanguage for logic programming. In (Tärnlund, 1980) pp. 73-79.

Gallaire, H. and Lasserre, C. (1982).   Metalevel control for logic programs. This volume.

Gallaire, H. and Minker, J. (Eds). (1978).   "Logic and Data Bases" Plenum Press, New York.

Garami, P. (see Balogh, K. and -).

Gentzen, G. (1934).   Untersuchungen uber das logische schliessen. Mathematische Zeitschrift, 39. pp. 176-210.

Gero, P. (see also Halmay, E. and -).

Gero, P. and Halmay, E. (1980). Computer Aided Supervision as a Training of Programmers. (Hungarian) SZAMOK report.

Giraud, F., Pique, J.F. and Sabatier, P. (1980).   Manuel d'Utilisation de la Banque de Données MICROSIAL. Contract with CAP SOGETI Logiciel, Groupe Intelligence Artificielle, Université Aix-Marseille II. October.

Goguen, J.A. (see also Burstall, R. and -).

Goguen, J.A. and Tardo, J. (1979). OBJ-0 Preliminary User Manual. Semantics and theory of computation Report, UCLA.

Goldberg, A. and Kay A. (Eds). (1976). "Smalltalk-72 Instruction Manual". The Learning Research Group, Xerox Palo Alto Research Center, March.

Goodwin, J.W. (see Komorowski, J. and -).

Green, C.C. (1969). Theorem proving by resolution as a basis for question-answering systems. In "Machine Intelligence" 4, Edinburgh University Press, pp. 183-205.

Green, C.C. (1969b). The Application of Theorem Proving Question-Answering Systems. Ph.D. Thesis. Stanford University. Stanford, California.

Gregory, S. (see also Clark, K.L. and -).

Gregory, S. (1980). Toward the Compilation of Annotated Logic programs. Research report 80/16. Department of Computing, Imperial College.

Gries, D. (see Owicki, S. and -).

Griesmer, J.H. and Jenks, R.D. (1971).   SCRATCHPAD/1 - An interactive facility for symbolic mathematics. Proc. 2nd Symp. on Symbolic and Algebraic Manipulation. (Ed. Petrick, S.). New York.

Gross, M. (1977). Grammaire transformationnelle du francais, syntaxe du nom. Collection langue et langage, Larousse.

Guttag, J.V. and Horning, J. (1980). Formal specification as a design tool. Proc. of the ACM Symposium on Principles of Programming Languages, pp. 251-261.

Guttag, J.V., Horowitz, E. and Musser, D.R. (1978). Abstract data types and software validation. C ACM 21, 1048-1063.

Gödel, K. (1931).   Uber formal unentscheidbare Sätz der Principia Mathematica und verwandter Systeme, I. Monatsh. Math. 38, 173-198.

Halmay, E. (see also Gero, P. and - , Kofalusi, V. and -).

Halmay, E. and Gero, P. (1981). The PROGART Program System. (Hungarian) SZAMOK report.

Hansson, A. (1980). A Formal Development of Programs. Ph.D. Thesis. Department of Information Processing Computer Science, The Royal Institute of Technology and The University of Stockholm.

Hansson, A. and Haridi, S. (1981). Programming in a natural deduction framework. Proc. Functional Languages and their Implications for Computer Architecture, Göteborg, Sweden.

Hansson, A., Haridi, S. and Tärnlund, S-A. (1980). Some aspects of a logic machine prototype. In (Tärnlund, 1980). pp. 53-60.

Hansson, A., Haridi, S. and Tärnlund, S-A. (1982). Properties of a logic programming language. In this volume.

Hansson, A. and Tärnlund, S-A. (1979a). A natural programming calculus. Proc. 6th IJCAI, Tokyo Japan.

Hansson, A. and Tärnlund, S-A. (1979b). Derivations of programs in a natural programming calculus. Electrotechnical Laboratory, Tokyo.

Haridi, S. (see also Hansson, A. and -).

Haridi, S. (1981). Logic Programming Based on a Natural Deduction System. Ph.D. Thesis. Department of Telecommunication and Computer Systems, The Royal Institute of Technology, Stockholm, Sweden.

Hayes, P.J. (see also McCarthy, J. and -).

Hayes, P.J. (1973). Computation and deduction. Proc. 2nd MFCS Symposium. Czekoslovak Academy of Sciences.

Hayes, P.J. (1977). In defense of logic. IJCAI 5. pp. 559-565.

Hearn, A.C. (1971). REDUCE-2 - A system and language for algebraic manipulation. Proc. 2nd Symp. on Symbolic and Algebraic Manipulation, (Ed. Petrick, S.). New York.

Henderson, P. and Morris, J.H. (1976). A lazy evaluator. Proc. 3rd ACM Symp. on POPL. pp. 95-103.

Herenyi, I. (see Balogh, K. and -).

Hewitt, C. (see also Kahn, K. and -).

Hewitt, C. (1972). Description and Theoretical Analysis (Using Schemata) of PLANNER: a Language for Proving Theorems and Manipulating Models in a Robot. AI Memo 231, MIT Project MAC.

Hewitt, C. (1977). Viewing control structures as patterns of passing messages. Journal of Artificial Intelligence 8. No. 3.

Hill, L. (1974). Lush Resolution and its Completeness. DCL memo 78. University of Edinburgh.

Hogger, C. (1978). Program synthesis in predicate logic. Proc. AISB/GI Conf. on AI, Hamburg. pp. 18-20.

Hogger, C. (1979). Derivation of Logic Programs. Ph.D. Thesis. Department of Computing, Imperial College, London.

Hogger, C. (1980). Logic Representation of a Concurrent Algorithm. Imperial College. London.

Hogger, C. (1981). Derivation of logic programs. Journal of the ACM 28. No. 2. 372-422.

Holnapy, D. (1979). On the Mathematical Foundations of the Automatized Technical Planning. ETI report.

Horning, J. (see Guttag, J. and -).

Horowitz, E. (see Guttag, J. and -_,).

Huet, G. (1976). Resolution d'Équations dans des Langages d'Ordre 1,2,...,Omega. These de doctorat d'état, Université de Paris VII. Septembre.

Jaskowski, S. (1934). On the rules of suppositions in formal logic. Studia Logica 1. Warsaw.

Jenks, R.D. (see Griesmer, J.H. and -).

Johansson, A-L. (see Eriksson, A. and -).

Kahn, G. (1974). The semantics of a simple language for parallel programming. Proc. IFIP 74.

Kahn, G. and McQueen, D.B. (1977). Coroutines and networks of parallel processes. Proc. IFIP 77.

Kahn, K. (1979). Director Guide. MIT AI Memo 482b.

Kahn, K. (1980). Intermission, actors in PROLOG. In (Tärnlund, 1980). pp. 33-44.

Kahn, K. (1981). Uniform -- A language based upon unification which unifies (much of) Lisp, Prolog, and Act 1. IJCAI-81.

Kahn, K. and Hewitt C. (1978). Dynamic graphics using quasi parallelism. Computer Graphics 12, No. 3, pp. 357-362.

Kanoui, H. (see Colmerauer, A. and - , Bergman, M. and -).

Kaposi, A.A. and Markusz, Z. (1979). PRIMLOG - the case for augmented PROLOG programming. Proc. of Informatica'79, Bled, Yugoslavia.

Kaposi, A.A. and Markusz, Z. (1980). Introduction of a complexity measure for control of design errors in logic-based CAD programs. Proc. of CAD'80, Brighton.

Kay, A. (1977). Microelectronics and the personal computer. Scientific American. September.

Keenan, E.L. (1972). On semantically based grammar. Linguistic Inquiry 111, no 4.

Keleti, K. (see Matrai, G. and -).

Kiss, V. and Simor, G. (1978). A Preliminary Specification of an Architecture Design Environment and the Analysis of the Programming Tools Applicable in the Environment. (Hungarian) SZKI report.

Kiss, V. and Simor, G. (1979). On a Simulator for Evaluating the Design and Experimental Testing of Higher Level Architectures - DELBOLSIM". (Hungarian) SZKI report.

Kiss, Z., Proszeki, G. and Toth, L. (1979). Morphological Analysis of Hungarian Texts with Computer. (Hungarian) MTA NYTI report. SOFTTECH D41, SZAMKI. (An English version to appear in Computational Linguistics and Computer Languages.)

Kofalusi, V. (1979a). On Simplification in Mathematical Structures. (Hungarian) SOFTTECH D42, SZAMKI, pp. 12-86.

Kofalusi, V. (1979b). A PROLOG Program for Generating the First n Formal Derivatives of Given, Real Multi Variable Analytic Functions of Great Complexity. (Hungarian) SOFTTECH D42, SZAMKI, pp. 104-127.

Kofalusi, V. (1982). The state space set and its applicativity in PROLOG language. To appear in Computation Linguistics and Computer Languages.

Kofalusi, V. and Bartha, F. (1979a). On a Possible Application and Extension of PROLOG: Applications Based on State Space Sets. (Hungarian) SOFTTECH D42, SZAMKI.

Kofalusi, V. and Bartha, F. (1979b). Numeric Analysis of Ligand Bonding Systems. (Hungarian) MTA SZBK report. SOFTTECH D42, SZAMKI, pp. 128-132.

Kofalusi, V. and Halmay, E. (1981). State-space Sets, State-space Graphs - Logic Based Symbolic Mathematical Computational Approach. Manuscript.

Kohegyi, J. (see Ban, P. and -).

Komorowski, H.J. (1979). Qlog Interactive Environment -- The Experience from Embedding a Generalized Prolog in Interlisp. Datalogi Research Report, Linkoeping University, Sweden.

Komorowski, H.J. (1980). Qlog - The software for Prolog and logic programming. In (Tärnlund, 1980). pp. 305-320.

Komorowski, H.J. and Goodwin, J.W. (1981). Embedding Prolog in Lisp: An Example of a Lisp Craft Technique. Software Systems Research Center, Linkoeping University.

Kornfeld, W. (1979). Using Parallel Processing for Problem Solving. MIT EECS Master Thesis.

Kosa, M. (see Bendl, J. and -).

Koster, C.H.A. (1977). CDL - a compiler implementation language. Proceedings of Conference on Methods of Algorithmic Language Implementation. In "Lecture Notes in Computer Science" No. 47. Springer-Verlag, Berlin, Heidelberg, New York.

Koves, P. (see also Bendl, J. and - , Darvas, F. and -).

Koves, P. (1978). BS2000 PROLOG Users' Reference Manual. V2.4. (Hungarian) SZKI report.

Koves, P. (1979). A Preliminary Users' Manual of Debugging and Trace Subsystem of MPROLOG. (Hungarian) SZKI report. SOFTTECH D32, SZAMKI.

Kowalski, R.A. (see also Bowen, K. and - , van Emden, M. and - , Deliyanni, A. and -).

Kowalski, R.A. (1970). Studies in the Completeness and Efficiency of Theorem Proving by Resolution. Ph.D. Thesis. University of Edinburgh. Edinburgh.

Kowalski, R.A. (1974). Predicate logic as programming language. Proc. IFIP-74 Congress. North-Holland. pp. 569-574.

Kowalski, R.A. (1978). Logic for data description. In "Logic for Data Bases" (Eds Gallaire, H. and Minker, J.). Plenum Press. New York. pp. 77-102.

Kowalski, R.A. (1979a). "Logic for Problem Solving". Artificial Intelligence series, (Ed. Nilsson, N.J.). North Holland.

Kowalski, R.A. (1979b). Algorithm = logic + control. C ACM 22. 424-431.

Kowalski, R.A. (1980). Logic as a computer language. Proc. Infotech State of the Art Conference of Software Engineering. London.

Kowalski, R.A. and Keuhner. (1971). Linear resolution with selection function. Artificial Intelligence 2 (3/4) pp 227-260.

Labadi, K. (see Balogh, K. and - , Szeredi, P. and -).

Landin, P. (1965). The correspondence between ALGOL 60 and Church's lambda notation. Part I. CACM 8 no 2.

Lang, I. (1978). On the generation of data processing ANSI-COBOL programs in PROLOG. (Hungarian) Proc. of the Conf. Programming Systems'78, Szeged (Hungary), pp. 364-368.

Lasserre, C. (see also Gallaire, H. and -).

Lasserre, C. and Gallaire, H. (1980). Controlling backtrack in Hornclause programming. In (Tärnlund, 1980). pp. 286-292

Laufer, T. (1979). DOS PROLOG Users' Reference Manual. (Hungarian) Technical High School report, Pecs (Hungary).

Lee, R.T.C. (see Chang, C.L. and -).

Levi, G. (see also Bellia, M. and -).

Levi, G. and Pegna, A. (1982). Top-down mathematical semantics and symbolic execution. To appear in RAIRO Informatique Theorique.

Levi, G. and Sirovich, F. (1975). Proving program properties, symbolic evaluation and logical procedural semantics. Proc. MFCS '75. In "Lecture Notes in Computer Science". Springer Verlag. pp. 294-301.

LeVine, S. (1980). Questioning English Text with Clausal Logic. Univ. of Texas, Dept. of Comp. Sci., Thesis, Austin.

Lieberman, H. (1981). A Preview of Act 1. MIT AI Memo 625.

Lopata, A. (see Darvas, F. and -).

Loveland, D.W. (1968). Mechanical theorem proving by model elimination. JACM 15, 236-251

Loveland, D.W. **(1978).** "Automated Theorem-Proving". North-Holland.

Lucena, de., G.J. (see also van Emden, M. and -).

Lucena, de., G.J. **(1978).** Studies in Temporal Abstraction as a Programming Method. Ph.D. Thesis, University of Waterloo.

Luger, G. (see Bundy, A. and -).

Lugosi, Gy. (see Bendl, J. and -).

Lyness, J.N. **(1970).** SQUANK (Simpson quadrature used adaptively, noise killed), Algorithm 379. CACM 13 No. 4.

Manna, Z. **(1974).** "Mathematical Theory of Computation". McGraw-Hill Inc.

Manna, Z. and Waldinger, R. **(1971).** Toward automatic program synthesis. CACM 14, no 3, 151-165.

Manna, Z. and Waldinger, R. **(1975).** Knowledge and reasoning in program synthesis. Artificial Intelligence Journal 6, No. 2, 175-208.

Manna, Z. and Waldinger, R. **(1978).** A Deductive Approach to program Synthesis. Technical Report. Computer Science Department. Stanford University.

Markusz, Z. (see also Bendl, J. and - , Kaposi, A. and -).

Markusz, Z. **(1977a).** How to design variants of flats using programming language PROLOG, based on mathematical logic. Proc. of IFIP 77, Toronto, pp. 885-890.

Markusz, Z. **(1977b).** The application of the programming language PROLOG for panel house design. (Hungarian) Informacio-Elektronika XII. No. 3. 124-230.

Markusz, Z. **(1980a).** The application of the programming language PROLOG for many storied panel house design. (Hungarian) Informacio-Elektronika XV. No. 5. 256-263.

Markusz, Z. **(1980b).** An application of PROLOG in designing many storied dwelling houses. In (Tärnlund, 1980). pp. 249-260.

Markusz, Z. **(1980c).** Logic Based Programming Method and its Applications for Architectural Design Problems. (Hungarian) Ph.D. Thesis. Eotvos Lorand University, Budapest.

Markusz, Z. **(1981).** Design in Logic. Working paper, SZTAKI, AP/13.

Martelli, A. and Montanari, U. **(1976).** Unification in Linear Time and Space. University of Pisa. Internal report B76-16.

Martin-Löf, P. **(1979).** Constructive Mathematics and Computer Programming, Department of Mathematics, University of Stockholm.

Matrai, G. (see also Darvas, F. and -).

Matrai, G. **(1979).** The Application of PROLOG for Search of Similar Substructures of Enzyme Sequences. (Hungarian) MTA SZBK report.

Matrai, G. **(1980).** Primary structure activity of dehidrogenases. To appear in J. of Mol. Bio. No. 5.

Matrai, G., Darvas, F. and Keleti, K. (1980). Homologous Subsequences in Dehidrogenases. (Hungarian) MTA SZBK report.

McCabe, F.G. (see also Clark, K.L. and -).

McCabe, F.G. (1978). Programmer's Guide to IC-PROLOG. Dept. of Computation and Control, Imperial College, London.

McCarthy, J. (see also Cartwright, R. and -).

McCarthy, J. (1979). First-order theories of individual concepts and propositions. In "Machine Intelligence" 9. (Ed. Michie, D.). University of Edinburgh Press.

McCarthy, J. and Hayes, P. (1969). Some philosophical problems from the standpoint of artificial intelligence. In "Machine Intelligence" 4. (Ed. Meltzer, B.). University of Edinburgh Press, pp. 463-502.

McCord, M.L. (1980). Using Slots and Modifiers in Logic Grammars for Natural Language. Technical Report 69A-80. Department of Computer Science. University of Kentucky.

McDermott, D. (1980). The PROLOG phenomenon. SIGART Newsletter 72, July, pp. 16 - 20.

McDermott, D. and Doyle, J. (1980). Non-monotonic logic I. Artificial Intelligence 13, 41-72.

McQueen, D.B. (see Kahn, G. and -).

Mellish, C.S. (see also Bundy, A. and -).

Mellish, C.S. (1980). An Alternative to Structure-Sharing in the Implementation of a PROLOG Interpreter. Research Paper 150, Department of Artificial Intelligence, University of Edinburgh.

Mellish, C.S. (1982). An alternative to structure sharing in the implementation of a PROLOG-interpreter. In this volume.

Mellish, C.S. and Cross, M. (1979). The UNIX Prolog System. Software Report 5, Department of Artificial Intelligence, University of Edinburgh.

Meloni, H. (see Battani, G. and -).

Minker, J. (see also Gallaire and -).

Minker, J. (1977). Control Structure of a Pattern Directed Search System. TR 503 Department of Computer Science. University of Maryland.

Montague, R. (1974). "Formal Philosophy". Selected Papers. (Ed. Thomason, R.H.), Yale University Press.

Montanari, U. (see Martelli, A. and -).

Monteiro, L.F. (see Pereira, L.M. and -).

Montgomery, C. (see Silva, G. and -).

Moon, D. (see Weinreb, D. and -).

Moore, J.S. (see Boyer, R.S. and -).

Morris, J.H. (see Henderson, P. and -).

Moss, C. (1980). A Comparison of Several PROLOG systems. Imperial College. London.

Musser, D.R. (see also Guttag, J. and -).

Musser, D.R. (1979). Abstract data type specification in the AFFIRM system. Proc. Specification of Reliable Software Conf., Boston.

Naszvadi, L. (see Bendl, J. and -).

Nemeti, I. (see Andreka, H. and -).

Nilsson, N. (1980). "Principles of Artificial Intelligence". Tioga Publishing Company. Palo Alto, California.

Nordström, M. (1978). Lisp F3 User's Guide. Datalogilaboratoriet, Uppsala University.

Operating Systems, Inc. (1979). A Knowledge Based Automated Message Understanding Methodology for an Advanced Indication System. OSI R79-006. Woodland Hills, California.

Owicki, S. and Gries, D. (1976). An axiomatic proof technique for parallel programs. Acta Informatica $\underline{6}$.

Palmer, M. (see Bundy, A. and -).

Parikh, R. (1971). Existence and feasibility in arithmetic. J. Symbolic Logic $\underline{36}$.

Pasero, R. (see also Colmerauer, A. and -).

Pasero, R. (1973). Représentation du Francais en Logique du 1ér Ordre en Vue de Dialoguer avec un Ordinateur. Thèse de 3ème cycle, Groupe Intelligence Artificielle, Université Aix-Marseille II.

Paterson, M.S. and Wegman, M.N. (1976). Linear unification. Proc. 8th ACM Symp. on Theory of Comp. pp 181-186.

Pegna, A. (see Levi, G. and -).

Persch, G. (see Winterstein, G. and -).

Pereira, F. (see also Warren, D. and -).

Pereira, F. and Warren D. (1980). Definite clause grammars for language analysis -- A survey of the formalism and a comparison with augmented transition networks. Art. Intell. $\underline{13}$, 231-278.

Pereira, L.M. (see also Bruynooghe, M. and - , Coelho, H. and - , Warren, D. and -).

Pereira, L.M. (1979). Backtracking Intelligently in AND/OR Trees. Departamento de Informatica, Universidade Nova de Lisboa.

Pereira, L.M. and Monteiro, L.F. (1981). The semantics of parallelism and coroutining in logic programming. Colloquim on Mathematical Logic in Programming, Salgotarjan, Hungary. North Holland. pp. 611-657.

Pereira, L.M. et al. (1978). User's Guide to DECsystem-10 Prolog. Divisao de Informatica, Laboratorio Nacional de Engenharia Civil, Lisbon.

Pereira, L.M. and Porto, A. (1979a). Intelligent Backtracking and Sidetracking in Horn Clause Programs: The Theory. Departamento de Informatica, Universidade nova de Lisboa.

Pereira, L.M. and Porto, A. (1979b). Intelligent Backtracking and Sidetracking in Horn Clause Programs: The Implementation. Departamento de Informatica, Universidade Nova de Lisboa.

Pereira, L.M. and Porto, A. (1980a). An interpreter of logic programs using selective backtracking. In (Tärnlund, 1980).

Pereira, L.M. and Porto, A. (1980b). Selective backtracking for logic programs. In "Springer Lecture Notes in Computer Science" No. 87. Fifth Conference on Automated Deduction, (Eds Bibel, W. and Kowalski, R.) pp. 306-317.

Pereira, L.M. and Porto, A. (1980c). Selective Backtracking at Work. Departamento de Informatica, Universidade Nova de Lisboa.

Perichaud, L. (1981). Consultation en Francais d'une Banque de Donnees sur Fichiers et Mise en Place du Systeme Prolog Necessaire. These de 3eme cycle, Groupe Intelligence Artificielle, Université Aix-Marseille II.

Pique, J.F. (see also Colmerauer, A. and - , Giraud, F. and -).

Pique, J.F. (1975). Interrogation en Francaise d'une Base de Donnees Relationelle. Diplome d'Etude Approfondies, Groupe Intelligence Artificielle, Université Aix-Marseille II.

Pirotte, A. (1978). High level data base query languages. In "Logic and Data Bases" (Eds Gallaire, H. and Minker, J.). Plenum Press, New York, N.Y. pp. 409-436.

Poppelstone, R. (see Burstall, R. and -).

Porto, A. (see Pereira, L.M. and -).

Pratt, V.R. (1977). The competence/performance dichotomy in programming. Proc. Fourth ACM Sigart/Sigplan Symp. on Principles of Programming Languages. pp. 194-200.

Prawitz, D. (1965). Natural Deduction. A Proof-Theoretical Study. Ph.D. Thesis. Almqvist and Wiksell. Stockholm.

Proszeki, G. (see Kiss, Z. and -).

Quam, L.H. et al. (undated). Stanford Lisp 1.6 Manual. Stanford AI Laboratory, Operating Note 28.7.

Rabinowitz, P. (see Davis, P. and -).

Redei, J. (see Darvas, F. and - , Futo, I. and -).

Reiter, R. (1978). On closed world data bases. In "Logic and Data Bases" (Eds Gallaire, H. and Minker, J.). Plenum Press New York. pp. 55-76.

Reiter, R. (1980). On reasoning by default. Artificial Intelligence 13, 81-132.

Riesbeck, C. (see Schank. R. and -).

Roberts, G. (1977). An Implementation of PROLOG. M.Sc. Thesis, University of Waterloo.

Robinson, J.A. (1965). A machine-oriented logic based on the resolution principle. Journal of the Association for Computing Machinery 12, 23-41.

Robinson, J.A. (1979). "Logic: Form and Function". Edinburgh University Press and Elsevier North Holland.

Robinson, J.A. and Sibert, E. (1980). Logic Programming in LISP. School of Comp. and Inf. Sc., Syracuse University.

Rosen, B.K. (1974). Correctness of Parallel Programs: the Church-Rosser Approach. T.J. Watson Research Centre, Yorktown Heights (N.Y.), IBM Research Report RC5107.

Roussel, P. (see also Colmerauer, A. and -).

Roussel, P. (1975). PROLOG, Manuel de Reference et d'Utilisation. Groupe Intelligence Artificielle, Université Aix-Marseille II. September.

Sabatier, P. (see Giraud, F. and -).

Sacerdoti, E.D. et al. (1976). Qlisp, A Language for the Interactive Development of Complex Systems. SRI AI Center, Technical Note 120.

Sandewall, E. (1978). Programming in an interactive environment: the "Lisp" experience. Computing Surveys 10, No. 1.

Santane-Toth, E. (see also Balogh, K. and - , Szeredi, P. and -).

Santane-Toth, E. (1979). PROLOG Applications in Hungary 1979. (Hungarian) SZKI report, SOFTTECH D42, SZAMKI.

Schank, R. and Riesbeck, C. (1980). Inside Natural Language. LEA.

Schank, R. and Abelson, R. (1977). "Scripts, Plans, Goals and Understanding", Wiley, New York.

Šebelík, J. and Štěpánek, P. (1980). Horn clause programs suggested by recursive functions. In (Tärnlund, 1980). pp. 348-359.

Sergot, M.J. (1980). Programming Law: LEGOL as a Logic Programming Language. Department of Computing. Imperial College, London.

Shoenfield, J. (1967). "Mathematical Logic". Addison-Wesley. Reading. Mass.

Sibert, E. (see Robinson, J.A. and -).

Sickel, S. (see also Clark, K.L. and -).

Sickel, S. (1978). Invertibility of Logic Programs. Technical Report 78-8-005. Information Sciences. University of California, Santa Cruz.

Sickel, S. (1979). Invertibility of logic programs. Proc. 4th Workshop on Automated Deduction, Austin. pp. 103-109.

Silva, G., Montgomery, C. and Dwiggins, D. (1979). An application of automated language understanding techniques to the generation of data base elements. Proc. Ass. Comp. Ling., San Diego.

Simmons, R.F. and Chester, D. (1980). Relating Sentences and Semantic Networks with Clausal Logic. Mss. Univ. Texas., Dept. Comp. Sci., Austin.

Simor, G. (see Kiss, V. and -).

Sirovich, F. (see Levi. G. and -).

Stamper, R.K. **(1979).** LEGOL: Modelling legal rules by computer. Proc. CREST Course on Computer Science and Law. Swansea.

Štěpánek, P. (see Šebelík, J. and -).

Suhai, Gy. (see Ban, P. and -).

Szalo, P. (see Futo, I. and -).

Szenes, K. (see Futo, I. and -).

Szeredi, J. (see also Darvas, F. and -).

Szeredi, J. **(1978).** On the Application of Mathematical Logic in Computer Techniques. (Hungarian). Ph.D. Thesis.

Szeredi, P. (see also Balogh, K. and - , Bendl, J. and - , Darvas, F. and - . Futo, I. and -).

Szeredi, P. **(1975).** On a high-level programming language based on logic. (Hungarian) Proc. of the Conf. Programming Systems'75, Szeged (Hungary). pp. 191-209.

Szeredi, P. **(1977).** PROLOG - a very high-level language based on predicate logic. Preprints of second Hungarian Computer Science Conference, Budapest. pp. 853-856.

Szeredi, P. and Futo, I. **(1977).**   PROLOG reference manual. (Hungarian) SZAMOLOGEP, <u>VII</u>. No. 3-4. pp. 5-130.

Szeredi, P., Futo, I., Labadi, K. and Balogh, K. **(1979).** (Ed. Szeredi, P.) On the Implementation Methods and Theoretical Foundations of the PROLOG Language. (Hungarian) NIM IGUSZI and SZKI report. SOFTTECH D34, SZAMKI.

Szeredi, P., Balogh, K., Santane-Toth, E. and Farkas, Z. **(1980).** LMD-Logic based software development methodology. In (Tärnlund, 1980). pp. 160-171.

Tardo, J. (see Goguen, J.A. and -).

Tärnlund, S-Å. (see also Clark, K.L. and - , Hansson, Å. and -).

Tärnlund, S-Å. **(1975).**   Logic Information Processing. Report TRITA-IBADB.1034 Department of Information Processing Computer Science, The Royal Institute of Technology and The University of Stockholm, Sweden.

Tärnlund, S-Å. **(1977).** Horn clause computability. BIT <u>17</u>. pp. 215-226.

Tärnlund, S-Å. **(1978).**   An axiomatic data base theory. In "Logic and Data Bases" (Eds Gallaire H, and Minker, J.). Plenum Press.

Tärnlund, S-Å. **(1980).**   (Ed.). Proceedings of the Logic Programming Workshop, Debrecen, Hungary.

Tärnlund, S-Å. **(1981).** A Programming Language Based on a Natural Deduction System, UPMAIL Report, Computing Science Department, Uppsala University.

Teitelman, W. **(1979).** Interlisp Reference Manual. Xerox-Palo Alto, California.

Toth, L. (see also Kiss, Z. and -).
Toth, L. (1974). Comparative Analysis of the Very High Level Programming Languages. (Hungarian) NIM IGUSZI report.
Trum, P. and Winterstein, G. (1978). Description and Practical Comparaison of Unification Algorithms. Internal report, University of Kaiserslauten.
Turing, (1937). On computable numbers, with an application to the Entscheidungsproblem. Proc. London Math. Soc., ser. 2, <u>42</u>.
Tyurin, J. (see Andreka, H. and -).
van Caneghem, M. (see Colmerauer, A. and -).
van Emden, M.H. (see also Andreka, H. and - , Aot, K. and - , Kowalski, R. and -).
van Emden, M.H. (1977). Programming in resolution logic. In "Machine Intelligence" <u>8</u>, 266 - 299.
van Emden, M.H. (1978). Computation and deductive information retrieval. In "Formal Description of Programming Concepts". (Ed. Neuhold, E.). North-Holland. pp. 421-440.
van Emden, M.H. and Kowalski, R.A. (1976). The semantics of predicate logic as a programming language. J ACM <u>23</u>. No. 4. 733-743.
van Emden, M.H. and de Lucena, G.J. (1979). Predicate Logic as a Language for Parallel Programming. Report CS 79-15 University of Waterloo.
van Emden, M.H. and de Lucena, G.J. (1982). Predicate logic as language for parallel programming. In this volume.
Varga, K. (see Bendl, J. and -).
Veszpremi, A. (see Ban, P. and -).
Visnyovszky, J. (see Balogh, K. and - , Bendl, J. and -).
Vuillemin, J. (1974). Correct and optimal implementations of recursion in a simple programming language. J CSS <u>9</u>.
Wadsworth, C. (1971). Semantics and Pragmatics of the Lambda-Calculus. Ph.D. Thesis, Oxford.
Waldinger, R. (see Manna, Z. and -).
Warren, D. (see also Pereira, F. and -).
Warren, D. (1976). Generating conditional plans and programs. Proc. AISB Summer Conference, Edinburgh. pp. 344-354.
Warren, D. (1977). Implementing PROLOG - Compiling Logic Programs. 1 and 2. D.A.I. Research Report No 39, 40, University of Edinburgh.
Warren, D. (1980). An improved PROLOG implementation which optimises tail recursion. In (Tärnlund, 1980).
Warren, D. (1981). Efficient processing of interactive relational database queries expressed in logic. Proc. VLDB conference.
Warren, D. and Pereira, F. (1981). An Efficient Easily Adaptable Queries. DAI research paper no 155, Departement of Artificial Intelligence, University of Edinburg.

Warren, D., Pereira, L.M. and Pereira, F. (1977). Prolog - the language and its implementation compared with Lisp. Proc. Symp. on AI and Programming Languages, SIGPLAN Notices 12, No. 8, and SIGART Newsletter 64, pp. 109-115.

Warren, D., Pereira, F. and Pereira, L.M. (1979). User's Guide to DECsystem-10 Prolog.. Occasional Paper 15, Department of Artificial Intelligence, University of Edinburgh.

Wegman, M.N. (see Paterson, M.S. and -).

Weinreb, D. and Moon, D. (1978). Lisp Machine Manual. MIT AI Laboratory.

Weyhrauch, R. (1980). Prolegomena to a theory of mechanized formal reasoning. Artificial Intelligence 13, 133-170.

Winterstein, G. (see also Trum, P. and -).

Winterstein, G., Dausmann, M. and Persch, G. (1980a). Deriving different unification algorithms from a specification in logic. In (Tärnlund, 1980). pp. 274-285.

Winterstein, G., Dausmann, M. and Persch, G. (1980b). A Method for Describing Concurrent Problems Based on Logic. Research Report, Institut fur Informatik II, Univesity of Karlsruhe.

Wise, D. (see Friedman, D. and -).

Zloof, M.M. (1975). Query-by-example. Proc. AFIPS 1975 NCC 4. AFIPS Press, Montvale, New Jersey. pp. 431-348.

Zsako, L. (see Ban, P. and -).

SUBJECT INDEX